1986

Arcana Mundi

ARCANA

MUNDI

*Magic and the Occult in the Greek
and Roman Worlds*

*A Collection of Ancient Texts
Translated, Annotated, and Introduced by*

GEORG LUCK

THE JOHNS HOPKINS UNIVERSITY PRESS
BALTIMORE AND LONDON

This book has been brought to publication
with the generous assistance of
the David M. Robinson Publication Fund and the Andrew W. Mellon Foundation.

© 1985 The Johns Hopkins University Press
All rights reserved
Printed in the United States of America

The Johns Hopkins University Press, 701 West 40th Street,
Baltimore, Maryland 21211
The Johns Hopkins Press Ltd, London

The paper in this book is acid-free and meets the guidelines
for permanence and durability of the Committee
on Production Guidelines for Book Longevity
of the Council on Library Resources.

Library of Congress Catalog Card Number 84-28852
ISBN 0-8018-2523-7 (hardcover)
ISBN 0-8018-2548-2 (paperback)

For Harriet

Contents

List of Texts

Preface

Arcana Mundi, the title of this book, may be translated as "secrets of the universe." The phrase appears in Seneca's tragedy *Hercules Furens* (v. 596), and Lucan, who perhaps borrowed it from his uncle, used it in his epic poem, *Pharsalia* (5.196). Both Seneca and Lucan were deeply interested in occult phenomena—an interest that was characteristic of the whole Neronian age—and to both we owe important testimonies.

One cannot really understand the world of the ancient Greeks and Romans without some knowledge of what is today called "folklore"—what used to be called, in a derogatory sense, "superstition." Most modern historians do not pay much attention to the subject, and for a long time it was fashionable to ignore these darker and, to us, perhaps, unfamiliar aspects of everyday life in Greece and Rome: somehow all this hocus-pocus does not seem to fit the exalted concept of the "glory that was Greece" and the "grandeur that was Rome." But we can no longer idealize the Greeks and their "artistic genius" or the Romans and their "sober realism." Magic and witchcraft, the fear of daemons and ghosts, the wish to manipulate invisible powers—all were very much a part of life in the ancient world.

Recent work in the fields of anthropology, folklore, and comparative religion has demonstrated the need for a new look at the ancient beliefs and customs associated with magic. Linguistics also has made a contribution. To mention one example, the latest *Complete English-Maori Dictionary,* compiled by Bruce Biggs and published, in 1981, by the Oxford University Press, lists roughly nineteen synonyms for *incantation* in general, and at least two dozen entries for more specific types of magical operations such as "incantation and rite to cause death," "incantation to be used by a rejected suitor," or "incantation for moving a canoe." The Maoris also seem to have special words for different kinds of dreams—for instance, "a dream involving the appearance of one dead" or "a dream of a person floating in the air."

The wealth of synonyms or near-synonyms in a language reflects the interests of its speakers. Small differences in meaning can be very important. What comparative mythology suggested long ago is confirmed by the linguistic evidence: people of different societies and cultures the world over think and feel and react in similar ways. They have the same types of dreams, hopes, fears, problems, and obsessions, and all this is reflected partly in language, myth, and literature, partly in folklore, ritual, and religion.

My interest in occult phenomena goes back a long time. When I was a schoolboy in Switzerland, my teacher and friend Fritz Schneeberger introduced me to the medicinal herbs that grow in the mountains, and he showed me the use of the pendulum, a simple magical tool. Later I read Alfred Fankhauser's books on magic and astrology and began to explore the world of medieval and Renaissance "occultism" through the old Latin tomes in the Municipal Library in the city of Bern. At about the same time I read C. G. Jung, whose doctoral dissertation was entitled *The Psychology and Pathology of So-called Occult Phenomena;* this curious work was first published in German, in 1902, and is now available in English in the Bollingen Series of Jung's Psychiatric Studies. Jung's later works helped me understand the ways in which the experiences and theories of ancient magicians, alchemists, and astrologers shed new light on the structure of the human psyche.

As a student of theology at the University of Bern, I attended the classes of Max Haller on the history and phenomenology of religions; it was Haller who made me read Karl Beth's very useful book on religion and magic.

In the late forties I went to Paris as a student of classics and took, at the Ecole Pratique des Hautes Etudes, a course entitled "Descent of the Soul," which was taught by Father Festugière. At that time, Father Festugière was collaborating with Arthur Darby Nock on the Budé edition of the *Corpus Hermeticum,* and he recommended me for a fellowship that permitted me to study at Harvard University with Nock, who later became a colleague and friend.

Although I have never met E. R. Dodds, I have read and reread his books with admiration. In a sense, then, he too has been my teacher.

When I first taught the course "Magic and Occult Science in Antiquity" at Johns Hopkins in 1972, it occurred to me how useful a source book, a collection of texts in translation, would be. As I continued to teach this course, sometimes twice a year, I translated such texts, adding brief introductions or comments. The book that has resulted is not an exhaustive treatment. I have tried simply to come to terms with a difficult subject by taking a close look at the ancient texts and interpreting them, within their historical framework, by drawing on modern research.

Mine is a tentative approach, but I hope that the texts themselves and the bibliographical references will be useful to others.

I am very grateful to the anonymous reader for his helpful comments and to Eric Halpern, Humanities Editor of the Johns Hopkins University Press, for his advice. Penny Moudrianakis, my copy editor, has read the manuscript with great care and improved it in many ways; I am much indebted to her. David Azzolina has saved me time by introducing me to a computer at the Milton S. Eisenhower Library. As usual, I must acknowledge a very special debt to my wife, Harriet. My daughter, Annina, has helped me in organizing and typing the manuscript. Patricia Steccone also has typed a number of pages. To all of them I am deeply grateful.

Arcana Mundi

·I·

MAGIC

Introduction

Settling on a precise definition of magic is not easy; so let me begin with a practical interpretation. According to Lynn Thorndike, magic includes "all occult arts and sciences, superstitions and folklore." [1] In truth, however, this is not a satisfactory definition, for magic is but one of the occult sciences. Moreover, Thorndike uses the vague term *superstition*, which characterizes the attitudes of a supposedly more enlightened age and civilization. Finally, he includes *folklore*, which in itself is not an occult art, although folk tales are often *about* witches, sorcerers, and the like. In the present context, I would define magic as a technique grounded in a belief in powers located in the human soul and in the universe outside ourselves, a technique that aims at imposing the human will on nature or on human beings by using supersensual powers. Ultimately, it may be a belief in the unlimited powers of the soul.

The multitude of powers can, perhaps, be reduced to the notion of power, or *mana*. The Greek equivalents, found in Hellenistic texts, are *dynamis* 'power', *charis* 'grace', and *aretē* 'effectiveness'. This magical *mana* is freely available; all it needs is a vessel or a channel, and the true *magus* is such a medium—even his garments or something he touches can receive and store the *mana*.

In a polytheistic society such as Greece or Rome it was only natural that the one Power took on the forms and names of many powers—gods, daemons, heroes, disembodied souls—who were willing, or even eager, to work for the *magus*. When the *magus* summoned these powers by means of his magical knowledge and technique, he could either help and heal or destroy and kill.

One important concept in all magic is the principle of cosmic sympathy, which has nothing to do with compassion but means something like "action and reaction in the universe." [2] All creatures, all created

3

things, are united by a common bond. If one is affected, another one, no matter how distant or seemingly unconnected, feels the impact. This is a great and noble idea, but in magic it was mainly applied in order to gain control. Scientists think in terms of cause and effect, while *magi* think in terms of "sympathies" or "correspondences" in the sense defined above. The positions of the planets in the signs of the zodiac, as well as their aspects in relation to one another, govern the characters and destinies of human beings, not by some sort of direct mechanical influence but rather by a hidden "vibration." The microcosm reflects and reacts to the macrocosm because both share certain deep affinities. This doctrine was held, with variations, by Pythagoreans, Platonists, and Stoicists. Among the Stoicists, Posidonius of Apamea (c. 135–50 B.C.) should be mentioned, and among the Neoplatonists, Iamblichus (c. A.D. 250–325), whose treatise *On the Mysteries of Egypt* deals with *theurgy* 'higher magic', which he defines as an activity surpassing the understanding of man, an activity based on the use of silent symbols that are fully known only to the gods. In fact the higher *magus*, or theurgist, does not quite understand what he is doing; the "sympathy" somehow works through him. The secret is "power through sympathy" and "sympathy through power."

Can a clear distinction be drawn between religion and magic? Many approaches to the problem have been tried, but none seems to work well. Four fundamentally different positions on the relationship between magic and religion have been argued: (1) that magic becomes religion (K. T. Preuss); (2) that religion attempts to reconcile personal powers after magic has failed (Sir James Frazer); (3) that religion and magic have common roots (R. R. Marrett); and (4) that magic is a degenerate form of religion (P. Wilhelm Schmidt). It has been said that the religious person prays to a deity in a humble, submissive manner, while the *magus* compels his gods by means of threats, that the religious person relies more or less on the good will or mercy of a god, while the magician uses some special knowledge that gives him power (sometimes he knows the secret name to which a daemon will respond). This may be generally true. And yet we find a religious mood in magical texts [*no. 23*], and the *magi* use rituals and liturgies not unlike those performed in the great religions of the present and the past. Their concerns are the same: health, wealth, good looks, children, protection from dangers or disasters, and so on. For the *magi*, however, there is such a thing as black magic, whereas almost by definition religion itself can do no harm. Still, the threatening of deities is not unknown in religious contexts. When Germanicus, the adopted son of Emperor Tiberius (and much more popular than his adoptive father) died a mysterious death, Tacitus [*no. 13*] did not exclude magical operations, and when the people of Rome heard the news, they stormed into the temples and kicked the statues of the gods into the streets.[3] It is said that even in more recent times Italian fishermen treated the statues of their saints in the same way. Whenever they made a good catch, they offered the saints the usual incense, flowers, and candles; but when the catch was not good, they cursed the statues and kicked them. The law of "sympathy" is in effect: if you kick the statue of your saint or god, he will feel the pain somehow and will react.[4]

Hence some scholars believe that there is no fundamental difference between religion and magic. There may be one: praying for something,' giving thanks for something, is conceivable in magic, but not the consciousness of sin and the prayer for forgiveness.[5] The *magus* does not recognize sin; he is, in a way, above morality and the law, a law unto himself. In a society in which practically everyone believed in magic and practiced it in one form or another, this contempt for conventional morality and the laws of the state could have encouraged criminal behavior, but the reasons why magicians and astrologers—along with philosophers— were periodically discriminated against in the time of the empire were mainly political.

The roots of magic are no doubt prehistoric. There is reason to believe that some fundamental magical beliefs and rituals go back to the cult of the great earth goddess.[6] In historical times, she was worshiped in Greece and other Mediterranean countries under a variety of names: Ge or Gaia, Demeter, Ceres, Terra Mater, Bona Dea, Cybele, Ishtar, Atargatis, and so on. There must have been an important cult of an Earth Mother in prehistoric Greece long before the Indo-European invaders known as the Hellenes arrived. No doubt the ancient Greeks' own Demeter owes something to that pre-Greek deity, and it is conceivable that the parts of the ritual (human sacrifices, for instance) that were rejected later on survived in secret. The fact that iron knives are generally taboo in magical sacrifices suggests that they may have originated in the Bronze or Stone Age. In other cases the Greeks gave a new interpretation to existing sanctuaries of Mother Earth, for instance in Delphi, where they attached to the old Earth oracle, with its prophetess, their god Apollo. The inevitable conflict between an old and a new religion may help to explain why magic, as a profession, remained suspect and feared among the Greeks and why the great witches of Greek mythology, Medea and Circe, are portrayed as evil or dangerous. In fact, they may have been goddesses of a former religion or priestesses of the Mother Earth cult. Their knowledge of roots, herbs, and mushrooms—gifts of the earth—may have been part of their priestly training. Here again we have the interpretation of a new civilization that conquered an old one.

The early Greeks may well have misunderstood the nature of some foreign religions and cults—they seem to have made very little effort to understand them. Hence, a good deal of magical lore may simply reflect the beliefs and rituals of ancient religions in countries of which the Greeks had only some vague knowledge. One such "creative" misunder-

standing has apparently given us the very word *magic*, which is derived
from *magoi*, a Median tribe or caste recognized in ancient Iran as spe-
cialists in ritual and religious knowledge. Sometimes they are associated
with the cult of fire. As we know from Apuleius' *Apology*, the Greeks and
Romans saw in the *magoi* the priests of Zoroaster (Zarathustra) and Ormazd (Ahura Mazda), but these two divine or semidivine beings were
also considered the inventors of magic [*no. 28*]. This may simply reflect a
Greek prejudice dating from the fifth century B.C. The doctrines and rites
of a foreign religion were probably reported in a misleading way and
understood not as religion but as a sort of perversion of religion. At the
same time, since this religion (or whatever it might be) was so exotic, so
different, so ancient, the Greeks must have speculated that the *magoi* had
access to secret knowledge.[7]

Incidentally, the borrowing of names, concepts, and rituals from
foreign religions is one of the characteristics of ancient witchcraft, as the
magical papyri attest. Even though cities like Alexandria and Rome were
already full of sanctuaries of exotic deities, apparently there was still
room for more speculation and more experiment. No doubt the religions
of ancient Egypt were similarly misinterpreted or at least simplified by the
Greeks of the Hellenistic period who lived in Egypt, and these religious
practices survived, through a series of transformations, in the main-
stream of magical doctrine.[8]

Ancient history shows us a succession of great empires—Egypt,
Persia, Athens, Macedonia, Rome—and each of these had its Pantheon of
divine powers. As one culture conquered another, it took over some of its
gods, usually the ones that could be identified with a native deity, or the
ones suitable to become at least the attendants, the courtiers as it were, of
native deities. The truly outlandish elements in a foreign religion seem to
have been rejected and despised by the conquerors and classified as
witchcraft, but the witchcraft continued to have a life of its own. The
Greek witches came from Thessaly or the Black Sea, that is, from countries at the end of the world. The Marsi, a tribe or nation of central Italy,
maintained their identity until the late second century B.C., it seems.
Their civilization apparently was just different enough from the Roman
one to make them look somewhat bizarre. Hence, Marsian magicians
(perhaps priests of some of their local deities) enjoyed a great reputation
in Rome: they were especially famous for curing snakebites.

Finally, when the victorious Christian Church began to hunt
witches and wizards, its actions were often directed against surviving
pagan cults. In continental Europe, as well as in Britain, some worshipers
of the ancient Celtic and Greco-Roman gods had refused to convert to
Christianity, and the rites they performed (by necessity in secret) were
interpreted as magical rites. The Celts worshiped a horned male god that

may have reminded the Romans of the god Pan, a minor god to be sure, but one who could drive you into a "panic" terror when you encountered him at noontime. This combination of horned gods, one Celtic, one classical, produced a very powerful deity around which the *pagani* rallied. Indeed, so powerful was this god that the Christian priests cast him as the prototype of the Devil, with horns, hoofs, claws, a tail, and a generally shaggy appearance. These groups also preserved knowledge of the powers of herbs, roots, and mushrooms, and although this knowledge was not included in the fashionable medical science of the day, patients given up by their doctors probably consulted the local witch, and if she cured them, her practice most likely grew.

If this Celto-Roman deity was cast as the Devil, his female worshipers or priestesses naturally were labeled witches, and this may have been the origin of the witch craze in medieval Europe and in early Colonial America. To us, the medieval Church looks monolithic, universal, unshakable, but there must have been just enough evidence of dissension, schism, and this kind of underground paganism for the Church to take the measures it did. There could be no tolerance of anything outside the Church—*extra Ecclesiam nulla salus*—and if these unfortunates resisted conversion, they offered proof of the power the Devil had over them, a power that had to be broken, if not in this world, at least in the next.

Magic as a Social Phenomenon and a Science

There is, in fact, a form of cooperation, or symbiosis, between established religion and magic. The ability to predict the future is certainly an occult power, a form of magic. We hear of many ancient soothsayers and prophets, some of them highly respected, some of them considered mere fortunetellers; but without question the most important places of divination were the great sanctuaries.

In Delphi, the method of divination practiced by the Pythia, the priestess-prophetess who sat on top of a deep crack in the ground, receiving her trance and her visions from inside the earth, had nothing to do with the cult of the god Apollo. She was a medium who received impulses and messages from the Great Mother, who of course knew the future of the earth and of all mankind. The trance, the ecstasy of the priestess, her unintelligible language (probably not unlike the *glossolalia* of the early Christians), were alien to the whole Apollonian myth and form of worship as we understand it. But the oracle was so old that the priests of Apollo kept it going, under their control, and over the centuries turned it into one of the most powerful religious, political, and economic centers of the ancient world. Perhaps the priests of Apollo were suspicious of the ancient method, but for many reasons they recognized its value and sanctioned it. Generally speaking, such occult phenomena as trance, visions, and ecstasy were tolerated only within the context of a sanctuary and had to be supervised by the priests of a recognized religion.[9]

It has recently been argued that a drug was used to induce programmed hallucinations during the initiation rites at the temple of Demeter in Eleusis.[10] But use of that same drug at private parties by privileged Athenian playboys like Alcibiades and his set was considered a profanation and desecration. In a religious context the magical drug was tolerated—in fact was indispensable—but outside of that context it was condemned.

There has been enormous interest in the exorcism of daemons in recent years. Exorcism is the ancient magical technique of driving out daemons from patients who are thought to be possessed. It was practiced in antiquity by "medicine men" and miracle workers long after Hippocrates had established the foundations of scientific medicine. Christ exorcised, and in the early Church the ability to drive out daemons was considered a spiritual gift, like speaking in tongues. Today, exorcism is still a prerogative of the Roman Catholic Church, and only ordained priests may practice it. This reveals the same tendency to concentrate and institutionalize magical powers within a larger religious context that we observed above.

Thus magic may be called a religion that has been distorted and misinterpreted beyond recognition by a hostile environment almost from the beginnings of history. The environment changed, but the tradition of magic continued through many metamorphoses. By the time of Christ it had become a science, without completely losing its religious character. This process probably took place in Egypt, a country that acted as a melting pot of different civilizations and traditions, combined influences from East and West, and gave birth to an abundance of mystical systems. We will discuss the role of Egypt later. At this point, it may be useful to consider the scientific elements that magic had from the earliest times.

Magic, as a science, has always tried to locate the secret forces in nature (*physis*), their sympathies and antipathies. In a sense, the *magi* were scientists (*physikoi*) whose work was not recognized by the "modern" scientists of the day, though they probably borrowed from them. The *magi* were less interested in pure science than in manipulating the powers (*dynameis*) of nature. At the same time, they explored the human soul, its conscious and unconscious states and expressions. They clearly knew about the psychedelic effects of certain plants, but they probably also practiced hypnosis; they used the techniques of fasting, deprivation of sleep, and prolonged prayers. Certain religions used the same techniques. What is today considered to be science or philosophy was at times part of religion or magic in antiquity and was often presented as a vision or a revelation sent by a god:

Religion [in late antiquity] made science its underling. The so-called science of late Antiquity is speculative and mystical and appeals to revelations and dealings with the supernatural world. But, like magic, it always has a practical aim and does not research for the sake of researching. The fundamental idea was the concept of sympathy. . . . The analogies with which Greek rationalism worked shot up like weeds in the hothouse of mysticism.[11]

Ancient magic could arrive at the same results as science, but it did not attribute them to human reasoning or experimentation; rather, it credited them to direct or indirect contact with a supernatural power. Ancient magic usually dealt with the material world, but that world was thought to be governed and controlled by invisible presences. These presences had to be controlled by the *magus*, who wanted to gain knowledge and power through them to change the present and to predict or influence the future. Hence magic in ancient times was an esoteric technique as well as a science, something which was not accessible to everyone but which had to be revealed by a god or learned through a process of initiation. There could not be many *magi* within one environment, and these *physikoi* accepted few disciples.

Ancient magic may have been based on "primitive" ideas, but the form in which it was handed down to us was by no means primitive. On the contrary: magic in this sense existed only within highly developed cultures and formed an important part of them. Not only the lower classes, the ignorant and uneducated, believed in it, but the "intellectuals" down to the end of antiquity were convinced that dangerous supernatural powers operated around them and that these powers could be controlled by certain means.

Magic as a Literary Theme

The best way to look at ancient magic is, perhaps, to survey various literary texts. The Greek and Roman poets were interested in magic and they provide some good descriptions of magical operations. The first magical operation that was recorded in Greek is found in Book 10 of the *Odyssey* [*no. 1*]. It is one of many adventures that the hero of the epic had to endure on his way back from Troy. The epic itself was probably composed in the eighth century B.C., but it reflects the heroic age of Greece, which coincided roughly with the second part of the second millennium B.C. Homer, in other words, is writing about things that were supposed to have happened about five hundred years before he was born. He works from oral tradition—from folktales, myths and legends, and perhaps folk ballads in verse form. The witchlike character, Circe, seems to be characteristic of folk tales in many cultures.

One should note that Circe's witchcraft consists in the use of a wand and that Odysseus' defense against her involves an herb called *moly,* which is revealed to him by the god Hermes. Several requisites of magic are here combined: a mysterious tool that looks like a stick but that is obviously endowed with special powers; an herb that was not easy to find; and a god who reveals to one of his favorites a secret that will save him. Thus, at the beginning of recorded Greek literature we find the three elements that will characterize magic as a system in the Hellenistic Age: a magical tool, a magical herb (starting a long tradition of herbaria), and a god who reveals an important secret.

Circe is a beautiful woman—a seductress or temptress like Calypso—whom Odysseus visits on her island and who changes his companions into swine. It is not clear why she does this: perhaps because she hates men; perhaps because she represents a more ancient matriarchal society; perhaps because she is just a semidivine power left over from an older culture, a relatively harmless power if one keeps one's distance, but very dangerous if one comes within her reach. This last explanation may have some support in the story of Lucius, as told by Apuleius in the *Metamorphoses* [*no. 29*]: the hero of that novel gets into trouble only when he actually visits the country of witches, Thessaly. Presumably, if Odysseus had stayed away he would have been safe. But if you believe or half-believe in witchcraft, to enter the territory of a witch is to invite trouble. Although Circe changes Odysseus' companions into swine, she has no power over Odysseus himself, because Hermes has given him a magical herb, the *moly,* whatever it means. But even Hermes cannot protect Odysseus from Circe's physical charms; when Circe realizes that she has no power over Odysseus, she offers him her bed, they become lovers, and he stays for a while.[12]

Circe is a daughter of the Sun, one of the Titans, just as Medea is the granddaughter of the Sun. The Titans represent an earlier generation, or dynasty, of the gods. Not only can Circe transform men into beasts but she can predict the future. This is another magical power. Through her predictions and instructions Homer links Circe with the other magical motif of the epic, the necromantic scene in Book 11 of the *Odyssey* [*no. 50*]. Following Circe's instructions, Odysseus digs a trench, pours out as an offering to the dead a drink consisting of honey, milk, wine, and water, and slaughters two black sheep in such a way that their blood runs into the ditch. This attracts the shades of the dead in flocks, and by drinking the blood they regain, for a short time, the ability to communicate with the living.

In the centuries after Homer a number of men with supernatural powers emerged who cannot be labeled or classified precisely. They belong partly to the history of Greek philosophy and science, partly to the realm of Greek religion, but they are also *magoi,* or miracle-workers. In his important book *The Greeks and the Irrational*, E. R. Dodds has suggested for them the term *shaman*, and it is certainly possible to see in them highly sophisticated medicine men.[13] The word *shaman* is derived from Tungusian *saman* 'priest', 'medicine man'. *Shamanism*,[14] which is based on animism and ancestor worship, was practiced as a religion by the Indians of North America. To become a *shaman* required strict training and harsh asceticism, which led up to a kind of delirium, or trance, during which a vision came. Isolation from the community, fasting and praying, and monotonous exercises such as whirling could help produce this experience, but certain drugs were probably also used. In his well-known books *The Teachings of Don Juan* (1968) and *Tales of Power* (1974), to name only two of a series, Carlos Castaneda describes the world of Don Juan, a Yaqui *shaman* of the twentieth century.

Perhaps the three most famous Greek *magoi*, or *shamans*, between Homer and the Hellenistic period, when magic became an applied science, were Orpheus, Pythagoras, and Empedocles. All three are strikingly similar, but each clearly has an identity of his own. Pythagoras and Empedocles lived in the fifth century B.C. Orpheus was a more mythical figure, but Orphism, the religious movement named after him, was a reality, and such movements usually have a founder and leader.

Orpheus and Pythagoras are associated with important philosophical and religious groups or schools in the history of Greek culture, while Empedocles remains more of a solitary phenomenon, though he did have disciples. The Sicilian medical school that Empedocles is thought to have founded flourished for a long time. All three men are known to have expressed their ideas in poetry and prose, and at some point many of these compositions must have been written down by their followers, but few of these writings are extant. What we have are fragments or substitutions by later authors. The similarities between these three spectacular figures suggests the existence, in Greek civilization, of a type of miracle-worker who was also an original thinker and a great teacher, someone who offered a philosophical theory to explain the universe and the human soul—macrocosm and microcosm—and who may also have been a poet. In all three instances we seem to face the image of the *shaman*, known from more primitive cultures but superimposed on a great philosopher, teacher, or poet.

Shamanism is a useful term because it is more neutral than *magus* or *thaumaturge* (miracle-worker). Anthropologists, folklorists, and scholars in the field of comparative religion have been working with it for a long time, but it was E. R. Dodds who introduced it into the history of Greek culture. As Dodds writes, a *shaman* is a "psychically unstable person" who has received a call to the religious (or philosophic) life, who undergoes ascetic discipline (fasting, long periods of praying in solitude), and who acquires supernatural powers and sometimes also the ability to write poetry, which is really such a power (at least it was to the ancients).[15] He can heal the sick, understand the language of animals, be at different places at the same time, and so on.

This definition fits Orpheus, Pythagoras, Empedocles, and a number of others—including Apollonius of Tyana, who appears much later—quite well. Dodds has been able to show, in particular, that tradition has given Orpheus the main characteristics of a *shaman:* he was a poet, *magus*, religious teacher, and oracle-giver or prophet.[16] With his music (a kind of magical charm in itself) he could summon birds, soothe wild beasts, and even make trees follow him as he sang and played on his instrument. Like *shamans* in other cultures, he was able to descend alive into the underworld and return. His magical self lived on as a singing head that continued to give oracles for many years after his death.

The attribution of magical powers to Pythagoras, as recorded in the days of Aristotle, has been discarded by many historians of Greek philosophy of science, but scholars such as W. Burkert tend to accept it as part of the genuine tradition.[17] Pythagoras had a golden thigh; he was greeted by rivers with a resounding "Hail, Pythagoras!"; he had the gift of prophecy; and he could be at different places at the same time. Like Orpheus, he had power over animals, and he, in turn, respected them to the degree that he preached a strict vegetarianism. All these characteristics indicate that Pythagoras was no ordinary human being; he was a "divine man," *theios anēr*—or *shaman*, to use the more objective term.[18]

Empedocles ascribed to himself the powers to heal the sick and rejuvenate the old; he also claimed he could influence the weather (produce rain in a drought or calm a storm) and summon the dead. It is evident that he—or his disciples—thought of him as a miracle-worker. How could he also be a great scientist? Did he start as a magician who lost his nerve and took to natural science, or was he a scientist who later in life converted to a form of Orphism or Pythagoreanism? This is the way Dodds amusingly states the problem, but he adds, in a more serious vein, that we should not ask these questions, for Empedocles was a *shaman*—a combination of poet, *magus*, teacher, and scientist. To him, there was clearly no contradiction between these various skills or vocations; they formed a unity.[19]

After Empedocles, the scale of these unusual gifts in exceptional individuals seems to shrink; *shamanism* becomes one-dimensional, so to speak, or specialized. One either has the gift of healing or the gift of prophecy, but no longer the universal range of supernatural powers with which the early *shamans* were blessed. This specialization, or limitation of spiritual gifts, was observed in antiquity by Paul in his First Letter to the Corinthians and by Plutarch in his essay *On the Cessation of Oracles*. Compared to the great thaumaturges of archaic Greece, most of the later practitioners of one occult science or another (dream interpreters or soothsayers) seem like *shamans* who have lost the full range of their powers. It was therefore a great step forward when Dodds taught us to see Orpheus, Pythagoras, and Empedocles as *shamans*, each sharing with the other two (and with some minor figures, such as Abaris) the distinctiveness of such a personality, but each with his own specific role and message and his personal way of expressing it.

Pythagoras, through both his legend and his doctrine, had great influence on Platonism, but Plato himself says little about magical practices. That he believed in astrology (and other forms of divination) is strongly suggested by the *Timaeus*, and that he believed in daemons is reasonably clear from the Platonic School tradition. In his *Laws* (933A–E) he takes healers, prophets, and sorcerers for granted. These practitioners existed in Athens and no doubt in other Greek cities, and they had to be reckoned with and controlled by laws. But Plato adds that one should not be afraid of them. Their powers are real, but they themselves represent a rather low form of life.

Aristotle is convinced that the planets and the fixed stars influence life on earth, and, in principle at least, he too believed in the existence of daemons. In his *History of Animals* (a better title would be *Biological Researches*, because *historia* originally meant "research," not "history" in the modern sense) he already suggests the magical theory of sympathies and antipathies in the animal world, under the influence of the stars, a theory that reflects a good deal of ancient Greek folklore. Some of these pseudoscientific theories are found in Books 7–10 of the *History*, but because they do not fit our image of Aristotle, there are serious doubts concerning their authenticity. Book 10, for instance, is missing in the oldest extant manuscript; but even though Aristotle himself may not have written it in this form, it seems to reflect the teaching of his school. Books 7 and 9 have also been rejected by modern editors, but it seems that Book 7 uses material from respectable Hippocratic writings and that Book 9 relies on Theophrastus; hence these portions cannot lightly be discarded as later fabrications.[20]

In his collection *Characters*, Aristotle's pupil Theophrastus (c. 370–285 B.C.) has given us the wonderful "Portrait of the Superstitious Person" [*no. 2*]. In Greek, *superstition* is *deisidaimonia*, literally "fear of supernatural powers." Some of the powers mentioned by Theophrastus are bona fide deities that had cults in Athens, and the priests of these deities probably encouraged some of the sentiments the subject of the sketch displays. In addition to the priests, however, the superstitious person consults the "advisers." These are doubtless the more obscure practitioners of the occult arts, but even they appear to be more rational than he. Surely not all Athenians of Theophrastus' time were so haunted by fears, but his portrait is based on personal observation and represents a sort of scientific study.

The Hellenistic period (roughly the last three centuries before Christ) is characterized by a new interest in magic. From this period we have an abundance of texts in Greek and Latin, some literary and some for practical use. Although the magical papyri that are extant were written in the first centuries of the Christian era, their concepts, formulas, and rituals reflect this earlier period, the time when all the occult sciences were developed into one great system. This systematization probably took place in Egypt. The Greeks who lived in Egypt had an opportunity to observe native religions and forms of worship, folklore, and superstition, and being Greek, they must have tried to make sense of what they saw. Since we owe remarkable descriptions of magical operations to two Hellenistic poets who lived in Egypt in the early third century B.C., it seems appropriate to discuss them first and the magical papyri later, before we try to say something about Hellenistic magic in general.[21]

Apollonius of Rhodes (so called because he spent the last years of his life on the island of Rhodes, though he was born in Egypt) is famous for the epic *Argonautica*, one of the main characters of which is Medea. Our text [*no. 3*] is taken from the account of the return of the Argonauts from the Black Sea. They landed on the island of Crete, but its shores were guarded by a monster called Talos, "a bronze giant who broke off lumps of rock to hurl at them." Talos is introduced by the poet as a leftover from the Bronze Age, as if people then had really been made of bronze; he had survived into the heroic age (the age of myth, in which all this happened), and Zeus had given him to Europa as a guard. It is easy to see why Talos was associated with Crete: on this island Daedalus, the great craftsman, created statues that were so lifelike that they might have walked away had they not been chained to the floor. (This, by the way, is a humorous exaggeration of the realism of Minoan art as seen by the Greeks of a later period. To create such statues seemed a kind of magic in itself. No wonder, Daedalus was also the first human being to fly.) Talos naturally terrified the Argonauts (great heroes that they were). They would have rowed away had Medea not come to their rescue. It was obviously time for her magic, and this quasi-magical monster was a real challenge to her. She knew she could destroy Talos unless there was immortal life in him, that is, unless he was a god. A product of magic could be destroyed by countermagic.

Our text describes the struggle between Medea and the monster. She won because the powers of evil in and around her, which she could control and channel into a single force, were so strong that the monster was literally knocked over. Medea worked herself into a state of trance during which her hatred became material and the "images of death" that she had conceived assumed a reality all their own. This is perhaps the first explicit description of the power of the evil eye and of black magic. We owe it to a very sophisticated Greek poet who professed to be shocked by the mere thought that someone could be hurt by magical operations. Whether or not Apollonius himself believed it, we can be almost certain that most of his contemporaries did.[22]

Theocritus (c. 310–250 B.C.) is mainly known as a pastoral poet, but he also wrote several pieces describing everyday life in the great modern capital Alexandria.[23] One of these (nr. 2 in modern editions) has the title *Pharmakeutria*, which is the feminine equivalent of *pharmakeutēs* and means "witch" or "sorceress"; it is derived from *pharmakon* 'drug', 'poison', 'potion', or 'spell'. Any herb, chemical, or requisite used in medicine or magic could be called *pharmakon*. We do not know whether Theocritus himself or an ancient editor gave the poem this title, but it is appropriate, even though the woman is certainly not a professional. Our text [*no. 4*] is a long monologue. Simaetha, a young Greek woman who lives in a city, presumably Alexandria, is in love with a young athlete. It was love at first sight, and for some time they were happy together. But now he has not shown himself at her house for eleven days, and she decides to draw him back by magical means, threatening more powerful measures if this love magic does not work. She has already consulted the professionals, of which there may have been quite a few: "Did I skip the house of any old woman who knows magic songs? But this was a serious matter." Then, according to the do-it-yourself principle, she sets up, with a few fairly simple prerequisites, a magical operation at her house. The ingredients she uses are barley groats, bay leaves, bran, wax, liquids (wine, milk, or water) for libations, coltsfoot (an herb), and pulverized lizard (used by alchemists throughout antiquity and the Middle Ages). Her tools are a magic wheel, a bull-roarer, and a bronze gong. She also keeps a fringe from her lover's cloak—in magical thought any object belonging to a person represents that person—and she shreds it and throws it into the flames. She then addresses various spells and incantations to the full moon in the sky and to Hecate in the underworld, though in some mysterious way the two are identical.

Theocritus' account of this magical ceremony is poetic, not factual, yet there is an amazing degree of truth in it, for extant magical papyri, amulets, and curse tablets, although from a later period, illustrate almost every phase of the operation as he records it, which he does without getting tedious or obscure, as such documents often do.[24]

Literature and Reality

The poets observed magical operations from the outside; but we also have the testimony of the insiders, the professionals. By the end of the last century B.C., Hellenistic magic was fully formed as a system, and all the occult practices that we know of—astrology, alchemy, daemonology—had become applied sciences that could be taught and learned to a certain extent. Much of the instruction was probably carried out in secret, with small groups of disciples studying with a master. The Egyptian priests were supposed to be the keepers of ancient mysteries that they never shared with outsiders, and thus we have practically no information on this kind of apprenticeship. We do have, however, many handbooks and treatises on the more technical sciences, such as astrology and alchemy, and we have a substantial body of recipes and formulas for practical use— that is, the magical papyri. The trend toward specialization continued. The professional astrologer was now usually not a practicing *magus;* as these sciences became more complex, it became more difficult to master them in a lifetime. No doubt some "sorcerers" dabbled in more than one of these arts, and, as an ideal at least, the Faustian type of magician, who is also a great astrologist, alchemist, daemonologist, and physician, was recognized. He was not unlike the "pure" scientist who trained in the school of Aristotle, and he was interested in the whole physical world, in living creatures, plants, stones, and metals; but his experience and methods were different.[25]

Even when the various subjects are kept separate, they explain and interpret one another from our point of view. The astrological texts from Egypt, which F. Cumont discusses, reveal the superstitions that people in late antiquity shared—the hopes and fears, the desires and ambitions, of ordinary men.[26] The magical papyri show us the sort of power that men wished to have over others, and the amulets that people wore, also preserved, indicate how the would-be victims defended themselves. Then as now, people wished for themselves and for their loved ones health and good looks, wealth, success in business, politics, sports, and love, and, if they had been hurt or humiliated, revenge. It is curious that in Hellenistic Egypt the ancient native gods (Isis, Osiris, Horus, Anubis, Typhon) became the sources of magical powers. Their names and attributes were borrowed by practitioners of magic who probably took no part in regular Egyptian cults. Similarly, the formula "Jesus, god of the Hebrews" appears in a spell that obviously was not used by a Jew or a Christian. The Lord's Prayer also appears as a magical formula. It is the same phenomenon that we noted earlier: the gods of a foreign culture are not addressed as proper gods, but since they seem to work for that other culture, they are suspected of having powers that could be useful in magical operations.[27]

Later we shall discuss some literary texts (Horace, Virgil, Apuleius, Lucian, and others) that inform us of magical doctrine and rituals. At this point it seems most convenient to look at the magical papyri, those scrolls and leaves from Egypt which, taken together, formed a practicing magician's collection of spells. Although their date is relatively late (third or fourth century A.D.), they reflect much older ideas, and the doctrines and techniques they embody were probably developed in the late Hellenistic period. Many are considered to be copies of copies; in fact, some of them (e.g., the London Papyrus 46) seem to derive from at least two earlier texts, and one (the Oslo Papyrus) appears to be an approximation of a barely legible earlier specimen.[28]

The first magical papyri discovered in Egypt were brought to Europe by Johann d'Anastasy, the Swedish vice-consul in Cairo from 1828 to 1859. He bought a whole collection that had been discovered, he was told, in a grave near Thebes, but no one seemed to know exactly where or when. This amazing collection contained recipes and formulas for all types of magic: love magic, exorcism, curses. At the time it must have created no less of a sensation than the discovery of the Dead Sea Scrolls or of Menander's *Dyskolos,* and its importance should not be underestimated today. One may think of it as the working library of a magician, a library that was buried with him (some time in the fourth century A.D.) to provide him with magical knowledge in the other world.[29] Some of these papyri were acquired by the Leiden Museum of Antiquities in the early nineteenth century, others by museums in London, Paris, and Berlin. The Great Magical Papyrus, for instance, is in Paris; it consists of 36 sheets covered with writing on both sides, or a total of 3,274 lines.[30]

What we have is no doubt only a fraction of the magical literature available at one time or another in antiquity. From Acts 19:18–20 we know that Paul made many Ephesians bring out their magical books (which were worth a great deal of money) and burn them; Ephesus was apparently one of the centers of magic, and *Ephesia grammata* are "magical words." The language of the magical papyri would require a separate study. They reflect various levels of literary skill, but generally they are standard Greek; they are not incorrect, but presumably they are closer to the spoken language than to poetry or artistic prose. Many terms are borrowed, it seems, from the mystery cults; thus magical formulas are sometimes called *teletai* (literally, "celebrations of mysteries"), or the magician himself is called *mystagōgos* (the priest who leads the candidates for initiation).

Often the texts are written in the form of a recipe: "Take the eyes of a bat . . ." [*no. 24*]. These recipes, along with the appropriate spells and gestures, are supposed to produce a variety of effects: they guarantee revealing dreams and the talent of interpreting them correctly; they send out daemons to plague one's enemies; they break up someone's marriage or kill people by insomnia. There is a definite streak of cruelty in some of these ceremonies, and Theocritus, in the text discussed above [*no. 4*] shows how love magic, which seems harmless enough, can turn into hate magic if the victim does not respond. The same is true for Dido's magical ceremony at the end of *Aeneid* 4 [*no. 9*]. The magician seems to think: "If you won't love me, I'll kill you," a feeling that has caused countless tragedies in literature and in real life.

The magical ostraca are a variety or subspecies of the magical papyri, but the material used (broken pots) was cheaper (some papyri actually recommend the use of ostraca), and the texts had to be shorter. They range chronologically from the fourth century B.C. to Byzantine times, and they operate along the same lines as the spells on the magical papyri. A love spell from Oxyrhynchus, for instance, is designed to break up a woman's marriage and attract her to the sorcerer instead.

The "curse tablets," *tabellae defixionum,* are another important primary source of our knowledge of magic. The term *defixio* is derived from the Latin verb *defigere,* which means literally "to pin down," "to fix," but which also had the more sinister meaning of delivering someone to the powers of the underworld. Of course, it was possible to curse an enemy through the spoken word, either in his presence or behind his back, and this was thought to be effective. But for some reason it was considered more effective to write the name of the victim on a thin piece of lead (other materials were used as well) with magical formulas or symbols and to bury this tablet in or near a fresh tomb, a place of execution, or a battlefield, to give the spirits of the dead—which were presumed to hover around such sites on their way to the underworld—power over the victim. Sometimes the curse tablets were transfixed by a nail (the *defixio* dramatized), or they were thrown into wells, springs, or rivers.[31]

The curse tablets cover a much wider range of time than the magical papyri: the first examples are from the fifth century B.C.; the last, from the fifth century A.D.; they are particularly frequent in the Hellenistic period and toward the end of antiquity. The oldest examples are very simple: "X, bind Y, whose mother is Z," where X is either a (Hellenic) god or a daemon and Y is the victim. It is curious that the victim is identified by his or her mother rather than by the father, as might be expected, since this was the common form of introducing someone. Moreover, it is remarkable that familiar Greek gods can be substituted for magical daemons. Later, as the texts become more elaborate, they contain magical diagrams, series of vowels, and names of foreign gods who are probably considered more powerful than the native ones. Often the curse tablets were aimed at an athlete, a charioteer for instance, to prevent him from winning. The populace was usually divided in its loyalty to an athlete or a team, and since, no doubt, large bets were placed on the victory or defeat of one or the other, emotions ran high.

Amulets were worn as protection against curses, the evil eye, and evil powers in general.[32] These tokens were often made of cheap materials, but precious stones were thought to have special powers; they were also more durable, and so thousands of carved gems that had a magical rather than an ornamental function have survived.[33] One might wear them around the neck or on a ring. On an Egyptian jasper, for instance, there might be carved a snake biting its own tail, two stars, the Sun, and the words *Abrasax, Iaô,* and *Sabaôth* (*Abrasax* being a magical word, and *Iaô* as well as *Sabaôth* being different names for the supreme Jewish-Christian deity).

The word *amulet* is probably derived from *amolitum* (see Pliny *NH*, 28.38, 29.66, 30.138), whereas *talisman* could be an Arabic transformation of Greek *telesma* 'initiation'. Any devotee of magic, whether gentile, Jew, or Christian, could wear amulets, with their mixture of Babylonian, Egyptian, Greek, and cabalistic elements, regardless of his faith or affiliation.[34] The amulets carry the same formulas as the papyri, though these inscriptions were probably copied from the papyri in a more abbreviated and concentrated form. Again, it seems that the papyri were the working texts of the professional sorcerer and could be put to various uses.[35]

The world of the ancients was full of magical powers, acting in all directions, and many people must have felt constantly threatened. To protect oneself by wearing an amulet was probably not safe enough, and since attack is the best defense, a good deal of black magic was probably performed as a simple measure of precaution: if you suspected someone of putting a curse on you, you put a curse on him and let it be known. Hence a sort of equilibrium was established in which one could exist and pursue one's everyday business.

Something should be said about magical ingredients, tools, and devices. Magical tools were used again and again, just as the spells and incantations were repeated on each occasion. Herbs and other ingredients, however, were used up and had to be replenished. Plant magic and the use of a wand are as old as Homer. Theocritus' amateur witch also used herbs, and in addition a magical wheel, a bull-roarer, and a gong. Moreover, special plates and rings were to be worn during the ceremony. Such a magician's kit, probably dating from the third century A.D., was discovered in Pergamon. It consisted of a bronze table and base covered with symbols, a dish (also decorated with symbols), a large bronze nail with letters inscribed on its flat sides, two bronze rings, and three black polished stones inscribed with the names of supernatural powers. This kit seems to have worked on the principle of a roulette table.[36]

The Roman historian Ammianus Marcellinus (29.1.25–32) describes a kind of ancient Ouija board that was used in a séance in A.D. 371 with very unfortunate results for all the participants.[37] It consisted of a metal disk on whose rim the twenty-four letters of the Greek alphabet were engraved, supported by a tripod made of olive wood. To consult this portable oracle, one had to hold a ring suspended on a light linen thread. After lengthy prayers and incantations addressed to an anonymous "deity of divination" (perhaps Apollo), the ring began to swing from one letter to another, forming words and names, sometimes even sentences in verse form. Two questions that were no doubt frequently asked during such séances were clearly asked during this one—and this made the whole experiment definitely illegal and subversive: "When will our emperor die?" and "Who will be our next emperor?" The first question was answered by the oracle poetically (but accurately it appears); as for the second question, the ring spelled *thēta*, then *epsilon*, then *omikron* (giving 'Theo-'). At this point an impatient participant jumped to the conclusion that the oracle was about to spell out *Theodorus*, and the group stopped the whole procedure right there. Somehow the authorities learned of the secret gathering, and all those involved—including Theodorus, who denied all knowledge of it—were arrested, tried, and executed. Seven years later it became evident that the oracle had tried to get the truth across. The emperor Valens was killed, and the name of his successor was Theodosius!

The use of symbols, numbers, and strange words in magic must be very old, though the abracadabra formula is not attested before Serenus Sammonicus, the author of a work *Res Reconditae (Secret Matter)*, who was murdered in A.D. 212.[38] Symbols are signs that preserve human experience and can create powerful reactions, sometimes more powerful than the reality they represent.[39] Numbers are symbols too, and number mysticism is well attested in Hellenistic magic.[40]

What emerges from the evidence is the permanence and universality of magic in the ancient world. Although some testimonies may be relatively late, the doctrines and practices they reveal are often much older. Certain formulas and recipes were handed down for generations, perhaps with minor changes, and though they are found on tablets and papyri dating from the early Christian era, they probably had been practiced for centuries. Moreover, it is clear that the same type of magic was practiced throughout the Roman Empire.[41]

Types of Magical Operations

Our material permits a division of magical operations into two main kinds, theurgical and goetic. The word *theurgia* calls for a brief explanation. In some contexts it appears to be simply a glorified kind of magic practiced by a highly respected priestlike figure, not some obscure magician. Dodd says: "Proclus grandly defines theurgy as 'a power higher than all human wisdom, embracing the blessings of divination, the purifying powers of initiation, and in a word all the operations of divine possession'" (Procl., *Theol. Plat.* [=63 Dodds]). It may be described more simply as magic applied to a religious purpose and resting on a supposed revelation of a religious character. . . . So far as we can judge, the procedures of theurgy were broadly similar to those of vulgar magic."[42] Here again we see how difficult it is to separate magic from religion: if Dodds' definition is valid, any theurgical operation must have both a religious and a magical aspect. In a typical theurgical rite the divinity appears in one of two ways: (1) it is seen in trance, in which case the soul of the theurgist or medium leaves the body, ascends to heaven, sees the divinity there, and returns to describe the experience; (2) it descends to earth and is seen by the theurgist either in a dream or when he is fully awake. In the latter case, no medium is needed; only certain "symbols" and magical formulas are required. The "symbols" could be an herb, a stone, a root, a seal, or an engraved gem, and the formulas might include the seven vowels of the Greek alphabet, representing the seven planetary gods.[43] Sometimes the divine presence manifests itself more indirectly, through a medium or a requisite such as the flame of a lamp or the water in a basin.

The term *goeteia* is a synonym for *mageia*, but has even more negative undertones, it seems, just as *theurgia* is definitely more exalted than either. Perhaps these three terms reflect a long battle between believers and nonbelievers, and the attempt by the various groups of practicing believers to distinguish their "magic" from the lower types or techniques that existed at all times. Hence, it could be argued that the term *theurgia* was introduced to make magic a respectable practice for the philosophers of late antiquity, who would have been horrified to be called *magoi* or *goetes*, especially the latter, since that term could also designate a juggler or charlatan—the gypsylike type of fraud who was out to make a quick profit at fairs and festivals all over the Greek world.

The philosophers who were interested in magic described themselves at theurgists, and the lower-class practitioners as *magoi* or *goetes*. According to Plotinus (*Enn.* 4.4.26), theurgy aims at establishing sympathy in the universe and uses the forces that flow through all things in order to be in touch with them. He admits that it works, but he rejects some of its claims and practices (*Enn.* 4.3.13; 4.26.43–44). Thus, the theurgist achieves in reality what the philosopher can only think (Iambl., *Myst.* 3.27).

The term *theurgist* seems to have been introduced by Julianus, a Hellenized Chaldean who lived under Marcus Aurelius. Theurgists formed a late pagan religious sect. They not only talked about the gods as the theologians did; they performed certain actions by which, they claimed, the gods were affected. "Theurgy, like spiritualism, may be described as magic applied to a religious purpose and resting on supposed revelations of a religious character."[44] Their sacred book, *The Chaldean Oracles*, is lost, but parts of it can be reconstructed. They used mediums. Thus, there was an important difference between the theurgists and the theologians; the latter mainly thought and talked about the gods; the former tried to influence them, forced them to appear, even created them.[45]

These theurgical operations appealed to the Neoplatonists, who believed that by ascetic exercises and proper initiation they could either bring divine powers down to earth or make their own souls ascend to heaven. Thessalus of Tralles (first century B.C.) was granted a personal vision of the god Asclepius by an Egyptian priest in Thebes.[46] In other words: theological or philosophical thought is not enough; certain actions, procedures, or rites have to be followed.

But is theurgy really different from magic? In a sense, it is. Franz Cumont called it "a respectable form of magic, an enlightened type of sorcery,"[47] and we may add that the great theurgists of antiquity were highly educated men and women of impeccable reputation, totally different from the sellers of curses and spells.[48]

We know very little about the ritual itself, no doubt because it was kept secret, but it was apparently based on the doctrine of sympathy between things visible and things invisible, beings of this world and beings of another world. The initiation of the emperor Julian[49] gives us an impression of the ritual, but the report we have is sketchy, almost incoherent, full of symbolism and allusions that would make sense only to fellow-initiates:

> Voices and noises, calls, stirring music, heady perfumes, doors
> that opened all by themselves, luminous fountains, moving
> shadows, mist, sooty smells and vapors, statues that seemed
> to come to life, looking at the prince now in an affectionate,
> now in a threatening manner, but finally they smiled at him
> and became flamboyant, surrounded by rays; thunder,
> lightning, earthquakes announcing the arrival of the supreme
> god, the inexpressible Fire . . .

How all these effects were produced is unknown, but they are reminiscent of initiation rites that were required in the mystery religions.[50] There is no evidence that everything was fraud, and it is hard to believe that mechanical tricks, elaborate staging, and so on could fool a man like Julian. It makes much more sense to assume that Julian submitted to some kind of "programming" (months of indoctrination, ascetic exercises, etc.), which, through the use of drugs, either ingested or inhaled, produced an altered state of consciousness at the crucial moment.

In addition to the spoken word (*to legomenon*), certain requisites and rites (*to dromenon*) were necessary. Porphyry gives us a portrait of a theurgist (actually a statue, but the implications are unmistakable, I think), his head wreathed with bandages and flowery branches, his face anointed or actually made up, a laurel twig in one hand, magical symbols on his shoes.[51] And Iamblichus writes:

> The theurgist, by virtue of mysterious signs, controls the
> powers of nature. Not as a mere human being, or as [one who]
> possesses a human soul, but as one of a higher rank of gods,
> he gives orders that are not appropriate to the condition of

man. He does not really expect to perform all these amazing
things, but by using such words he shows what kind of power
he has and how great he is, and that because of his knowledge
of these mysterious symbols he is obviously in touch with the
gods.[52]

It seems that even Iamblichus, a believer in theurgy, makes certain distinctions: not everything the great theurgist says and does will have an
immediate magical effect; much of it serves to create a mood, an atmosphere that prepares the faithful for greater things to come, such as
autopsia, the appearance of the divine light without any shape or form.
    Theurgy could therefore be defined as an attempt to reestablish,
through indoctrination, training, ritual—in short, through "programming"—and possibly through the use of certain drugs, the status of the
great *shamans* of archaic Greece such as Pythagoras (whose biography
Iamblichus wrote).
    To read about magical operations can be a tantalizing experience.
The reader is often led up to a certain point, but the real secret—the
words or rites that make the magic work—seems to lie beyond that point.
Obviously, there are things that our texts do not reveal, and it makes
sense that the magician would not entrust everything to papyrus but
would reserve what he considered an essential element to private instruction. Astrology is perhaps the only "occult" science that could be learned
from a good handbook. Nevertheless, none of the texts that have survived from antiquity gives us a complete introduction; there are always
gaps, perhaps left on purpose, so readers would have to study with a
professional astrologer. The same is true for alchemy: the texts are either
too general or too technical, and if one wanted to pursue the subject, one
would have to be close to an experienced practitioner, watch him, consult
him, use his equipment and his books.[53] There are, at every step, allusions, symbols, a kind of mystic shorthand that would be intelligible and
useful only to the initiated and that would have to be explained by a
master. It seems safe to venture the statement that magic "worked" only
within a group—often a very small group—of devotees and practitioners
who gave one another mutual support even when, from an outsider's
point of view, their magic failed.
    Even the relatively simple, early forms of magic such as those
attested in Homer and in Apollonius of Rhodes [*nos. 1* and *3*] involve a
kind of ritual. By the end of the Hellenistic period this ritual had become
very complex. It generally included *klēsis* 'invocation' and *prāxis* 'ritual',
properly speaking.[54] The invocation summoned a divine power by name,
though sometimes the name was not written in, in our documents: it was
either kept secret or left open, a blank for the *magus* to fill in. The name of
the god or goddess was not enough; it had to be accompanied by a string

of epithets describing the powers of the divinity (*aretalogia*). The *magi* wanted such lists to be as complete as possible, for it might be dangerous to omit one epithet that the god was particularly fond of; hence the lists tended to grow and grow. The invocation was also a means of reminding the divine power of past occasions when he or she had helped the operator in a striking way or performed some sort of miracle. It might also include a specific request for a specific occasion—for example, what the divinity was expected to do for the operator now.

The *prāxis* tended to be just as complex as the *klēsis*. Long litanies were recited mainly in Greek, but sometimes in a kind of nonlanguage consisting of strings of magical words. Presumably they were recited in a way that could be learned only from an acknowledged teacher. The gestures had to be performed correctly, the right kind of equipment had to be used. Some of these ceremonies must have lasted for several days and nights. Substances (sulfur, for example) were sniffed, libations were poured, visual and acoustic effects were produced—and no doubt drugs were used to help induce a state of trance. We read about weird sounds made by the *magus:* clucking, sighing, groaning, smacking of lips, taking a deep breath and letting it out with a hissing sound.[55] In some cases it was even necessary to eat the magical text, as *PGM* 1.14 prescribes: "Write these names with Hermes ink. After having written them as told, rinse them off in spring water from seven springs, drink it on an empty stomach during seven days, when the moon is ascending. But drink a sufficient amount!" Magicians also wrote certain words or names in their own blood.[56]

It seems paradoxical that for certain periods we are better informed on magical rituals than on religious ones. Moreover, although the magical rituals often betray what appears to be a genuine religious feeling, the elements of pressure, blackmail, and sinister threats often build up in and are reinforced by the rituals.

Hellenistic magic represents a conglomerate of many different influences. It borrowed freely from the religions and occult sciences of different cultures (Greek, Jewish, Egyptian, Persian, etc.), but even the religious elements were selected for a practical purpose: the gods of witchcraft were worshiped not for the sake of their glory but for the help they could offer in specific situations. Often these gods were asked to fulfill wishes that the operator would not acknowledge openly; hence, magical prayers and spells were usually "whispered" or "hissed," whereas in the temples of a god or goddess legitimate prayers were uttered aloud. But the syncretism of Hellenistic magic had a parallel in the syncretism of Hellenistic religions in Egypt, a country where many different cultures coexisted, a country that had been open to Eastern influences for centuries and that now, under Greek rulers, had been given a capital,

Alexandria, that would become one of the intellectual centers of the world.

Let us turn, then, to the Persian origins of magic. Persian priests, the *magoi,* were supposed to have inherited the lore of the Chaldeans. Chaldea, or "the land of the Chaldeans," was the name of a country (according to Genesis it was the home of Abraham), but a Chaldean could also be an astrologer or an interpreter of dreams, originally perhaps a member of a priestly caste that studied occult rituals and handed them down. Zoroaster (sixth century B.C.) was the greatest teacher, priest, and magician (a figure comparable to Orpheus in some ways) in the early Persian Empire. He lived during the reign of the Achaemenids and wrote many works on magic, astrology, divination, and religion. He is considered the creator of a system of daemonology that was adopted at various stages and in various forms of Jews, Greeks, and Christians. Another great Persian *magus,* Ostanes, accompanied Xerxes on his campaign against Greece (480 B.C.), no doubt as an adviser to the king. After his defeat at Salamis, the king left Ostanes behind, and Ostanes became the teacher of Democritus (born c. 470 B.C.), apparently encouraging his pupil to travel to Egypt and Persia. Democritus is chiefly known as a great scientist (his atomistic theory of the universe anticipates modern physics and chemistry); he may have transmitted Persian magic in one of his many works.

The *magoi,* who came to Palestine from a distant oriental country to offer their adoration to the new-born child in Bethlehem, are represented as kings and as wise men. Clearly they are skilled in astrology, for a star or an unusual constellation has told them of the birth of a king.

Zoroaster, Ostanes, and the three *magi* mark half a millennium. During that time and for centuries to come, the Western world associated Persia with magic and secret lore.

In Egypt, according to our theory, a kind of curriculum of occult sciences was created during the Hellenistic period. To the Greeks living there, many religious ceremonies must have appeared to be magical operations. Then, too, the Greeks probably considered to be magic certain manufacturing processes that the Egyptians kept secret. From the beginning, alchemy seems to have been a mixture of magic and real technology, but the secrecy that enveloped both probably exaggerated the role of the former. Some typically Egyptian features of Hellenistic magic are: (1) Magic is not practiced primarily as a necessary protection from the evil powers that surround the individual; rather, it is a means of harnessing good or evil powers in order to achieve one's goals and desires. (2) The operator of the magical papyri pretends to be a god in order to frighten the gods. This attitude of pretending, of temporarily assuming a supernatural identity, is highly characteristic of magic in general. (3) Magical power is linked to certain words that are clearly differentiated from normal language; they are pronounced in a certain way or written on gems, papyri, and the like, along with certain signs and diagrams. (4) Power is also linked to certain gestures and rites; these rites are similar to the ones used in religious cults, but, one would assume, are sufficiently different and distinctive to avoid misunderstandings. It was common, for instance, to sacrifice black animals to the powers of the underworld to make sure that none of the heavenly gods would claim it for himself.

The Greek influence on Hellenistic magic can only be sketched at this point. In a sense, Hellenistic magic was a Greek creation on Egyptian soil: Greek philosophers had given it a basis and built it into a system. In terms of specifics, however, while the magical operations are familiar, the roles of the gods are not. Hermes becomes identified with the Egyptian Thoth, not only as the patron of science and of learning in general, but also as the god who leads souls into Hades. Hecate, the most ancient goddess of the underworld, becomes, along with Persephone, the divinity *par excellence* of the witches, as does the moon goddess, Selene, who presides over their nocturnal rites. Apollo, the official god of the Delphic oracle, becomes tied to divination in many forms. Pan, as god of the witches, furnishes the traditional image of the Devil; hence he must have played an important role in magical ceremonies in later antiquity, although the texts do not give a coherent picture of this development.

We should also consider the influence of Judaism, and especially Jewish magic, on Hellenistic magic.[57] Alexandria had a large Jewish population in the later Hellenistic period, and it seems to have contributed a good deal to Hellenistic culture in general. On one level we have the daemonology of Philo, a Jewish Platonist, and on another level, all sorts of popular superstitions.[58]

The Old Testament gives us a certain amount of information on magical practices and beliefs, and the very fact that they were outlawed indicates that they existed.[59] In turn, toward the end of the Hellenistic period, Jewish magic was strongly influenced by Greek and Egyptian ideas.[60] By that time many Jews—like the Greeks and Romans—believed in the evil eye, the power of certain words and phrases and of spittle, the *omina* given by birds, the protection afforded by amulets, and so on.[61] The difference between black magic and white magic was understood. Necromancy was practiced (necromancers were called "bone-conjurers"), as was exorcism (since diseases in general and madness in particular were explained by possession), usually as a last resort when medical science failed.[62]

Because he practiced exorcism and because of some popularized versions of the Gospels, Jesus was considered a magician by some Talmudic teachers and no doubt appeared as such to many Romans who did not think of him as a religious leader.[63] It is easy to see how even Moses, in later antiquity, could appear to be a powerful magician in addition to being a great teacher and leader, the inventor of philosophy, learning, writing, and so on, like the Egyptian Thoth. Moses and Aaron perform magic in the Egyptian style before Pharaoh (Exodus 7:8–14; 8:1–15) to compete with the Egyptian sorcerers, and though the sorcerers can duplicate the Jewish magic up to a certain point, Moses and Aaron win the contest because they receive their guidance from the Lord. Magical books were ascribed to Moses in antiquity (*PGM* 13).

Solomon's great wisdom was supposed to include magic, and a magical text, the Testament of Solomon, circulated under his name; it was probably composed in the early third century A.D., but the manuscripts attesting it were not written before the fifteenth and sixteenth centuries.[64] The much better known Wisdom of Solomon, a biblical book considered apocryphal by Jews and Protestants, was probably composed in the first century B.C. In it Solomon says: "God . . . gave me true knowledge of things, as they are: an understanding of the structure of the world and the way in which elements work, the beginning and the end of eras and what lies in-between . . . the cycles of the years and the constellations . . . the thoughts of men . . . the power of spirits . . . the virtues of roots. . . . I learned it all, secret or manifest." Clearly, Solomon is pictured as the greatest scientist, but also the greatest occultist, of his time: he has studied astrology, plant magic, daemonology, divination, but also *ta physika* 'science'. Some translators obscure this fact; they write, for instance, "the power of winds" when the context shows that daemons are meant. Josephus certainly understood the passage in this way. He writes (*Antiq. Jud.* 8.45): "God gave him [Solomon] knowledge of the art that is used against daemons, in order to heal and benefit men." He even adds that Solomon was a great exorcist and left instructions on how to perform this kind of healing. This could mean that in Josephus' time, a magical text existed which taught how to exorcise daemons in the name of Solomon.[65] In Justin's *Dialogue with Trypho* (85.3) a Jewish magician is addressed as follows: "If you exorcise a daemon in the name of any of those who once lived among you—kings, righteous men, prophets, patriarchs—it will not obey you. But if you exorcise the daemon in [the name] . . . of the God of Isaac and the God of Jacob, it may obey you. No doubt your exorcists apply magical techniques when they exorcise, just like the Gentiles, and they use fumigations and incantations."

In later antiquity, the Jews had the reputation of being formidable magicians, and the various names of their deity—Jao for Yahweh, Sabaoth, Adonai—appear frequently in the magical papyri. Many outsiders must have thought of Yahweh as a secret deity, for no image could be seen and his real name was not pronounced. Here again we see a misunderstood theology or religious ritual at the basis of speculations on magic.[66]

The roots of *cabala* 'received tradition' are believed to reach back into the first century A.D., when the first tracts appeared in Palestine.[67] The cabala is best explained as a system or method of Jewish mystical devotion having certain magical elements. It flourished in Spain in the twelfth and thirteenth centuries but is much older. The cabalists believed in the possiblity of direct communion with God, the descent and incarnation of the soul, and the transmigration of souls. They extracted hidden meanings from the Bible by interpreting it allegorically or by using numerology, giving each Hebrew letter in a word or sentence a numerical value. The world, according to them, is inhabited by daemons, and men need amulets to protect themselves. In brief, the cabalistic tradition has preserved, in a systematic and coherent form, blended with Platonist and Neoplatonist doctrine, a good deal of occult science from late Hellenistic times.

Having surveyed the "real" magic, the practical, everyday witchcraft of the period, we can now return to the literary texts.

Other Literary Texts

In his eighth eclogue, Virgil (70–19 B.C.) gives us a free translation or adaptation of Theocritus' second poem [*no. 8;* cf. *no. 4*]. He leaves out a number of details and gives it a happy ending—the magic works and the lover returns—but otherwise, he is quite faithful to the original. Poems such as these describe the life of the so-called lower classes (shepherds and peasants) with a kind of poetic realism, but they are addressed to a highly sophisticated audience. Virgil's amateur witch cannot be assigned to any social class; one would assume that she is a farm girl, but her passion is noble, romantic like that of any Greek heroine, and she speaks in accomplished Latin verse. Undoubtedly, this kind of magic was practiced in Italy as well as in Greece and Egypt. Virgil may have left out something here and there or added some color, but the magical operation as a whole sounds authentic.

A more serious magical ceremony is described by Virgil at the end of Book 4 of the *Aeneid* [*no. 9*]. The hero of the epic, Aeneas, has landed on the coast of North Africa, where he meets Queen Dido, who has just begun to build a new city, Carthage. She is not at all like a witch, but rather resembles an oriental fairy tale queen with a tragic past. She falls in love with Aeneas and wants him to stay with her as her prince consort. One is reminded of the Circe episode in the *Odyssey* [*no. 1*] and of the encounter of Jason and Medea in Apollonius' *Argonautica.* In all these epics, a traveling hero with a mission meets a beautiful, exotic woman who is potentially dangerous, although kind and hospitable as long as her love for the hero lasts. When Aeneas leaves Dido because Fate demands that he found an empire of his own, Dido's love turns to hate.

Determined to destroy her faithless lover, she stages a complex magical rite. She builds a gigantic pyre in the main courtyard of her palace and prepares, with the assistance of a famous priestess-witch, an elaborate sacrifice to the powers of the underworld. She realizes that no love magic can bring Aeneas back to her and, despairing, kills herself, giving an ultimate emphasis of doom to her curse. It was commonly believed that suicides, murder victims, men killed in battle—in short, all those who died before their time—could unleash enormous powers of destruction at the moment of their death and for some time afterward. Dido had thus both sealed and extended her curse through her death. She did not destroy Aeneas, who, like Odysseus, was protected by his own gods and reached the coast of Italy safely after many other adventures, but her curse lingered on. Generations later, Rome was almost conquered by Hannibal and his Carthaginian army, but once more the gods of Rome prevented the worst from happening.

In her last wish to hurt Aeneas—and Rome—Dido is more like Medea than Circe [see *no. 11*]. But she also resembles Cleopatra, the queen of Egypt, who in Virgil's lifetime had love affairs with two great Romans: Julius Caesar and Mark Antony. Cleopatra's image was so distorted by contemporary Roman propaganda that her power over these two men could be explained as witchcraft, an art she could easily have learned in the country of her birth. Virgil thus borrowed something from the mythical heroines Circe and Meda and something from a historical person, Cleopatra.[68]

Horace (65–8 b.c.) was Virgil's contemporary and friend. Two of his poems (*Epodes* 5 and *Satires* 1.8) deal with witchcraft. The fifth epode [*no. 6*] is remarkable because here a child is murdered by witches for magical purposes. A clique of witches led by Canidia has kidnapped a Roman boy of noble birth and buried him up to his chin in the ground. Close to his head they place a dish of food which he cannot reach. They intend to starve him to death and then to remove his liver, which, they believe, will grow because of his growing hunger. In vain does the child plead with the degenerate hags: they want his liver in order to brew a particularly powerful love potion. The intended victim of this potion is a man called Varus, who has not yet responded to Canidia's usual spells and brews, and she assumes that he has rubbed himself with a magical unguent given to him by a redoubtable rival of hers. Realizing that he will not be spared, the boy directs a terrible curse against the witches. This curse is a form of magic, too, for the spirits of those who die young or who die a violent death can turn into daemons of vengeance.

Satires 1.8 [*no. 7*] deals with witchcraft in a more humorous vein. Here, the wooden statue of the god Priapus is speaking. The statue has been placed in a beautiful modern park on the Esquiline in Rome as a threat to thieves and birds. But this park was once a cemetery for the poor, and at night, in the light of the moon, the witches, again led by Canidia, still haunt the place, digging for human bones or calling up the shades for necromantic purposes. They also perform other kinds of magic, and these rituals are so revolting that even Priapus, who is not a very refined god, loses his nerve and lets out a resounding fart. This works like a charm: the witches run away screaming; one of them loses her wig, the other her false teeth.

After a careful reading of these two pieces, it is difficult to say whether an educated man and famous author like Horace actually believed in witchcraft. In one poem he seems to take it quite seriously; in the other he makes fun of it. Naturally, the fact that he writes about Canidia with such intense feeling gives her a special kind of reality and makes her, along with Medea and Lucan's Erictho, one of the great witches of ancient literature. That witchcraft was practiced in ancient Rome by women who looked more or less like Horace's Canidia cannot be doubted; that many people were afraid of these women is equally certain. On the whole, however, they seem to have lived underground, so to speak, in the slums of Rome, threatened by laws which, though not always enforced, provided for drastic punishment.

Instead of following a strict, chronological order, it might be better to discuss briefly Seneca, the philosopher and playwright (c. 5 B.C.–A.D. 65), and his nephew, Lucan (A.D. 39–65), the epic poet, because they continue the literary tradition of the superwitch. Seneca's tragedies reflect the taste for the horrible, cruel, and grotesque which seems so characteristic of the early Roman Empire. He selects some of the most gruesome Greek myths for dramatic treatment (*Thyestes*), and he spins out the theme of magic, necromancy, and the like where it is given by the mythical tradition (*Medea* [see *no. 11*]) and even where it is barely indicated (*Heracles on Mount Oeta* [see *no. 10*]). From the dialogue between Deianira and her nurse [*no. 10*] we learn that it was quite common for jealous wives to consult a witch (Seneca projects this into the age of myth); as it turns out, the nurse, very conveniently, is a witch herself. Deianira offers to help by plucking rare herbs in remote places, but she is not sure that magic will work in the case of her unfaithful husband, Heracles; there is at least an implication here that a great hero such as he cannot be influenced by magical means. In the end he is overcome by a deadly poison that Deianira gives him, believing it to be a love charm.

In the two selections from Seneca's *Medea* [*no. 11*] it is remarkable how the image of Medea has changed in the three centuries since Apollonius wrote his epic [*no. 3*]. Her invocations and incantations are no longer left to the reader's imagination: they are spelled out. Her power of hating, which she can switch on, so to speak, and intensify at will, is still the dominant theme, but Medea now has her cabinet of horrors from which to select the most efficient engines of destruction. Her magic now involves the whole universe; she claims that she can force down the constellation of the Snake.

The magical papyri illustrate the sense of power that filled the operator during the course of the ritual. Seneca must have known such texts, but he gives them a rhetorical build-up, a literary polish of which the professional magicians were hardly capable. Like Horace, he endows the magical arts with a poetical and terrifying reality. Whether these plays were performed on the stage or were simply recited, they must have shocked a contemporary audience, and shock, *ekplēxis*, was supposed to have a therapeutic value. It is probably fair to say that Seneca created horror not for horror's sake but because, as a Stoic philosopher, he believed that the shock produced by horror cleansed the soul of all the emotions that interfere with peace of mind. As a Stoic, Seneca also believed in cosmic sympathy, and thus some of the tenets of magic would have made sense to him, even though he may not have accepted their exaggerated claims.

The ultimate horrors and powers of witchcraft are portrayed by Lucan in Book 6 of the *Pharsalia* [*no. 58*], no doubt in an effort to surpass his uncle, Seneca. Before the decisive battle of Pharsalus (48 B.C.), in which the forces of Julius Caesar defeated those of Pompey, the two armies had been moving through Thessaly, the classical country of witchcraft. There, one of Pompey's sons consults the famous witch Erictho about the outcome of the impending confrontation. In Lucan's epic, Erictho is the most powerful witch, although she is also the most loathsome and disgusting. More powerful and horrible than Medea, she can compel some of the lesser gods to serve her and cause them to shudder at her spells. Through his encounter with Erictho, this frightening apparition, the reader is again supposed to experience shock. In the end he will wonder whether such a monster should be hated or respected: to love her would be impossible, and in this respect she is totally different from Circe, Medea, and Dido, who were all loved, although briefly, by traveling heroes. Shelley admired Lucan greatly, and it is possible that this passage from a poet whom her husband placed above Virgil gave Mary Shelley the idea for her novel *Frankenstein*. The idea of an artificially created human being or a revived corpse may be older, but Lucan was much more accessible than any tract of the ancient alchemists who were experimenting with this.

At this point we should probably discuss three historical persons of the first century A.D. who seem to have had at least some of the powers of the *shaman* documented in earlier times by Orpheus, Pythagoras, and Empedocles. It is almost as if this old tradition of *shamanism* had been briefly revived. The three men I propose to compare with each other, from a purely historical point of view, on the basis of controversial evidence and with all due caution are: Jesus of Nazareth, Simon Magus, and Apollonius of Tyana.[69]

It is difficult to describe Jesus in terms of this particular tradition, but since he was called a "magician" by Jews and Gentiles alike, it seems legitimate to examine some of these charges. From any outsider's point of view, Jesus may have looked like the typical miracle-worker. He exorcised daemons, he healed the sick, he raised the dead, he made predictions, but outside of walking on the waves, he never performed the kind of ostentatious magic that Moses and Aaron performed when they defied the Egyptian magicians. He did not, however, practice necromancy. Nevertheless, within three hundred years of his birth, he was accused of stealing the "names of the angels of might" from Egyptian temples (Arn., *Adv. Gent.* 1.43). The "angels of might" could be translated as "powerful daemons," and the Egyptian concept of "words of power" could be connected with Jesus' belief in angels close to the throne of the Father.[70] Jesus has power over the minds of men, and he represents a limit beyond which the human imagination cannot go. According to the Gospels, he does not practice necromancy, but his life story is colored by features that can be paralleled elsewhere: his divine origin, his miraculous birth, the annunciation and the nativity surrounded by unusual events; he is menaced in infancy; he is initiated into his own ministry by John the Baptist, an earlier evangelist who yields before him; he has to face Satan, a powerful daemon representing the evil forces in the world, and refuses to make a deal with him, winning in a trial of spiritual strength. These encounters and confrontations can be paralleled: Abaris yielded to Pythagoras, just as John the Baptist yielded to Jesus, and Zoroaster had to resist evil daemons.

The important point seems to be this, however: when Jesus was challenged to prove his divinity by performing the kind of magic that many people might expect from him, he refused to do so. He did perform "magic" of a kind spontaneously, but he did so out of compassion, not merely to impress the skeptics or score a point; in fact, he is sometimes slightly impatient with those who need "signs and wonders" to believe in him. It almost seems that magic "flows" out of him, not as a conscious effort, as the result of complicated rituals, but simply because of a power (*dynamis*) that he transmits. Jesus' healing power works when the patient and the bystanders have faith in him (Luke 8), but it also works even when the patient is unaware of being healed (Matthew 8). On the whole, faith does not seem to matter—the power still works, and then faith is created; it is not always a condition. Faith can generate the miracle, but the miracle also generates faith.

It should be noted that Jesus never claimed to perform miracles all by himself; rather, he taught that his power came from the Father and was readily available, without complex sacrifices and incantations. There was no mumbo-jumbo, no hocus-pocus. Moreover, Jesus did not accept any fees for what he did: he considered it part of his ministry to heal the sick, and he passed the gift on to his disciples. Clement of Alexandria (*Strom.* 6.3) says that the pagans were wrong to deny the miracles recounted in the Gospels, for God is infinitely great and can easily perform miracles at any time, without any help from magical arts.

Matthew's report that Jesus was taken to Egypt as an infant was used by hostile sources to explain his knowledge of magic; according to a rabbinical story, he came back tattooed with spells.[71] It is also pointed out in the rabbinical tradition that Jesus was "mad," which probably means "emotionally unstable," one of the characteristics of the *shaman,* or occasionally "in a state of trance," (e.g., when receiving a vision). The Gospels speak of the "descent of the spirit," the outsiders of "possession by a daemon," and both are possibly describing the same mystic phenomenon, the former as Jesus would explain it, the latter in a negative way. It has even been suggested that Jesus' claim to be "the Son of God" is a formula used in magical rites by the operator who identifies himself closely with the supernatural power that he invokes.[72]

A word of caution should be added here concerning these and similar theories, for that is what they are, theories, not facts. Some of the material comes from sources hostile to Jesus and the early Church; words and facts were either invented or distorted in order to discredit him. The parallels from the magical papyri, even if they were conclusive, are of doubtful value, for they may have been influenced by stories circulating about Jesus. We have seen how eager the magicians were to add to their repertory of formulas, rites, and names, especially if they seemed to work within the context of a new religious movement. At least some contemporary magicians clearly were not just traditionalists; they observed what was going on in the world and added new material to their stock-in-trade. To them Jesus must have appeared to be a very powerful fellow-magician from whom they could learn a lot. This certainly does not mean that he was a magician. The outsiders were incapable of realizing what was new and different in Jesus' life and teaching, and they reduced it to their own level. Certain aspects of Jesus' ministry can perhaps be illustrated by certain things contemporary magicians did or said, but the whole of his ministry has no parallel. It is precisely the nonmagical dimension in Jesus that made the early Church grow strong in such a short time; if it had been magic, history might have taken a different course.

Simon is the name of a *magus* mentioned in Acts 8:9ff. and elsewhere.[73] He was active in Samaria about the time of the Crucifixion, and his disciples called him "the power of God which is called the Great Power."[74] Simon was deeply impressed by the apostle Philip's cures and exorcisms and by the gift of the Spirit which came from the apostles' laying on of hands; therefore, he not only "believed and was baptized" but he asked the apostles to sell him their special gift so that he could practice it too. This is the typical attitude of the professional magician, and it illustrates what has been said above. To Simon, the charisma of this new religion is a kind of magic that can be purchased, for a price, and he is prepared to pay for it as he probably had before for the kind of magic he had learned. The sharp rebuke that he draws from Peter—and that he is flexible enough to take in good grace—shows how the early Church drew a line between itself and practitioners of magic such as Simon.[75]

We hear about Simon again from Justin Martyr (e.g., *Dialogue with Trypho*, ch. 120), who says that he was a *magus* born in Samaria, that his followers worshiped him as the supreme God, and that a Phoenician woman, a former prostitute called Helen, lived with him; she was considered the "primary notion" emanating from him, though in a different context. She was a fallen power for whose salvation he had appeared. Justin also reports that in Rome a statue was erected in his honor on Tiber Island, with the inscription SIMONI DEO SANCTO, "To Simon, the Sacred God." By an amazing coincidence a monument bearing an inscription that begins with the words SEMONI SANCO DEO was found in Rome, but this was clearly a statue of a very old Italic deity known as Semo Sancus, who had a cult on Tiber Island, perhaps nearly extinct by this time, and it is possible that the followers of Simon used the old statue for their own worship. Or perhaps Justin simply misunderstood the inscription SEMONI SANCO DEO for SIMONI DEO SANCTO.

According to other early Christian writers (e.g., Epiph., *Adv. Haeres*. 6.21.2ff.), Simon established his own Trinity, in which he was the Father, Jesus was the Son, and Helen was something like the Holy Spirit; but in another sense, Simon really was all three. This remarkable bit of theology would seem to show how skillfully Simon adapted the Gospel to his own needs. Indeed, it looks as if he started out as a *magus* and then, inspired by the example of Jesus, developed into a cult figure by borrowing from Christianity whatever suited him. He and Helen were worshiped before statues of Zeus and Athena; this, no doubt, was designed to make the ritual more palatable to the Gentiles. The priests of Simon's religion were said by some early Christian writers to practice both magic and free love—a combination of charges which appears throughout history.

From the testimonies that we have, Simon Magus emerges as a kind of *shaman*, a practitioner of occult science (which he was supposed to have learned in Egypt) with Christlike aspirations. Unlike Jesus, he used daemons for his own purposes, practiced necromancy, and even claimed, according to the *Clementine Recognitions*,[76] to have created a human being. The text may be corrupt, but on the whole the meaning seems clear: Simon claimed to have invoked the soul of an innocent boy who had been murdered and commanded it to enter a new body that he had made from air, thus forming a new human being. He boasts that this was a far nobler achievement than the creation of Adam by God the Father, "for he created a man from earth, but I from air—a much more difficult thing." When people demanded to see this *homunculus*, Simon answered that he had already made him disappear into air again.

The moment of truth came when, according to Acts, Simon and Peter challenged each other before the emperor Nero in Rome. Like earlier confrontations between a mere magician and a true religious leader,[77] it was a contest of spiritual powers. Simon actually managed to fly through the air for a short time, impressing Nero, but Peter broke the spell and made the magician crash to earth so badly that he never recovered. His resurrection within three days, which he himself had predicted (provided he was buried alive), never took place, "because he was not the Christ," Hippolytus notes sarcastically (*Haer.* 6.20.3.).

The third *magus* of this period was Apollonius of Tyana, who was born in Cappadocia a few years after Jesus, it seems, and survived into the reign of Nerva (c. A.D. 97). About a century later, Flavius Philostratus wrote a comprehensive *Life of Apollonius of Tyana* [see *no. 26*], which, though not exactly trustworthy, is still our most important source.[78] Philostratus, a professional writer, was a protégé of the empress Julia Domna, mother of the emperor Caracalla. This beautiful and cultured lady was interested in philosophy, religion, and science; Galen, the great physician and medical author, was another of her protégés. She owned a document that claimed to be the memoirs of a certain Damis of Niniveh, a disciple of Apollonius; this she gave to Philostratus as raw material for a polished literary treatment. Philostratus complied, and from his biography, which is eminently readable, the strange, ascetic, traveling teacher and wonder-worker called Apollonius emerges. He is usually labeled a Neo-Pythagorean; actually he is more like a new Pythagoras. He certainly represents, in a different age, the same combination of scientist, philosopher, and *magus*, even though he explains this kind of "magic" as a science. A revival of Pythagoreanism took place in the first century A.D.; its centers were Alexandria and Rome. If we can trust his biographer, Apollonius traveled as far as India, where he exchanged ideas with the Brahmins, who were considered to be true Pythagorean philosophers.

What we know of Apollonius' teaching is fairly consistent with traditional Pythagorean doctrine. Animals have a divine soul, just like human beings; hence it is a sin to kill an animal, either to eat it or use its fur or skin for clothing or to offer it to the gods as a sacrifice. Vegetarianism and a pure, ascetic life in general are necessary. Apollonius also believed in the transmigration of the soul and claimed to remember his own previous existences, but he explicitly denied certain astonishing feats that were ascribed to him by Philostratus (*Life of Apollonius of Tyana*

8.7)—for example, that he had descended into the underworld and that
he could raise the dead. Since he was arrested on charges of magic twice,
once under Nero and again under Domitian, he must have had every
reason to reduce the miracles he was credited with to reasonable dimensions. His disciples probably made him into more of a thaumaturge than
he himself wanted to be. In some ways Apollonius resembles Socrates: he
enjoyed lively philosophical debates and was very good at using an opponent's premises against him, leading him on *ad absurdum*. Like Socrates,
he had a *daimonion* [see *no. 53*]. Unlike Socrates, he published; we know of
one treatise, *On Sacrifices*.

     In the early fourth century A.D. a new effort was made to discredit
the Christians, perhaps in order to justify the persecutions ordered by
Diocletian. A high official in his administration, Hierocles of Nicomedia,
wrote an anti-Christian pamphlet entitled *The Lover of Truth*, in which he
tried to show that Apollonius ranked above Jesus both as a teacher and as
a miracle-worker. His thesis was rejected, probably soon after A.D. 310, by
the Church historian Eusebius, himself a survivor of the persecutions.[79]

     Apollonius was worshiped by his followers as a holy man or a
divine being, and he had a shrine in his birthplace, Tyana. At one time, a
statue of him stood in the private chapel of a Roman emperor, along with
statues of Abraham, Orpheus, Jesus, and others.[80] But even the enthusiasm of the empress Julia Domna, her son, Caracalla, and the fine literary
style of Philostratus could not spread his cult throughout the empire.
Julian, an earnest believer in theurgy and a defender of paganism, never
mentions Apollonius.

     Something should be said about the spiritual movements of later
antiquity, which, although often not clearly distinguishable from one
another, were, at the time, different. Although they were more like exclusive theologies, and their followers did not necessarily practice magic,
they can be labeled "occult sciences."

     First we shall discuss Gnosticism.[81] The term is derived from
gnosis 'knowledge'—not just any knowledge, but knowledge *par excellence*, "knowing God." To the followers of this ideal, the highest goal in
life was to escape from the evil environment surrounding them, to ascend
to the realm of the good, which is, at the same time, the ultimate reality.
To escape from the visible world by "knowing God" is to be saved. To be a
Gnostic meant to rise above all earthly things and thereby to lose interest
in the body, its needs, functions, and emotions. Everything else followed
from this; hence it was not necessary to design a system of ethics for the
problems of everyday life, as imperial Stoicism and the early Church did.

     It has been suggested that Gnosticism derived from Orphism but
was also influenced by Babylonian astral religion and by Hermeticism.
This is hard to prove, however, because by that time Orphism, like
Pythagoreanism, had lost much of its original character.

Some Gnostic leaders—for instance, Carpocrates of Alexandria (c. A.D. 120)—apparently used incantations, drugs, and messages from spirits or daemons, but since much of this information has come down to us through Christian authors who were hostile to the Gnostics, it is not considered reliable. There seems to have been a genuine interest within Gnosticism to reconcile Christianity with contemporary philosophy and occult science, but on the whole the Gnostics were more concerned about understanding how the cosmic mechanisms worked than about switching them on and off.[82]

Hermeticism is a related movement. We have a considerable body of Hermetic writings that promise mankind deeper knowledge of and control over nature.[83] Magic, astrology, and alchemy were all part of Hermeticism. The name itself is derived from Thoth, the Egyptian manifestation of the Greek god Hermes, who is for some the most important god of Greece, Rome, and Egypt around the time of the birth of Christ, and is therefore honored by the title Trismegistus, "the thrice greatest." In an attempt to draw in Jewish proselytes, he was even associated with Moses (Euseb., *Praep. Evang.* 9.27.3).[84] Here we observe the tendency to elevate a relatively minor Greek god to the highest possible rank and enrich his image, so to speak, with features borrowed from other religions, especially the most ancient and venerable ones. Such a composite god would be a powerful rival to the popular goddess Isis.[85]

There must have been a good deal of rivalry and competition among these groups. They clearly had much in common, but each one had to have a distinctive feature that demanded total commitment on the part of the neophyte. At this distance it is difficult to see the distinctive features except through the polemic of Christian authors, which helped define the essence of Christianity.

The *Natural History* of Pliny the Elder (A.D. 23/24–79) is a voluminous survey of science, pseudoscience, art, and technology. Reflecting the state of knowledge of the late Hellenistic era, it is based on a hundred or so earlier authorities. This huge compilation deals with cosmology, geography, anthropology, zoology, botany, pharmacology, mineralogy, metallurgy, and their uses in ancient art. It is a mine of information and misinformation, but since almost all the sources that Pliny used are lost, it is of considerable value to us, and it had great influence on later scientific thought. Pliny himself was neither a philosopher nor a trained scientist in the modern sense of the word, but he had read a great deal, always taking notes, and had developed a philosophy, partly derived from Middle Stoics such as Posidonius, in which there was room for the forces of religion as well as those of popular and advanced magic. His attitude, his general curiosity, may be compared to that of Apuleius. He believed in ancient traditions and was convinced that the power of certain herbs or roots was revealed to mankind by the gods, although he also recognized the role of chance. Men stumbled upon the truth by accident; then they tested it by experiment. The divine powers, in their concern for the welfare of mankind, have ways of making us discover the secrets of nature, and this is really what is called progress today. In their wisdom and love the gods bring us gradually closer to their own status; this is the Faustian aspiration of "being like the gods." There will always be progress of this kind, according to Pliny.[86] How it works in the short term is not so important; in the long term it emanates from benevolent powers. This concept is firmly rooted in Middle Stoicism: here we have a "cosmic sympathy" that, if properly understood and used, operates for the good of mankind.

With all his learning, Pliny preserved many religious and magical beliefs and practices, and much of this tradition was folklore with a scientific pretense. He did not believe in the effectiveness of all magical arts; in fact, he felt that most claims of the professional sorcerers were exaggerated or simply false (25.59, 29.20, 37.75). The sorcerers would not have written down their spells and recipes unless they despised and hated mankind (37.40). If their promises were worth anything, the emperor Nero, who studied magic with the best teachers and had access to the best books, would have been a formidable magician, but in fact he did nothing extraordinary (30.5–6). Pliny's conclusion, however, is cautious: though magic is ineffective and infamous (*intestabilis*), it nevertheless contains at least "shadows of truth" (*veritatis umbras*) which are due to the "arts of making poisons" (*veneficae artes*). Hence, it is the drugs that really work, not so much the hocus-pocus of spells and ritual. Yet, Pliny states, "there is no one who is not afraid of spells" (28.4), and he seems not to exclude himself. The amulets and charms that people wore as a kind of preventive medicine he neither commends nor condemns. It is better to err on the side of caution, for, who knows, a new kind of magic, a magic that really works, may be developed somewhere this very minute. This is why the professional magicians, as we have seen, were always on the lookout for new ideas.

A large part of Pliny's enormous work deals with remedies and drugs to cure diseases. Most of them are herbal preparations. Pliny's medicine is primarily folk medicine, which does not mean that it is totally unsophisticated, for it has a long history that is enriched by valid scientific discoveries.[87] By the time of Pliny, many physicians were using drugs in addition to diet, exercise, baths in mineral springs, and reliance on *vis naturae medicatrix*, "the healing power of nature." There is one ingredient that Pliny mentions time and again, for both internal and external application, an ingredient whose value is recognized today: honey.

Altogether Pliny gives several thousand recipes for drugs and remedies (especially in Books 20–32). Personally, he prefers herbal simples, but he also notes mixtures, animal remedies, and even drugs concocted by the *magi*, although he dislikes and despises them heartily. Pliny devotes the beginning of Book 30 to the *magi* and refers to them here and there especially in Books 28 and 29.[88] To him they are basically sorcerers, but they might also be priests of a foreign religion, such as the Druids of the Celts in Britain and Gaul. He even includes Moses in a list of famous *magi*, as if he had heard the Old Testament story of Moses' performance before Pharaoh. According to Pliny, the art of the *magi* touches three areas: *medicina, religio*, and *artes mathematicae* (30.1), "healing power," "ritual," and "astrology." This is a curious definition, but perhaps essentially correct, for many professional magicians of that time were probably also healers, performing certain rites, addressing prayers to supernatural powers (*religio*), and many of them no doubt knew something of astrology, even though they did not practice other techniques of divination. Pliny's *religio* is not the same as our *religion*, however; sometimes he uses it in the sense of "superstition," sometimes in the sense of "expression of religious belief or custom" (11.250–51).

In the end, even a well-read, well-educated, enlightened man like Pliny is not sure of what to believe and what to reject. To be on the safe side and to make his work as useful as possible, he hands down, along with many drugs in which he has confidence, a number of superstitions and magical rituals about which he has serious doubts. He dislikes and distrusts professional magicians as a class and calls them "frauds" and "charlatans," and yet he seems to admit, almost grudgingly, that there are certain things they know and can do. His dilemma can best be illustrated by this sentence (28.85): "People agree that by simply smearing menstrual blood on the doorposts, the tricks of the *magi*, those worthless quacks, can be rendered ineffective. I would certainly like to believe this!"

To the Platonist philosopher Plutarch of Chaeronea (c. A.D. 45–125) we owe the treatise *On Superstition*, which reminds one here and there of Theophrastus' sketch [*no*. 2].[89] Plutarch defines *deisidaimonia* 'superstition' as "fear of the divinity or of the gods," though the examples he uses show that, like Theophrastus, he has in mind a kind of fear that becomes an obsession. Specifically, he mentions magical rites and taboos, the consultation of professional sorcerers and witches, charms and spells, and unintelligible language in prayers addressed to the gods.[90] Although Plutarch himself takes dreams (especially those of the dying) and portents seriously, he reserves the term *superstitious* for those who have excessive or exclusive faith in such phenomena. Clearly, it is a matter of discrimination. He also seems to take for granted other magical practices, such as hurting someone by the evil eye, and offers an explanation of that phenomenon (*Table Talk* 5.7). He also believes in daemons that serve as agents or links between gods and men and are responsible for many supernatural events in human life which are commonly attributed to divine intervention. Thus, a daemon, not Apollo himself, is the real power behind the Delphic oracle. Some daemons are good, some are evil, but even the good ones, in a fit of anger, can do bad things.[91]

In general, Plutarch, though he ridicules the excessive, morbid fear of supernatural powers, accepts a certain amount of what we would call "popular superstition," but he is anxious to select only what is compatible with his own philosophical doctrine, and what he selects he purifies and gives, as far as possible, a rational explanation. He does not discuss ritual magic in any detail, and he seems to reject astrology; in his biography of Romulus (ch. 12) he ridicules a friend of Varro's who tried to determine the date and time of Romulus' birth by working backward from his character and from certain known facts of his life. This operation also led indirectly to a secure date, the astrologer believed, for the foundation of Rome.

A later Platonist, Apuleius of Madaura (born c. A.D. 125), gives us a substantial amount of information on contemporary beliefs in occult science. We have the speech he delivered in his own defense against the charge of magic, c. A.D. 160, and from this *Apologia* (another title is *De Magia* [*On Magic*]) we learn how easy it was, at that time, for a scientist and philosopher to be accused of magical practices. We also learn that the accusation could be used as a pretext to destroy an enemy. Yet Apuleius may not have been completely above suspicion. In his novel, *Metamorphoses* (also known as *The Golden Ass*), a piece of fiction which seems to have autobiographical elements, the hero, Lucius, dabbles in magic as a young man, gets into trouble, is rescued by the goddess Isis, and then finds true knowledge and happiness in her mysteries.[92] It is the story of a conversion. As an extension of his normal philosophical curriculum, a talented, intellectually curious young man attempts to study magic, but he falls in with a group of professional witches who play nasty tricks on him. Delivered from distress and disgrace by the goddess Isis and cured of his unhealthy curiosity, he becomes a deeply religious person, though still a philosopher. To him, religion and philosophy (or science), cleansed of their magical elements, offer, as J. Tatum writes, "a means of making sense of an unpredictable and cruel world."[93] This was exactly the role that magic claimed, but in addition to "making sense" it attempted to "control" the negative powers in the world and promised all kinds of thrills and excitement to the neophyte, and in all this it obviously failed. What can be said of Apuleius can probably be said of many "intellectuals" (as we would call them today) of his period. Magic held tremendous attractions for them, but the more deeply they studied it, the more aware they became of its dangers.

The transformation of Lucius, the hero of the novel, into an ass is described in Book 3 [see *no. 29*]. The main characters are Lucius, the eager young student of magic who is determined to learn the secret of transformation, though he had been warned of the risks; and Photis, the attractive young witch whose mistress, Pamphila, a more advanced sorceress, has a kind of magical workshop on the roof of her house—a wooden shelter hidden from view but open to the winds and crowded with her requisites: herbs, metal plates inscribed with magical characters, various ointments in little boxes, and, most gruesome of all, parts of dead bodies stolen from cemeteries or places of execution (*Met.* 1.10; 2.20–21).

Around A.D. 160 Apuleius came to Oea, a city in North Africa, where an illness forced him to stay longer than he had planned. A friend with whom he had studied in Athens introduced him to his mother, a rich widow by the name of Pudentilla, who was about ten years older than Apuleius. When the two got married, the relatives of her first husband feared for the inheritance they expected, and when Apuleius' friend suddenly died in mysterious circumstances, they accused him of murder, later changing this charge to witchcraft. The speech that he delivered in court not only tells us a great deal about magical beliefs and practices, folklore, and superstitions, but it reflects what people thought witches and magicians did in secret. If Apuleius had not convinced the court of his innocence, the presiding Roman magistrate could have sentenced him to death.

In his speech, Apuleius totally rejects the kind of black magic that had been proscribed by Roman Law ever since the Twelve Tables, but he also maintains that some of the greatest philosophers have been unjustly accused of magical practices. He mentions, among others, Orpheus, Pythagoras, Empedocles, and the Persian Ostanes (*Apol.* 27.31). We have seen that these men represented *shamanism* in early Greece, and that it is difficult to separate philosophy (or religion) from magic in their case. Unlike the ordinary sorcerers, however, they never practiced black magic; this is probably what Apuleius wants to say, for he also includes in his list Socrates (whose *daimonion* was considered a strange sort of god by his accusers) and Plato. It seems clear that the ignorant masses and the educated elite could never agree about the differences between witchcraft and some of the more esoteric philosophic or scientific doctrines.

Like Plutarch, his fellow Platonist, Apuleius firmly believed in the existence of daemons, the intermediaries between men and the gods. They populated the air and were, in fact, formed of air. They experienced emotions just like human beings, and their mind was rational. In a sense, then, the human soul was also a daemon, but there were daemons who never entered bodies.[94] In his treatise *On Socrates' God* Apuleius presented a complete, systematic version of daemonology that was acceptable to later Platonists. The discussion is not always easy to follow, and one can see the dangers of distortions and misunderstandings for outsiders. Philosophers speculated about daemons—magicians invoked them—so what was the difference?

Lucian of Samosata was born about the same time as Apuleius (c.

A.D. 125) and died after A.D. 180. Like Apuleius, he traveled from city to city, giving lectures. He also studied philosophy, though he did not belong to any particular school. His philosophical dialogues show the influence of the Platonic dialogues, but he is not a Platonist, and his writings are never as technical as those we have under Apuleius' name. He admires the Epicureans because they fight superstitions in every form.

One of the themes of Lucian's writings is the folly of superstition. It appears, for instance, in a satirical account of the founder of a new cult, Alexander of Abonuteichus, a contemporary of his. Lucian's essay *Alexander, or The Pseudoprophet*, obviously hostile, is our main source of information.[95] Alexander claimed to control a new manifestation of the god Asclepius in the form of a snake called Glycon. Thanks to this divine agent, he dispensed oracles and conducted mysteries to which outsiders, especially Christians and Epicureans (a strange combination), were not admitted. He did have a fairly large number of followers, many women and at least one prominent Roman among them. In his essay Lucian takes great pleasure in revealing the "magic" tricks that Alexander performed in order to impress the ignorant and credulous. For example, the questions submitted to the oracle were sealed and came back with an answer, the seal apparently unbroken; Alexander had several methods of opening them, adding a response, and replacing the seal.

Alexander of Abonuteichus was probably just one of many accomplished impostors of later antiquity. If Lucian is right, Alexander knew how to manipulate crowds by his appearance, his delivery of some kind of message, and his skillful use of mechanical devices to produce sham miracles.

Another fraud is ridiculed in Lucian's dialogue *The Lovers of Lies*. Several philosophers, including a Stoic, a Peripatetic, and a Platonist, along with a physician, talk about miracle cures. Some amazing examples are quoted [*no. 45*]. This leads to a discussion of love magic [*no. 27*] and other astonishing feats. Here we find the original version of the story of the sorcerer's apprentice as told by the apprentice himself. His name is Eucrates, and he had studied with a great magician called Pancrates, who had spent twenty-three years underground learning magic from Isis. Pancrates needed no servants: he took a piece of wood—for instance, a broomstick—dressed it in some clothes, and made it into a sort of robot that looked like a human being to all outsiders (Lucian, *The Lovers of Lies*, pars. 34ff.). One day the apprentice overhears the master whispering a magic formula of three syllables, and when the master is away, tries it on the broomstick. The results are well known from Goethe's poem *The Magician's Apprentice*. At the end of this conversation, even the skeptic (Lucian himself, presumably) is confused and has lost faith in the venerable philosophers who teach the young and perpetuate ancient superstitions. Still, he is not quite sure what to believe and what not to believe.

As far as the story of the great Hyperborean magician is concerned [*no. 27*], Lucian seems to put his finger on the main problem. The magician charges an enormous fee for performing a feat that would have taken place anyway, due to purely natural causes. But the prestige he has, the build-up in front of the audience, the whole hocus-pocus—the public-relations job, as one would say today—are all so impressive that people willingly pay and gladly give him credit, though needless to say he is a fraud.

In another dialogue, *The Ship*, one of the participants tells the others about his fantasies. What he really wants is magical rings from Hermes, rings that will give him eternal youth and the power of inspiring love in those who attract him.[96] This case of wishful thinking is part of the folklore of many countries and finds expression in fairy tales and legends. Such a ring might be compared to the cap that makes one invisible or the wings that enabled Hermes of Daedalus to fly through the air. In response to such fantasies, magic offered an inadequate substitute that seemed to work somehow, with a great deal of faith. It is only fair to say, however, that some very bold short-cut solutions offered by magic have been realized more slowly, but more reliably, by science and technology.

In his dialogue *Menippus*, or *The Necromancy*, Lucian uses motifs from Homer's *Odyssey* [*no. 50*], but he produces a more complex picture of a necromantic ceremony. The satirist Menippus, one of Lucian's heroes, wishes to visit the underworld, and he travels all the way to Babylon to consult one of the *magi*. The preparations he has to make are formidable: purification by ablutions and fumigations, strict diet, sleeping out of doors, taking special precautions. Some of the details seem rather fantastic, others might be part of the long, slow formation of the *shaman*; it is Lucian's technique to mix fantasy with "reality," but by the admixture he shows how little "reality" he thought there was to begin with.

The *magi* of later antiquity could be called "Men with the Double Image."[97] Lucian tapped the potentialities of the occult, and he recognized that there are two different ways of making one's way in the world. He engaged in what a psychoanalyst might today call "objective identification" (i.e., he became the god he invoked: "For you are I, and I am you").[98] The people who pointed their finger at him were "Men with the Single Image." They may have envied the *magus'* way of life, his apparent success; they may have been afraid of his power; but they resented his existence, declared his activities illegal, and tried to entrap him.

It is still difficult to draw the line between philosophers (or scientists) who were just that and philosophers who were also "into magic," to use the contemporary idiom. The archaic combination of both survives on a lower level, as it were. A Neo-Pythagorean like Apollonius of Tyana, a Platonist like Apuleius of Madaura,[99] could be accused of magical practices and in their defense simply say: "As a philosopher [or scientist] I am interested in everything and ready to investigate every phenomenon under the sun. If there is such a thing as magic—and almost everyone seems to believe there is—I want to find out whether it works or not. But let me assure you that I am not a magician, and any miracles that I seem to perform can be explained in scientific terms."

The professional sorcerers of later antiquity were consulted by women and men of all classes, but among their best clients were the *demi-monde* of popular performers, such as athletes and actors who had to give their best in a limited period of time and were naturally afraid that their rivals or the supporters of their rivals might put a spell on them just then.

Apuleius, accused of witchcraft, was a highly educated man, but most real magicians apparently were not. Augustine (*c. Acad.* 1.7.19ff.) was impressed by Albicerius, a sorcerer who had helped him find a lost silver spoon; this man could also "thought-read" lines from Virgil in the mind of a proconsul. But according to Augustine, he lacked education; hence, he could not be "good." This may seem a curious verdict to us, but ever since Cicero the word *humanitas* had had two meanings: "higher education" and "human feeling"; to lack the first would exclude one to a certain degree from the second.

But even among the educated, magic was popular because it helped explain misfortune.[100] For Christians and pagans alike, any sort of misfortune—an accident, an illness, even a nightmare—could be the work of superhuman agents, daemons who either acted on their own or were manipulated by an enemy. The Christian Church, in fact, found it convenient to attribute misfortune to the power of witchcraft. Some theologians believed that God had given the daemons authority to act as his "public executioners" (Origen, *c. Cels.* 8.31), to punish the human race for Adam's sin. Thus the world had become a playground for daemons, an area where they could release their destructive urges: "He has sent upon them the anger of His indignation and rage and tribulation and possession by evil spirits" (Psalms 78:49).

Libanius, a contemporary of Augustine's, reacted to bad dreams as if they were symptoms of magical spells and curses.[101] Whenever a person felt inadequate in relation to his or her image (a lecturer forgot the speech he had memorized; a highly respectable lady fell in love with a man socially far beneath her), black magic was thought to be at work. Thus it is not always just misfortune, but misfortune accompanied by a sense of shame or guilt, that leads one to suspect magical interference.

Gregory the Great (end of the sixth century A.D.) warned that any woman who slept with her husband on the eve of a religious procession was practically inviting a daemon to possess her, and that a nun who ate lettuce without first making the sign of the cross on it might swallow a daemon perched on its leaves. Daemons were everywhere, and only the Church could give protection.[102]

Theodoret (*Hist. Rel.* 13 [= *PGM* 82, 1405ff.]) tells the story of a girl who had become the victim of a love spell, and of St. Macedonius, who was brought in to exorcise her. The daemon who had taken possession of her excused himself, and naming the sorcerer who had summoned him, declared that he could not leave her easily because he had entered her under great stress. The girl's father then lodged a complaint against that sorcerer before the governor, but Saint Macedonius managed to chase the daemon away before it could be used as a witness in court.[103] The story shows that the Church was able to deal with daemons, but it also shows that the Church accepted the fact of possession by the agency of witchcraft. These daemons had been sent by someone outside the Church, and it was the Church's duty to counteract their evil power.

The belief in daemons is much older than Plato, but it found a home in Platonism and Neoplatonism, and if philosophers, on the authority of Plato, spoke of daemons as real, it is clear that the common people, Christians and pagans alike, also were looking for ways in which to deal with them. The Bible did not offer much technical knowledge— Jesus' exorcisms are always unique and could not be duplicated from any information given in the Gospels—so even the Christians sought guidance elsewhere, in the ancient magical traditions.

The Neoplatonists—at least some of them—became the most ardent defenders of ritual magic and theurgy, perhaps as part of a last effort to suppress Christianity. Plotinus (c. A.D. 205–270), the founder of the school, seems to have had psychic powers [*no. 31*] and certainly took magic seriously [*no. 30*], though it is doubtful he should be called a magician.[104] He believed that the soul was clothed in an ethereal covering, the *ochēma*, which was illuminated by divine light so that spirits and souls (or daemons) could be seen. The soul itself could ascend toward the Absolute through ecstasy. Perhaps one could say that certain inexplicable things happened around him, and no doubt after his death his students speculated a great deal about what had really happened.

Porphyry (c. A.D. 232–304) in his *Letter to Anebo*, criticizes the exaggerated claims of certain Egyptian theurgists: they threatened to frighten not only the daemons, or the spirits of the dead, but the Sun and the Moon and other divine beings of a higher order; they pretended to be able to shake the heavens, to reveal the mysteries of Isis or interfere at a distance with her sacred rites. How can blatant lies force the gods to tell the truth? And why do the Egyptian theurgists insist that Egyptian is the only language these gods understand? What Porphyry attacks is not the theory that magic works, but the techniques employed by its Egyptian practitioners and their blatant self-advertisement.

Iamblichus (c. A.D. 240–330), another Neoplatonist, replies to Porphyry's letter in a work entitled *On the Mysteries of Egypt* [*no. 32*], which is basically a defense of ritual magic and theurgy and which deals, from a philosophical point of view, with the techniques of inducing the presence of daemons or gods.[105] Iamblichus firmly believes that the world is managed by a host of daemons and that the magician-priest, if he has been duly initiated and trained, can get in touch with these subordinate deities and control them to a certain degree. In this work, which is an important source for understanding religious feeling in antiquity, Iamblichus describes in detail the visions he has had of spirits, probably hallucinations in a half-waking state.

The full-scale persecution of magic by the state begins in the fourth century A.D.[106] The emperors clearly felt uncomfortable at the thought that astrologers might be able to predict their death accurately and that magicians might put a curse on them. At times even the wearing of an amulet was considered a crime. In a parallel movement, the Church now also condemned witchcraft, but for different reasons. The fears of the Church were not unfounded, for the emperor Julian, "the Apostate" (A.D. 361–363), hated the Christian faith and tried to restore the old religion. From that point on, the two ruling forces of the empire, Roman law and the Church, combined to fight witchcraft, and this alliance continued into the Middle Ages.

Ancient Magic and Psychic Research Today

Many phenomena described in ancient texts as magical feats might now be called paranormal, supernormal, or parapsychical.[107] Today, parapsychology has become an academic subject, and experiences similar to those reported by ancient authors have been observed and studied over a long period of time. Experiments have been conducted in order to understand the nature of extrasensory perception (ESP), telepathy, psychokinesis, and the like, and the literature that is available is enormous. In some ways we have come a little closer to understanding the stories and speculations that have reached us from antiquity. If telepathy is real, we can no longer dismiss as fraud stories like the vision of Sosipatra [no. 49]. Of course, there were cases of fraud: supernatural lights and voices could be created by simple devices. From Hippolytus (Haer. 4.35) we hear of a glass-bottomed cauldron of water that was placed over a small skylight, and of a seer who, gazing into the cauldron, saw in its depths various daemons, who were actually the magician's accomplices in the room below.[108] People wanted to see daemons, so a clever operator gave them daemons. Whenever a magician makes grandiose claims, charges a fee, and then produces certain special effects, we ought to be suspicious. But there also seem to be cases that are above suspicion.

Labeling phenomena reported by Greek and Roman writers with modern terms does not really explain them, and it can confuse the issue.

Telepathy, for instance, is derived from two Greek words (*tēle* 'at a distance' and *pathos* 'experience'), but, coined in the nineteenth century A.D., it was never used by the ancient Greeks. Similarly, *medium* looks like a Latin word and is a Latin word, but it was never used by Latin authors in antiquity to describe a person who helped the living communicate with the spirits of the dead; in this sense this term too was coined only in the last century. These terms are useful, but they do not explain what really happens. *Mediumship* may be a real supernormal phenomenon and yet have nothing to do with messages or manifestations from the spirit world. In short, such things may happen, but the traditional explanation is false.

The main difficulty consists in applying modern terms to events and experiences described by ancient sources, for even if the modern term seems to fit, we should not assume that simply because it has a label the phenomenon is now explained once and for all. Where an ancient author speaks of his visions, we might use the term *state of consciousness;* where an ancient author uses the term *ecstasy,* we might prefer *trance.* Ever since William James breathed in nitrous oxide for the first time, we have known that our normal waking consciousness is but one particular state of consciousness, and that there are others, potential or real, that are separated from it only by a screen, as it were.

Thus the psychical research[109] done over the last century or so is valuable for our understanding of occult science in the ancient world as long as we keep these difficulties in mind. Moreover, as Dodds has pointed out, there is a difference between the occultist and the psychical researcher:

> The occultist, as his name betokens, values the occult *qua* occult: that is for him its virtue, and the last thing he will thank you for is an explanation. . . . The genuine psychical researcher . . . is attracted to [occult phenomena] because he believes that they can and should be explained, being as much a part of nature as any other facts. . . . Far from wishing to pull down the lofty edifice of science, his highest ambition is to construct a modern annex which will serve, at least provisionally, to house his new facts.[110]

Much of this cannot yet be explained. Dodds quotes from Augustine (*De Gen. ad Litt.* 12.18) as follows: "If any one can trace the causes and modes of operation of these visions and divinations and really understand them, I had rather hear his views than be expected to discuss the subject myself."[111] But Augustine does not doubt the reality of the visions themselves.[112]

Telepathy, mediumship, and *automatism* are among the most useful terms in our attempt to understand "occult" phenomena in the ancient world, but they do not all belong in the sphere of "magic." Telepathy could be discussed in the chapter on divination. For a Greek or a Roman, mediumship would have been a case of possession, and hence might seem to belong in the chapter on daemonology. The question is: should we put ourselves in the position of the ancients and use their concepts and terms? Up to a point this might be useful, but there is also some value in testing the modern terms by applying them to experiences that were felt to be "magical" or "miraculous" by the ancient narrators.

The vision of Sosipatra, as reported by Eunapius (*Lives of the Philosophers and Sophists* [*no. 49*]), is a good example of supernatural knowledge of an event that happened (at that very moment, it would appear) at a distance from the seer and was verified soon afterward. Livy relates how his friend, the augur Caius Cornelius, actually saw Caesar's victory over Pompey at Pharsalus, thousands of miles away (Plut., *Caes.* 47; Gell., *Noct. Att.* 15.18), and there are other stories of this kind, usually involving important battles. Should this be called "telepathy" or "clairvoyance"? Or is it that "sixth sense" which, according to Democritus,[113] "animals, wise men, and gods" have in common? Or should we simply call it the *psi* faculty, the term parapsychologists use today?

Like Freud, Dodds believed that before the development of language there was an archaic method by which individuals understood one another, a kind of shared consciousness, going back, perhaps to a time when human beings were not yet aware of themselves as individuals.[114] Once this awareness developed and language came into use, that other faculty functioned at an unconscious level and was used only under special circumstances, in an emergency. Normally this faculty manifested itself in dreams or in states of mental dissociation; in fact, the normal consciousness rejects any "occult" communication from outside.

The standard definition of *telepathy* as "the communication of impressions of any kind from one mind to another, independently of the recognized channels of sense" (F. W. H. Myers) would fit a number of cases reported from classical antiquity, and it seems that Democritus (c. 400 B.C.) based his account of divination on that concept. He believed that images are constantly flowing through space, some of them sent out by living persons. These images penetrate the body of the recipient and appear to him, for instance, in a dream. The more excited or emotional the sender, the more vivid the images.[115] In our age of television the idea of images traveling through space at tremendous speed is not unfamiliar. Democritus' sender of telepathic images could be compared to a television station, the recipient to a television set. The comparison does not explain anything, of course, but it seems clear that Democritus, who also anticipated the modern atomic theory, observed genuine cases of telepathy and tried to explain them scientifically.

King Croesus of Lydia's testing of the famous oracles of the Greek world by making them guess a bizarre event that took place under his control, at a certain moment, was an experiment in telepathy (Herodotus 1.47).[116] The king assumed that the oracle who guessed right would also advise him best about the future. Croesus' envoys to the seven greatest oracles were to ask, on a prearranged day, "What is the King of Lydia doing on this very day?" Only the Delphic oracle came up with the correct answer: the King of Lydia was cooking a most unusual dish consisting of lamb and tortoise, in a copper pot. The story has a sad ending, however. After this rather frivolous or, as some Greeks thought, blasphemous experiment, Croesus put his trust in the Delphic oracle, asked a crucial question, received an ambiguous answer, attacked Persia, and was defeated. This story may be a Greek invention, but the idea of such an experiment may well have occurred to a Middle Eastern ruler of that time.

The "Tale of the Wicked Innkeeper" is quoted by several Stoic philosophers as an example of the truth that is revealed to us, under certain circumstances, in dreams.[117] Two travelers arrive at Megara together. One has to stay at an inn, the other spends the night at the house of a guest-friend. The second man has a vivid dream: he sees his fellow traveler being killed by the innkeeper, jumps out of bed to run to his aid, but then says to himself that it was only a dream and goes back to bed. But now he has a second dream, in which the other man informs him that he has, indeed, been murdered and tells him to go to one of the city gates early in the morning: there he must stop a dung cart because his body is hidden in it. This the man does, the corpse is found, and the innkeeper is arrested as a murderer. Whether the story is genuine or not we cannot tell, though it does sound authentic. How to explain it, as Dodds says,[118] is even more difficult: is it telepathy from a man being murdered (in the case of the first dream) and clairvoyance on the part of the dreamer (in the case of the second dream), or are there other explanations?

Psychokinesis has received a good deal of attention in recent years. It can be defined as the moving or alteration of objects without direct physical contact. This ability is attributed to daemons in some legends of early saints,[119] and in Philostratus' *Life of Apollonius of Tyana* (4.20), the daemon, after having been forced to leave a possessed youth, overthrows a statue nearby. There is a story of a walking statue in Lucian's *Lovers of Lies* (ch. 21), but this seems to be a joke aimed at the belief in animated statues.[120] Some cases that have been reported could be considered instances of the "poltergeist" phenomenon. The house in which the future emperor Augustus was nursed as a baby—some said he was born there—was supposed to be inhabited by such a force, and when a new owner, either in ignorance or because he was too curious, tried to sleep in a certain room, he found himself ejected, mattress and all, by a "sudden, mysterious force" (Suet., *Aug.* 6).

There are various states of "mental dissociation," as they are called today: dreams, slight distractions, hallucinations of the dying and the mentally disturbed, and "mediumistic" states voluntarily induced.[121] For a Greek or Roman, any form of dissociation may have been considered a case of possession. As Dodds, from his personal experiences as well as from his knowledge of the ancient sources, points out, the "more extreme symptoms" are interpreted as signs of possession, and the experience of symbolic physical phenomena confirms the religious authority of the possessed and his or her utterances. Lights are seen, not always by all witnesses, at the moment when the medium is falling into trance or emerging from it; this means, no doubt that these sittings were usually held in dark or semidark rooms.[122] Levitation of the medium when in trance is also reported,[123] but this seems to have a religious rather than a magical significance, because in different cultures it is consistently the mark of a good and holy person: Indian sages (i.e., fakirs or yogis), Jewish rabbis, Christian saints—even Jesus, according to the apocryphal Acts of Peter (32)—had the gift.[124]

Phenomena of materialization are also described as "spirit forms," which are shapeless or take on a recognizable shape;[125] they have been compared to the "ectoplasm" that some modern spiritualists claim to have seen emerge from and return to the body of a medium.[126]

Automatism is another modern term applied to certain occult phenomena. It means, essentially, that someone else or something else is taking over and that one loses, for awhile, control over a sense or a muscle. Dodds distinguishes four main types of automatism: (1) visual, (2) auditory, (3) motor or muscular, and (4) vocal, actually a subspecies of (3) because, in speaking, muscles are used.[127]

Visual automatism[128] is the modern term for scrying or crystal-gazing—that is, the technique of seeing images in crystal balls, mirrors, or water which reveal the future or, less frequently, secrets of the past and present. *Catoptromancy,* the use of a mirror for this purpose, was already practiced in Athens in the fifth century B.C.[129] When water is used, the terms are *hydromancy* (divination by water) or *lecanomancy* (divination by means of a bowl). The latter method seems to have originated in Babylonia, where oil was poured on water, and the shapes it formed were observed and interpreted. A similar custom has survived in Europe into the twentieth century: the pouring of melted lead into a pan of water on Halloween or New Year's Eve to see what the New Year will bring (Halloween is the Celtic New Year's Eve). The oil or lead is not necessary, for the scryer ought to be able to see figures in the water. Nor is this technique always used for divination: the theurgist may use catoptromancy or hydromancy to see God. In ancient times this technique was used for the most mundane of purposes, such as recovering money or valuable objects that had been stolen or lost, but it was also practiced by magician-priests, within an established sanctuary, as part of a mystic ritual to produce visions of gods.

Auditory automatism[130] is the hearing of supernormal voices. Technically speaking, an Old Testament prophet hearing the voice of Yahweh is a case of this kind of automatism. The phenomenon was more frequent among the Jews than among the Greeks and the Romans, it seems, but Socrates' *daimonion* is a notable exception; though it did not deliver long messages to his inner ear which he could share with others, it always stopped him from doing one thing or another. Whether he actually heard anything at all or just felt a kind of restraint, we cannot know. Later texts such as the pseudoplatonic *Theages* make him deliver oracles, but they seem to be the work of authors who did not know Socrates himself.

It would be wrong to say that an individual who experiences visual or auditory automatism is entirely passive, just the recipient of visions and voices. There is also a more active, "muscular" or "motor" automatism, which, according to Dodds, accounts for automatic writing and drawing, table-tilting, and the so-called Ouija board.[131] Actually, vocal automatism or mediumship could also be treated as a form of "muscular automatism," though, as Dodds says, it involves "a much more profound degree of dissociation than the types so far considered, and has correspondingly made a much deeper impression on the popular imagination of all periods."[132] The type of Ouija board described earlier is a good example; it is an experiment that can easily be reproduced today.

Eighty Egyptian priests moving the statue of a god at the oracle of Zeus Ammon "wherever the will of the god directed them" (Diod. Sic. 17.50.6) must have been an even more impressive sight, but it involved the same unconscious muscular movement or pressure that activates the Ouija board. Though the technique had its origin in Egypt, it was practiced in Antium (not far from Rome), in the sanctuary of Fortuna, as late as the fifth century A.D. Macrobius (*Sat.* 1.23.13) describes the "moving statues of the Fortunes which give oracles" at Antium.[133] The details are not known, but we may imagine several statues, each one representing Fortuna, the goddess of Chance, each one carried by a group of priests in a certain direction, "as the deity moved them." One direction perhaps meant "yes," another one "no," but the spectacle must have been striking, and since there were several statues, more applicants could be dealt with. It is possible to think of the whole operation as a kind of gigantic Ouija board.

Automatic speech or *mediumship*[134] are modern terms that have been used to explain cases of possession reported from ancient times, and in a sense the Pythia at Delphi, a woman in trance who spoke with a voice not her own, was a case of possession; the only question was, who possessed her—Apollo himself or some minor daemon? All we can say is that her state of consciousness was autosuggestively induced, and that she had very little control over it. Not everyone was suitable to serve as a medium, but "young and unsophisticated persons" were the best candidates.[135] How they were put into trance we do not know, but a simple ritual such as the putting on of special vestments, sitting in a holy place, touching holy water, reciting prayers, or chanting hymns may have operated as an autosuggestion. At this distance in time it is difficult to determine whether this phenomenon was spontaneous or induced. "Speaking with tongues" (glossolalia) was, in a sense, an early Christian equivalent of the unintelligible utterances of pagan prophets and prophetesses; an interpreter who was also psychic, but in a different way than the medium, was needed (see 1 Corinthians 12:10).

Hypnotism was probably practiced in antiquity, though no detailed account of its use has survived.[136] The technique of inducing (in the absence of drugs) a trancelike state in a person and thus rendering that person more susceptible to external suggestions and directions is probably very old and may have been handed down as a secret in certain sanctuaries in Egypt and Greece. In more recent times, the Austrian physician Franz Anton Mesmer (1734–1815) discovered in himself a quality he called "animal magnetism" and he used it to cure or relieve certain disorders. After Mesmer that trancelike state was called "mesmerism." Then, in 1842, the Scottish surgeon James Braid coined the term neurohypnotism, which is still used in shortened form. Although it is derived from the Greek word hypnos 'sleep', hypnosis was never used in the modern sense by any ancient writer. Instead, the Greek word ekstasis 'stepping outside oneself' was used to describe this trancelike state, whether spontaneous or induced, hypnotic or mediumistic.

It would be tempting to investigate the relationship between the ancient magi of the Western world and the yogis and fakirs of India, who seem to be able to control the automatic processes of the body, can live without food and drink for days, have visionary and telepathic experiences, and are said to perform miraculous feats. Such paranormal happenings are documented but remain largely unexplained. There are peculiar parallels between the Greek and Latin texts and modern eyewitness reports from India. Is it possible that some of the early Greek shamans learned their techniques in India, where these traditions are still alive? A discussion of the whole problem would require a book in itself.

We have seen the many different forms magic took in classical antiquity. It is a great distance from Homer's Circe to Lucan's Erictho, and there are many differences between the *magi* of early Greece and the sorcerers of later centuries, but they all have one thing in common: they all personify the desire of man to impose his will on nature and to become, like Prometheus, like Doctor Faustus, "equal to the gods." Much of ancient magic in a sense anticipates (as a dream, at least) modern science and technology; but much of it also reveals man's continuous yearning for *gnosis*, the knowledge or understanding of mystical things.

Notes

1. Thorndike, *A History of Magic and Experimental Science*, 1:2.
2. Festugière, *La Révélation d'Hermès Trismégiste*, 1:76, 89.
3. Suet., *Calig.*, ch. 5.
4. R. Ehnmark, in *Ethnos* 21 (1956): 1; E. R. Goodenough, *Jewish Symbols in the Graeco-Roman Period*, 13 vols. (New York: Pantheon Books, 1963–68), 2:155; M. Smith, *Jesus the Magician* (New York: Harper, 1978), ch. 1 passim.
5. M. Smith, *Jesus the Magician*, ch. 1.
6. A. Dieterich, *Mutter Erde*, 3rd ed. (Leipzig: Teubner, 1925); I. F. Burns, in *Encyclopaedia of Religion and Ethics*, ed. J. Hastings, 12 vols. (New York: Scribner, 1908–21), 4:145 (hereafter cited as *ERE*), E. O. James, *The Cult of the Mother Goddess* (London: Thames and Hudson, 1959).
7. Bidez and Cumont, *Les Mages hellénisés*; R. N. Frye, *The Heritage of Persia* (London: Weidenfeld and Nicolson, 1962), p. 75.
8. P. Ghalioungui, *Magic and Medical Science in Ancient Egypt* (London: Hodder and Stoughton, 1963), p. 18.
9. R. Wasson, C. A. P. Buck, and A. Hofmann, *The Road to Eleusis* (New York: Harcourt, Brace, Jovanovich, 1978).
10. D. MacDowell, in his commentary on Andocides, *On the Mysteries* (Oxford: Clarendon Press, 1962), app. N.
11. M. P. Nilsson, *Greek Piety*, trans. H. J. Rose (New York: Norton, 1969), pp. 14–15.
12. C. M. Bowra, *Homer* (New York: Scribner, 1972), pp. 125–28.
13. Dodds, *The Greeks and the Irrational*; W. K. C. Guthrie, *A History of Greek Philosophy*, 6 vols. (Cambridge: Cambridge University Press, 1962–81), 1:146ff., 2:12ff.
14. On *shamanism* see, among others, J. A. MacCulloch, in *ERE*, 11:441ff.; M. Eliade, *Le Chamanisme et les techniques archaïques de l'extase* (Paris: Payot, 1951); H. Findeisen, *Schamanentum* (Stuttgart: Kohlhammer, 1957).
15. Dodds, *The Greeks and the Irrational*, p. 140.
16. Ibid., p. 147.
17. Arist. frag. 191 Rose (3rd ed.) (= pp. 130ff. Ross).
18. Burkert, *Lore and Science in Ancient Pythagoreanism*, pp. 162ff.
19. Dodds, *The Greeks and the Irrational*, pp. 145–46.
20. Thorndike, *A History of Magic and Experimental Science*, pp. 26ff.

21. Apollonius of Rhodes and Theocritus, both of whom represent the Alexandrian style in Greek poetry.
22. On the evil eye see F. T. Elworthy, in *ERE*, 5:608ff.; E. A. W. Budge, *The Mummy: Chapters in Egyptian Funereal Archaeology*, 2nd ed., repr. (New York: Biblo and Tannen, 1964), pp. 316ff.
23. H. Schweizer, *Aberglaube und Zauberei bei Theokrit* (Basel, 1937).
24. Similar rituals have been observed in other cultures. In his *Popular Antiquities of Great Britian*, 2 vols. (London: J. R. Smith, 1870), 1:379ff., John Brand quotes and illustrates a poem by Thomas Gray:

> Two hazel nuts I threw into a flame,
> And to each nut I gave a sweetheart's name:
> This with the loudest bounce me sore amaz'd,
> That in a flame of brightest colour blaz'd.
> As blaz'd the nut, so may thy passion grow,
> For 'twas thy nut that did so brightly glow.

This appears to be a magical guessing game. A girl throws nuts into a fire, giving to each the name of a young man, in order to find out which one truly loves her. This is not real love magic, as in Theocritus, but is closely related to it.
25. Festugière, *La Révélation d'Hermès Trismégiste*, 1:189.
26. F. Cumont, *L'Egypte des astrologues* (Brussels: Fondation Egyptol. Reine Elizabeth, 1937).
27. Bell, *Cults and Creeds in Graeco-Roman Egypt*, pp. 71ff.; A. D. Nock, in *Journal of Theological Studies* 15 (1954): 248ff.
28. Hull, *Hellenistic Magic and the Synoptic Tradition*, pp. 23ff.
29. K. Preisendanz, in *Zentralblatt für Bibliothekswesen* 75 (1950): 223ff.
30. The Greek magical papyri were published by K. Preisendanz, E. Diehl, S. Eitrem, and others (Leipzig: Teubner) in 3 vols.: 1 (1928), 2 (1931), 3 (1941). Only a few copies of volume 3 survived the Second World War. A new edition of the whole work is presently being prepared by A. Henrichs of Harvard University. Counting the more recent discoveries, almost two hundred magical papyri have been published to date. The London and Leiden papyri (= *PGM* 61) were published by Bell, Nock, and Thompson in *Proceedings of the British Academy* 17 (1931): 235ff.
31. On curses see A. E. Crawley, in *ERE*, 4:367ff.; G. van der Leeuw, *La Religion dans son essence* (Paris: Payot, 1948), pp. 395ff.
32. See C. Bonner, *Studies in Magical Amulets* (Ann Arbor: University of Michigan Press, 1969).
33. On these gems see S. Eitrem, in *Symbolae Osloenses* 19 (1939): 57ff. Their use must be old; see Saggs, *The Greatness That Was Babylon*, pp. 303ff.
34. F. C. Burkitt, *Church and Gnosis* (Cambridge: Cambridge University Press, 1932), pp. 35ff., deals with Gnostic amulets.
35. These texts gave the magician elaborate instructions for his own operations, but brief excerpts could be used for the amulets the magician then sold to his customers.
36. R. Wünsch, "Antikes Zaubergerät aus Pergamon," *Jahrbuch des deutschen Archäologischen Instituts, Ergänzungsheft* 6 (1905). In a little-known article,

"Die pergamenische Zauberscheibe und das Tarockspiel" (*Bulletin de la Société Royale de Lund* 4 [1935–36]), S. Agrell tries to establish a connection between the symbols found in the three concentric circles round the edge of the dish and the twenty-two cards of tarot.

37. E. R. Dodds, "Supernatural Phenomena in Classical Antiquity," first published in *Proceedings of the Society for Psychical Research* 55 (1971) and reprinted, with additions, in his book *The Ancient Concept of Progress*, pp. 156ff.

38. *Abraxas*, another magical word, is often found on gems. *Hocus-pocus* appears much later, and its etymology is controversial; some derive it from the pseudo-Latin formula *Hax Pax Max Deus Adimax*, which was first used in the Middle Ages by vagrant scholars who performed magical tricks; others see in it a parody of *hoc est corpus*, "this is the body," which is spoken by the priest during Holy Communion.

39. C. Wilson, *The Occult* (New York: Random House, 1971), p. 106. The pentagram as protection against evil spirits seems to be very old, and it survives far into the Middle Ages; see M.-T. d'Alverny, in *Antike und Orient im Mittelalter*, ed. P. Hilpert (Berlin: De Gruyter, 1962), pp. 158–59.

40. Reitzenstein, *Poimandres*, pp. 256ff.

41. J. M. R. Cormack, "A Tabella Defixionis in the Museum of . . . Reading," *Harvard Theological Review* 44 (1951): 25ff.

42. Dodds, *The Greeks and the Irrational*, p. 291.

43. These symbols were secretly placed by the operator in the hollow inside the statue of a god; see ibid., p. 292.

44. Dodds, *The Ancient Concept of Progress*, pp. 200–201; see also idem, *The Greeks and the Irrational*, appendix.

45. See E. des Places, in *Entretiens de la Fondation Hardt* 21 (1975): 78–79.

46. See Festugière, *La Révélation d'Hermès Trismégiste*, 1:56ff.

47. F. Cumont, *Lux Perpetua* (Paris: Geuthner, 1949), p. 362.

48. See Thorndike, *A History of Magic and Experimental Science*, 1:319ff.

49. J. Bidez, *La Vie de l'empereur Julien* (Paris: Les Belles Lettres, 1930), p. 79.

50. See J. E. Harrison, in *ERE*, 7:322; G. Luck, in *American Journal of Philology* 94 (1973): 147ff.

51. See Porphyrius, *De Philosophia ex Oraculis Haurienda*, ed. G. Wolff (Leipzig, 1856), pp. 164–65; and Euseb., *Praep. Evang.* 4. 50ff., in the edition of E. des Places (*Sources Chrétiennes* 262 [1979]), where O. Zink discusses the fine robes, the liquids and flowers, and the gestures used in magical operations of this kind.

52. Iambl., *Myst.* 6.6.

53. The correct manner of uttering certain sounds and words was an orally transmitted secret; see Dodds, *The Greeks and the Irrational*, p. 292. Oral tradition obviously played an important role in the teaching of magic and other occult techniques, and our knowledge must remain incomplete or uncertain because that tradition has been lost.

54. Hull, *Hellenistic Magic and the Synoptic Tradition*, pp. 42–43.

55. *PGM* 7:786ff., 13:946.

56. d'Alverny, in *Antike und Orient im Mittelalter*, p. 164.

57. L. Blau's *Das altjüdische Zauberwesen* (Strassburg, 1898) is still useful.

58. A. A. Barb, in *The Conflict between Paganism and Christianity in the Fourth Century,* ed. Momigliano, pp. 118–19.

59. J. Dan, in *Encyclopaedia Judaica* (1971), s. v. "Magic."

60. Blau, *Das altjüdische Zauberwesen,* pp. 27, 43.

61. Ibid., pp. 96ff.

62. Ibid., p. 53.

63. Hull, *Hellenistic Magic and the Synoptic Tradition,* p. 129; M. Smith, *Jesus the Magician,* pp. 45ff. The thesis of S. Eitrem in *Die Versuchung Christi* (Oslo: Gröndahl, 1924) that the purpose of the Temptation, according to the synoptic Gospels, is to *induce* Christ to *become* a magician should have received much more attention than it did; but see H. J. Rose's comments in *Classical Review* 38 (1924): 213.

64. Cf. C. C. McCown, ed., *The Testament of Solomon* (Leipzig: Teubner, 1922); K. Preisendanz, in *PW,* suppl. vol. 8 (1952): 684ff.

65. See D. Winston, trans., *The Wisdom of Solomon,* Anchor Bible Series, vol. 43 (Garden City, N.Y.: Doubleday, 1979), pp. 172ff. The author of this apocryphal book was clearly familiar with Middle Platonism and may have belonged to the circle of Philo of Alexandria.

66. Hull, *Hellenistic Magic and the Synoptic Tradition,* p. 31.

67. See G. Scholem, in *Encyclopaedia Judaica* (1971), 10:489ff.; B. Pick, *The Cabala* (La Salle, Ill.: Open Court, 1974).

68. It seems worthwhile to note that Aphrodite, Circe, Medea, and Dido live on in Germanic mythology in at least two versions, the tale of Tannhäuser and the tale of the Lorelei. Tannhäuser was a knight-errant and minstrel who spent—not altogether against his will—many years with Frau Holde (or Hulda, or Holle) in the mountain of Venus. Frau Holde ("the lovely woman") appears to be a pagan goddess (related to Aphrodite) who, with her whole court, survived the victory of Christianity over paganism. Living deep inside a mountain, she could be found by privileged heroes such as Tannhäuser. (Incidentally, the dwarfs and elves of European fairy tales also live in mountains; they are usually interpreted as ancient nature daemons who were driven from society but not completely eliminated by the Church.) Tannhäuser is spellbound by this ancient yet eternally beautiful and seductive goddess, but finally he manages to tear himself away and goes on a pilgrimage to Rome, where he confesses his sins to Pope Urban. According to the old German ballad, Tannhäuser says to the Pope: "Lady Venus is a beautiful woman, lovely and graceful, and her voice is like sunshine and the scent of flowers. . . . If I owned all of heaven, I would gladly give it to Lady Venus; I would give her the sun, I would give her the moon, and I would give her all the stars." The Pope replies: "The devil whom they call Venus is the worst of all. I could never save you from her beautiful claws."

   In the end, Tannhäuser is saved by a miracle that even the Pope has to acknowledge. He has been forgiven. But according to the ancient folk tale, the pagan goddess of love has been degraded to the role of an evil witch, though the Church still recognizes her great power over men. Tannhäuser, the poet, returns to the pagan cult of beauty but must humble himself before the head of the Church. In his study *The Science of Folklore* (pp. 106ff.) Krappe maintains that the whole story is un-German, that it never was popular in the Middle Ages, and that it is Celtic in origin, even though Tannhäuser is a German name. It may be Celtic, but the main point seems to be that it replaces the Greek island on which an ancient goddess survived as a witch, by a mountain in the North which serves as the underground domicile of a formerly powerful Roman goddess.

Similarly, the Lorelei is a seductive woman who sits on a rock in the Rhine, combing her golden hair, luring to their death the boatmen who cannot take their eyes off her. She is arrested and tried as a witch, but the bishop who presides over the ecclesiastical court is so moved by her loveliness that he lets mercy prevail. Again, Krappe (p. 92) feels that this is not a genuine German folk tale. It is apparently not attested in any medieval source, and it might indeed be, as Krappe thinks, a creation of the Romantic era, at least in the form in which we know it. Heine's haunting song

> Ich weiss nicht, was soll es bedeuten,
> dass ich so traurig bin;
> ein Märchen aus uralten Zeiten,
> das kommt mir nicht aus dem Sinn

has made it popular since then, but the Romantic poet is right: It is a story from times immemorial; Homer's Circe is still alive.

69. A. D. Nock, in *Beginnings of Christianity*, vol. 5, ed. F. J. F. Jackson and K. Lake (London: Macmillan, 1933), pp. 164ff.; P. de Labriolle, *La Réaction païenne*, 6th ed. (Paris: L'Artisan, 1948), pp. 175ff.; E. M. Butler, *The Myth of the Magus* (Cambridge: Cambridge University Press, 1948), pp. 66ff. See also note 78 below.

70. See Hull, *Hellenistic Magic and the Synoptic Tradition*, p. 38.

71. See M. Smith, *Jesus the Magician*, pp. 150ff.

72. Ibid., p. 151.

73. See R. S. Casey, in *Beginnings of Christianity*, 5:151ff. See also G. N. L. Hall, in *ERE*, 11:541ff.; and P. Carrington, *The Early Christian Church*, 2 vols. (Cambridge: Cambridge University Press, 1957).

74. The formula, curious as it seems, has an authentic ring; perhaps it is an adaptation of some of Jesus' sayings.

75. There is a parallel story in Acts 13:6–12. While they were at Paphus, on Cyprus, Paul, John, and Barnabas met a Jewish *magus* and pseudoprophet called Elymas. He was part of the household of the proconsul, Sergius Paulus, a Roman who was anxious to "hear the word of God." When the Jewish *magus* tried to influence the Roman proconsul against the Christian missionaries, Paul, "filled with Holy Spirit," looked at him, cursed him, and struck him with blindness, whereupon the proconsul became a believer. This event can be dated within a year or two of A.D. 45; see Nock, in *Beginnings of Christianity*, 5:182ff. Nock's discussion of Jewish *magi* of the period—the role that someone like Elymas might have played in the household of a Roman official (a kind of spiritual adviser), the scene of confrontation before someone in authority, and the fate of the *magus* beaten at his own game—is still important.

76. *Recogn. Clement.* 2.15; *Homil. Clement.* 2.26. These passages are quoted in P.

M. Palmer and R. P. More, *Sources of the Faust Tradition* (New York: Octagon Books, 1978), p. 16. The implications are that Simon killed the boy; see the witches in Horace's fifth epode.

77. Moses and the Egyptian magicians before Pharaoh (Exodus 7); Paul and Elymas before the proconsul (Acts 13:6–12).

78. See note 69 above; cf. Thorndike, *A History of Magic and Experimental Science*, 1:242ff.; T. Whittaker, *Apollonius of Tyana and Other Essays* (London: Sonnenschein, 1906); and W. R. Halliday, *Folklore Studies* (London: Methuen, 1924), ch. 6.

79. A French scholar of the seventeenth century wrote an *Apology for All Great Men Who Were Wrongly Accused of Magic* (first published in French, Paris, 1625). Among those defended are Pythagoras and Socrates; Apollonius is characterized as a religious leader who patterned himself after Christ; and Philostratus' *Life of Apollonius of Tyana* is presented as an imitation of the Gospels.

80. S.H.A., *Sev.* 29.2; see M. Smith, *Jesus the Magician*, pp. 88–89.

81. See C. H. Dodd, *The Bible and the Greeks* (London: Hodder and Stoughton, 1935); R. Bultmann, *Das Urchristentum im Rahmen der antiken Religionen* (Zurich: Artemis, 1949), pp. 181ff.; W. C. van Unnik, *Evangelien aus dem Nilsand* (Frankfurt: Scheffler, 1960); R. M. Grant, *Gnosticism: A Source Book* (New York: Harper, 1961).

82. New Gnostic texts have been found in the Coptic Library of Nag Hammadi. See G. MacRae, in *Interpreter's Dictionary of the Bible*, suppl. vol. (Nashville, Tenn.: Abingdon, 1976), pp. 613–19.

83. Festugière and Nock, *Corpus Hermeticum*, 4 vols.

84. Witt, *Isis in the Graeco-Roman World*, p. 207.

85. On the survival of Hermeticism see W. Shumaker, *The Occult Sciences of the Renaissance* (Berkeley and Los Angeles: University of California Press, 1972), pp. 201ff.; F. A. Yates, *Giordano Bruno and the Hermetic Tradition* (Chicago: University of Chicago Press, 1978), passim.

86. Pliny, *HN* 2.62; Manil., *Astron.* 1.95ff.; Sen., *QNat.* 6.5.3; 7.25; Dodds, *The Ancient Concept of Progress*, p. 23.

87. Aspirin, the most widely used drug in the world and one of the least expensive, has been called a "magical" drug because medical science does not know exactly how it works. Its active ingredient, salicylic acid, has been used in the form of willow-bark in scientific medicine since Hippocrates (c. 400 B.C.) and in folk medicine—for instance, by the American Indians—for many centuries. See *The World Almanac Book of the Strange* (New York: New American Library, 1977), pp. 13–14.

88. See W. H. S. Jones, in *Proceedings of the Cambridge Philological Society* 181 (1950/51): 7–8.

89. J. E. Harrison, *Prolegomena to the Study of Greek Religion*, 3rd ed. (Cambridge: Cambridge University Press, 1922), pp. 4ff.

90. F. E. Brenk, *In Mist Apparelled: Religious Themes in Plutarch's "Moralia" and "Lives"* (Leiden: E. J. Brill, 1977), p. 59.

91. J. Dillon, *The Middle Platonists* (Ithaca, N.Y.: Cornell University Press, 1977), pp. 216ff.

92. J. Tatum, *Apuleius and the Golden Ass* (Ithaca, N.Y.: Cornell University Press, 1979), pp. 28–29; he refers A. D. Nock, *Conversion* (Oxford: Clarendon Press, 1933), pp. 138ff., a detailed treatment of Book 11 of Apuleius' *Metamorphoses*.

93. See Tatum, *Apuleius and the Golden Ass*, pp. 62ff., for a discussion of "spiritual serenity and the surrounding world." Philosophy and science are both ingredients of a higher kind of magic.

94. Dillon, *The Middle Platonists*, pp. 317ff.

95. Elymas (see note 75 above) is called *pseudoprophetes*, which corresponds to Lucian's term *pseudomantis*. But Elymas is also called, in Acts, *magos*, while Alexander is labeled *goes*. At this period, the terms must have been almost synonymous, though *goes* tends to be more negative. The essential information on Alexander is found in H. J. Rose's excellent article in the *Oxford Classical Dictionary*, 2nd ed., p. 42.

96. See M. Caster, *Lucien et la pensée religieuse de son temps* (Paris: Les Belles Lettres, 1937), pp. 307ff.

97. This is the term used by P. Brown in *Religion and Society in the Age of St. Augustine* (New York: Harper, 1972), p. 124.

98. Dodds, *Pagan and Christian in an Age of Anxiety*, pp. 72ff.

99. A. Abt, *Die Apologie des Apuleius von Madaura und die antike Zauberei* (Giessen: Töpelmann, 1908), pp. 108ff.

100. This concept was introduced in a classic work by E. E. Evans-Pritchard, *Witchcraft, Oracles, and Magic among the Azande* (Oxford: Clarendon Press, 1937), passim; it has been applied to later antiquity by Brown, *Religion and Society in the Age of St. Augustine*, p. 131.

101. Libanius' *Autobiography* (ed. J. Martin [Paris: Les Belles Lettres, 1979]) is remarkable; see esp. pars. 245ff. His speech "On Witchcraft" (nr. 36) also is very revealing; cf. C. Bonner, "Witchcraft in the Lecture Room of Apuleius," *Transactions and Proceedings of the American Philological Association* 63 (1932): 34ff.

102. Gregory the Great, *Dial.* 1.4, 30. The best edition is that by A. de Vogüé (= *Sources Chrétiennes* 251 [1978]). There are many curious tales of the supernatural in the *Dialogues*.

103. Brown, *Religion and Society in the Age of St. Augustine*, p. 37.

104. Merlan, in *Isis* 44 (1953): 341ff.; Armstrong, in *Phronesis* 1 (1955): 73ff.

105. Iamblichus, *Les Mystères d'Egypte*, ed. and trans. E. des Places (Paris: Les Belles Lettres, 1966); cf. Dodds, *The Greeks and the Irrational*, pp. 278ff.

106. Barb, in *The Conflict between Paganism and Christianity*, pp. 102ff.

107. See Dodds, *The Ancient Concept of Progress*, pp. 156ff. In a letter to Dodds, M. P. Nilsson had written in 1945: "I am persuaded that the so-called parapsychical phenomena played a very great part in late Greek paganism and are essential for understanding it rightly."

108. Dodds, *The Ancient Concept of Progress*, pp. 191–92.

109. See Wilson, *The Occult*; A. Koestler, *The Roots of Coincidence* (London: Hutchinson, 1972).

110. E. R. Dodds, *Missing Persons: An Autobiography* (Oxford: Clarendon Press, 1977), pp. 97ff. This is a charming book.

111.   Ibid., p. 111.
112.   In fact, Augustine was a careful observer of occult phenomena, as P. Brown (*Augustine of Hippo* [London: Faber, 1967], pp. 413ff.) has shown; cf. Dodds, *The Ancient Concept of Progress*, p. 174, n. 1.
113.   H. Diels and W. Kranz, *Die Fragmente der Vorsokratiker*, 12th ed. (Berlin: Weidmann, 1966), 68A.116; cf. Dodds, *The Ancient Concept of Progress*, p. 162.
114.   Dodds, *Missing Persons*, pp. 109ff.
115.   Diels and Kranz, *Die Fragmente der Vorsokratiker*, 68A.77; Dodds, *The Ancient Concept of Progress*, pp. 161–62.
116.   Dodds, *The Ancient Concept of Progress*, pp. 166–67.
117.   For testimonies from Chrysippus, Cicero, and other authors, see ibid., pp. 172–73.
118.   Ibid., p. 172.
119.   Ibid., p. 158, n.1; p. 206, n. 2.
120.   P. Boyancé, in *Rev. Hist. Rel.* 147 (1955): 189ff.
121.   Dodds (*The Ancient Concept of Progress*, p. 204) points out that dissociation is a psychological state that occurs in all cultures.
122.   Iambl., *Myst.* 3.5; Dodds, *The Ancient Concept of Progress*, pp. 203ff.
123.   Iamblichus was apparently capable of this; cf. Eunap., *Lives of the Philosophers and Sophists*, p. 458 Boissonade.
124.   Dodds, *The Ancient Concept of Progress*, p. 205.
125.   For instance, Proclus, the Neoplatonist, in his commentary on Plato's *Republic* 1.110.28 (ed. Kroll, 1899).
126.   Dodds, *The Ancient Concept of Progress*, p. 204.
127.   Ibid., pp. 186ff.
128.   Ibid.
129.   Aristoph., *Ach.* 1128ff.; A. Delatte, *La Catoptromancie grecque et ses dérivés* (Paris: Droz, 1932), pp. 133ff.; Dodds, *The Ancient Concept of Progress*, pp. 186ff.
130.   Dodds, *The Ancient Concept of Progress*, pp. 191ff.
131.   Ibid., pp. 193ff.
132.   Dodds discusses "motor automatism" and "vocal automatism" or "mediumship" (ibid., p. 193).
133.   Ibid.
134.   Ibid.
135.   Iambl., *Myst.* 3.19, quoted by Dodds in *The Ancient Concept of Progress*, pp. 193ff.
136.   Dodds, who was an experienced hypnotist, was inclined to dismiss the experiment described by the philosopher Clearchus (frag. 7 Wehrli); whereby a "soul-dragging" wand rendered a sleeping boy insensitive to pain (*The Ancient Concept of Progress*, pp. 193ff.). Apuleius' description of boys "lulled to sleep either by spells or soothing odors (*Apol.* 43) is, to Dodds, more suggestive of hypnosis.

Texts

1

The oldest Greek text in which a magical operation is mentioned forms part of Homer's *Odyssey*. In this episode the hero confronts a sorceress, Circe, on her own territory. Her power is established when she transforms some of Odysseus' companions into swine. She accomplishes this by mixing a magical drug into the special cheese mixture that she serves them, and by touching them with her magic wand. Here we see the typical *modus operandi* of the witch (no chant or formula is mentioned, just a direct order), but unlike later witches, Circe is beautiful. This leads one to suspect that in mythological terms she is not really a witch, but a minor goddess, a survivor from an earlier generation of gods, removed—like Kronos—to a distant island and of no great concern to anyone, except, of course, if one enters her territory. Her power, whatever it may be, is inferior to that of the ruling dynasty of gods, the Olympians, and one of them, Hermes, equips Odysseus with a magical antidote, the mysterious herb *moly*, and provides the necessary instructions.

It is clear that witchcraft was part of Greek folklore from the earliest times. Some of Homer's material may go back to the Bronze Age, and an epic like the *Odyssey*, with its rich heritage of folk tales and sailors' yarns, would have been incomplete without a tale of magic and, no less important, countermagic, for wherever people believe in witchcraft, they believe in ways of protecting themselves. They wear an amulet because they are convinced that they need it, to be on the safe side.

Homer, *Odyssey* 10.203–47

[*Odysseus is speaking.*]

I counted up my strong-greaved companions, divided them into two groups, and appointed a leader for each group. One of them I led myself, the other was led by godlike Eurylochus. Quickly we shook lots in a bronze helmet. The lot of the great-hearted Eurylochus jumped out. So he left, along with his twenty-two men, all weeping. We who were left behind wept too.

In a clearing in the woodland glen they discovered the house of Circe; it was put together with well-polished stones. All around it were mountain wolves and lions. She had bewitched them by giving them evil drugs. They did not attack my men, but stood up on their hind legs, wagging their long tails, as dogs go fawning about their master when he comes from dinner, for he always brings them some treats. With such affection did the wolves with their strong claws and the lions fawn about my men. But they were scared when they saw the terrifying beasts. They stood before the gate of the goddess with the neatly braided hair and heard Circe singing melodiously inside as she walked up and down at her great, immortal loom, weaving a delicate, lovely, shining fabric, as goddesses do.

Polites, a natural leader, one of my dearest friends, said to the others:

"Friends, inside a woman is singing beautifully, walking up and down at her great loom—the whole building echoes—either a goddess or a woman. Come on, let us call her."

They shouted and called her. At once she opened the shining doors, came out, and invited them in. They were naïve enough to follow her, all of them except Eurylochus, who waited outside, suspecting some treachery. She led them inside, asked them to sit on high chairs and benches, and mixed for them a dish of cheese and barley, clear honey, and Pramnian wine. But into the mixture she also put some dangerous drugs that would make them forget completely their native land. After she had given this to them and they had drunk it, she quickly struck them with her wand and drove them into her pig pens. They had the head, the voice, and bristles, and the shape of a pig, but their minds were the same as before. So they went in, crying. Circe cast before them acorns, chestnuts, and cornelian fruit, the kind of food that pigs, who sleep on the ground, usually eat.

Eurylochus returned to the fast black ship to tell the story of his companions and their tragic fate. He was unable to bring out a single word, though he tried; his heart was struck with great anguish, his eyes were filled with tears, and he only wanted to lament. We were all shocked and asked him questions. Finally he told us of the disaster that had befallen his companions:

"Glorious Odysseus, we went, as you had ordered, through the woods and discovered, in a clearing in the woodland glen a beautiful house constructed of polished stones. Inside, somebody—a goddess or a woman—sang sweetly as she walked up and down at her great loom. We shouted and called her. Quickly she opened the shining doors and came out, inviting us in, and all the others, naïve as they were, followed her. But I stayed outside, suspecting some treachery. They all vanished completely, and none of them reappeared, though I sat there waiting for a long time."

I slung my great bronze sword with the silver studs and my bow across my shoulders. I told him to lead me along the same path he had taken before. But he clasped my knees in both hands and implored me in a plaintive voice, saying:

"Son of Zeus, I do not want to go; please do not force me, but let me stay here. I know that you will not come back yourself and that you will not bring back any of your companions. Let us rather flee, those of us that are left; it is still possible to escape our doom."

I answered:

"Eurylochus, you may stay right here and eat and drink near the hollow black ship. But I am going. It is absolutely necessary."

I left the ship and the shore. As I went through the awesome woods and was approaching the great house of the sorceress Circe, Hermes with the golden rod met me as I came close to the house, looking like an adolescent in the flower of manhood, with a new-grown beard. He took my hand, spoke my name, and said to me:

"Where are you going, my poor friend, through the wild woods, all by yourself, not knowing the place? Your companions move around in Circe's house, looking like swine, crowded into her pig pens. Are you going there to set them free? I tell you, you will not come back; you will stay there with the others. But look, I will help you and rescue you from your troubles. Here, take this fine medicine—it will give you strength and protect you from evil—and enter Circe's house. I will tell you all about Circe's deadly tricks. She will prepare a potion for you and mix drugs into the food, but in spite of it she will not be able to bewitch you, for the fine medicine which I will give to you will prevent her. Let me explain the details. As soon as Circe strikes you with her long wand, you must draw from beside your thigh your sharp sword and pounce on her as if you wanted to kill her. She will be frightened and ask you to sleep with her. Do not reject the bed of a goddess, but let this set your companions free and be pleasant for you. You must make her swear a great oath by the gods not to plan any more evil against you, lest she weaken and unman you once you are naked."

The Argus-killer gave me an herb which he had plucked out of the ground and explained its nature to me. It was black at the root, and its flower was like milk. The gods call it moly. It is difficult for mortal men to dig it up. But to the gods everything is possible.

Then Hermes went away, over the wooded island, to great Olympus, and I went to Circe's house; my heart was agitated as I went. I stood at her gate and shouted; the goddess heard my call. Quickly she opened the shining doors and came out, inviting me in; I followed her nervously. She led me in and asked me to sit down on a beautiful, well-made chair with silver nails; there was a stool under my feet. In a golden dish she prepared a potion for me to drink; but with evil thoughts in her mind she had slipped a drug into it. After she had given it to me and I had drunk it, unbewitched, she struck me with her wand and called out, saying:

"Go now to the pig pen and lie down there with your friends."

I drew my sharp sword from beside my thigh and pounced on Circe as if I were about to kill her. She let out a loud scream, ran under my stroke, clasped my knees, and wailed:

"Who are you? Where are you from? What is your city? Who are your parents? I am amazed: you drank the poison, yet you are not bewitched. No other man could ever resist my poison once he had drunk it and it had passed the fence of his teeth. There is a mind in your breast that cannot be bewitched. You must be the resourceful Odysseus! The Argus-killer with the golden staff has always told me that you would come here from Troy in a fast black ship. But please, sheathe your sword, and then let us go to bed to make love and learn, in love, to trust each other."

I answered:

"Circe, how can you expect me to be kind to you? You have turned my companions into swine in your house, and now that you have me here you ask me deceitfully to come into your bedroom and go to bed with you, in order to weaken and unman me once I am naked. No, I do not want to go to bed with you, goddess, unless you agree to swear a great oath to plan no further mischief against me."

She swore immediately what I had asked her to swear. When she had sworn the oath and completed it, I climbed into the beautiful bed of Circe.

2

Theophrastus (c. 370–285 B.C.) studied with Aristotle, whom he succeeded as head of the school in Athens. In addition to a large number of specialized philosophic, scientific, and critical works, most of which are lost, he wrote for a larger public a collection of thirty character sketches, portraits of the miser, the garrulous type, the superstitious person, and so on. These sketches were doubtless based on his own amused observations of real people, but they also show the influence of contemporary Greek comedy with its repertory of psychological "types," the braggard and the grouch, among others. Many of Menander's plays are titled after the particular type whose habits and principles are presented on the stage. Theophrastus must have been an avid theater-goer, and since he was a contemporary of Menander's (some thirty years older, but he survived him), he had an opportunity to see all of Menander's plays performed, and probably many of those produced by Menander's colleagues and rivals. Comparatively few of these comedies have survived, either in the original or in Latin adaptations. If we had more of them, we would get an invaluable picture of Athenian society in the postclassical period. Since literally hundreds of plays are lost, however, an "extract," like that by Theophrastus, must fill a few gaps.

In his "Portrait of the Superstitious Person" Theophrastus begins, as he learned from his teacher, Aristotle, with a definition of superstition; only then does he list the characteristic features of the psychological type he is describing. Reading his account, his contemporaries would recognize with pleasure certain of their friends or acquaintances. In a sense, these sketches may have been born out of gossipy, malicious conversations about local characters, but then much good literature is gossipy and can be malicious!

Today we would probably say that the superstitious type, as described by Theophrastus, is a neurotic person weighed down and hemmed in by an unusual number of taboos—not only the normal, contemporary, local taboos, but some ancient and rather exotic taboos as well. There are taboos that one has to respect in any society, but there is no limit to the number of taboos one may impose upon oneself. Theophrastus is saying that some people need more taboos than others in order to function.

Theophrastus, *Characters*, "Portrait of the Superstitious Person" (ch. 28 Jebb)

Superstition would seem to be simply exaggerated fear of supernatural powers.

The superstitious type is the sort of person who will wash his hands at a fountain and sprinkle himself from a temple font. He will take a laurel leaf into his mouth and walk around like this all day. If a weasel crosses his path, he will not walk any farther until someone else has passed him or until he has thrown three stones across the road. When he sees a snake in his house, he will invoke the god Sabazius if it is the "red snake"—but if it is the "sacred snake," he will at once establish a shrine on the spot. Whenever he passes a "pile of smooth stones" at the crossroads, he will pour oil from his flask on them, and he will fall on his knees and worship them before he continues on his way. If a mouse gnaws a hole in a barley sack [in his house], he consults his "adviser" and asks him what to do. If the "adviser" tells him to take the sack to a cobbler and have it stitched up, he will not pay attention to his advice but will go his own way and offer a special sacrifice. He is capable of purifying his house quite often, saying that it has come under a spell of Hecate. If he startles an owl as he walks along, he may shout "Glory be to Athena!" before he continues. He will never walk on a [flat] tombstone or come near a corpse or a woman who has just given birth, saying that it is better for him not to be polluted. On the fourth and seventh days of the month he will order his servants to mull wine, while he goes out to buy myrtle wreaths, frankincense, and smilax; when he comes back to his house he will put wreaths on the busts of Hermaphroditus all day long. Whenever he has had a dream, he will consult the interpreters of dreams, the seers, the augurs, to find out to which god, to which goddess, he ought to pray. Once a month he will go to see the priests of the Orphic Mysteries, taking his wife along or, if she is busy, his children and their nursemaid.

This is the kind of person who will sprinkle himself thoroughly with sea water. Whenever he sees someone at the crossroads who is crowned with garlic [reading *estemmenon tina*, with Kayser], he will go away, pour water over his head, call the priestesses [of Hecate], and make them carry a squill or a puppy round him for purification. If he sees a madman or an epileptic, he shudders and spits into his bosom.

3

This episode from a Hellenistic epic, the *Argonautica*, by Apollonius of Rhodes (early third century B.C.), is based on old folk tales and myths. Medea is in the same class as Circe; later ages have labeled her a witch, but she may be a minor goddess from a distant age, a remote civilization. She has fallen in love with Jason, the leader of the Argonauts, helps him win the Golden Fleece and protects him and the other heroes on the way back to Greece. At one point they are threatened by a bronze monster called Talos, who patrols the shores of Crete, where they would like to land. Talos is a sort of robot, himself a magical creature, unless he is a survival of an earlier, more powerful race of men. The men of the heroic age are helpless against him, but Medea destroys him with her evil eye and by her knowledge of ritual magic.

This is the oldest extant Greek text that describes the effect of the evil eye and gives a tentative explanation of the powers involved. We see that magic was, by Apollonius' day, understood as a science. Apollonius had lived in Egypt, where he no doubt had had an opportunity to study occult arts.

Apollonius of Rhodes, *Argonautica* 4.1635–90

Rocky Carpathus greeted them from afar. They were planning to cross over from there to Crete, which is the biggest island in the sea.

But Talos, a bronze man who broke off lumps from a massive rock, prevented them from tying the rope to the land, as they entered the shelter of Dicte's harbor. He had been left over from the Bronze Race of men who had sprung from ash trees, and he survived into the Heroic Age. Zeus had given him to Europa to be a guard of the island by running three times around Crete on his bronze feet. Well, the rest of his body and his limbs were made of bronze and invulnerable, but way down under a tendon near his ankle he had a blood vessel; it was covered by a thin membrane, and to him it meant the difference between life and death.

The Argonauts, though overcome by fatigue, were terrified and quickly put the ship astern, rowing away from the shore. They would have been driven away from Crete in a gloomy mood, thirsty and exhausted as they were, had not Medea spoken to them as they pulled back:

"Listen, I think that I and I alone can kill for you that man, whoever he is, even if his body is completely of bronze, provided that there is no immortal life in him. But do what I tell you and keep the ship where it is, outside the range of his rocks, till I have finished with him."

Rowing hard, they wrenched the ship out of range of his missiles, waiting to see what novel scheme Medea would carry out.

She held a fold of her purple cloak close to both cheeks and went up on deck. Grasping her hand in his, Jason accompanied her as she passed between the benches.

Then she sang songs of incantation, invoked the Daemons of Death, the swift Hounds of Hell that whirl around the air everywhere and fall on living creatures. On her knees she called them three times in song, three times in prayer. She put herself into a sinister mood, and with her own evil eye she put a curse on the eye of Talos. She gnashed at him her devastating fury and hurled forth images of death in an ecstasy of rage.

Father Zeus! It comes as a great shock to my mind that fearful death does not face us by illness and wounds alone but that someone can hurt us from a distance! Yes, he was brought down helplessly, though made of bronze, by the force of Medea, the cunning sorceress. As he was lifting up some heavy lumps to prevent them from entering the anchorage, he nicked his ankle on a sharp rock. His divine blood ran out of him like molten lead. For a short time he remained there, on the jutting cliff on which he stood. But like a tall pine tree high up in the mountains which the woodmen left half-felled from their sharp axes before they came down from the wooded hills—first it is shaken by the winds in the night, but then it breaks at the bottom and crashes down—thus he stood for a little while, swaying sideways on his sturdy legs, but then he fell down helplessly with a mighty crash.

That night the heroes camped on Crete.

4

Theocritus lived in Alexandria at some time during the first quarter of the third century B.C. and had a good opportunity to observe the middle-class

Greeks who had settled in the new capital of Ptolemaic Egypt. This stay inspired a few realistic poems about daily life in the great city. They are numbered among Theocritus' *Idylls*, though they are not "idyllic" at all; the Greek word *eidyllion* originally meant "short text," but since Theocritus was chiefly known as a pastoral poet, the name attached itself to the genre and, by extension, to most of Theocritus' poems that have come down to us. This particular poem is more like a mime, and its dramatic form (one long monologue) made it ideal for recitation. The monologue of Simaetha is dramatic in character (though it was probably not delivered on a stage), with another character, her maid, Thestylis, present and the ingredients she mentions ready at hand. The imagination of the audience had to supply all this. It was a special art (like that of the mime today, but using the words of a poet) to make the audience actually see everything as the story was told.

Theocritus may not have been a believer in magic himself, but he must have been familiar with magical practices, for almost every detail he mentions can be documented from the magical papyri and other sources. The ceremony he describes dramatizes Simaetha's passion for the handsome young athlete, Delphis, who treats her rather coolly. Simaetha's love is so overpowering that she would literally do anything to get Delphis back; and if she cannot have him, she threatens to harm him—like Dido in the *Aeneid* [*no. 9*].

Theocritus, *Idylls* 2

[*Simaetha is speaking.*]

Where are the bay leaves? Bring them, Thestylis! Where is the love magic? Tie a thread of fine purple wool around the bowl that I may bind with a spell my lover who is so cruel to me. For eleven days he has not visited me, the scoundrel, and does not even know whether I am alive or dead; nor did he—heartless as he is—knock at my door. Of course Eros and Aphrodite have carried his fickle heart elsewhere. Tomorrow I will go to Timagetus' wrestling school and reproach him for the way he treats me. But now I will bind him with fire magic. Shine brightly, Moon; I will softly chant to you, Goddess, and to Hecate in the Underworld—the dogs shiver before her when she comes over the graves of the dead and the dark blood. Hail, grim Hecate, and stay with me to the end; make these drugs as powerful as those of Circe and Medea and golden-haired Perimede.

Draw to my house my lover, magic wheel.

First, barley groats must cook on the fire. Throw them on, Thestylis! Idiot, where are you with your thoughts? Has it come to the point that even you make fun of me, scamp? Throw them on and say at the same time: "I throw on Delphis' bones."

Draw to my house my lover, magic wheel.

Delphis brought me trouble, and for Delphis I burn this bay leaf. As it crackles in the flames with a sharp noise and suddenly catches fire and we don't even see its ash, so may Delphis' flesh melt in the flame.

Draw to my house my lover, magic wheel.

Now I shall burn the husks of corn. Artemis, you have the power to move even the steel in Hades or anything else that is hard to move. . . . Thestylis, the dogs are howling around the town: the Goddess is at the crossroads. Quick, bang the gong!

Draw to my house my lover, magic wheel.

Look, the sea is still and the winds are still, but never stilled is the pain deep in my heart; I am all on fire for the man who made me a wretched, useless thing, who took my maidenhood but did not marry me.

Draw to my house my lover, magic wheel.

As I melt, with the goddess's help, this wax, so may Delphis of Myndus waste at once from love. And as this bronze rhombus whirls by the power of Aphrodite, so may he whirl about my door.

Draw to my house my lover, magic wheel.

Three times I pour a libation, mighty Goddess, and three times do I cry: "Whether it is a woman who lies with him now or a man, may he forget them as clean as Theseus once in Dia, they say, forgot Ariadne with the lovely locks."

Draw to my house my lover, magic wheel.

Coltsfoot is an Arcadian herb, and because of it, all the fillies and the swift mares run madly over the hills. May I see Delphis in such a state, coming to this house like a madman from the bright wrestling school.

Draw to my house my lover, magic wheel.

Delphis lost this fringe from his coat: I now shred it and cast it into the wild flames. Ah, cruel Love, why do you cling to me like a leech from the swamps and drain all the dark blood from my body?

Draw to my house my lover, magic wheel.

I shall crush a lizard and bring him an evil drink tomorrow. Thestylis, please take these magic herbs and smear them on his threshold while it is still night, and whispering say: "I smear the bones of Delphis."

Draw to my house my lover, magic wheel.

Now that I am alone, how can I lament my love? Where shall I begin? Who brought this curse upon me? Eubulus' daughter, my friend Anaxo, went as a basket-bearer to the grove of Artemis, in whose honor on that day many wild animals, among others a lioness, were led around in the procession.

Tell me, Moon goddess, how my love began.

Theumaridas' Thracian nurse—she died not long ago—who used to live next door, begged me and urged me to see the procession, and I, poor wretch, went with her in my nice long linen dress and Clearista's wrap over it.

Tell me, Moon goddess, how my love began.

I was halfway down the road, near Lycon's place, when I saw them walking together, Delphis and Eudamippus. Their beards were more golden then helichryse and their breasts much shinier than you, Selene; for they came directly from their athletic workout at the gymnasium.

Tell me, Moon goddess, how my love began.

One look, and I lost my mind, and my poor heart was aflame. My beauty faded. I was no longer interested in the procession, and I have no idea how I got home, but a dry fever shook me, and I was in bed ten days and ten nights.

Tell me, Moon goddess, how my love began.

Sometimes my complexion would be like fustic, and all the hair on my head fell out, and all that was left of me were skin and bones. Whose place did I not visit? Did I skip the house of any old woman who knows magic songs? But it was a serious case, and time went by.

Tell me, Moon goddess, how my love began.

So I told my maid the true story: "Please, Thestylis, find me some remedy for this bad disease. The man from Myndus possesses me completely; it is terrible. Go to Timagetus' wrestling school and keep watch, for there he goes and there he likes to sit."

Tell me, Moon goddess, how my love began.

"And when you are sure that he is alone, give him a quiet nod and tell him: 'Simaetha invites you' and lead him here." This is what I said. She went and brought smooth-skinned Delphis to my house. When I saw him stepping lightly across the threshold of my door—

tell me, Moon goddess, how my love began—

I felt chillier than snow all over, and from my forehead the sweat ran damp like dew, and I was unable to make a sound, not even as much as a baby whimpers in his sleep to his dear mother. My beautiful body went stiff all over like a doll's.

Tell me, Moon goddess, how my love began.

My faithless lover looked at me and then fixed his eyes on the ground, sat down on a couch and said: "Really, Simaetha, your invitation beat my coming to you by no more than I recently beat charming Philinus in a race."

Tell me, Moon goddess, how my love began.

"I would have come, I swear it by sweet Eros, with two or three friends, in the evening, carrying in my pocket apples of Dionysus and on my head white poplar leaves, the holy plant of Heracles, twined all around with crimson bands."

Tell me, Moon goddess, how my love began.

"If you had let me in, that would have been very nice, for I am considered agile and handsome among young men, and if you had only let me kiss your lovely lips, I could have slept. But if you had pushed me out and barred the door, then, believe me, axes and torches would have marched up against you."

Tell me, Moon goddess, how my love began.

"But now I must first say thanks to Cypris and after Cypris to you, lady, because you have rescued me from the fire, already half-burned, by inviting me to this house. You know, Eros sometimes kindles a hotter blaze than Hephaestus on Lipara."

Tell me, Moon goddess, how my love began.

"With dangerous madness Eros scares a maiden from her bedroom and makes a young bride leave her husband's bed when it is still warm."

This he said, and I—so easily persuaded—took him by the hand and drew him down on the soft couch. Body quickly warmed to body, and cheeks burned hotter than before, and we whispered sweetly to each other. To make a long story short, dear Moon-goddess, our main purpose was achieved, and both of us came to our desire. He found no fault with me till yesterday, nor I with him. But today, when the horses of rosy Dawn ran up the sky, bringing her out of the Ocean, the mother of Philista, our flute-player, and of Melixo came to see me. She said she did not know for sure whether it was love for a woman or a man, only this: he constantly called for unmixed wine, and his toast was "To Love!" and finally he left in a hurry, saying that he must decorate that house with garlands. This is the story my visitor told me, and she is no liar. For I swear he used to come three or four times a day, and often he would leave his Dorian oil flask with me. But now it has been eleven days that I have not seen him. Does this not mean that he has found other delights and has forgotten me?

Now I will bind him with my love magic, but if he still causes me pain, he shall beat on the gate of Hades, such evil drugs, I swear, I keep for him in my box; it is something, Goddess, that I have learned from an Assyrian stranger.

But farewell, Queen! Turn your horses toward the Ocean. I shall bear my desire as I have endured it till now. Farewell, Selene, on your shining throne! Farewell, all you other stars that follow the chariot of silent Night.

5

The following Roman spells can be roughly ascribed to three different periods: one is from the second century B.C., one is from the first century B.C., and the third is somewhat later (Marcellus Empiricus?). Nevertheless, they are very similar, and they show that this kind of folk medicine was old and did not change much over the centuries. Cato the Elder (who distrusted doctors) takes us back to a time when the owner of an estate was an authority on everything and, if an accident happened, had to administer some kind of first aid. The symbolism of the split reed and the iron is fairly obvious, and the impressive mumbo-jumbo of pseudo-Latin also fulfilled its purpose. The daily recitation of the second formula made it necessary for the owner to visit the patient every day. Clearly this magic had some kind of rational basis.

Varro's formula is more "magical" because it involves a superior power—the "you" that is mentioned. It also uses the concepts of analogy and transmission: the feet that touch the earth communicate their pain to the earth. Spittle is often used in healing, and to be sober during a religious or magical ritual is a form of ascetic discipline.

This last point is also stressed by Marcellus in the third spell (if he actually wrote it). The real Marcellus, as the title of the text shows, was a professional physician. The spell is like a form: one has to fill in the appropriate words ("swelling in tonsils"). Here the magical gesture is as important as the words spoken. The language is obscure toward the end, but this is no doubt intentional.

A: Cato, *On Agriculture,* par. 160

If something is out of joint, it can be set by the following spell: Take a green reed, four or five feet long, split it in the middle, and let two men hold it to their hips. Begin to recite the following formula: *moetas vaeta daries dardaries astataries dissunapiter,* until the parts come together. Put iron on top of it. When the two parts have come together and touch each other, grip them with your hand, make a cut left and right [on the reed?], tie it onto the dislocation or the fracture, and it will heal. But you must recite every day [the formula] *huat huat huat ista sistas sistardannabou dannaustra.*

B: Varro, *On Agriculture* 1.2.27

If your feet hurt [you must say]: "I think of you; heal my feet. Let the earth retain the illness, and let health remain here." This you must recite nine times, touch the earth, and spit. Must be recited sober.

C: [Marcellus Empiricus?] *De Medicamentis* 15.11
(= 113.25 Niedermann)

To be recited when sober, touching the relevant part of the body with three fingers: thumb, middle finger, and ring finger; the other two are stretched out.

"Go away, no matter whether you originated today or earlier: this disease, this illness, this pain, this swelling, this redness, this goiter, these tonsils, this abscess, this tumor, these glands and the little glands I call forth, I lead forth, I speak forth, through this spell, from these limbs and bones."

6

In his *Epodes* (the title can be translated as "incantations") Horace describes a fantastic human sacrifice performed by witches. The victim is a boy whom the witches have kidnapped. In an ordinary sacrifice, the liver was considered an important organ because it gave clues to the future; in this case the witches want to use the boy's liver in a love potion they are planning to prepare. The boy, realizing the fate that awaits him, first pleads with the witches, and when this has no effect, curses them. His curse is an act of black magic in itself. In it, the boy distinguishes between right and wrong on the one hand and human fate on the other. The witches then commit the criminal act of killing an innocent child, and they seem to get away with it—that is, they escape the arm of worldly justice— but sooner or later they will be punished for their vicious deed.

Scholars have wondered why Horace in this piece and in the next [*no. 7*] makes such an effort to paint witchcraft as loathsome and despicable. He seems to hate Canidia (who appears here and there in his poems) with a passion, almost as if he had loved her once. The answer may be that Augustus (whose ideas Virgil and Horace often translated into poetry) was planning drastic legislation to stamp out witchcraft in the Roman Empire and that, through Maecenas, he enlisted the aid of two great poets of his age, Virgil and Horace. Little is known about the legislation itself, but it seems to have been in effect over the following centuries and to have served as the government's main tool in prosecuting the occult sciences.

Horace, *Epodes* 5

[*The kidnapped boy speaks.*]

"By all the gods in heaven who rule over the earth and mankind, what does this tumult mean? What is the meaning of the fierce looks of all these women, fixed on me? I implore you by your children—if you really ever gave birth to any, assisted by Lucina, whom you called—I beg you by this useless purple ornament of mine and by Jupiter, who must disapprove of all this, why do you stare at me like a stepmother or a wild beast wounded by a spear?"

The boy made these complaints with a trembling voice. He stood there, his badge having been taken away from him. His childish body would have softened the heart of a Thracian. But Canidia, small vipers braided in her hair on her unkempt head, ordered wild fig trees torn from graves, funeral cypresses and eggs smeared with the blood of a loathsome toad and the feathers of a screech owl that flies by night, the herbs which Iolcus and Hiberia, rich in poisons, send, and bones snatched from the mouth of a hungry bitch, all to be burned in Colchian flames.

Sagana, her robes tucked up, sprinkled water from Avernus throughout the house. Her rough hair bristled like a sea urchin or a running boar. Veia, totally unscrupulous, was digging up the floor with a solid spade, groaning as she labored. They wanted to bury the boy in such a way that only his face would stick out, like that of a swimmer who seems suspended on the water by his chin. Then they would slowly torment him to death by making him look at food that was changed twice or three times a day. Finally, when his eyes, fixed on the food denied to him, dimmed, they intended to cut out his marrow and his parched liver to make a love potion.

In Naples, where people have time to gossip, and in all the neighboring towns, it was believed that Folia from Rimini, known for her masculine lust, was there too. She can force down the stars and the moon from heaven by singing magic songs in Thessalian.

At this point savage Canidia began to gnaw her uncut thumb nail with her yellow teeth. What did she say? What did she not say?

"Night! Diana, who rules over silence when secret rites are performed! You are the faithful witnesses of my doings. Now is the time to help me. Now you must turn your wrath and your divine power against the house of my enemy. Now that the wild beasts, relaxed in sweet slumber, hide in the fearful forests, let the dogs of the Subura bark at the aging playboy, drenched with a perfume more perfect than my hands ever made! Let everybody laugh at this. But what happened? Why are the horrible drugs of barbarian Medea not as powerful as they once were? She used them to take revenge on her husband's arrogant mistress, the daughter of great Creon—and got away! A robe she sent as a gift, saturated with poison, took off the young bride in a blaze of fire. And yet I have not missed any herb or root growing in a rough spot. But he, he sleeps in the perfumed bedroom of every harlot, without a thought of me. Ah! Ah! he moves around, protected from me by a song of a witch who knows more than I do.

"Varus! You are about to shed many tears, and you will hurry back to me, drawn by extraordinary drugs, and even the recitation of Marsian spells will not help you recover your sanity. You scorn me, but I will prepare a more potent drug; I will pour you a more potent drink. As surely as the sky will never drop below the sea and the earth never float above, as surely must you burn with passionate love for me like pitch in sooty flames!"

When he heard this, the boy no longer tried, as he had before, to appease the ruthless hags with gentle words. Though he did not know what to say, he broke the silence and poured out a malediction worthy of Thyestes:

"Magic drugs can upset right and wrong; they cannot upset human destiny. I shall pursue you with curses: a deadly curse cannot be undone by any sacrificial victim. So I am doomed to die. But when I have breathed my last I shall haunt you as a terrifying appearance in the night; I shall, as a ghost, attack your faces with hooked talons, for such is the power of the divine Manes. Crouched on your anguished hearts I shall terrorize you and rob you of your sleep. In every quarter of the city a crowd will gather, throw stones at you, and crush you, you filthy old hags. Your unburied limbs will then be scattered by the wolves and the vultures that live on the Esquiline. I hope that my parents, who must, alas! survive me, will not miss that show."

7

Horace's other witchcraft piece is funnier, less frightening. Here the god Priapus delivers a monologue, telling us what happened one night as he was guarding the new park established on the Esquiline. Since the park had once been a cemetery for the poorest of the poor, witches still frequented it to dig for bones and herbs and to conjure up the souls of the dead. They also performed some black magic on the spot. Priapus is so anguished and disgusted that he has to interrupt the goings on.

In this text the witches are made to look ridiculous and pathetic. Because a minor god like Priapus can chase them away, the power they claim for themselves cannot be real.

Horace, *Satires* 1.8

[The statue of Priapus is speaking.]

Once I was the trunk of a fig tree, a useless piece of wood. A craftsman, not sure whether he would make a bench or a Priapus, decided that it was to be the god. So I am a god, a holy terror to thieves and birds: my hand and the red shaft that sticks out indecently from my crotch threaten the thieves; the bundle of reeds planted on my head frightens the birds— they are a nuisance!—and forbids them to settle in what is now a park. Once the bodies of slaves, thrown out of their narrow cells, were carried here in cheap coffins by their fellow slaves to be buried. This place served as a common grave for the poorest of the poor. Here a tombstone gave to that clown Pantolabus and to Nomentanus, the big spender, "A thousand feet in front, three hundred deep" and announced, "This plot does not go to the heirs." Now the air is clean on the Esquiline, and people can live here and go for walks on the sunny embankment where not so long ago they found it depressing to look at a field disgraced by white bones. But I have to worry and watch out not so much for the thieves and the wild animals that are accustomed to haunting this place as for women who work on the minds of men with magic songs and potions. There is no way in which I can wipe them out or, once the wandering moon has shown her graceful face, keep them from gathering bones and poisonous herbs.

With my own eyes I have seen Canidia walk barefoot, her black dress tucked up over her knees, hair undone. She and her elder sister, Sagana, were howling. Their pale faces made them horrible to look at. They began to dig up the earth with their fingernails and to tear a black lamb to pieces. The blood ran into a ditch, to summon up the souls of the dead and make them answer questions. They had two dolls—one of wax, the other, larger one of wool; [the wool one] was meant to punish the smaller, waxen one, which stood submissive like a slave about to be put to death. One of the witches called "Hecate!," the other "Dreadful Tisiphone!" You could see serpents sliding, hell hounds running. The moon blushed because she refused to be witness to all this and hid behind some large monuments. If I tell not the whole truth, let white turds of crows disgrace my head, and let Ulius and frail Pediatia and that thief Voranus come to piss and shit on me!

Must I go into more detail and tell how the ghosts—they sounded shrill, desolate—carried on a conversation with Sagana, how the witches furtively buried a wolf's beard together with teeth from a spotted snake, how the wax doll blazed with larger flames, how horrible it was for me to witness the things that those two Furies said and did? But revenge was near: I made a fart that split my figwood buttocks; it sounded like a pig's bladder exploding. They ran back to town: Canidia lost her teeth, Sagana her pompous wig, and they dropped their herbs and magic bracelets. What a joke! You would have laughed, had you seen it.

8

Virgil's eighth eclogue ("pastoral poem") is an adaptation of Theocritus' second idyll [no. 4]. Although it was written over two hundred years after Theocritus' poem, it stays very close to the original story line in many details. Most of the magical ingredients are the same, though the bull-roarer and the magical wheel are replaced by two dolls, one made of clay, the other of wax. Virgil also introduces the werewolf theme: Moeris, a local warlock who has sold Simaetha some powerful herbs, is a werewolf. Virgil leaves out the whole love story that Simaetha tells in Theocritus' idyll, but he adds a happy ending: the magic works, Daphnis comes back. The skillful use of the refrain (suggesting magical chants that are repeated over and over again) is another technique Virgil has learned from Theocritus. Poems like these are realistic and accurate in the details they represent, but they are not meant to be factual reports of a real ceremony. Rather, they create an atmosphere that makes the reader feel the meaning of the goings on. In this sense, poetry is a kind of magic in itself: the Latin word *carmen* means "poem" as well as "magical chant."

Virgil, *Eclogues* 8.64–109

Bring water, tie a soft fillet around this altar, and burn on it fresh twigs and male frankincense that I may succeed in turning my lover from sanity to madness by magic rites: all we need now is songs.

Draw home from the city, my songs, draw Daphnis home.

Songs can even draw the Moon from heaven; by songs Circe transformed Odysseus' men; by singing the cold snake in the meadow bursts.

Draw home from the city, my songs, draw Daphnis home.

To begin with, I shall twine around you three strands composed of three threads, each of a different color, and three times I shall carry your image around the altar; the divinity likes the odd number.

Draw home from the city, my songs, draw Daphnis home.

Tie the three colors with three knots, Amaryllis; please, tie them and say: "I tie the bonds of Venus."

Draw home from the city, my songs, draw Daphnis home.

As this clay gets hard and as this wax gets soft in one and the same fire, so may Daphnis from love of me. Sprinkle barley meal and kindle the fragile laurel twigs with pitch. Cruel Daphnis makes me burn: I burn this laurel for Daphnis.

Draw home from the city, my songs, draw Daphnis home.

With love possessed is the heifer that has been searching for the young steer through the woods and the tall groves and sinks, weary and lost, in the green rushes near a water bank and forgets to go away when the night falls: may such love possess Daphnis, and may I not care to heal him.

Draw home from the city, my songs, draw Daphnis home.

My faithless lover once left behind these clothes, dear pledges of himself. Earth, I now commit them to you, right under the threshold: these pledges must bring Daphnis back to me.

Draw home from the city, my songs, draw Daphnis home.

Moeris himself gave me these herbs and poisons gathered near the Black Sea (they grow in abundance near the Black Sea). I have often seen Moeris turn into a wolf by their power and hide in the forest, and often seen him conjure up souls from the depth of their tombs and move to other fields the crops that had been sown.

Draw home from the city, my songs, draw Daphnis home.

Bring ashes, Amaryllis, and throw them over your head into the running brook, and don't look back! With these will I attack Daphnis; he cares nothing for gods, nothing for songs.

Draw home from the city, my songs, draw Daphnis home.

"Look: the embers on the altar have caught, all by themselves, with a flickering flame while I was slow to fetch them. Let this be a good sign!"

It must mean something . . . and Hylax is barking in the doorway! May we believe it? Or do lovers make up dreams for themselves?

Spare him, my songs! Daphnis is coming from the city! Spare him, my songs!

9

In his *Aeneid*, Virgil returns once more to the theme of love magic and its potential transformation into black magic. Simaetha in Theocritus' second idyll threatens to hurt her unfaithful lover; the woman in Virgil's eighth eclogue hints at this possibility; Dido in Book 4 of the *Aeneid* actually curses Aeneas because she realizes that love magic will not work, and then she kills herself.

Dido, deserted by Aeneas, is the victim of different emotions: hate and love, frustration, shame, and anger. The conflict between these feelings is so strong that Dido goes into a deep depression, as we would say, and resolves to take her own life. To mask the preparations for her suicide she stages an elaborate magical ceremony under the supervision of a famous priestess who is also a powerful witch. As a great and noble queen she is opposed to magic, but in this situation she is willing to give it a try.

Although the magic is intended at least partly for show, most ancient readers of this passage would have felt that it worked. Dido's curse does not harm Aeneas himself, for, like Odysseus, he has powerful divine protectors, and he has not left her frivolously, but because he had a mission. The curse comes true many generations later, when the descendants of Aeneas, the Romans, become involved in three murderous wars against the Carthaginians, and Dido's "avenger"—none other than Hannibal—comes very close to total victory.

Dido's self-sacrifice has a magical meaning. By killing herself, she releases her own spirit and turns it into a daemon of revenge, thus lending additional emphasis to her curse. In ancient times, everyone was thought to have special powers at the moment of death, and the souls of those who died before their time or died a violent death (Dido fits into both categories) were especially suitable for black magic.

Virgil has created a magnificent scene in which magic is only one element. The psychological portrait of Dido in her despair is drawn with great understanding, and the reader, though he may be shocked by her thirst for revenge, nevertheless feels compassion for the unfortunate queen.

Virgil, *Aeneid* 4.450–705

At this point poor Dido, frightened by her fate, prayed for death. She could no longer stand the sight of the arch of heaven, and she saw something which made her even more anxious to carry out her plan and leave the light: when she placed offerings on the altars on which incense was burning, she saw—horrible to say—that the sacred liquid turned black and that the wine she had poured turned into ghastly blood. She told no one what she had seen, not even her sister.

There was also in the palace a marble shrine of her former husband which she tended with very special reverence; it was decorated with snow-white fur and festive leaves. Now she thought she heard a voice coming from its inside—the words of her husband, who was calling her. It was the time when dark night covered the earth, and only the screech owls on the roof tops delivered their funeral laments, again and again, drawing out the mournful notes.

Moreover, many predictions of ancient prophets terrified her with their sinister meaning.

In her dreams she was pursued by cruel Aeneas himself, rushing madly after her. Constantly she dreamed of being left by herself, of going without companions on a long trip, seeking the people of Tyrus in a desert land, just as Pentheus, driven out of his mind, sees the swarm of the Eumenides and a double sun and a double vision of Thebes, or as Orestes, the true son of his father, Agamemnon, is driven across the stage, fleeing before his mother, who is armed with torches and black snakes; and the Avenging Furies crouch on the doorstep.

Overwhelmed by grief, she conceived a mad scheme and decided to die. She worked out by herself the time and the method. She approached her sister, who was still sad, and talked to her; her face did not betray her plan, and the way she looked even left room for hope:

"Dear sister, I have found a way—wish me luck—which will either bring Aeneas back to me or help me get rid of my love for him. Near the far end of the Ocean, where the sun sets, at the limits of Ethiopia, is a place where Atlas, the giant, turns on his shoulders the axle that is fitted to the sphere of the burning stars. A priestess of the Massylians who lives there has been recommended to me: she is the custodian of the temple of the Hesperides, and she used to bring the dragon his food and guard the sacred boughs on the tree, sprinkling liquid honey and sleep-inducing poppyseed. She guarantees that she can relax with her incantations all those she wishes to, but she also threatens to inflict harsh pains on others.

She says that she can stop the flowing of a river and turn the course of the stars around. She conjures up ghosts by night. You might hear the earth roar under her feet and see ash trees marching down from the mountains. I swear by the gods, my dear, and I take you as a witness, darling, that I hate to get involved in magic arts. Please raise secretly a pyre in the inner courtyard, under the open sky, and place upon it the weapons of my lover which he left hanging in my bedroom—how faithless he is! Put all his clothes on top and our conjugal bed, which has been death for me. It is very important to wipe out all traces of that horrible man, says the priestess."

She fell silent. Her face turned pale. And yet Anna could not believe that her sister would conceal her death under strange rites, nor could she understand such a fantastic scheme, nor did she fear anything more serious than what had happened at the time of Sychaeus' death. So she arranged everything as she was told.

When the huge pyre was constructed of piled faggots and cleft ilex in the innermost part of the palace, under the open sky, the queen hung the room with garlands and funeral boughs. On top she placed Aeneas' clothes, the sword he had left behind, and, on a bed, his image. She knew very well what would happen. Altars were all around. The priestess, her hair undone, called three times with a thundering voice the gods, the Erebus, the Chaos, Hecate with her three heads, and the three faces of the virgin goddess Diana. She sprinkled water that was supposed to have come from the springs of Avernus. Potent herbs with the milk of black poison that had been cut with bronze sickles by moonlight were obtained. They also obtained the love magic torn from the forehead of a filly at birth before the mother could snatch it.

Dido herself, the holy cake in her pure hands, stood near the altars, one of her feet bare, her robes flowing loose. In the hour of her death she called on the gods and the stars that knew her fate. She also prayed to any just and mindful divinity that might care for abandoned lovers.

Night fell. Weary creatures enjoyed restful sleep all over the earth. The woods and the cruel sea were at rest. It was the time when the stars are halfway in their gliding course, when all the fields are silent and the beasts and colorful birds that live on smooth lakes or in thorny thickets all rest peacefully under the silent night. But not so the Phoenician lady in her distress: she never relaxed in sleep or drew the night into her eyes or her heart. Her pain grew twice as intense, her frantic love swelled once again, and she was tossed up by a high wave of anger.

She began to express the various feelings that stirred in her heart:

"What shall I do? Shall I try my luck with my former suitors and risk being laughed at? Shall I humbly beg to become the wife of one of the Nomad chiefs whom I have rejected so many times as husbands? Well, perhaps I ought to follow the fleet of the Trojans and obey their most outrageous orders? They, of course, are happy that I, at one time, gave them help and assistance, and the memory of the favor I once did them is no doubt still fresh in their minds. But even if I wanted to do this, who would want me? Would they let a hateful woman—arrogant as they are—travel on their ships? Ah, you fool, you still don't know, you still don't understand the treachery of the descendants of Laomedon! And then? Shall I alone, an exile, follow the cheering sailors? Or shall I join them, surrounded by the men of Tyrus and my whole army, and order my people to set the sails to the winds, forcing them to cross the sea once more? It was hard enough for me to uproot them from their former city, Sidon. No. Die as you deserve, and let the sword end your pain. Sister, you started it all. I was mad, but you gave in to my tears, burdened me with all this misery and cast me before an enemy. Why was it not possible to live, the way animals do, a blameless life, without getting married again and without getting involved in such problems? I have not kept the faith that I promised to the ashes of Sychaeus."

These were the heavy laments that burst out from her heart.

[In the meantime the god Mercury appears to Aeneas in a dream, warns him of Dido's wrath and thoughts of revenge, and urges him to sail at once. Aeneas obeys the divine order.]

Dawn left the saffron-colored bed of Tithonus and spread her early morning radiance over the earth. From her watchtower the queen saw the early light turn white and Aeneas' ships depart with their sails squared to the wind. She noticed that the harbor was empty, not an oarsman left. Three, four times she struck her lovely breasts and tore her golden hair and cried:

"God! He is leaving! A foreigner may mock my kingdom? Will nobody fetch arms? Won't my men from all over the city pursue him? Won't they drag their ships out of the dockyards? Let's go! Hurry! Carry torches, hand out missiles, pull on the oars! But what am I talking about? Where am I? What madness transforms my mind? Poor Dido, have you finally realized what crime has been committed? You should have realized it earlier, when you offered him your kingdom! There is faith and loyalty for you! And they say he took his household gods with him and carried his old weary father on his shoulders! Why could I not tear his limbs apart and throw them into the sea? Why not kill his companions, why not kill his son Ascanius and serve him as food for his father's meal? The outcome of the fight would have been doubtful. All right, but whom was I to fear, since die I must? I should have thrown firebrands into his camp, heaped flames on his decks, destroyed father and son and the whole race and flung myself on top of everything! Sun god, you let your flames shine over all the works of the world! Juno, you know my sorrows and understand them! Hecate, they howl at you in the night at the crossroads in the cities! Avenging Furies! Gods of dying Elissa! Listen to me! Turn your power to my misfortune: it deserves your attention! Listen to my prayers! If it is preordained that this hateful man must reach a harbor and may land somewhere, if Jupiter's fates demand this, if this is predestined, then let it happen. But let him be harassed in a war against a fierce, aggressive nation! Let him be driven homeless from his country! Let him be torn from the embrace of Iulus! Let him beg for help! Let him see the tragic deaths of his people! And once he has yielded to the harsh terms of a peace treaty, may he not enjoy his kingdom and a pleasant life! May he die before his time and lie unburied somewhere in the sand! This I pray. These are my last words, poured out with my blood. But then, men of Tyrus, you must pursue his race and all his descendants with your hatred. This sacrifice you must offer to my ashes. Let there be no friendship, no treaties between our peoples! Avenger, whoever you are, arise from my bones! Attack the Trojan settlers with the torch and the sword! Do it whenever an opportunity makes you strong! I pray: let shores fight against shores, sea against sea, arms against arms! Let this and future generations carry on the war!"

These were her words. Her thoughts moved in various directions. She wanted to end as soon as possible the life she hated. Briefly she spoke to Barce, Sychaeus' old nurse, for her own nurse was buried, a heap of black ashes, in the old country:

"Dear nurse, please go and bring me my sister Anna. Tell her to quickly sprinkle river water over herself and bring along the cattle, the sacrificial offerings I mentioned. Yes, let her come. And you must cover your head with a pure fillet. I am determined to go through with the sacrifice to the god of the underworld which I prepared and began in the ritual manner. I want to end my sorrows and hand over to the flames the pyre of the Trojan leader."

This she said. The old woman ran eagerly as fast as she could. Dido, trembling and almost overcome by her enormous endeavor, staring out of bloodshot eyes, with spots here and there on her quivering cheeks that were marked already with the pallor of impending death, burst into the innermost courtyard of the palace and in a state of madness climbed up the pyre, pulling out the Trojan sword, a gift not meant for such use. At this moment she saw the clothes of the Trojan and the familiar bed. She paused for a while to think and weep, then sank on the bed and spoke her very last words:

"Clothes, you were dear to me while fate and the gods allowed it. Now take my soul and deliver me from my distress. I have lived long enough to finish the course that Fortune gave me. I will go now, a majestic shade, underground. I have built a splendid city, seen my ramparts rise; I have punished my wicked brother to revenge my husband; and I would have been happy, oh, too happy! if only the Trojan ships had never come near our shores."

She buried her face in the pillows and cried:

"I shall die unavenged, but die I must. Yes! Yes! I want to go into the darkness. May the cruel man from Troy enjoy the sight of this fire, and may he carry away my death as an evil foreboding!"

Still speaking, she collapsed; she had stabbed herself. The attendants saw it, saw the sword foaming with blood, her hands splattered. Their cries went up to the palace roof. The news spread wildly through the city. The whole palace trembled with the laments, the sobbing and howling of the women, and the echo of the loud wailing resounded from heaven. It seemed as if Carthage or ancient Tyrus had fallen from an enemy attack, wild flames rushing across the tops of houses and temples.

Dido's sister heard it. She almost fainted from the shock but ran hysterically through the crowd, goring her face with her nails and beating her breasts and calling her dying sister:

"Dido! What is this, dearest? Did you want to trick me when you called me? Is this—oh no!—what your pyre, your fire, your altars meant? You have left me. How can I say what I feel? You died and would not let your sister join you? But you should have called me to share your death! The same pain inflicted by the sword, the same hour would have carried both of us away. Did I build the pyre with my own hands and call on the gods of our fathers—to be left out when you lay down, cruel sister? You have destroyed yourself and me, the people of Sidon, its leaders, and your city! Bring water: I want to wash her wounds and catch with my lips her last breath if it still lingers."

She climbed up the high steps, embraced and caressed her dying sister, and sobbing dried the dark blood with her robes. Dido tried to open her heavy eyes, but her strength failed her; a hissing came from the deep wound in her breast. Three times she tried to raise herself on her elbow; three times she fell back on the bed. With wandering eyes she searched for the light in the sky, and when she found it, she moaned.

Great Juno felt sorry for her drawn-out suffering and painful death and sent Iris down from Olympus to free her struggling soul from the body to which it clung. Since she was dying neither by fate nor by a death she had deserved, but before her day, poor woman, and fired by sudden madness, Proserpina had not yet taken from her head the blond lock nor handed her over to Orcus below. So Iris, covered with dew, flew down through the sky on crocus-colored wings, displaying in the sunlight a thousand different colors. She stood near Dido's head and spoke:

"I take this lock, as I was told to do, as an offering to Dis, and I release you from this body."

She cut off the lock. All at once the warmth drained from Dido's body, and her life vanished into the air.

10

The story of Heracles' death through a kind of love magic has been drama-tized by Sophocles in *The Women of Trachis* and by Seneca in *Heracles on Mount Oeta*. The myth itself embodies the ancient belief that certain drugs can kill even if they are absorbed by the skin rather than ingested. Hera-cles' wife, Deianira, was carried across a river by the Centaur Nessus. When he tried to make love to her in midstream, Heracles shot him from the other side with his poisoned arrows. The dying Centaur persuaded Deianira to preserve some of his blood, telling her it was a potent love charm, to be used whenever she felt that Heracles was unfaithful to her. This happens; she impregnates a new garment with the Centaur's poi-sonous blood and sends it to her husband, who then dies a slow and painful death. According to one version, he cannot die and has to burn himself alive on a gigantic pyre constructed on Mount Oeta; perhaps Virgil had this scene in mind when he described Dido's suicide; both Dido and Heracles were victims of love.

Although the myth reflects magical concepts, Seneca (unlike Sophocles) has stressed this by making Deianira's nurse—that is, her confidante—a witch. But even her powers are not sufficient to restore Heracles' love, and in the end Deianira has to resort to the dead Centaur's magic.

Seneca, *Heracles on Mount Oeta*, vv. 449–72

[*Deianira wants to regain Heracles' love.*]

DEIANIRA'S OLD NURSE: Has your love for illustrious Heracles vanished?

DEIANIRA: No, it has not vanished, nurse: it remains with me and sits deeply, firmly in my heart, believe me. But angry love hurts very much.

NURSE: It often happens that wives pull their marriage together by magic arts and prayers. I once ordered a landscape to bloom in the middle of winter; I have stopped a thunderbolt in its flight; I have shaken the sea, though there was no wind, and smoothed the stormy ocean. The dry earth opened up in fresh springs; rocks began to move; doors were forced open by me. Shades stood still; the Manes spoke; the hound of hell fell silent; for my prayers are an order. The sea, the earth, the sky, and Tartarus obey me. Midnight saw the sun, and the day saw night. When I begin my chants the laws of nature lose their power. Let me change his mood: my songs will find a way.

DEIANIRA: Do you want me to gather the poisonous herbs that grow beside the Black Sea or on high Pindus in Thessaly to break his will? Sooner will the moon desert the stars and come down to earth, forced by a magic song; sooner will the winter solstice see a harvest; sooner will a fast thunderbolt be stopped by an incantation; sooner will everything be turned upside down; sooner will noon be bright with all the gathered stars: but he alone will never change.

11

In his tragedy *Medea*, Seneca presents the heroine as a witch whose power has no limits. These two scenes are typical. In the first one she invokes various deities in order to curse her enemies. Like Deianira, like Dido, she feels abandoned and betrayed by the man she loved, and she is determined to hurt him as deeply as she can. What distinguishes her from Deianira and Dido is the fact that she is a professional witch, not just an amateur, and she knows exactly what she is doing.

The second passage probably inspired Lucan's necromantic scene. In it Medea invokes the powers of the underworld while she cooks in her cauldron all kinds of magical herbs.

Much of both scenes is sheer rhetoric, designed to create a mood. To us it is just one tedious detail after another, but contemporary audiences probably experienced the kind of *frisson* that one gets nowadays from horror movies. It is not great literature, perhaps, but it catered to a need. It dramatized aspects of the old myths that had not been shown before.

A: Seneca, *Medea*, vv. 6–23

[*Medea invokes various gods to curse her enemies.*]

MEDEA: . . . and Hecate with the three bodies! You offer your light, which knows all, to secret rites. Gods by whom Jason made his vows to me! Gods to whom Medea must pray in particular: Chaos of eternal night! Realms remote from the heavenly gods! Shades of the sinners! Ruler of the gloomy kingdom! Queen whom he abducted but kept more faithfully than Jason kept me! I pray to you with a voice that threatens doom. Now, now is the time to help me, avenging goddesses, your hair bristling freely with snakes, black torches in your bloody hands! Appear in the same horrible shape you had when you once stood in my bridal chamber! Bring death to my husband's new wife, death to her father and to the whole royal house! And let me wish an even more terrible curse on the bridegroom: to live, wandering from city to city in foreign lands, poor, exiled, anguished, hated, homeless! May he wish to have me back as his wife!

B: Seneca, *Medea*, vv. 670–843

[Medea prepares a deadly poison.]

MEDEA'S OLD NURSE (*observing Medea*): I am frightened, horrified. Something terrible is going to happen. It is amazing how her anger grows, inflames itself, and renews its former strength. Often have I seen her mad, assailing the gods, pulling down the sky, but now Medea plans something more monstrous, yes, more monstrous than ever before. As soon as she hurried away, out of her mind, and entered her cabinet of horrors, she spread all her materials, even those she had long been afraid to use, and unfolded a host of terrors, secret, occult. She touched with her left hand a magic utensil and invoked all the plagues which the hot sands of Libya produce and which the Taurus, covered with arctic snow, imprisons; she invoked every monstrosity on earth. Drawn by her magic incantations, a whole army of reptiles appears from their hiding places. A fierce dragon hauls its enormous body, darts its triple tongue, and looks around for victims to kill. It hears the magic song and stops and wraps its bloated, knotty rump in spirals around itself. Medea cries: "Small are the evils, weak the weapons that hell can produce: I shall claim my poison from heaven. It is time, high time, to carry out a most unusual scheme. I want the Snake that lies up there to come down here like a gigantic torrent. I want the two Bears—the big one, useful to Greek ships, and the small one, useful to Phoenician ships—to feel the Snake's enormous coils. Let the Snake-Keeper at long last relax the tight grips of his hands, and let the poison pour out. I want Python, who dared to challenge the Twins, to obey my song and appear! I want Hydra and all the snakes that Hercules killed to come back, renewed from their death. Leave Colchis and come here, watchful snake, put to sleep for the first time by my songs!" After she had summoned up all kinds of snakes, she stirred together poisonous herbs: whatever impassable Eryx produces on its rocks; what the Caucasus, sprinkled with Prometheus' blood, grows on peaks covered with eternal snow; the poisons that the warlike Medes and the fast Parthians carry in their quivers; the poisons that the rich Arabs smear on their arrows; the juices that Suebian noblewomen gather in the Hyrcanian forest under a cold sky; whatever the earth sprouts in spring, when birds build their nests, or later, when the numbing winter solstice has destroyed the beauty of the landscape and shackled everything with icy frost; every kind of plant that blooms with deadly flowers; every virulent juice in twisted roots that causes harm. All this she takes. Mount Athos in Thessaly has contributed some poisonous herbs, huge Pindus others; some tender leaves were cut on the peaks of Pangaeum with a bloody sickle; some grew near the Tigris, lord over deep currents; some near the Danube; some near the Hydaspes, which runs lukewarm water and carries many gems; some near the Baetis, which gives its name to a country and sluggishly joins the Hesperian Sea. This plant was cut as Phoebus started the day; that stalk was lopped off deep in the night; this crop was mown with a magic fingernail. She plucks the deadly herbs and squeezes out the poison of the snakes and mixes them with hideous birds: the heart of the night owl, which brings sorrow, and the vitals of hoarse screech owls, cut out alive. The mistress of crime sorts out other ingredients and arranges them: this one has the ravening power of fire, that one the paralyzing cold of icy frost. The words she speaks over her poisons are not less frightening. Listen: her frenzied step has sounded. She sings. The whole world trembles at her first words.

MEDEA: I pray to the silent crowd, to the gods of doom, the dark Chaos, the shadowy house of gloomy Dis, the caves of horrible Death circled by the banks of Tartarus. Shades, your torments have ceased: hurry to this new kind of wedding! The wheel that tortures Ixion's limbs must stop and let him touch the ground; Tantalus must drink undisturbed the water of Pirene. A heavier punishment should weigh on my husband's father-in-law alone. Let the slippery stone make Sisyphus roll backwards over the rocks. You, too, Danaids, whose wasted efforts are mocked by your pitchers full of holes, assemble! You are needed today.

Come now, star of nights! My offerings call you. Come, wearing your most sinister expression, threatening with all your faces.

For you have I loosened my hair from its band, according to the custom of my people. On bare feet have I wandered through remote groves and conjured water from dry clouds. I have pushed the seas down to the bottom. I have conquered the tides, and the Ocean has sent its heavy waves farther into the land. I have upset the cosmic laws, and the world has seen at the same time the sun and the stars. The Bears have touched the sea, which was forbidden to them. I have changed the order of the seasons: my magic chant made the summer earth bloom, and compelled by me, Ceres saw a winter harvest. Phasis has turned its rushing streams back to its source, and the Danube, split into so many mouths, has checked its currents and become a sluggish river in all its beds. The waves have roared, the sea swelled madly, but there has been no wind. The framework of an ancient grove lost its shadows at the command of my voice. The day was over, yet Phoebus still stood in the middle of the sky. Moved by my magic songs, the Hyades are falling. Phoebe, it is time to present at your sacred rites.

For you my bloody hands are wreathing these garlands, each entwined with nine serpents; to you I present these limbs which rebellious Tiphys had when he shook the throne of Jupiter. This contains the blood of Nessus, the treacherous ferryman: he offered it as he died. These are the ashes left from the pyre on Mount Oeta: it drank the poisoned blood of Hercules. Here you see the torch of Althaea, the avengeress: she was a good sister, but a bad mother. These are the feathers that the Harpy left in her unapproachable lair after she had fled from Zetes. And finally you have the quill of the Stymphalian bird after it had been wounded by the arrows of Lerna.

Altars, you made a sound. The goddess is favorable. I can see how her approach moves my tripods.

I see the fast chariot of Trivia. It is not the chariot that she drives in the night when her face is full and shining. It is the one that she drives when she stays closer to the earth, troubled by the threats of Thessalian witches, her face sad and pale. Yes! Pour out from your torch a gloomy, pallid light through the air! Frighten the peoples with a new kind of horror! Let precious Corinthian bronze gongs sound to help you, Dictynna! On the bloody turf I bring you a solemn offering. A torch snatched from the middle of a funeral pyre illuminates the night for you. For you I toss my head, bend my neck, speak my words. For you I have tied loosely, as is the custom at a funeral, a fillet round my flowing locks. For you I wave the branch of sorrow from the Stygian stream. For you I will bare my breasts and, like a Maenad, slash my arms with the sacrificial knife. Let my blood flow to the altar. My hand must learn to draw the sword, and I must learn to endure the sight of my own blood. There! I have cut myself and given my sacred blood.

If you resent the fact that I call on you to often in my prayers, please forgive me, daughter of Perses: the reason why I call on your bow again and again is always the same: Jason.

Poison now the robes of Creusa! As soon as she puts them on, let a hidden flame burn her marrow deep inside. Within this dark-golden box lurks an invisible fire. Prometheus gave it to me: he stole the fire from heaven and pays for this with his ever-growing liver. He taught me by his art to store magic powers. Hephaestus gave me fires covered by a thin layer of sulfur, and from my cousin Phaethon I received powerful shafts of lightning. I hold contributions from the middle part of Chimaera; I have flames that were snatched from the parched throat of the bull; those I mixed thoroughly with Medusa's gall, and I told them to preserve secretly their deadly effect.

Add your sting to these poisons, Hecate, and preserve in my gift the seeds of fire that are hidden in it! Let them deceive the sight and endure the touch; let the heat penetrate Creusa's heart and veins; let her limbs melt and her bones go up in smoke, and let the bride, her hair on fire, shine brighter than the wedding torches!

My prayers have been heard: three times has fearless Hecate barked, and she has sent out the fire of damnation from her torch that brings sorrow.

12

Encolpius ("Bosom Pal"), the narrator and antihero of Petronius' novel *Satyricon*, describes an embarrassing episode. A beautiful woman by the name of Chrysis ("Goldie") had offered herself to him, but he had completely failed in her arms. Now he is most anxious to restore his sexual powers. First he tries the conventional remedies of the day: a spicy meal of onions and snails (considered an aphrodisiac) and a little wine—not too much. He goes for a leisurely stroll and abstains from sex with his boyfriend, Giton. The next day, at the rendezvous with Chrysis, he discovers that she, too, has given the problem some thought and has brought her own witch with her. First the witch ties a kind of amulet around his neck, for his temporary impotence might have been caused by black magic. The threads of different colors (probably black, white, and red) remind us of the threads in Virgil's eighth eclogue [*no. 8*]. Spittle is often used in healing rites, and the spell, of course, is necessary to ask for supernatural help. The pebbles might have been just ordinary stones, but certain minerals were thought to have magical properties, just like herbs. The purple cloak wrapped around them is supposed to enhance their power to form another amulet. The magic works instantly.

Petronius, *Satyricon*, ch. 131

I now devoted myself to that body of mine that had been of so little use to me. Instead of taking a bath, I applied a little perfume, and then I ate a fortifying meal: onions, snails' necks without sauce, and just a little wine. Before going to sleep I went for a very leisurely stroll and then to bed without Giton; I was so anxious to soothe the lady that I was afraid to let the dear boy give me a workout. The next day I got up, physically and emotionally in one piece, and went down to the grove of plane trees where we had met before, although that ill-omened place made me nervous. Under the trees I then began to wait for Chrysis, my guide. I had only walked a few steps and sat down at the place where I had been yesterday when Chrysis appeared, dragging a little old woman with her. She greeted me and said: "How about it, my delicate lover: have you made up your mind to be normal today?" The old woman pulled a string made from threads of different colors from her dress and tied it around my neck. Then she took some dirt, mixed it with her spittle, and with her third finger made a mark on my forehead in spite of my resistance. . . . After having recited a spell, she told me to spit three times and to drop inside my garment three times in a row some pebbles over which she had said a spell and which she had wrapped in purple cloth. Then she tested the power of my loins by touching me there. . . .

13

After the mysterious death of Julius Caesar Germanicus, the adopted son
of the emperor Tiberius, at Antioch in A.D. 19, a gruesome discovery was
made. According to Tacitus, workmen who searched Germanicus' residence found under the floor and between the walls a collection of objects
obviously put there by someone who wanted the commander out of the
way. Even though Germanicus was almost universally popular, he had at
least two enemies: Gnaeus Calpurnius Piso, governor of Syria; and Piso's
wife, Plancina. As Germanicus lay dying, he expressed the belief that
these two had poisoned him, but his friends suspected black magic. Piso
was later prosecuted by the Senate and took his own life; his wife escaped
condemnation in A.D. 20 but was accused again years later and also
committed suicide. Tacitus, the historian, does not commit himself, although the list of objects allows no other interpretation: someone who
believed in the powers of black magic planted them in order to destroy the
prince. Whether poison was used for good measure we do not know.

     This is a fairly well documented example of the interaction be-
tween the world of politics and the world of magic. No doubt this sort of
thing happened very often; we just do not hear about it very often from
reliable sources.

Tacitus, *Annals* 2.69

[Under the floor and between the walls of Julius Caesar Germanicus'
residence workmen found] the remains of human bodies, spells, curses,
lead tablets engraved with the name Germanicus, charred and blood-
smeared ashes and other implements of magic by which, it is believed,
the soul [the life force] of a person can be devoted [surrendered, deliv-
ered] to the powers of the grave.

14

The language of this inscription from the late first century A.D. is very
formal, but the story is clear. The city of Tuder had been in grave danger
because a curse had been placed on several members of the city council.
The inscription does not explain how this became public knowledge, but
someone may have started a rumor. By suggesting that some of the
councillors were in danger, it was possible to frighten all of them. In
magical operations the victims were often allowed to know that something was going on. This gave them a last chance to pray to the gods for
protection, unless they wished to launch a magical counterattack. In this
instance the man who set up the inscription, L. Cancrius Primigenius,
made a vow to Jupiter Optimus Maximus. He vowed to set up the inscription in the temple (and probably to offer a sacrifice) if more details about

the curse, especially the names of the intended victims, came to light. Thanks to Jupiter this happened—we are not told how—and the details were duly recorded. The names of victims had been written on tablets and the tablets had been buried near some tombs. The communal slave, who may have had a grievance against the city council, is not identified, but no doubt he was convicted of sorcery and executed.

CIL 11.2.4639

For having saved the city, the city council, and the people of Tuder, L. Cancrius Primigenius, freedman of Clemens, member of the committee of six men in charge of the worship of the Augustans and the Flavians, has fulfilled his vow to Jupiter Optimus Maximus, because through his divine power he has brought to light the names of the members of the city council which, by the unspeakable crime of a worthless communal slave, had been attached to tombs so that a curse could be put upon them. Thus Jupiter has freed the city and the citizens from the fear of danger.

15

This is an authentic curse tablet, and its victims are two teams of charioteers. The chariot races in the circus—and most major cities throughout the Roman Empire had one—were among the most popular of spectator sports, and emotions ran high during these events. At the time of our inscription there were four teams. Distinguishable by the color of their uniforms, they were known as the Reds, the Whites, the Greens, and the Blues. This tablet was obviously inscribed by a fan of the Blues and the Reds, for he delivers the opposite teams—riders and horses—to an anonymous daemon. He strengthens the spell by invoking the name of the Jewish deity: *Iaô* and *Iasdao* seem to be variants of *Yahweh* (Jehovah). *Iasdao* was perhaps pronounced with a hiss, *susurrus magicus;* the series of vowels *a e i a* often appears in magical texts.

Lead tablet from Africa, late Empire (= nr. 286 Audollent)

I conjure you, daemon, whoever you may be, to torture and kill, from this hour, this day, this moment, the horses of the Green and the White teams; kill and smash the charioteers Clarus, Felix, Primulus, Romanus; do not leave a breath in them. I conjure you by him who has delivered you, at the time, the god of the sea and the air: *Iao, Iasdao . . . a e i a.*

16

The following section of the Great Magical Papyrus in Paris is entitled "Astonishing Love Magic." The papyrus was written in the early fourth century A.D., but it contains ideas and materials that are older. Like most magical "recipes," it follows the format "take this," "do this," "say this," and so on. It is a rather elaborate love charm, and some parts of it remind one of Theocritus [*no. 4*], while others are reminiscent of Horace [*no. 7*]. The magician has to fashion two dolls, one representing himself, the other the woman he desires. The doll respresenting the woman then has to be pricked with thirteen iron needles at certain spots, and the appropriate formulas have to be recited. The symbolism is fairly obvious, and there is a certain weird logic behind the whole thing. Such were the working papers of the professional sorcerer.

This so-called love charm has nothing to do with love, however. It is a tool that was used to possess and subjugate a woman who, presumably for good reasons, had rejected the suitor who ordered this performance. There is certainly a cruel, vindictive, and aggressive tone throughout the charm. It continues with more prayers, formulas, and rites, and one has the feeling that after a certain amount of all this either the magician or his customer (who may have been present) or both must have been exhausted.

The Great Magical Papyrus in Paris (= *PGM* 1:83–87)

Take wax or clay from a potter's wheel and shape it into two figures, one male and one female. Make the male look like Ares in arms. He should hold a sword in his left hand and point it at her right collarbone. Her arms must be tied behind her back, and she must kneel. Attach the magic substance to her head or neck. On the head of the figure representing the woman whom you wish to attract write: [magical words].

[list of other parts of her body, including the genitals, on which magical words must be written]

Take thirteen iron needles, stick one into her brain and say: "I prick your brain, X."

[list of other parts of the body to be pricked; each time the magician has to say: "I prick this part of the body of X, to make sure that she thinks of no one but me, Y."]

Take a lead plate and write the same formula on it and tie it to the figures in three hundred sixty-five knots with thread from a loom and recite the "Abrasax, hold tight" formula, which you know, and deposit this at sunset near the tomb of someone who died before his time or died a violent death, with flowers of the season. The spell that must be written and recited is this:

"I deposit this binding spell with you, gods of the underworld [magical words] and the Korē Persephone Ereschigal and Adonis, the [magical words] Hermes of the underworld, Touth [magical words] and powerful Anubis, who holds the keys of those in Hades, the gods and daemons of the underworld, those who died before their time, male and female, youths and maidens, year after year, month after month, day after day, hour after hour. I conjure all the daemons at this place to assist this one daemon. Wake up for me, whoever you are, male or female, and go to every place, to every street, into every house, and fetch and bind. Bring me X, the daughter of Z, whose magical substance you have, and make her love me, Y, the son of A. Let her not have intercourse, neither from front nor from behind, and let her not have pleasure with any other man except me, Y. Let her, X, not eat, not drink, not love, not be strong, not be healthy, not sleep, except with me, X, because I conjure you in the name of the terrifying one, the horrifying one. When the earth hears his name, it will open up. When the daemons hear his awful name, they will be afraid. When rivers and rocks hear his name, they will burst. I conjure you, daemon of the dead. . . .

Yes, drag her by her hair, her entrails, her genitals, to me, Y, in every hour of time, day and night, until she comes to me, Y, and remains inseparable from me. Do this, bind [her] during my whole life [to me] and force her, X, to be my slave, the slave of Y, and let her not leave me for a single hour of time. If you fulfill this wish, I will let you rest at once.

For I am Adônai [magical words], who hides the stars, the brightly radiating ruler of the sky, the lord of the world. . . .

"Fetch her, tie her, make her love and desire me, Y, . . . because I conjure you, daemon of the dead, by the terrible, the mighty one [magical words], to make you fetch X and make her join head to head, lips to lips, body to body, thighs to thighs, black to black, and do her job of making love with me forever and ever. . . ."

17

King Psammetichus, to whom this text is dedicated, may be as fictitious as Nephotes, the magician who addresses him, but the magic itself is probably much older than the papyrus. The kings of Egypt were thought to live forever (hence the spectacular tombs built for them), and during their life on this earth they must have had the best magicians money could buy—witness their confrontation with Moses, in Exodus 7. The Pharoah learns from them how to have visions in a bowl of water, how to hear voices, and how to receive revelations from "the ruler of the universe." But even the Pharaoh needs a "mystagogue"—that is, a guide to initiate him into the higher mysteries, and he apparently has to pretend to be a mummy and to create or reproduce a whole mythology in his prayer. Obviously, to arrest the great Osiris and bring him before an even greater god is no mean feat.

The first part of the ritual is supposed to produce a specific vision (that of the seahawk), which, in itself, is only a signal to proceed with another ritual. The real vision appears in a bowl of water on whose surface there is a film of olive oil. This is the technique of *lecanomancy*, here incorporated into an elaborate ritual. Watching the shapes forming on the surface of the water, the magician falls into a state of trance, during which he hears voices. The gods who send these voices then must be properly released.

The Great Magical Papyrus in Paris (= *PGM* 1:76–79)

Nephotes sends his greetings to Psammetichus, King of Egypt, the ever-living.

Since the great god established you as the ever-living king, and since nature made you an outstanding scientist, I wanted to prove to you my dedicated work, and I have sent to you this magic recipe, which achieves without any trouble supernatural results. When you examine them you will be astonished at the miracle of this process. You will see, by means of a basin giving you an immediate vision on any day or any night you wish, and in any place, in the water, the god. You will hear a voice, talking in [oracular] verses from the god, as you wish. You will also see the ruler of the universe and everything else you may wish to see. He will tell you everything about all the other things that you may wish to find out.

To be successful in getting an oracle you will have to do these things. First you must communicate with Helios as follows (it can be on any sunrise, provided the Moon is in her third day): Climb up on the top of your house and spread a clean linen sheet on the floor. Do this in the presence of a mystagogue. Put on a garland of black ivy. When the Sun is in the middle of the sky, in the fifth hour, lie down naked on the linen sheet, face upward, and command that your eyes be veiled with a black strap. Have yourself wrapped as if you were a corpse [a mummy?], close your eyes, and start saying these words:

(PRAYER) "Mighty Typhon, scepter-holder and ruler of the scepter-power above! God of gods! Lord! ABERAMEMTHÔOU. Shaker of darkness! Bringer of thunder! Stormy one! Night-lightener! Breather of cold and warm! Shaker of rocks! Shaker of walls! Raiser of waves! Raiser and mover of the deep sea! IÔERBÊT AU TAUI MÊNI.

I am he who, along with you, searched the whole earth and found the great Osiris, whom I have brought before you in chains. I am he who fought at your side against the gods. I am he who shut the double folding doors of heaven and put to sleep the dragon whose sight nobody can endure. I stopped the sea, the streams, the flowing of rivers, until you became ruler of this kingdom. I, your soldier, was overcome by the gods, and because of their vain wrath I was hurled to the ground. Raise me, your friend, I beseech you, I entreat you! Do not throw me on the ground, lord of the gods. AEMINAEBAROTHERRETHORABEANIMEA. Give me strength, I beseech you, and grant me this favor that, whenever I order in my incantations one of the gods themselves to come, he will come and show himself to me. NAINE BASANAPTATOU EAPTOU MÊNÔPHAESME PAP-TOU MÊNÔPH · AESIMÊ · TRAUAPTI · PEUCHRE · TRAUARA · PTOUMEPH · MOURAI · ANCHOUCHAPHAPTA · MOURSA · ARAMEI · IAÔ · ATHTHARAUI · MÊNOKER · BOROPTOUMÊTH · AT TAUI MÊNI CHARCHARA · PTOUMAU · LALAPSA · TRAUI TRAUEPSE MAMÔ PHORTOUCHA · AEÊIO IOU · EAI AEÊI ÔI IAÔ AÊI AI IÂO.

When you have said this three times there will be the following sign of communion (but you, armed as you are with that magic soul of yours, must not be shocked): A sea hawk will pounce on you and hit your body with his wings, signifying that you should stand up. Stand up and dress yourself in white robes and offer uncut incense drop by drop as a sacrifice on an altar made of earth, and say: "I have had communion with your holy image. I have received strength from your holy name. I have partaken of the flow of your blessings, lord, god of gods, ruler, divine beings, ATHTHOUIN THOUTHOUI TAUANTI · LAÔ APTATÔ." When you have done all this, you will be in control of your godlike nature. Descend [return?] in order to perform through this communion the dish oracle that will give you a vision and conjure up the dead.

VISION. If you wish to see things, take a bronze vessel, a cup or a bowl of any kind. Pour water into it: rain water if you wish to call the heavenly gods; sea water if you wish to call the gods of the earth; water from a river if you wish to call Osiris or Sarapis; spring water if you wish to call the dead. Hold the vessel on your knees. Add oil from green olives and, bending over the vessel, say the following prayer and call any god you wish and ask him about anything, and he will answer you and tell you everything. After he has spoken, release him by the formula of release. If you apply this prayer, you will be amazed.

(PRAYER SPOKEN OVER THE VESSEL) AMOUN AUANTAU LAIMOUTAU RIPTOU MANTAUI IMANTOU LANTOU LAPTOUMI · ANCHOMACH · ARAPTOUMI · Come here, god X Y Z, appear to me now in this hour. Do not shock my eyes. Come here, god X Y Z. Listen to me, for he who wants this and commands this is ACHCHÔR ACHCHÔR · ACHACHACH PTOUMI CHACHCHÔ CHARACHÔCH · CHAPTOUMÊ · CHÔRACHARACHOCH · APTOUMI · MÊCHÔ-CHAPTOU · CHARAPTOU · CHACHCHÔ · CHARACHÔ · PTENACHÔCHEU [one hundred letters].

18

This prayer of thanksgiving comes as a surprise in a body of magical recipes and spells. It seems to contradict the theory that the magician uses gods as his tools, compelling them to perform, whereas the religious person approaches them humbly, asking for help. The god addressed in this prayer is very much like the Judaeo-Christian God, and since this text

was written down as late as the fourth century A.D., it is quite possible
that its author was influenced by Christian theology, though not a Christian himself. The success of Christianity may have persuaded him that
here was a powerful magic that might be used to good advantage, especially if the ancient magic did not work anymore. If so, this text is
another example of the flexibility of the magicians: they were always on
the lookout for new methods, even if they involved a kind and benevolent god rather than the threatening daemon of earlier days. For a similar
text see *Corpus Hermeticum* (edited and translated by Festugière and
Nock), 2:353ff.

The Great Magical Papyrus in Paris (= *PGM* 1:56–58)

We are grateful to you with all our soul and in our heart, which goes out to
you, the unspeakable name that is honored by the appellation "god" and
praised through the divine holiness by which you show to everybody and
to everything your fatherly benevolence, love and friendship, and your
most benign work by having given us mind, speech, and insight: mind, in
order to know you; speech, in order to call upon you; insight, in order to
understand you. We are glad that you have shown yourself to us, even
though we are still embodied. There is only one way in which men can
show their gratitude to you: by understanding the greatness that is you.
We have understood it, O womb of all knowledge; we have understood it,
O womb fertile by the father's production; we have understood it, O
everlasting presence of a fertile father. After having worshiped your infinite goodness, we can pray for only one thing: Preserve us in our knowledge of your existence, and help us never to go astray from this, our way
of life.

19

Here is another example of love magic from the Great Papyrus in Paris.
Similar to an earlier text [*no. 16*], it illustrates the total power over a
woman which the magician (or his client) desires. The spell is written in
the form of an impassioned monologue directed at vessel of myrrh, which
is burning during the whole operation. There is a kind of poetry in the
intensity of the appeal to the magical substance and the detailed anticipa-
tion of its effect, and there is the same lack of compassion for the victim,
who is treated as a mere sex object, not as human being.

The Great Magical Papyrus in Paris (= *PGM* 1:121–24)

Magic to deliver someone, to be said over smoking myrrh.
        Let it [the myrrh] smoke on coals, and recite the spell.
        The spell: "You are Zmyrna [i.e., myrrh], the bitter and effective

one, the one that reconciles people who fight with each other, the one that roasts those who do not recognize (the power of) love and forces them to love. Everyone calls you Zmyrna, but I call you Eater and Burner of the Heart. I am not sending you far away to Arabia; I am sending you to X, daughter of Y, to serve me against her and bring her to me.

"If she is sitting, she may not sit; if she is talking to someone, she may not talk; if she is approaching someone, she may not approach; if she is walking around, she may not walk; if she is drinking, she may not drink; if she is eating, she may not eat; if she is kissing someone, she may not kiss; if she is enjoying something, she may not enjoy it; if she is sleeping, she may not sleep. She may think only of me, Z, desire only me, love only me and fulfill my every wish.

"Do not enter her by her eyes, nor by her ribs, nor by her nails, nor by her navel, nor by her limbs, but enter her through her soul and remain in her heart and burn her entrails, her breast, her liver, her breath, her bones, her marrow, until she comes to me, Z, to love me and fulfill my every wish.

"I urge you, Zmyrna, by the three names Anochô, Abrasax, Trô, and by those that are even more appropriate and more powerful—Kormeioth, Iaô, Sabaôth, Adônai—to make sure that you carry out my orders, Zmyrna. Just as I am burning you and you are potent, just so you must burn the brain of X, the woman I love, burn it completely and rip out her entrails and shed her blood, drop by drop, until she comes to me, Z, the son of A."

20

For this magical operation a cat must be "made into an Osiris," that is, killed. The euphemism originates from the belief that Osiris represents the dead Pharaoh and therefore, by extension, any dead creature. To be "osirified," therefore, means to be given a new life in another world, for, as the spell shows, the dead cat is capable of attracting a daemon. The magician blames the death of the cat on his enemies—the names are to be filled in—because they forced him to engage in magical rites in the first place. This is very ingenious. The last few lines show that this magic can be used to influence the outcome of the races in the circus. A simple drawing of the circus, the chariots, and the charioteers, is sufficient.

The Great Magical Papyrus in Paris (= PGM 1:30)

Take a cat and make him an Osiris by putting his body into water. As you drown him, say over his back . . . "Come here, you who control the shape of Helios, you, the cat-faced god, and look at your shape that has been insulted by your adversaries . . . , because I conjure you by your

names [magical words] . . . awake now, cat-faced god and do such and
such a thing."

Take the cat and stuff three scraps of paper into him—one into his
behind, one into his mouth, one into his throat. Write the appropriate
formula with vermilion on clean paper and then [draw] the chariots and
the charioteers and the seats and the race horses and wrap them around
the cat's body and bury it. Light seven lights over seven unbaked bricks
and give him a smoke offering of gum resin. And be of good cheer. . . .

21

This papyrus is entitled "Sacred Book, Called the 'Monad,' or 'Eighth
Book of Moses,' about the Holy Name." It was written down in the fourth
century A.D., but the material seems to be at least two centuries older.

The first rite described is to be used for an exorcism. Sulfur and
bitumen ("Jew's pitch," found in antiquity in Palestine and Babylon) are
strong-smelling substances that are believed to have the power to drive
daemons away. The "Name" is probably the holy name of the Old Testament, Yahweh.

The second ritual invokes the snake Apyphys, in Egyptian myth
the enemy of the sun god. By calling a snake by this name, the magician
will enlist the sun god's help. To bring a corpse back to life requires an
appeal to a daemon, a reference to the Egyptian god Thayth and a recitation of the Name, presumably Yahweh.

The last spell includes Christ (but the reading is not certain), as
well as the Name (Yahweh?), but also Helios and an Egyptian formula.
The syncretism is obvious: the deity or deities of a single religion were no
longer thought to be sufficient, and two or three different names had to be
invoked.

The Magical Papyrus in Leiden (= *PGM* 2:98–102)

If someone is possessed by a daemon, say the Name and hold sulfur and
bitumen under his nose. He will speak at once, and the daemon will go
away.

If you want to kill a snake, say "Stop. You are Apyphys." Take a
green palm branch and take the marrow, split it into two parts, say the
Name over it seven times, and the snake will at once be split in two or
burst.

How to awaken a dead body. "I conjure you, spirit walking in the
air; come in, fill him with your breath, give him strength, wake up this
body through the power of the eternal god, and let him walk around at
this place. For it is I who perform this operation through the power of
Thayth, the holy god." Say the Name.

How to unshackle fetters. [Say] "Hear me, Christ [or, Helpful

One] in my torture. Help me in my predicament, for your are compassionate in the hour of violence and the most powerful in the universe, and you have created Pressure and Punishment and Torture."

For twelve days [?] whistle three times and say the whole name of Helios eight times, beginning with the Achebykrôm: "Let every fetter be opened . . . let all irons break, every rope, every leather strap, every knot, every shackle be opened, and let no one restrain me, because I am [say the Name]."

22

To send dreams to someone, the magician has to draw a rather complicated figure on a linen sheet and recite a formula. This forces a minor daemon to go to the bedroom of X and give him a dream—the dream to be specified by the operator. The minor daemon is threatened by the authority of a major one in drastic terms. The "sending of dreams" is not a common magical operation, but it may have been practiced whenever a dream was required to reveal the future. The priests at Epidaurus must have used similar methods to induce sleep and significant dreams in their patients and in themselves (incubation), because everything depended on having those dreams.

The Magical Papyrus in Leiden (= PGM 2:66–67)

Ziminis of Tentyra, the Sender of Dreams

Take a clean linen sheet and paint on it with myrrh solution—according to Ostanes—a human figure with four wings. It should show the left hand stretched out along with the two left wings; the other hand should be bent, the fingers, too. It should have a diadem on the head and a garment around the elbow and two folds in the garment. On top of the head bull's horns, and on the behind the winged behind of a bird. The right hand should touch the throat, holding it, and there should be a sword sticking out of both heels. Also write on the sheet the following names of the god and whatever you want X to see, and how [magic words]: "I am telling you [daemons], and you [in particular], most powerful daemon, go into the house of X and tell him this." Then take a lamp that is not painted red, that is not painted at all, put a wick into it and fill it with cedar resin, and as you light it say the following three names of the god [magic words]: "Holy names of the god, hear me, and you, benevolent spirit, whose power is the greatest among the gods, listen to me, and go to X, into his house, where he sleeps, into his bedroom and stand over him, frightening him, making him tremble with the great, powerful names of the god, and tell him this . . . I conjure you by your power, by the great god Seith, by the hour in which you were born as a great god, by the god who will now give me an oracle, by the three hundred and sixty-five names of the great god—go to X right now, this night, and tell him in his dream the following. . . . If you do not listen to me and do not go to X, I shall tell the great god, and he will pierce you and chop you limb by limb and will give your flesh to the mangy dog on the dung heap to eat. So listen to me right now, right now, quick, quick, and don't force me to say all this once more."

23

The following texts are invocations of a supreme deity for magical purposes. In the first text (A), some qualities and attributes of the god are given (*aretalogia*), then he is identified as the "invisible Aion of Aion." Originally *aiōn* meant "a very long, unlimited time" (either past or still to come), but in Biblical Greek it also designated a limited period of time (e.g., "the present age"), and in Late Hellenistic Greek in general its meaning was "the world" (a time concept having become a space concept) or even the god that rules over time and space (the concept having become a person) and over all other gods.

In the second text (B), an unnamed deity is addressed in similar terms. The real name of a divine power was often kept secret and not committed to writing, but sometimes there is a cumulation of names, to reinforce the effect.

A: The Magical Papyrus in Leiden (= *PGM* 2:89–90)

I invoke you, you who are greater than all, who have created all, you the self-created who sees everything but cannot be seen. You have given the sun all its glory and power, you have told the moon to wax and wane and move in a steady course; you have not taken away anything of the former darkness, but you have given it equal measure. For when you appeared, the universe was and light appeared. To you all things are subject, and none of the gods can see your true form. You can transform yourself into all beings and you are the invisible Aion of Aion.

B: The Magical Papyrus in Leiden (= *PGM* 2:74–76)

Come here, you from the winds, you supreme ruler of the universe, you who have breathed spirit into men to give them life, lord of all beauty in the world. Listen to me, lord, you who have the secret, the unspeakable name—the daemons tremble when they hear it. . . .

Who has shaped the forms of living creatures? Who has found the paths? Who is the begetter of fruits? Who piled up the mountains? Who told the winds to do their work, year after year? Which age supports age and commands ages?

24

As one reads this text, one discovers that it is another type of love charm, for the sending of sleepless nights to a woman is not the ultimate purpose of this spell: she is supposed to lie awake, thinking of the sorcerer or the client who ordered this. The symbolism of the puppy dog and the bat's eye is fairly obvious: bats are awake at night and see in the darkness, and barking dogs keep people awake. The three-forked roads outside ancient cities were useful for magical purposes because there were usually tombs nearby, and Hecate as well as Korē (i.e., Persephone), the goddess of the underworld, were thought to appear at these places at night. Both Hecate and Korē are invoked in this spell, along with some more obscure deities and daemons (although Brimo is often identified with either Persephone or Hecate).

The text is uncertain at the very end of the passage, but since provisions are made to remove the magical device from its spot near the crossroads, one may assume that the sleepless nights are not intended to last forever but can be ended as soon as the woman discovers her love for the magician.

The Great Magical Papyrus in Paris (= PGM 1:167–68)

Take the eye of a bat and release it alive. Take unbaked dough made from wheat flour, or wax that has not burned, and shape a puppy dog. Put the right eye of the bat into the right eye of the puppy and the left eye of the bat into the left eye of the puppy. Take a needle and stick the magic substance onto it. Prick the eyes of the puppy with the needle and make sure that the magic substance remains visible. Throw it [the puppy] into a new drinking vessel, put a label on it, seal it with your own signet ring, which has on it (two) crocodiles turning their heads toward each other, and hide it on a three-forked road, after having marked the place so you may find it when you want to take it away. Prayer written on the tablet [i.e., the label on the vessel]: "I conjure you three times in the name of Hecate PHŌRPHŌRBA BAIBŌ PHŌRPHŌRBA to make X loose the fire in her eyes or become sleepless and have no one in her mind except me, Y. I conjure you by Korē, who became the goddess of the three-forked roads and who is the true mother of (write the names of any daemons) whom you like: PHORBEA NĒRĒATO BRIMŌ DAMŌN · BRIMŌN SEDNA · DARDAR· all-seeing one, IOPĒ, make X be sleepless because of me forever and ever" [or, "and love me passionately"; there is a gap here in the papyrus].

25

Kronos, younger son of Heaven and Earth, father of Zeus, was the leading deity of an earlier generation of gods, the Titans, his brothers. He probably belongs to a pre-Greek civilization. After Zeus and the other Olympian gods took over, the Titans were driven from heaven. What happened to their leader, Kronos, is told in different versions. According to one story (reflected here) he was chained and imprisoned; according to another one he was exiled on a distant island, where he fell into an everlasting sleep, dreaming the destinies of the world.

In our spell, Kronos is presented as a god in chains who is therefore full of resentment and needs to be soothed and flattered. Naturally, he can be dangerous to the magician too, but the magician can protect himself by wearing the white linen robe of a priest of Isis and fashioning an amulet of the shoulder blade of a boar (very durable material) by scratching a picture of Zeus on it—Zeus with the sickle, the emblem of power that he took away from his father. This will humiliate Kronos and render him harmless to the wearer of the amulet.

The Great Magical Papyrus in Paris (= *PGM* 1:172–74)

An oracle of Kronos that is much in demand:
The so-called Little Mill.

Take two measures of sea salt and grind them in a manual mill, reciting the prayer many times, until the god appears to you. Perform the operation at night, at a place where grass grows. If you hear, as you recite the spell, someone's heavy footsteps and the clanking of iron, it is the god who comes, fettered with chains, carrying a sickle. Do not be afraid, for you are protected by a protective device that will be explained to you. You must wrap yourself in pure linen like the one the priests of Isis wear. Present to the god a smoke offering with the heart of a cat and the droppings of a mare. The prayer that you should recite, as you grind, is the following:

Prayer: "I am calling you, the great one, the holy one, the founder of the whole inhabited world, who was treated unjustly by his own son, who was bound by Helios with steel fetters to save the universe from collapsing. Male-female one, father of thunder and lightning, who rules even over those in the underworld [magical words], come, lord, and tell me by force of necessity all about the matter in question. For I am the one who has withheld from you [magical words]."

This is what is said over the grinding of the salt.

The spell that compels him is this:

[magical words].

Say this when he enters in a threatening manner, to soothe him and to make him reveal to you what you want to know. The much-desired protective device against this is the following: On the shoulder blade of a boar you must scratch a [picture of] Zeus carrying a sickle and this name [magical word]. The shoulder blade must come from a black, leprous, castrated boar.

Dismissal [magical words]: "Go away, ruler of the world, progenitor, and withdraw into your own region, to keep the universe safe. Be gracious to us, lord."

26

Apollonius of Tyana, philosopher and miracle-worker of the first century A.D., was reported to Tigellinus, Nero's "chief of police," we would say today, and was promptly arrested. But the charges against him, written on a scroll, disappeared magically. Tigellinus then interrogated him in secret and was so impressed by the man that he released him.

It is clear from the story told in document A that Apollonius could have been executed at the order of Tigellinus, as so many others were, even without a trial. Apollonius consistently denies having any supernatural abilities—for instance, the gift of divination. Like Apuleius, about a century later, he claims that he is merely a philosopher, a scientist who observes certain natural phenomena and interprets them correctly. But according to his biographer, Philostratus, he sees things that no one else sees, and he certainly believes in daemons, for he deals with them: but then, many serious philosophers of the time believed in daemons, and Pythagoras, whose doctrine Apollonius professed to teach, was that strange combination of philosopher and miracle-worker which we call "shaman."

In document B, Apollonius is in a similar situation, but here his biographer gives us his formal *Apologia* before the emperor Domitian. In many respects it corresponds to Apuleius' *Apologia*, delivered in court about a century later, but unlike Apuleius' speech it can hardly be considered authentic; Philostratus no doubt composed the sort of speech that Apollonius *might* have delivered under the circumstances, though it is possible that he found some of the material in his source.

Apollonius was accused of witchcraft because he predicted a plague at Ephesus. The argument of the prosecutor was that only a wizard could have made such a prediction. The fact that Apollonius also saved the people of Ephesus from the plague did not interest the court. In maintaining that this kind of foreknowledge is not supernatural, Apollonius compares himself with two "pre-Socratics," Thales and Anaxagoras (since he calls them both Ionians, he may be thinking of Anaximander, or perhaps the name is corrupted, in the textual tradition), and with Socrates himself.

How does Apollonius explain his "psychic" abilities? First, by his diet. Though he does not explain it here in detail, it is clear that he was a vegetarian and probably avoided wine. This is in accordance with Pythagoras' teaching, but it is also something that Apollonius might have learned in India, where he lived for a while. In modern terms, he might be called a practitioner of yoga.

Another argument Apollonius presents in his defense is the fact that he gave credit to Heracles for ending the plague; he dedicated a temple to the god. A real magician would have claimed all the credit for himself. This is an important distinction. By paying tribute to a god, Apollonius removes the miracle from the sphere of magic and places it in the religious sphere. The fact that he actually *saw* the plague in human shape is puzzling, but for Apollonius evil daemons were responsible for diseases whether they affected a person or a whole community.

Finally, Apollonius rejects the charge or insinuation that he offered human sacrifices to perform black magic. He is against *all* bloody sacrifices (i.e., he would never ritually kill an animal, much less a human being). He describes the magician as "the sort of person who prays with his eye on a knife" (an interesting and rather unusual detail), meaning that the magician promises in his prayer to the god the gift of sacrifice he is about to offer with the knife. Apollonius argues that if he himself had done any such thing, his *daimonion* would have left him long ago; the fact that it still advises him proves that he is pure.

A: Philostratus, *Life of Apollonius of Tyana* 4.44

An epidemic broke out in Rome, called a "flu" by the doctors; its symptoms: coughing, and when the patient tried to speak, his voice was affected. The temples were full of people supplicating the gods because Nero had a swollen throat and his voice was hoarse. Apollonius thundered against the ignorance of the crowd, though he did not chastise anyone in particular; in fact, he talked sense to Menippus, who was furious at this sort of thing, and restrained him, telling him to forgive the gods if they enjoyed the farces of clowns. This remark was reported to Tigellinus, who sent the police to take him to prison and summoned him to defend himself from the charge of impiety against Nero. A prosecutor was appointed in his case who had already ruined many people and had quite a record of such Olympic victories. He held in his hands a scroll in which the charge was written out, and he brandished it against Apollonius like a sword, saying that it had been sharpened and would destroy him. But when Tigellinus unrolled the scroll and did not find in it a single trace of writing, but looked at a perfectly blank book, he began to suspect that he was dealing with a daemon. Apparently Domitian later felt this way about Apollonius, too.

Tigellinus now led Apollonius into the secret tribunal where magistrates of his rank try in private the most important cases. He told everyone else to withdraw and kept asking Apollonius questions. "Who are you?" Apollonius gave his father's name and that of his country and explained why he practiced philosophy: he said that he practiced it in order to know the gods and to understand human beings, because it was more difficult to know someone else than to know oneself. Tigellinus asked: "How do you drive out daemons and ghostly phantoms, Apollonius?" He answered: "In the same way as I would drive out the murderous and the impious." This was a sarcastic remark aimed at Tigellinus, for he had taught Nero every kind of cruelty and perversion. Tigellinus asked him: "Could you prophesy, if I asked you to?" Apollonius answered: "How could I, seeing that I am no prophet?" "And yet," Tigellinus remarked, "they say you predicted that some great event would happen and yet not happen." "What you heard is true," Apollonius answered, "but you must not ascribe this to any gift of divination, only to the wisdom which god reveals to the wise." Tigellinus asked: "Why are you not afraid of Nero?" Apollonius answered: "Because the same god who made him seem so terrifying also gave me the gift of being without fear." Tigellinus asked: "What do you think about Nero?" Apollonius said: "I have a better opinion of him than the rest of you; for you consider him worthy to sing, but I consider him worthy to be silent." Tigellinus was astonished and said: "You may go, but you must post a bond for your person." Apollonius asked: "And who might post a bond for a person that no one can bind?" These answers struck Tigellinus as being divinely inspired and above the nature of man, and since he was afraid of fighting with a god he said: "You may go wherever you wish, for you are too powerful to be controlled by me."

B: Philostratus, *Life of Apollonius of Tyana* 8.7.9–10

My prosecutor says that I am not accused of having saved the city of Ephesus from the plague, but for having predicted that it would be visited by an epidemic. This, he says, is beyond science and represents a miracle, and that I could never have reached such a degree of truth if I were not a magician, an unspeakable creature. Well, what would Socrates say, at this point, of the knowledge that he received from his *daimonion?* What would Thales and Anaxagoras say, both Ionians, one of whom predicted an abundant olive crop, the other a series of dramatic changes in the weather? That they predicted these things because they were magicians? And yet they were brought before courts of law on different charges, and we never hear of anyone accusing them of witchcraft simply because they had the gift of foreknowledge. That would have seemed ridiculous, an improbable charge against scientists, even in Thessaly, where women had a bad reputation for pulling the moon down to earth.

How, then, did I sense the coming disaster at Ephesus? You have heard the statement made by the prosecution that my life style is different from that of others, that I follow a diet of my own which is light and more pleasant than the luxurious meals of the others. I have said that myself at the beginning of my speech. This diet, Your Majesty, keeps my senses in a kind of mystic atmosphere and prevents them from coming in contact with any interference, but allows me to see, as if in the shining surface of a looking glass, everything that is happening or will happen. For the true scientist will not wait for the earth to send up its exhalations nor for the air to be polluted, if the evil influences should come from above, but he will sense these things when they are imminent—not as soon as the gods, of course, but sooner than the ordinary person. For the gods perceive the more distant future, men what is happening, scientists what is about to happen. Please ask me privately about the causes of epidemics, Your Majesty; they are too scientific to be discussed in public. Is it then my life style alone which makes my sense perceptions so subtle, so keen, that they take in the most spectacular, the most miraculous, phenomena? You can look at the facts from different points of view, but especially from what happened in Ephesus in connection with that epidemic. I actually saw the physical appearance of the epidemic—it looked like an old beggar—and once I saw it, I captured it and did not so much bring the disease to an end as eradicate it. And who was the god to whom I had prayed? The sanctuary that I founded in Ephesus to commemorate the event shows it, for it is dedicated to Heracles, the "Averter of Evil." I chose him for my helper because he is the god whose technique and courage once purged Elis of a plague, when he washed away the miasma that used to rise from the ground when Augias was king.

Your Majesty, would you think that someone whose ambition it is to be considered a sorcerer would ever attribute his own achievement to a god? Who would admire his magic if he gave credit for the miracle to a god? And what magician would pray to Heracles? For these accursed men attribute such miracles to the trenches they dig and to the gods of the underworld, from which Heracles must be separated, for he is a pure god and kind to men. Another time I prayed to him in the Peloponnesus, too, for there was an apparition of a Lamia; it haunted the surroundings of Corinth and devoured handsome adolescents. Heracles helped me in my struggle and did not ask for extraordinary gifts—just a honey cake and some frankincense and the opportunity of working for the good of mankind. For in the days of Erechtheus, too, this had been the only reward for his labors. Your Majesty need not resent my mentioning Heracles; Athena had him under her special care because he was good and a savior of mankind.

But since you command me to justify myself in the matter of the sacrifice—I know that this is what your gesture means—please listen to my defense: it is the truth. In everything I do I have the salvation of mankind at heart; yet I have never offered any sacrifice on their behalf nor will I ever offer one nor will I ever touch one that has blood in it; I am not the sort of person who prays with his eye on a knife or offers the kind of sacrifices [i.e., human sacrifices] that the prosecution alleges. The prisoner who stands before you is not a Scythian, Your Majesty, nor a native of some savage country. I have never mixed with Massagetes and Taurians, and if I had, I would have converted them from their traditional sacrifices. But what degree of madness would I have reached if—after talking so much about divination and the conditions under which it works or does not work, and understanding better than anyone else that the gods reveal their plans to holy and wise men, even if they have no prophetic gifts—I would become guilty of murder and operate with entrails that are an abomination to me and wholly unacceptable to the gods? If I had done such a thing, the divine voice of the *daimonion* would have left me as being impure. . . .

27

Lucian of Samosata, a satirist of the second century A.D., has left some eighty pieces, most of them short dialogues. Because of his wit and his irreverent criticism of contemporary customs and institutions he has been called "the Greek Voltaire." He makes fun of popular religious ideas (e.g., in the *Icaromenippus* and in the *Assembly of the Gods*) and of certain superstitions (as in *The Lovers of Lies*). It is clear from the present passage that Lucian himself did not believe in magic, though many of his contemporaries, even educated men, still did.

　　The person who tells the story is, as a matter of fact, a teacher of philosophy who tutors a young man in the doctrine of the Aristotelian school. (Incidentally, we are informed that the works of the master were studied in this order: *Analytics*, i.e., Logic, then *Physics*—to be followed no doubt by *Metaphysics*, i.e., "that which comes after *Physics*.") This philosophy teacher finds himself in the curious role of having to procure a magician for his pupil. The magician is found and produces first, for a fee, the ghost of the young man's father, and then the living body of the lady he loves. The description of the ritual is full of ironic distortions and exaggerations of details which, in themselves, are not implausible. Clay figures were used in magic, but this one can actually fly, and so on.

　　The fact that the whole ceremony—though it worked literally like a charm—was unnecessary, is another of Lucian's jokes. A famous exorcist is then mentioned, the "Syrian from Palestine," who healed many people for a fee.

　　Finally, one of those present affirms his belief in spirits. The narrator (Lucian himself, one assumes) each time intersperses his doubt in the politest possible Attic manner.

Lucian, *The Lovers of Lies*, pars. 14–18

"Very soon after Glaucias' father had died and he had taken over the property, he fell in love with Chrysis, the wife of Demeas. He had hired me as his philosophy tutor, and if that love affair had not kept him so busy, he would have mastered already the whole Peripatetic doctrine, for even at the age of eighteen he did Analytics, and he had studied Physics from beginning to end. Well, he was at his wit's end with this love affair and told me everything. It was only natural—after all, I was his teacher— for me to bring to him that Hyperborean magician at a fee of four minas down (an advance toward the cost of the sacrifices was required) and sixteen more if he should find Chrysis' favor. The magician waited for the moon to wax, for this is the time when such rites are usually performed. Then he dug a pit in an open court of the house. Around midnight he first conjured up for us Alexicles, the father of Glaucias, who had died seven months before. The old gentleman was against this love affair and grew quite angry, but finally he told his son to go ahead and love her. Then the magician produced Hecate, who brought Cerberus along with her. He also drew down Selene [the moon], who presented a variety of apparitions: first she looked like this and then like that. First she appeared in the shape of a woman, then she was a handsome bull, and then she looked like a puppy dog. Finally the Hyperborean formed a kind of miniature Cupid out of clay and said to him: 'Go and fetch Chrysis.' The clay [figure] flew away, and shortly afterward the lady stood at the threshold, knocked at the door, came in, embraced Glaucias as if she were madly in love with him, and stayed with him until we heard the cocks crowing. Then, as dawn was approaching, the moon flew back to the sky, Hecate plunged into the earth, all the other phantoms disappeared, and we sent Chrysis off. If you had seen this, Tychiades, you would no longer have doubted that there is much power in magic."

"You are right," I said. "I would have believed this, if I had seen it, but as things are, you will perhaps forgive me if I am not quite as clear-sighted as you. I do, however, know the Chrysis of whom you speak; she is an amorous lady and quite willing, and I don't see why you needed the clay ambassador and the magician from the land of the Hyperboreans and the moon in person in order to get her, when for twenty drachmas you would have brought her to the Hyperboreans! For the lady is very responsive to that kind of spell [i.e., money], and her reaction is totally different from that of phantoms: if they hear the clinking of bronze or iron, they take off—so you say yourselves—but when she hears the clinking of silver [coins] anywhere, she moves in the direction of the sound. Moreover, I am amazed at the magician; he was able to make the richest ladies love him and take whole talents [large sums] from them, and yet he was so penny-wise that for only four minas he made Glaucias irresistible?"

"It is ridiculous of you," Ion said, "to doubt everything. You know, I should really like to ask you what you have to say about all those who deliver men possessed by daemons from their terrible predicament by—there is no doubt about it—exorcising them! No need for me to dwell on this. Everybody knows about the Syrian from Palestine, the expert in these matters, and how many people he took care of—those who collapsed before the full moon, those who rolled their eyes, those whose mouths filled with foam—and yet he made them well and sent them home in a normal frame of mind, having healed them from whatever plagued them, for a substantial fee. They lie there and he stands beside them and asks, 'Where do you come from? Whence did you enter this body?' The patient himself says nothing, but the daemon answers, either in Greek or in a foreign language, depending on the country he comes from, and tells him how and from where he entered this person. Then he swears an oath, and if the daemon does not obey, he threatens him and drives him out. As a matter of fact, I saw one coming out, all black and smoky."

I said: "So what? You see that sort of thing, but even the ideas that Plato, your founding father, defines, are a hazy vision to those of us whose eyes are weak."

"Do you mean," said Eucrates, "that Ion is the only one who has seen that sort of thing? Are there not many others who have met spirits, some at night and some by day? I have seen things like that not only once but practically hundreds of times. At first I was upset by them, but now, having gotten accustomed to them, I no longer think that I am seeing anything abnormal, especially since the Arab gave me the ring made of iron from crosses and taught me the spelling of many names. But perhaps you won't believe me either, Tychiades?"

I said: "How could I not believe Eucrates, the son of Deinon, a learned and distinguished [text and meaning uncertain] gentleman, when he freely expresses his own opinions in his own home?"

28

Apuleius, a Platonist and traveling lecturer of the second century A.D. who had a certain interest in occult science, found himself accused of witchcraft. In the North African town of Oea (Tripoli today) he was visited during an illness by a friend, Sicinius Pontianus, and met through him his mother, Pudentilla, a wealthy and not unattractive widow a few years older than Apuleius. When Apuleius married Pudentilla, he was accused of witchcraft by his wife's relatives, who apparently were unwilling to let her fortune go to a foreigner.

In the trial held at Sabrata, before the Roman proconsul, Claudius Maximus, Apuleius defended himself, and the speech he delivered in

court (or, more likely, a revised version) is preserved. It contains a great
deal of information on magic. Had Apuleius been convicted, the penalty
would have been death.

Apuleius' speech first deals with the vague rumors that had been
spread in the community to discredit him. Those rumors had led to the
formal charge that Apuleius was a *magus*. To reject this, Apuleius first
discusses the original meaning of *magus*. He even quotes from Plato's
Alcibiades and *Charmides* to show how highly the Persians regarded "magic" and the "magi": magic formed part of the education that the royal
princes received; hence it must have been a religion, a philosophy, rather
than some kind of witchcraft. The second testimony, taken from Plato's
Charmides, is doubtful; Zalmoxis seems to have been a god of the dead
worshiped by the Getae, a semicivilized Thracian tribe, and what Plato
says about the "healers of Zalmoxis" cannot be substantiated.

Apuleius then shows that even his accusers do not believe in the
reality of witchcraft and use it only as a pretext to destroy him; for if he
were the formidable magician they make him out to be, they would be
worried about their lives. There is no question that throughout the centuries the charge of witchcraft has been used again and again as a way of
disposing of someone who has become unpopular.

In refuting the other arguments of the prosecution, Apuleius
shows himself to be a skillful trial lawyer. The only serious charge is the
experiment with the boy, the altar, and the lantern. Boys were considered
natural mediums in antiquity; Apuleius gives an explanation for it and
refers to Varro's story concerning Nigidius Figulus, a contemporary of
Cicero's who was interested in the occult. The boy with whom Apuleius
experimented apparently went into a trance, which must have frightened
the eyewitness but could hardly have surprised Apuleius. To that extent
the experiment was successful, but Apuleius—for obvious reasons—
says nothing about any revelations.

Apuleius, *Apology,* or *On Magic,* chs. 25–43

I will now deal with the actual charge of magic. He [the accuser] has
spared no effort to light the flame of hatred against me, but he has falsely
raised everyone's expectations by some old wives' tales he told. I ask you,
Maximus [the judge]: Have you ever seen a fire started from stubble,
crackling sharply, shining far and wide, getting bigger fast, but without
real fuel, with only a feeble blaze, leaving nothing behind? This is their
accusation, kindled with abuse, built up with mere words, lacking proof,
and, once you have given your verdict, leaving no trace of slander behind.

Aemilianus' slander was focused on one point: that I am a sorcerer. So let me ask his most learned advocates: What is a sorcerer? I have
read in many books that *magus* is the same thing in Persian as *priest* in our

language. What crime is there in being a priest and in having accurate knowledge, a science, a technique of traditional ritual, sacred rites and traditional law, if magic consists of what Plato interprets as the "cult of the gods" when he talks of the disciplines taught to the crown prince in Persia? I remember the very words of that divine man [Plato]. Let me recall them to you, Maximus: "When the young prince has reached the age of fourteen, he is handed over to the royal tutors. There are four of them, chosen as the most outstanding among the Persian elders. One is the wisest, one the most just, one the most restrained, one the bravest. One of them teaches [the crown prince] the 'magic' of Zoroaster, the son of Ormazd, which is the worship of the gods. He also teaches [him] the art of being king." Listen to this, you who rashly slander magic! It is an art acceptable to the immortal gods, an art which includes the knowledge of how to worship them and pay them homage. It is a religious tradition dealing with things divine, and it has been distinguished ever since it was founded by Zoroaster and Ormazd, the high priests of divinities. In fact, it is considered one of the chief elements of royal instruction, and in Persia no one is allowed lightly to be a "magus" any more than they would let him be king.

Plato also writes, in a different context, about a certain Zalmoxis, a Thracian, but an expert in the same art, that "there is a certain mental therapy in incantations, and that incantations consist of beautiful words." If this is so, why should I not be permitted to learn the "beautiful words" of Zalmoxis or the priestly traditions of Zoroaster? But if my accusers, after the common fashion, think of a "magus" primarily as a person who by verbal communications with the immortal gods and through the incredible power of his incantations can perform any miracles he wants, why are they not afraid to accuse a man who, as they admit themselves, has such powers? For there is no protection against such a mysterious, such a divine, power as there is against other things. If you summon a murderer before the judge, you come with a bodyguard; if you charge a poisoner, you take special precautions with your food; if you accuse a thief, you watch your possessions. But if you demand the death penalty for a magus, as they define him, what escort, what special precautions, what guards, can protect you against an unexpected, inevitable catastrophe? None, of course, and so this is not the kind of charge a man who believes in the truth of this sort of thing would make.

But it is a fairly common misunderstanding by which the uneducated accuse philosophers. Some of them think that those who investigate the simple causes and elements of matter are antireligious, and that they deny the very existence of gods, as for instance, Anaxagoras, Leucippus, Democritus, Epicurus, and other leading scientists. Others, commonly called "magi," spend great care in the exploration of the workings of providence in the world and worship the gods with great devotion, as if they actually knew how to make the things happen that they know do happen. This was the case with Epimenides, Orpheus, Pythagoras, and Ostanes. Similarly, later on, the "Purifications" of Empedocles, the "Daemon" of Socrates, the "Good" of Plato, came under suspicion. I congratulate myself to be associated with so many great men.

I am afraid, however, that the court may take seriously the silly, childish, and naïve arguments brought forward by my accusers in order to substantiate their charges—for the simple reason that they have been made. My accuser asks: "Why have you tried to get specific kinds of fish?" Why should a scientist not be allowed to do for the sake of knowledge what a gourmand is allowed to do for the sake of his gluttony? He asks: "What made a free woman marry you after having been a widow for fourteen years?" Well, is it not more remarkable that she remained a widow for such a long time? "Why did she, before she married you, express certain opinions in a letter?" Well, is it reasonable to demand of someone the reasons for someone else's opinions? "She is older than you, but did not reject a younger man." But this alone is proof enough that no magic was needed: a woman wished to marry a man, a widow a bachelor, a mature lady a man her junior. And there are more charges just like that: "Apuleius has in his house an object which he secretly worships." Well, would it not be a worse offense to have nothing to worship? "A boy fell to the ground in Apuleius' presence." What if a young man, what if an old man, had fallen when I was there, perhaps stricken by illness, perhaps simply because the ground was slippery? Do you think you can prove your accusation of magic by such arguments, the fall of a little boy, my getting married to my wife, the purchase of fish?

[*Apuleius deals with the subject of fish and argues that he was motivated only by scientific interest; then he turns to the incident of the boy who suddenly fell down in his presence.*]

My accusers claim that I bewitched a boy by an incantation with no witness present and then took him to a secret place with a small altar and a lantern and only a few accomplices present, and there he was put under a spell and collapsed; he lost consciousness and was revived. They did not dare go any further with their lie. To complete their fairy tale they should have added that the boy uttered a lot of prophecies. For this, of course, is the prize of incantations. This miracle involving boys is not only a popular superstition but is confirmed by the authority of learned men. I remember reading in the philosopher Varro, a thoroughly learned and erudite man, stories of this kind, and especially this one. There was at Tralles an inquiry by means of magic about the outcome of the Mithridatic War: a boy was gazing at a reflection of Mercury in water, and then foretold the future in one hundred sixty lines of verse. Varro also tells that Fabius, having lost five hundred denarii, came to consult Nigidius, who inspired some boys by a spell to reveal where exactly a pot with part of the sum was buried and how the rest had been dispersed; one denarius actually found its way to the philosopher Marcus Cato, who acknowledged having received it from a servant as a contribution to the treasury of Apollo.

I have read these and many similar stories about boys in magical rituals, and I cannot make up my mind whether to believe them or not. But I do believe Plato when he says that there are divine powers that rank both by their nature and location between gods and men and that all kinds of divination and magic miracles are controlled by them. It also occurs to me that the human soul, especially a boyish, unsophisticated soul, can be lulled to sleep by soft music and sweet smells and hypnotized into oblivion of reality, so that gradually all consciousness of the body fades from memory and the soul returns and retreats into its own true nature, which, of course, is immortal and divine, and thus, as if it were in a kind of slumber, can predict the future. Well, no matter whether this is true or not, if one were to believe this sort of thing, the boy with the gift of prophecy, whoever he is, from what I hear, must be handsome and healthy, also intellectually alert and articulate, to make sure that the divine power takes up lodgings in him, as if he were a respectable house—if it is really appropriate for such a power to squeeze itself into the body of a boy! It could also be that the boy's mind, when awakened, quickly applies itself to the business of divination, which may be his natural, spontaneous gift, which can easily be picked up without being dulled or damaged by any loss of memory. For, as Pythagoras used to say, you must not carve a statue of Hermes from just any piece of wood. If this is true, please tell me who that healthy, sound, gifted, handsome boy was whom I chose to initiate by my incantation. As a matter of fact, Thallus— you mentioned his name—needs a physician rather than a magician.

29

Lucius, the hero of Apuleius' novel, *Metamorphoses,* traveled to Thessaly in order to study witchcraft, because Thessaly was traditionally considered the country of witches. Since we know that Apuleius was attracted to magic and got into trouble because of that, we might reasonably assume that the novel is partly autobiographical. Lucius, eager to learn important secrets, befriends Photis, the maid of a famous witch, and asks her to help him get transformed into a bird. Unfortunately Photis—it is not quite clear whether by accident or on purpose—gets the wrong ointment, and Lucius finds himself transformed into a donkey.

The antidote at first seems very simple: all Lucius has to do is eat some roses in order to regain his human shape. As the story goes on, however, obstacle after obstacle is placed between Lucius and roses. In the end he is saved by the intervention of the goddess Isis and decides to become one of her devotees. Thus, a rather frivolous and ribald novel ends with a conversion and an initiation scene. Cured of the curiosity that caused him so much hardship, Lucius literally finds salvation and is reborn into one of the great mystery religions of the ancient world.

Apuleius, *Metamorphoses*, or *The Golden Ass*, 3.21–28

In this delightful way Photis and I spent quite a few nights. One day she came to me trembling with excitement and told me that her mistress was still making no headway by normal means in her love affair and was therefore going to transform herself into a bird the following night to fly to her darling. So Photis urged me to prepare myself carefully to watch secretly this important event. Early in the night she led me on tiptoe, without making the slightest noise, to the upstairs bedroom and told me to peep through a chink in the door and see what was going on. First I saw Pamphile strip completely. Then she opened a small chest, took out several boxes, opened one of them, and took some ointment out of it. This she rubbed for a long time between her hands and then applied it to her whole body, from the tips of her toes to the top of her head. At the same time she had a long, secret conversation with her lamp and shook all her limbs vigorously. Her outlines began to fluctuate gently, and soft feathers began to sprout, strong wings grew, her nose became crooked, horny, her nails took on the shape of talons. No doubt about it: Pamphile had turned into an owl. She gave a plaintive hoot, hopped about a few times to test her flying ability, and then took off and flew away with powerful wing strokes.

Well, she had transformed herself by magic technique as she had wished; but I just stood there, glued to the spot, not bewitched by any spell, but hypnotized by what I had seen, and I was not at all sure that I was really Lucius. My mind was wandering, my stupor bordered on madness, I dreamed and was awake at the same time. I kept rubbing my eyes to find out whether I was really awake. At long last I regained my awareness of reality; I took Photis' hand, held it close to my eyes, and said: "Please, do me a great favor; this is a very special moment; show me that you love me by doing something very unusual but very important for me and let me have a tiny little bit of that ointment; I beg you by these lovely breasts of yours, my honey child. I am your slave! Do me a favor that I can never repay (I shall always be indebted to you) and help me! You are my Venus: I want to be your winged Cupid!"

"Oh, really?" she said. "My little fox, my darling, you want me to chop off my own legs? You are helpless as you are, and I can hardly protect you from those Thessalian she-wolves; where shall I find you, when will I see you again, after you have become a bird?" I protested: "The gods in heaven forbid that I commit such a crime! Even though I fly on the proud wings of an eagle across the whole sky, as the trustworthy messenger or the cheerful armor-bearer of great Zeus, I would always get rid of my feathery glory and fly back to my love nest. By that sweet knot in your hair in which my soul is tied up, I swear that I shall never love any other woman as much as my Photis. There is something else that occurs to me: once I have used the ointment and become a bird, I will have to stay far away from all houses, for what lady would like to have an owl—such a fine, pleasant bird!—as a lover? Don't we know that those birds of night, when they have flown into someone's house, cause great anxiety and are caught and nailed to the main door to pay by their own torments for the bad luck their ill-omened presence threatens to the household? But I almost forgot to ask: What do I have to say or do to get rid of the feathers and become good old Lucius again?" She replied: "Don't worry about this problem. My mistress showed me every single step by which such creatures can regain their human shape. But you mustn't assume that she did this out of kindness; she simply wanted me to be able to help her with an antidote after her return. Watch and you'll see what a tremendous effect is produced by quite ordinary little herbs: a small amount of anise, along with some laurel leaves, is put into spring water to make a bath and a potion."

She impressed this on me repeatedly and, trembling with fear, sneaked into the room to take one of the boxes out of the chest. I embraced and kissed her first; then I begged her to wish me a good flight; then I quickly took off all my clothes, greedily plunged my fingers into the box, dug out quite a lump and rubbed my whole body with it. After this I just stood there, flapping my arms, first one, then the other, trying to act like a bird, but no feathers, no wings, appeared anywhere. Instead my hair turned into bristles and my tender skin into hide; my fingers and toes seemed to shrink and contract into hooves, and from the end of my spine a long tail began to sprout. My face became enormous, my mouth enlarged, my nostrils dilated, my lips pendulous, my ears oversized and hairy. The only good thing about this wretched transformation was that my genitals had increased in size enormously; it had become difficult for me to satisfy Photis.

In despair I considered all the parts of my new body and I realized that I was not a bird but a donkey. I wanted to complain about what Photis had done to me, but I was deprived of human gestures and a human voice; and all I could do was to let my lower lip hang down and look at her sideways with moist eyes and reproach her silently. When she saw what shape I was in, she beat her face violently with her own hands and cried: "What an idiot I am! Oh, I could die! I was nervous and in a hurry and took the wrong box; the two looked exactly alike, and that fooled me. But fortunately there is a rather simple antidote to reverse this kind of transformation. You need only nibble some roses and you will at once get rid of your donkey's shape and become my dearest Lucius again. If only I had made some garlands last evening, as I always do, so you wouldn't have to wait even one night. Anyway, first thing in the morning the remedy will be brought to you in a hurry!"

She was very upset, and I, though by now a complete ass and a beast of burden instead of Lucius, still retained my human ability to reason. For a long time I intensely debated within myself whether or not to kick and bite that wicked, scheming bitch to death. But my better sense checked this reckless impulse; I was afraid to cut off all hope for a remedy by punishing her by death. I let my head hang and shook it sadly, but decided to swallow my humiliation for the time being and accept my cruel fate. I walked into the stable to join my trusty saddle horse; there I found another ass, one of Milo's (who had once been my guest-friend) that shared the stable. I thought that if animals had any sense, any instinct of loyalty, my horse would recognize me and, feeling sorry for me, would offer me hospitality and a cozy place. But let Jupiter, the god of hospitality, let the mystic divinities of faith, hear this! That fine horse of mine and Milo's put their heads together and formed at once a conspiracy against me; they were worried about their food, of course. As soon as they saw me approaching the manger they laid their ears back and attacked me furiously with their hooves. They chased me away, as far as they could, from the barley which I myself had offered the evening before to my grateful servant! This is the way they treated me! I was relegated to a remote corner of the stable. There I meditated on the rudeness of my colleagues, and since I was sure to be, with the help of the roses, Lucius again the next day, I planned my revenge on that disloyal horse. Suddenly I noticed at the very center of the middle column that supported the beams of the stable a statue of the horse goddess, Epona, sitting in a small shrine; the statue had been carefully adorned with rose garlands that were still fresh. I realized at once that here was the remedy, the help that I needed, and I abandoned myself to hope. I stood up on my hind legs and stretched my forelegs out as far as I could, and I made a tremendous effort to extend my neck and my lips in order to reach the garlands. But as I tried, my bad luck wanted it that my slave, who had been ordered to take care of the horse, suddenly saw me, jumped up, and shouted angrily: "I have had all I can take from this creature! Just a moment ago he was after the food of the other animals, and now he is after the statues of the gods! I'll be damned if I don't beat the disrespectful brute until he is too weak and too lame to move!" He looked around for some weapon and happened to find a bundle of faggots which was lying there; from that he picked a thick, knobby stick bigger than all the others and started whacking me with it (oh, it hurt!), and whacked me until someone made a tremendous noise and banged deafeningly against the door; at the same time people in the neighborhood, in a state of panic, shouted "Robbers!" This frightened him and he ran away.

Almost at once the main gate was forced open and a gang of robbers rushed in. Armed men searched all parts of the house; neighbors arrived in a hurry from here and there to help, but they were powerless against the fast action of the enemies. They all had swords and carried torches that illuminated the night; reflected on the steel, the flames were brighter than the rising sun. There was a storage room in the center of the house, well locked and well secured by solid locks; it was full of Milo's treasures. This room they attacked with heavy axes and broke it open. Once they had opened it they carried out the treasures, tied them quickly into bundles, and divided them among themselves. But there were more packages than men to carry them. Their overabundance of wealth totally defeated them, so they led us two donkeys and my horse out of the stable, loaded us with the heavier bundles, and, threatening us with sticks, drove us out of the house, which was empty by now.

30

In his philosophical treatises, Plotinus, who was himself credited with supernatural gifts, discusses magic. As usual, it is difficult to follow his train of thought, possibly because he developed his thoughts as he lectured to his class and did not like to revise his notes or those taken by students.

It is clear from the first sentence of this text, however, that Plotinus believes in magic, though he is not certain how and why it works. He first deals with the concepts of sympathy and antipathy. These forces, he argues, exist in the universe by themselves and are contained by it, and magic simply reinforces them.

Ritual magic, as Plotinus no doubt saw it performed, required a special costume and the recitation of special formulas. He compares magic to music, for both affect the irrational part of the human soul.

Plotinus makes it clear that magic is something that happens between people, though he does not exclude the influence of cosmic forces; again, the analogy of music helps us understand what is happening: the vibrating strings of one lyre set off vibrations in another instrument.

To pray to the stars (i.e., the planets named after gods) is meaningless, according to Plotinus, and yet the stars do have a certain influence on all life on our planet. This leads back to the concept of cosmic sympathy: "He who demands something from the universe is no stranger to it"—that is, magic works because we belong to the universe.

Some magicians are bad, but their magic works too, because the force is available; since they use magic for an evil purpose, however, they will be punished sooner or later. Whatever harm the magician may be able to do to human beings, he cannot affect the universe, and even his power on this earth is limited, because the "wise man" (a concept Plotinus has borrowed from the Stoics) certainly can defend himself against black arts. The life of contemplation—that is, "the philosopher's life"—is free from magical influence.

Plotinus, *Enneads* 4.4.40–44

How should one explain magical operations? Either by sympathy or by the fact that there is a natural harmony between similar things and disharmony between dissimilar things, or else by the fact that there are a great many different powers which together affect a single living creature [or, which collaborate toward the unity of a living being?]. For there are many attractions and magical operations without anyone to set them in motion. The true magic is "the love and its opposite, the hatred," in the universe [Empedocles]. The first sorcerer, the first witch doctor, is the one whom people know well and whose potions and spells they use against each other. For since it is natural for them to love, and since [everything] that makes them love attracts them to each other, a technique of love attraction [reading *holkes*, with Kirchhoff, for *alke* or *alkes* of most manuscripts] through witchcraft has originated, and the practitioners of this craft [simply] unite by physical contacts natures which are already drawn to each other and have an inborn love for each other. They [the practitioners] join one soul to another, just as if one were to join together [i.e., graft] plants that have grown at a distance from each other. They also use the figures that have power, by dressing up in certain ways [or, assuming certain attitudes?], and in certain ways they silently draw to themselves powers and are in one toward one [or, are in and for universal unity?]. For if one were to assume [the existence of] such a person [the magician] outside the universe, he would not attract nor draw down any [special powers] by his spells or incantations. But now, since he does not lead them elsewhere, as it were, he is able to lead them, knowing the ways by which in the living universe one creature is led to another.

  It is only natural for the soul to be directed by the tune and the specific sound of the incantation and the attire [or, attitude?] of the operator, for that sort of thing has its own attraction, just like clothes [or, attitudes?] and words that inspire pity. For it is not our will power nor our reason that is charmed by music, but the irrational part of our soul. That sort of magic is not extraordinary; yet an audience that is bewitched (by music) feels love, even if it does not demand this (effect) from the performing musicians.

  One should not believe that prayers [are fulfilled] because the will [of the gods] is listening. This is not what happens to those who are bewitched by incantations, nor does a man who has been bewitched when a snake puts a spell on people understand [what is happening to him], nor does he feel [it], but he knows, when it has already happened to the ruling part [of his soul, i.e., his intellect].

From (the one) to whom a prayer has been addressed, something has gone out to the person [who prayed] or to another. But the sun or any other heavenly body [to whom a prayer was addressed] does not listen [or, understand?].

The effects of a prayer are real because one part [of the universe] is in sympathy with a[nother] part, as [one may observe] in a properly tuned string [on a lyre]. When it has been struck in its lower part, the upper part vibrates as well. And it often happens that when one string has been struck, another one, if I may say so, feels this, because they are in unison and have been tuned to one and the same pitch. If the vibration travels from one lyre to another, [one can see] how far the sympathetic element extends. In the universe, too, there is one universal harmony [or, tuning?], even though it is made up of discordant notes. It is also made up of similar notes, and all are related, even the discordant ones. Everything that is harmful to men—passionate impulses, for instance, that are drawn, along with anger, into the nature of the liver [i.e., the liver as their physical organ and center]—did not come [into the world] to be harmful [to men]. If, for example, one were to take fire from fire and hurt someone, yet without approaching him with any evil intention [reading *allon, hoi me mechanesamenos elthen*, modifying Seidel's suggestion, after Ficino's translation], he who took the fire [would be] responsible, because, you know, he delivered, as it were, something from one place to another, and it [i.e., the accident] happened because the person to whom the thing was transferred was unfit to receive it.

For this very reason the stars will need no memory—our whole discussion leads up to this point—nor any sense perceptions transmitted to them. Hence they have no power of conscious assent to [our] prayers, but one must admit that with or without prayer their influence is real, since they [like us] are part of the One. Since there are many powers that are not guided by a conscious will, some spontaneously, some through a technique, and since this is happening in one living organism [the universe], some elements are helpful, some harmful, to one another, according to their nature. Medical art and magic art compel one element to surrender part of its own specific power to another element. In the same way, the universe also distributes something of itself to its parts, both spontaneously and because it feels the attraction of something else to part of itself which is essential to its own parts, because they share the same nature. After all, he who demands [something from the universe] is no stranger [to it].

He who demands it may be bad. This should not surprise you. Bad men draw water from a river too. The giver does not know the one to whom he gives; he simply gives. And yet the gift [reading *ha dedotai*] agrees with the nature of the universe. Therefore, if someone takes from that which is available to everyone, but he had no right to it, punishment will catch up with him according to the law of necessity.

One must admit, then, that the universe may be afflicted, although its ruling part must be admitted to be completely free of any affliction. Since affliction can come to its parts, we must admit that they can be afflicted. But since nothing that happens in the universe is against its nature, it must be free of affliction . . . [the meaning of the following words is uncertain]. The stars, too, can be afflicted, inasmuch as they are parts [of the universe], and yet they remain unafflicted because their will is not affected, because their bodies, their natures, remain unharmed and because, if they communicate something through their soul, their soul is not diminished, and their bodies are the same; if something is leaking from them, it escapes unnoticed, and whatever augments them, if anything augments them, is not noticed either.

What influence do witchcraft and magic drugs have on the wise man? As far as his soul is concerned, he is not affected by witchcraft, and his rational part could hardly be affected, nor would it change its conviction; to the extent he has in himself the irrational element of the universe, he might suffer to that extent, or rather this [element] might suffer [in him]. But (no one could provoke in him) love by magic drugs, for to be in love requires the assent of the one [i.e., the rational] soul to the affect of the other [i.e., the irrational] soul. Just as the irrational part is affected by incantations, thus he [the wise man] will cancel out those outside powers by counterincantations. He might suffer death from such [evil] influences or diseases or every kind of bodily affliction, for the part of the universe [which is in him] may be affected by another part of the universe itself— but his [real] self remains unharmed.—It is perfectly consistent with nature that one is not affected [by magic] right away, but at some later time.—Even daemons are not exempt from being affected in their irrational part—it is [, after all,] not unreasonable to attribute memory and sense perceptions to them and [to assume] that they are being charmed and led by natural [or, scientific?] ways and that those among them who are closer to our region listen to those who call them, [the more readily,] the closer their contact with our region. For everything that is in close contact with another is bewitched by the other; the thing with which it is in contact bewitches and leads it; only that which is in contact with itself cannot be bewitched. Therefore all action and the whole life of the man of action is influenced by witchcraft, for he moves toward the things that charm him. . . .

This leaves only the life of contemplation to be uninfluenced by witchcraft: for no one practices witchcraft on himself. . . .

31

Plotinus had an enemy, Olympius of Alexandria, who tried to hurt him through magic. This passage from Porphyry's biography of Plotinus offers a good illustration of Plotinus' own teaching concerning magic [*no. 30*]. First, we are told that the sorcerer in vain appealed to the stars; second, that Plotinus, being a "wise man," was able to resist the evil forces directed at him and, in fact, to redirect them against the very operator who had unleashed them. Thus, the very real anguish that Plotinus had felt at one point rebounded on the magician himself. This personal experience apparently helped shape Plotinus' ideas on magic in general.

Porphyry, *Life of Plotinus*, pars. 53–55

Olympius' scheming went so far that he even attempted to direct, through magical operations, the evil influences of stars at Plotinus. But he realized that his attempts fell back on himself, and he said to his friends that the psychic powers of Plotinus were so strong that the attacks of those who wished to hurt him rebounded on themselves. Plotinus did sense the attempts of Olympius and said that his body had felt, at the time, like a purse whose strings had been pulled together; his limbs had been squeezed just like that. Olympius, however, ran the risk of hurting himself rather than Plotinus, and so he gave up.

32

Iamblichus, a later Neoplatonist, discusses magic as a science. He actually uses the term *theurgy*, which has become a more exalted word for "ritual magic," implying, as it does, that higher gods, not mere daemons, are involved. His main problem is this: How can we use, for magical purposes, beings that are obviously superior to us? Why should they obey us? The answer is ingenious: We, as human beings, trained by great teachers, are complete entities in a sense that mere daemons are not, and we will always find even higher entities that will support us against the lesser ones, because we are more "in tune" with them.

Iamblichus, *On the Mysteries of Egypt* 4.2

What we will now discuss is something that we occasionally experience. It happens now and then that commands are addressed to spirits which do not use their own powers of reasoning and have no principle of judgment. This does not occur without a reason. For since our mind has the ability to reason and to judge reality, and since it concentrates in itself many different vital powers, it is used to giving orders to creatures that have no reason and are complete with the possession of only one faculty. So it calls on them as on superior beings, because it tries to draw away from the whole universe that surrounds us, the elements that contribute to the whole order of things, toward those which are contained within individual creatures. But it commands them as subordinate beings because certain parts of the world are often purer and more perfect by nature than those which spread all over the world. For example, if one being is intellectual and another entirely without soul or purely physical, the more limited one has greater authority than the one that stretches over a larger space, even if it is greatly surpassed by the other in size and power of control.

There is another principle behind this. All of theurgy has a double aspect: On the one hand it is practiced by men and keeps our natural place in the universe; on the other hand it is supported by divine signs and rises upward through them because it is connected with the higher powers; it moves harmoniously according to their directions and may indeed put on the appearance of the gods. In accordance with this distinction the magician naturally calls the powers of the universe superior ones, since he who calls them is a human being, but he also commands them, since he has assumed by his secret formulas the holy appearance of the gods.

33

The Christian writer Eusebius of Caesarea (c. A.D. 260–240) deals with magic in his *Preparation of the Gospel,* a work which is designed to show that even before the ministry of Jesus pagans had at least a glimpse of the word of God. He rejects what are, to him, the errors of paganism, but he does not dismiss all the claims made for magic.

For the pagans the statues of the gods in their temples actually were the gods and could be used for magical operations. Eusebius does not reject this outright, even though his questions show that he has some doubts.

He then submits that many "supernatural" events are not the work of gods or daemons but the result of human fraud.

Finally he suggests natural causes for seemingly supernatural effects, and this takes us very close to the modern point of view. We can only observe, not always explain, what happens in nature. After a sufficient body of data has been collected, the true explanation may be found, and then what seemed like witchcraft becomes science.

Eusebius also explains the psychological factors that enter into this process: A mood of expectation can be created in a certain way, an audience can be hypnotized, so to speak, but to Eusebius, who is deeply suspicious of paganism, all this is part of a fraudulent scheme.

Eusebius, *The Preparation of the Gospel* 4.1.6–9

Even for the pagans it is obvious that lifeless statues are not gods. . . . But let us [now] consider this question: How should one look at the powers lurking in statues? Can one have a pleasant relationship with them? Are they good and truly divine or the very opposite of all this?

If someone were to study this subject thoroughly, he might possibly come to the conclusion that everything is a mystification produced by sorcerers and consists of fraud. Thus he would demolish their [the sorcerers'] prestige by showing that the stories told about them are certainly not the work of a god, and not even the work of an evil daemon. For the oracles in verse, skillfully arranged, are the work of clever men; they are fictitious and designed to deceive; they are expressed in such a vague, ambiguous manner as to fit both of two possible outcomes of a prediction quite well.

One might also say that portents which seem miraculous and deceive the masses can be explained by natural causes. For in all of nature there are many kinds of roots, herbs, plants, fruits, stones, as well as the various forces inherent in matter, whether they are dry or humid. Some of them have the power of repelling and driving away; others are magnetic and attract; some can separate and split up, others can assemble and concentrate; others can relax, make wet, rarefy; some save and others destroy; some transform and bring about a change in the present condition, one way or another, for a short while or a long time; their effect may be felt by many people or only by a few; some of them lead the way, and others follow; some agree with others and increase and decrease along with them; some are conducive to health and belong in the realm of medical science, while others produce illness and are harmful. Thus certain phenomena are due to the necessary effect of natural causes, and they wax and wane with the moon.

There are thousands of antipathies between living beings, roots and plants: certain perfumes go to the head and make you sleepy, while others produce visions. Moreover, the places, the locations where something is going on, also contribute a great deal, not to mention the instruments and the apparatus which sorcerers have held ready long beforehand to help them in their art. They also benefit from all sorts of outside assistance to bring off their deceit: helpers who receive the visitors with a great show of interest and find out what their business is and what they wish to know. The inner sanctum and the recesses inside the temple, which are not accessible to the public, also hide many secrets. The darkness certainly helps them in their fraudulent scheme, and the mood of expectation, the fear the visitors experience when they think they are approaching the gods, and all the religious prejudices they have inherited from their ancestors. . . .

34

The following text deals mainly with "theurgy," a form of ritual magic that was apparently practiced in late antiquity by certain religious and philosophical groups. As we have seen [*no. 30*], Plotinus believes in magic, but he does not accept the claims of the Gnostics that they can control cosmic powers by magical rites and use them for specific purposes, such as curing a disease by exorcising a daemon. For Plotinus, this is an insult to the gods. Whatever actually happens, whatever makes magic work, the gods are not involved. Plotinus leans toward "natural" or "scientific" causes, and since magic, according to him, uses natural forces, it is a kind of science. He attacks the practice of exorcism and ridicules the concepts on which it is based. No doubt, at the time when this was written, exorcists were still in demand, but Hippocratic medicine, of which Plotinus must have been aware, had been in existence for six or seven centuries.

Plotinus, *Enneads* 2.9.14

There is another way in which they [the Gnostics] grossly insult the purity of the higher powers. When they write out incantations, as if they were addressing those powers—not only the soul, but the powers above as well—what else are they doing but, if I may say so [reading, with Müller, *hōs logō* for *kai logō*], forcing [the people] to obey magic, to be led by witchcraft, charms, and formulas spoken by them? [Would this] apply to any of us who is highly accomplished in the art of reciting such formulas in the right way—songs and cries, hissing and whistling—and everything else which, according to their writings, has control over the higher powers?

   If they are reluctant to put it this way, [let me ask,] how can incorporeal things be affected by sound? By the kind of phrases they use to make their theories look more sublime, they take away, without realizing it, the sublimity of those powers. They claim that they can cure themselves of an illness; if they mean that they can do this by self-discipline and a rational way of life, "fine," as the philosophers would put it. But in fact they assume that illness is caused by daemons, and they claim that they can exorcise the daemons by their words. When they claim this, they may look quite impressive in the eyes of the average person who is in awe of the powers ascribed to magicians, but they would scarcely convince any sensible person [when they assert] that illness does not have its origin in fatigue, or over-eating, or lack of food, or a process of putrefaction, or, generally speaking, in changes that have their origin inside or outside.

Their treatment of illness makes this clear. If the patient has diarrhea, or if a laxative has been administered, the illness passes through the downward passage and leaves the body. It is the same with bloodletting. Fasting also heals.

Does this happen because the daemon has been starving, or because the drug has made him waste away? Does he leave at once at times, and at times remain inside? If he remains inside, how is it [possible] that the patient is feeling better, even though the daemon is still inside? And if the daemon is there to stay, how is it [possible] that the patient feels all right, though he still has the daemon inside? Why did he leave—if he actually left? What happened to him? Did he perhaps thrive on the illness? In that case, the illness is different from the daemon. Moreover, if the daemon enters the body without any cause [i.e., in the absence of illness], why are we not always sick? And if there was a cause, why do we need the daemon to get sick? The cause is sufficient to produce a fever. It would be ridiculous to suppose that as soon as the cause operates, the daemon, standing by, moves in at once, as if to reinforce the cause. No, it is quite clear what they mean, what they intend, when they say all this, and for this reason above all—but for others too—did I mention this type of daemon.

35

Porphyry seems to describe here a kind of séance during which some people he knew asked the "higher powers" all sorts of trivial questions. Such questions were also presented sometimes to the great oracles. For Porphyry, as for his teacher, Plotinus, this procedure is absurd unless it is conducted as an experiment, "for the sake of research." How dare you bother the gods with such trivialities? he asks. They should be consulted only about serious questions—for instance, the nature of the Good, the nature of Happiness—but somehow they never are, or if they are, no profound answers ever come across. Porphyry admits that such séances could be fraudulent.

Porphyry, *Letter to Anebo*, ch. 46

I want you to show me the way to Happiness and explain to me what it is essentially. There is an intense debate going on in our group: we are trying to form an idea of the Good on the basis of human reasoning. Those who have established communications with the higher powers— unless they use this approach in a more casual way [?], for the sake of research—practice their craft in vain, for they bother the divine mind with such questions as where to find a runaway slave, or whether to buy a piece of land, or whether a marriage would work out or a business venture prosper. If all this is done in earnest, and "those present" [i.e., the powers summoned] give absolutely correct answers to the the usual sort of question but have nothing trustworthy, nothing reliable, to say about the question of Happiness, even though they give thorough reports on difficult matters that are unprofitable to men, they clearly are neither gods nor benevolent spirits, but the whole thing is a typical, well-known illusion [?], or else a human device, a fiction of mortal nature from beginning to end.

36

In this text Iamblichus tells us clearly that the theurgists of his day invoked the powers that dwell in heaven, on earth, and in the underworld. This apparently puzzled some philosophers and theologians, because they thought that the gods dwell only in heaven.

In a rather poetic way Iamblichus tries to explain that the power of the gods is like the power of light: it gives illumination as well as warmth, and it fills the whole universe, yet it is one. He calls the stars "the brilliant image of the gods." The divine element, so to speak, is everywhere, and it cannot be understood in terms of time or space.

Iamblichus, *On the Mysteries of Egypt* 1.9

I assume you are not asking the difficult question "If the gods dwell only in heaven, why do those who practice theurgy invoke as well the powers that dwell on earth and below the earth?" As to the first principle, that the gods dwell only in heaven, it is not true. Everything is full of them. You are asking instead "How can some be said to be in the water or in the air? And how is it that some were assigned different places than others? Were they somehow given, as if by fate, the dimensions of bodies, even though their powers are infinite, indivisible, incomprehensible? How will there be a union among themselves, seeing that they are separated by their own distinct dimensions and isolated from each other according to the different nature of the places and the bodies they inhabit?"

There is one great solution to all these problems and many, many more like them: to consider the ways of divine allotment. No matter whether it distributes parts of the whole, such as the sky or sacred cities and areas or sacred precincts or holy statues, it illuminates everything from outside with its rays. Just as light embraces everything that it makes brighter, thus the power of the gods embraces everything that partakes of it. And just as light is present in the air without mixing with it (proof: no light remains in the air once the light-giving element has withdrawn, but it still keeps warmth once the warmth-giving element has withdrawn), thus the light of the gods shines separately and proceeds, stabilized in itself, throughout the whole universe. The visible light is a continuum, the same everywhere. Thus it is impossible to cut off part of it or to confine it in a circle or to isolate it from its source.

According to the same principle, the whole universe, since it is divisible, can be separated in relation to the one and indivisible light of the gods. The light, too, is entirely and absolutely one. It is present as an indivisible entity for all those who are able to partake of it. By its perfect power it has filled everything; by its infinite superabundance of creativity it transcends everything in itself; in all respects it is united to itself and connects the end with the beginning. Imitating this process, the whole sky, the whole universe, goes through its circular motion. It is united with itself. It leads the elements in their circular whirl; it includes all beings that are within one another and move toward one another; it defines by equal measures even the parts that are located at the farthest ends. It produces one continuity, one harmony of the whole toward the whole.

If you looked at the brilliant images of the gods [i.e., the stars], united in this way, would you not hesitate to form a different opinion of the gods, their originators, to assume that they have sections and divisions and bodylike outlines? As far as I am concerned, I think that just about everyone feels that way. For if there is no principle, no symmetrical relationship, no shared substance, no connection, either potential or actual, between the organized and the organizing element, they have practically no reality, if I may say so, since no lateral tension, nor any internal tension or circumference in space, or division into parts, or any other equation of this type, is being generated in the presence of the gods. . . .

37

It is clear from this text that Iamblichus considers himself a theurgist and that, to him, theurgy is a very special experience that cannot be analyzed logically. He establishes a boundary line between a purely theoretical approach to theurgy and a deeper understanding of it. We hear the voice of a philosopher who sincerely believes in the power of the ancient gods and seeks for means and techniques to demonstrate this power to unbelievers, a man who assumes that the gods respond to goodness and perfection in man. All this is expressed in the terminology of the Neoplatonist school, with its curious transitions from things as they are to things as they should be, and vice versa.

Iamblichus, *On the Mysteries of Egypt* 2.11

The following problems, which you raise when you denounce the ignorance and fraud concerning these matters as a kind of wickedness and depravity, encourage me to expose the true doctrine about them. These problems are not controversial; everyone is in full agreement. For who would not admit that a science which concerns the being is most appropriate to the gods [leaving out three words of the Greek text, probably a gloss], whereas the ignorance which tends toward the nonbeing falls quite short of the divine cause of the true representations? But since I have not discussed this adequately, I will add [now] what I left out, and since my opponent defends himself more like a philosopher and a logician and not according to the operative technique of the priests, I feel I ought to speak about these matters as a theurgist.

Let us admit that ignorance and deceit are wrong and irreligious. At the same time, they do not necessarily give the lie to what one offers properly to the gods and to divine acts, for it is not thought, either, that connects the theurgists with the gods. For what could prevent those who philosophize from experiencing theoretically a theurgic union with the gods? In fact, things are quite different. It is the mystic realization of the unutterable things, the things that are achieved beyond all concept according to the divine will and the power of the silent symbols [that are] understood only by the gods, that bring about the theurgic union. Therefore, we do not achieve these effects by our thought, for in this way their effectiveness would be intellectual [only] and would depend on us. Neither of these is true. For even if we do not think [about it,] the signs themselves, by themselves, perform their proper operation, and the inexpressible power of the gods to whom they [the signs] belong recognizes itself, by itself, and its own images, without having to be awakened by our mental processes. It is not natural for the one containing to be shaken up by the one contained, the perfect by the imperfect, the whole by the parts. Therefore, the divine causes are not primarily called into action by our thoughts, but they [our thoughts], along with all the best dispositions of our soul and our purity, must be there first, as auxiliary causes of a sort. What properly awakens the divine will are the divine signs themselves. Thus the actions of the gods are stirred up by themselves and do not receive from any of the subordinate beings any kind of initiative for their proper energy.

I have discussed these things at length to make sure that you do not believe that the whole power of theurgic action comes from us. . . .

38

According to this anecdote, Iamblichus' disciples asked him to perform some special feat for them. He does not oblige them right away, but puts them off until a proper occasion arises. His first comment stems from his own doctrine: to demand a miracle from the gods is an act of arrogance and therefore dangerous. But he also believed—at least at one point—that miracles, as we call them, are not caused by the intervention of gods at all. In the end he succeeds in materializing two divine presences, Eros and Anteros. Eros is the god of love, but Anteros, in this context, cannot be the opposite of love, that is, hate. The prefix *anti* also suggests a substitute or surrogate for love, something like love, but not quite the real thing. The disciples are convinced by what they see, and from then on they accept everything their teacher tells them.

> Eunapius, *Lives of the Philosophers and Sophists*,
> p. 459 Boissonade

The disciples wanted to test Iamblichus in something more important, but he said: "No, it does not depend on me; we must wait for the right moment." Some time later they decided to go to Gadara. This is a place in Syria where there are hot springs, inferior only to those at Baiae in Italy, with which no other baths can be compared. So they traveled in the summer season to Gadara. Iamblichus happened to be bathing, his disciples were bathing with him, and they insisted on the same request as before. Iamblichus smiled and said: "It is irreverent to the gods to give this kind of demonstration, but for your sake it shall be done." There were two hot springs, smaller, but more pleasant than the others. He told his disciples to find out from the natives their ancient names. They did what he had told them and said to him: "This is not something we made up, but this spring is called Eros and the one next to it has the name Anteros." Right away he touched the water—he happened to be sitting on the ledge of the spring where the overflow runs off—recited a brief summons, and conjured up from the depth of the spring a boy. The boy had fair skin and was not too tall, his locks were golden and his back and breast shining, and he looked exactly like someone who was taking a bath or had just come out of a bath. The disciples were overwhelmed, but Iamblichus said: "Let's go to the next spring," and led the way, lost in deep thoughts. Then he went through the same sort of ritual at this other place and conjured up another Eros, similar to the former one in all respects except that his hair was darker and flowed in the sunlight. Both boys hugged Iamblichus and clung to him as if he were their real father. He sent them off to their proper places and went away, after completing his bath, while his disciples showed their reverence. After this the crowd of his pupils demanded nothing more, but considering the proofs that had been given to them, clung to him as if by an unbreakable chain and believed everything.

39

Maximus of Ephesus, the most famous theurgist of the fourth century A.D., had great influence on the emperor Julian, but was executed under Valens. Eunapius, the author of this biographical sketch, gives us his own impression of the great teacher and then refers to Eusebius (not the

Christian writer of Caesarea) and to Julian himself to show how Maximus' charisma worked. Apparently we face once more the type of philosopher-teacher-theurgist that seems to go back to Pythagoras. Without a miracle the message was not complete: the teaching was about miracles, and the miracles, when they happened, reinforced the teaching. Young Julian is looking for a teacher who combines these abilities, and through Eusebius he finds Maximus, but after Maximus he goes on to an even greater hierophant with prophetic powers.

Eunapius, *Lives of the Philosophers and Sophists*, pp. 473–75 Boissonade

When I was still young I met the old man [Maximus] and listened to his voice, which sounded like Homer's Athena or Apollo. The pupils of his eyes were winged, if I may say so, he had a gray beard, and his eyes revealed the urges of his soul. There was a harmony all over him when you listened to him and looked at him, and when you were around him you were overwhelmed through both of these senses because you could not stand the rapid movement of his eyes or the rapid flow of his speech. When there was a discussion, no one, not even the most experienced, the most eloquent, dared to challenge him, but yielded to him in silence and gave in to whatever he said, as if it had come from an oracle: such was the charm that sat on his lips. . . .

Chrysanthius had a soul very much like that of Maximus and, like him, he was ecstatic about working miracles, and he concentrated on occult science. . . .

[Eusebius, one of the teachers of Julian the Apostate, said:] "Maximus is one of our older and more advanced students. He is so enormously gifted and so articulate that he does not care about the normal kind of proof but gets some mad impulses. The other day he called us to the temple of Hecate and introduced many witnesses that were on his side. When we got there and had reverenced the goddess, he said to us: 'Be seated, dear friends, and watch what will happen, and judge whether I am different from the average person.' This is what he said. All of us sat down. He now burned a grain of incense and chanted to himself some sort of hymn from one end to the other, and his show was so successful that the statue of the goddess first began to smile and then even appeared to laugh. We were all shocked by this phenomenon, but he said: 'You must not be afraid of this, none of you, for in a moment even the torches that the goddess holds in her hands will light up.' Before he finished speaking, flames burst out of the torches in all directions. Well, for the time being, we left that spectacular miracle-worker, and we were impressed by the show. But you should not admire any of these things—neither do I. Rather, you should believe that purification through reason is something very important." But when the divine Julian heard this, he said: "All right, good-bye, and study your books; you have shown me the man I was looking for." After saying this he kissed the head of Chrysanthius and left for Ephesus. There he visited Maximus and hung on to the man and held on tightly to all that he [Maximus] could teach him. Maximus persuaded Julian to invite the divine Chrysanthius to join him, and when this had been done the two of them hardly sufficed to satisfy the boy's thirst for occult science.

Julian's studies went well, but he heard that there was, in Greece, a hierophant serving the Two Goddesses [Demeter and Persephone], and he rushed over there eagerly. I am not allowed to tell the name of the man who held the office of hierophant at the time, for he initiated the author of this book. He was descended by birth from the Eumolpidae. It was he who in the presence of the author of this book predicted the destruction of the temples and the downfall of all of Greece. . . . He reached such a degree of prophetic powers that he predicted that in his own lifetime the temples would be razed to the ground and ravaged . . . that the worship of the Two Goddesses would end before his own death. . . . And this actually happened. . . .

·||·

MIRACLES

Introduction

Miracles can be defined as extraordinary events that are witnessed by people, but that cannot be explained in terms of human power or the laws of nature. They are therefore frequently attributed to the intervention of a supernatural being. In this sense, an act of healing can be considered a miracle, for it involves a healer who is divine or who is especially favored by a higher being who acts through him.[1]

The definition, tentative as it may be, shows us how difficult it is to separate miracles from the power of performing magic (the Greek word *dynamis* covers both), since magic does produce miraculous effects, and miracles can be attributed to magic.

The problem is partly semantic, partly cultural, partly theological. We have seen that the word *magic* was borrowed by the Greeks from the Persians to describe religious rites totally foreign to them, totally different from their own, and therefore suspect. The word *miraculum* (from *mirari* 'to marvel'), on the other hand, is a Latin word with a long history; in the modern sense, it is attested only in later Latin and, contrary to expectation, not in the Vulgate.[2] The Latin Bible uses the term *signum* 'sign' to translate Gr. *sēmeion;* it uses *prodigium* 'marvel' to translate Gr. *teras,* and *virtus* 'power' to translate Gr. *dynamis,* as both the power to perform miracles and the resulting miracle itself.

The cultural problem has already been formulated. To rephrase it, one person's religion may be another person's magic.

The theological problem is related to the other two. A believer would readily accept the term *miracles* for what the New Testament calls "signs" and "wonders" (how to explain them is a different matter), but he would not use the term *magic;* from a different point of view, Jesus has been called a "magician" and put into the category of "wonderworkers" (*thaumatourgoi*) such as Apollonius of Tyana. Clearly, this is more than a semantic difficulty: it is ultimately a matter of faith.

One difference seems to be implied in many of the texts: magic can be performed privately, secretly; miracles, especially in the sense of "signs," have to be seen and experienced in the open by many people.

Another difference should not be overlooked: magic is often hard work; it may require hours, even days, of concentrated effort and sometimes an elaborate apparatus. Miracles tend to happen spontaneously and require only the miracle-worker and some very simple materials—a garment, for instance, which is thought to be charged with his *dynamis*. A miracle might be described as instant magic, but magic is not a continuing miracle; it is rather the exercise of a profession.[3]

Some characteristics of the miracle are *to paradoxon* 'the extraordinary' (in the sense of "the totally unexpected"),[4] *to teratōdes* 'the strange', and *to phoberon* 'the fearsome'. These words describe the emotions and comments of the people witnessing the miraculous event. Miracles, of course, are always welcome (while magic may be evil), but even so they inspire fear, because one is in the presence of a strange power.

One should keep in mind what Pierre Janet has said about miracles:

> From time to time it has been the fashion to laugh at miracles
> and to deny that they occur. This is absurd, for we are
> surrounded by miracles; our very existence is a perpetual
> miracle, and every science has begun by the study of miracles.
> What may be called miraculous is part of a very large category
> of phenomena which conflict with scientific determinism. . . .
> When such phenomena are rather indifferent to us, we
> describe them as "fate"; but when we welcome these
> undetermined phenomena, we speak of them as miracles. If I
> am told that some unknown person has won the first prize in a
> lottery, I say that he has done so by chance; but if I am myself
> the winner, I talk of a miracle.[5]

The Bible offers stories of miraculous cures. The miracles performed by Moses in his contest with the Egyptian wizards (Exodus 7) are magical in nature,[6] but for Josephus (*Ancient History* 2.284ff.) they are proof of divine authenticity; thus he makes Moses say that the deeds performed by him are superior to the magical art of the Egyptians because things divine are superior to things human. What Moses actually does is almost exactly what the Egyptian magicians were trying to do, except that he does it much better, and it is not magic for effect or profit, but a kind of miracle to demonstrate that his god is superior to their gods. Magic in itself would be suspect, but if it serves to confirm the supreme authority of a god, it is legitimate. This may explain why so many rites that we would call magical today were practiced in a sanctuary.

The Old Testament prophets were able to effect miraculous cures and even raise the dead, and Jesus, who was considered a prophet by some of his contemporaries, did the same. But this is only part of his ministry, for he is not a professional faith healer, and—unlike Apollonius of Tyana—he never gives any medical advice concerning diet, bathing, or exercise.

What we call "miracles" are very often extraordinary cures of diseases and physical conditions. The term *faith healing* is commonly used, but this is open to the objection that faith in the healer is not always necessary.[7] Hence the terms *divine healing* or *spiritual healing* have been suggested, and perhaps they are more useful. If diseases were caused by divine powers or by evil spirits, they could also be healed by a divine power acting through someone, or by a holy spirit driving out an evil one. Sometimes, as in the case of incubation discussed earlier (see Chapter 1), a ritual had to be followed, but very often the touch of the healer is sufficient. The healer is not always a religious figure; one of the prerogatives of royalty in antiquity (Pyrrhus of Epirus) as well as in the Middle Ages was the ability to effect miracles.[8]

Many patients whose miraculous cures are recorded had probably sought help from conventional medicine at one point, going to the healer as a last resort. Many, of course, would go to the healer in the first place rather than to a physician. Although what we would call scientific medicine had been practiced since Hippocrates (a contemporary of Socrates' [fifth century B.C.]), folk medicine continued to exist side by side with it. Presumably the upper classes would first consult a Hippocratic doctor, and only when his art failed would go to a healer.

A pilgrimage to Epidaurus is difficult to interpret in these terms. If you were deeply religious you might prefer this from the beginning. It should also be said that the priests were not really faith healers: they seem to have had some medical knowledge. Still, the miraculous cures recorded in the famous sanctuaries were ascribed to divine intervention: the priests' knowledge and the ritual they prescribed were only supposed to open the way, as it were, for the god to act upon the patient, and the miracle had to be recorded to the glory of the god. In this sense, the whole procedure, from the preparatory rites to the final recording of the cure on the walls of the temple, was very much a part of worship. The Egyptians apparently believed that anything left behind by a grateful patient had prophylactic powers. In this, as in other aspects, the cult of Asclepius seems to continue Near Eastern traditions.[9]

The ancient concept of "miracle" can best be explained in this way.[10] Nature is permeated by a divine power. We see the processes in the universe, the macrocosm, as analogies (on a much larger scale) of processes in the laboratory, the microcosm. The ancient alchemists wanted to achieve the ultimate miracle—the transformation of lead into gold, for instance—but they communicated with the gods in order to achieve this. Similarly, ancient physicians, although they prescribed diet, drugs, exercise, and other "natural" or "scientific" therapies, did not always exclude divine intervention. Either they identified God with Nature or they distinguished certain events which they thought they could explain in "natural" terms from those which seemed "spontaneous" because they could not be explained rationally. The latter might be called "miraculous." Thus, many ancient physicians from Hippocrates to Galen were probably opposed to the rites of exorcism and purification that were practiced by the *shamans*, but this does not mean that they were pure scientists in the modern sense of the word. The miraculous was part of their world, and it is unlikely that they discouraged their patients from making a pilgrimage to Epidaurus. Advice that would be considered "unprofessional" today was very much a part of Greek and Roman culture.

A miracle often implies an instant cure witnessed by astonished spectators; on the other hand, we have records of cures that required a certain amount of time, like those told by Aelius Aristides [*no. 44*] but that were still considered somewhat extraordinary. Of the fifty or so miracles ascribed to Jesus in the four Gospels, roughly three dozen can be called healings (excluding resurrections from the dead), and many of those refer to psychological states and psychiatric disorders.[11] Several cures of organic diseases are also recorded in the synoptic Gospels (Matthew, Mark, and Luke), and Matthew (8:5–13; see also Luke 7:1–10 and John 4:46b–54), along with Mark (7:24–30), deals with patients who did not know that they were being treated: one is the "boy" (son or slave) of the centurion (or royal official) of Capernaum; the other is the young daughter of the Syrophoenician (or, according to Matthew 15:21–28, Canaanite) woman.[12] These stories have one thing in common: the patient is closely associated with or related to a non-Jew, and Jewish readers might have been offended at the thought that Jesus had entered the house of one who was unclean. Yet he was so moved by their faith that he consented to cure the patient, even though it had to be done at a distance.

When Jesus commissions the Twelve (Matthew 10:1–15), he gives them authority over unclean spirits (daemons), the power to drive them out, and he charges his disciples to heal every disease and infirmity. Physical illness or emotional disturbances still had not been clearly separated from sin and could be considered a form of divine punishment. Therefore, salvation, the ministry of the Apostles, had to include physical, mental, and spiritual health. It has been suggested that one of the reasons for the growth of the early Church was its care for the sick (in other words, the sinful) who were neglected by the medical establishment of the period.[13]

In Book 22 of the *City of God* Augustine describes a long series of miracles, including some that he had witnessed or helped to bring about (ch. 8). One involved a high-level civil servant in Carthage who had suffered for a long time from a large number of fistulae in his rectum. He had been operated on already, but the surgeons said that one more operation was necessary. The patient, who feared the agonizing pain that he knew the surgeons' knives would inflict, begged Augustine and one of his associates—both not yet priests, but already, as Augustine writes, "servants of God"—two bishops, one priest, and several deacons to be present during the operation. They comforted him and prayed with him for a long time. What Augustine actually writes is this: "Whether the others prayed . . . I do not know; as far as I was concerned, I could not pray at all." He could only think: If God does not hear these prayers, what prayers does he hear? The next day the servants of God were there when the surgeons arrived, but the surgeons, after removing the bandages, could not find anything on which to operate. A miracle had happened literally over night.

In the texts translated here, it is mostly the so-called neurotic illnesses that are cured in such a way as to suggest divine intervention. Ancient Greek drama relates the tensions that existed within families or communities, and even though modern medical terms did not exist then, the problems were the same as those encountered today. Yet medical science, then as now, was more interested in particular physical symptoms that could be dealt with than in a patient's stress and anxiety.[14] The almost instant relief that successful operations afforded made surgeons rich and famous. Simple drugs, diet, exercise, and bathing in certain springs had curative powers, too, but their effects were less spectacular. Beyond such treatments, however, there was always the need for a sympathetic person to whom one could confess one's real problems or who might even grasp them intuitively.

Notes

1. See J. A. MacCulloch, in *ERE*, 8:676ff.
2. Isaiah 29:14 is difficult to interpret.
3. In Homer, miracles are sometimes performed by the will of a god, but the devices used may be magical; see E. J. Ehnmark, *Anthropomorphism and Miracle* (Upsala: Almqvist, 1939), p. 6.
4. See Weinreich, *Antike Heilungswunder*, pp. 198ff.
5. Pierre Janet, *Psychological Healing*, trans. E. and C. Paul, 2 vols. (New York: Macmillan, 1925), 1:21.
6. Hull, *Hellenistic Magic*, p. 46.
7. L. Rose (*Faith Healing* [Harmondsworth: Penguin Books, 1971], pp. 11ff.) admits the success of "unorthodox" medicine but claims that it has nothing to do with religious beliefs and practices; he prefers to consider it a form of

psychotherapy. See also E. Thrämer, in *ERE*, 6:540ff.; and Lawson, *Modern Greek Folklore and Ancient Greek Religion*, pp. 60ff.

8. See M. L. P. Bloch, *The Royal Touch*, trans. J. E. Anderson (London: Routledge and Kegan Paul, 1973). Pyrrhus of Epirus, Vespasian, and other ancient rulers were thought to have the "king's touch."

9. Rose, *Faith Healing*, p. 24.

10. C. J. Singer, *Greek Biology and Greek Medicine* (Oxford: Clarendon Press, 1922), passim; L. Edelstein, *Ancient Medicine,* ed. O. and C. L. Temkin (Baltimore: Johns Hopkins Press, 1967), pp. 205ff.

11. Rose, *Faith Healing*, p. 27.

12. Rose (ibid.) does not refer to the story in Matthew.

13. Ibid., pp. 28–29.

14. See U. Maclean, *Magical Medicine* (Harmondsworth: Penguin Books, 1974), p. 177.

Texts

40

The sanctuary of Asclepius at Epidaurus (a small city-state on a peninsula of the Saronic Gulf) was famous for its cures. Although the temple was built no earlier than the fourth century B.C., the cult seems to have been older. Around the temple there was a whole complex of other buildings, some of them designed for the convenience and entertainment of the patients, who often spent weeks or months there seeking relief. There were porticoes, baths, a gymnasium, at least one inn, and a theater, which has been preserved. Attached to the temple was a special dormitory, necessary for the procedure of "incubation" for which Epidaurus was famous, though it was also practiced elsewhere—for instance, at the oracle of Trophonius at Lebadea. The patients who spent the night in the dormitory received—perhaps not right away, but sooner or later—a vision of the god of healing, Asclepius, in their dreams. He inquired about their symptoms and indicated the therapy they needed. In principle, every god that a Greek or Roman believed in might appear to him, no matter where he slept, but only a few gods at a few places were thought to be able to give sound medical advice. On the other hand, incubation could be used for other purposes; the god then acted like an oracle, answering specific questions—for instance, telling the visitor where to find a lost article.

Incubation might be called "dreaming under controlled conditions," and it is still a mystery how the priests could practically guarantee dreams of this kind. Incubation must involve, somehow, a magic procedure, for a god is conjured or summoned by some ritual, but it is performed within a religious context, under the supervision of priests who may have had some medical knowledge. The details of the ritual itself are not known. There may have been ablutions, prayers, processions, and fasting, and it is said that the patient sometimes had to sacrifice an animal and sleep on its hide. The moods of hope and expectation were heightened by hundreds of inscriptions on the walls of various buildings recording previous cures and by the hymns of praise sung by aretalogists.

Trained physicians were probably available, for Asclepius was, after all, the patron god of Greek medicine, and it is said that the temple of Asclepius on the island of Cos—a rival institution—was founded by disciples of the great Hippocrates. But it also seems that many went to Epidaurus as a last resort, after the conventional medicine of their time had been unable to give them the help they wanted.

The god often prescribed specific diets, exercise, baths—just what a resident physician at one of the well-known spas in Europe might do today. Some sanctuaries were actually located near mineral or radioactive springs, and even though their healing powers are not quite established today, the Greeks and Romans believed in them. Sometimes the god would also prescribe a fairly simple drug.

Since the advice he gave usually made sense and since some cures took a long time, one should perhaps not speak of these cures as miracles, for miracles tend to happen suddenly, mysteriously. But the priests ascribed them to divine intervention, many patients seemed to accept this, and some of the stories—such as those of very long pregnancies—border on the miraculous.

The whole operation therefore has a magical, a medical, and a religious aspect, it seems. One wonders whether people with minor ailments went to Epidaurus for a vacation, just as the rich and the fashionable went to Baden-Baden in the nineteenth century.

The inscriptions mostly speak for themselves. Not all of the patients were firm believers (see the doubters of nrs. 3 and 4), but faith apparently was not absolutely necessary: the god did what he did and thus implanted a new faith in the person he had healed, but he also punished a man who defrauded him (nr. 7). As number 8 shows, the god also had a sense of humor.

IG 4.951–52 (= Dittenberger, Sylloge⁴ 1168–69)

God   Good Fortune   Cures of Apollo and Asclepius

1. *Cleo had been pregnant for five years.* When she had been pregnant for five years she turned to the god for help and slept in the inner sanctum. As soon as she came out of there and left the sanctuary she gave birth to a boy who, as soon as he was born, washed himself in the spring and walked around with his mother. After this happened to her, she had an inscription set up:

> It is not the size of the tablet that should be admired,
>   but the divine intervention.

Cleo bore her burden in her womb for five years
Until she slept here [in the temple] and he [the god]
    made her well.

2. *A pregnancy of three years.* Ithmonika of Pella [?] came to the
sanctuary and slept in the inner sanctum to find out about her child. She
had a vision: In her dream she asked the god to give her a baby girl. The
god told her that she was pregnant and that he would grant her any other
wish she might have, but she said that she had no further demands. She
became pregnant and remained pregnant for three years, until she approached the god, asking for help in giving birth. As she slept in the inner
sanctum she had a dream. She dreamed that the god asked her whether
she had not gotten everything she had wanted and whether she was not
pregnant, but about the baby he said nothing. But when he asked her
whether she needed anything else, he said he would do this, too. Since
she had come to him for help in this situation, he said he would grant her
that, too. After this she quickly left the inner sanctum and as she came out
of the sanctuary she gave birth to a baby girl.

3. *A man whose fingers, all but one, were paralyzed.* He came to the
god asking for help. When he looked at the tablets he did not believe in
the [miraculous] cures and made fun of the inscriptions. As he slept in the
sanctuary he had a dream. He dreamed that he was playing dice in the
temple and as he was about to make a throw, the god appeared to him and
leapt onto his hand and stretched out his fingers. As he left, still in his
dream, he clenched his fist and extended the fingers one by one. After he
had managed to stretch them all, the god asked him whether he still
refused to have faith in the inscriptions on the tablets around the sanctuary. He said "Yes." "All right," the god answered, "since you refuse to
believe what is not unbelievable, from now on your name will be 'The
Doubter.' " When it was day the man left and was cured.

4. *Ambrosia from Athens, who was blind in one eye.* She came to the
god seeking help, but as she walked around the sanctuary she laughed at
some of the cures, because it seemed implausible and impossible to her
that the lame and the blind could be healed simply by having a dream.
She slept in the sanctuary and had a dream. She dreamed that the god
stood close to her and said that he would make her well; in return he
asked her to dedicate in the sanctuary a silver pig as a memorial to her
stupidity. As he said this he cut open her weak eye and poured in some
medicine. When it was day she left and was cured.

5. *A dumb boy.* This boy came to the sanctuary to get his voice. As
he was presenting his preliminary sacrifice and performed the customary
ritual, the acolyte who carried the fire for the god looked at the father of
the boy and asked him: "Will you promise that if he gets his wish he will
bring within a year the sacrifice that he owes for his cure?" The boy at

once cried out: "I promise." The father was amazed and told him to say it again. He said it again and was well from that moment.

6. *Pandarus, a Thessalian, who had marks on his forehead.* He slept in the sanctuary and had a dream. He dreamed that the god put a bandage over the marks and told him to take the bandage off after he left the inner sanctum and dedicate it in the temple. When day came, the man got up and took off the bandage, and his face was clear of marks. He dedicated the bandage in the temple, and it had the marks from his forehead.

7. *Echedorus received the marks of Pandarus in addition to the ones he already had.* This man (Echedorus) had received from Pandarus a sum of money to offer to the god in Epidaurus on his behalf, but did not deliver it. As he slept in the sanctuary he had a dream. He dreamed that the god stood over him and asked him whether he had received any money from Pandarus to dedicate in the temple. He said that he had received nothing but that he would paint a picture and set it up if the god would heal him. After this the god tied a bandage around his marks and told him to take off the bandage when he came out of the inner sanctum, wash his face in the spring, and look at himself in the water. When it was day he came out of the inner sanctum and took off the bandage, but it did not have the marks. As he looked into the water he saw that his face had the marks of Pandarus in addition to the markings he already had.

8. *Euphanes, a boy from Epidaurus.* He suffered from stones and slept in the inner sanctum. He dreamed that the god was standing over him and asked him: "What will you give me if I make you well?" He replied: "Ten dice." The god laughed and said that he would relieve his condition. When day came he left and was cured.

9. A man was blind in one eye to such an extent that he had only the eyelids left, nothing in between; the socket was completely empty. Some of those who were in the temple blamed his naïveté in thinking that he would be able to see, even though nothing was left of his eye except the empty socket. As he slept in the inner sanctum he had a dream. He dreamed that the god prepared some medicine and then opened his eyelids and poured it in. When day came he left and was able to see with both eyes.

10. *The drinking vessel.* A porter who approached the sanctuary fell down near the Decastadion [a race course]. He got up and opened his pouch and looked at the broken objects in it. When he saw that the drinking vessel from which his master used to drink was shattered, he was upset and sat down to put the pieces together. A traveler passing by saw him and said to him: "Poor fellow, why are you wasting your time piecing that drinking vessel together? Even Asclepius of Epidaurus could not make it whole again." When the boy heard this he put the pieces into the pouch and went into the sanctuary. When he got there he opened his pouch and took out the drinking vessel and it was whole again. He told

his master what had happened and what had been said. When the master heard this he dedicated the vessel to the god.

41

Asclepiades of Prusa practiced medicine in Rome for many years and died there an old man c. 40 B.C. He had studied Epicurean philosophy as well as the medical science of the day, and he defined health as "a smooth flow of atoms through the body." Illness meant to him that somehow that flow had been blocked. He prescribed diets rather than drugs, and he taught that every kind of therapy should be safe, work fast, and be pleasant to take. Pliny, in his *Natural History* (Books 7 and 26) mentions him with approval.

This highly regarded practitioner who was trained as a physician and had studied Epicurean physics was also able to perform miracles, according to Apuleius. But was this really a full-fledged miracle? Asclepiades may have observed something, or his instincts may have told him that this body was still alive, though the man had been pronounced dead by other doctors. Such cases are known in medical history.

What makes this particular event a "miracle" is perhaps the drama staged by the great doctor: he obviously had not been consulted by the family, but now he stops the funeral, creates an uproar, forces the mourners to take sides, infuriates the heirs, and finally triumphs. All this happens in public, is witnessed by a large crowd, and the story naturally spreads and is magnified.

Asclepiades has this in common with the early Greek *shamans:* he is a miracle-worker as well as a scientist.

Apuleius, *Florida*, ch. 19

The famous Asclepiades, one of the greatest physicians—in fact, the greatest of all, with the exception of Hippocrates—was the first to discover, among other things, how to cure patients with wine, at the right time, of course, and he knew exactly when the time was right, because he carefully observed the irregularity or abnormal rapidity [reading *praeceleres*, with Stewech, for *praeclaros* of the ms. tradition] of the pulse beat in the veins.

One day, when Asclepiades returned from his country house to the city, he noticed, in a suburb, the preparations for an enormous funeral, with a great many people, a huge crowd, standing around to pay their respects, all looking very gloomy and wearing their oldest clothes.

He came closer, either to find out—he was human, after all— who it was, since nobody had answered his questions, or, perhaps, to find out whether his medical experience would allow him to discover anything . . . [text and meaning uncertain]. In any case, it was destiny that brought him to the person who lay there, stretched out and practically buried already. The poor creature's whole body had already been sprinkled with aromatic essences, the face already covered with a fragrant cream, and he had already been arrayed [in the customary way] for his funeral, prepared for the funeral pyre.

Asclepiades examined him very carefully, noted certain symptoms, palpated the body again and again, and discovered in him a hidden vein of life. At once he cried: "This man is alive! Throw away your torches! Take that fire somewhere else! Tear down that pyre! Move your funeral dinner from the tomb to the dining room!"

The crowd began to mutter. Some said that one should take the doctor seriously, but others, in fact, made fun of medical science. Against the protest of all the relatives [reading *omnibus*, with Stewech, for *hominibus* of the ms. tradition]—they either could hardly wait for their inheritance [reading *avebant*, with Colvinus, for ms. *habebant*] or they still did not believe him—Asclepiades with great difficulty and with a tremendous effort obtained a brief respite for the dead man, rescued him from the hands of the undertakers, and brought him back to his house, reclaimed from the underworld, if I may say so. There he quickly revived his breath and immediately stimulated by certain drugs the life force that had been languishing in the recesses of the body.

42

The Apellas Inscription (c. second century A.D.) is remarkable because it shows that this particular patient was almost constantly in touch with the god Asclepius. The god tells him to come to his sanctuary (to make a pilgrimage, as it were), gives him good advice as he sets out, and provides a weather forecast as Apellas enters the sanctuary. The god also prescribes a diet and a form of exercise right away. It all sounds very sensible, and divine care is evident, but one wonders whether part of the secret of these cures was not the total change of daily habits that was imposed on the patients. Someone who may have been accustomed to eating heavily spiced meat is told to eat only bread and cheese, with celery and lettuce, for a while; someone who may have been fond of Grecian wine is told to drink only milk with honey. If the patient adheres to this diet for a while he may feel better physically; this, after all, is the idea behind the diets that are fashionable today. Then he may go home and sin again, but the god at least gave him a chance.

We can only guess at the identity of the "Place Where Supernatural Voices are Heard." It could have been a hall where the patients meditated, concentrating on their medical problems, waiting for voices to speak to them. Or the patients may have heard the voices in a dream.

Before he leaves, Apellas is told by the god to write all this down, and that is what he did.

IG 4.955 (= Dittenberger, *Sylloge*[4] 1170)

I, Marcus Iulius Apellas, from Idrias (a suburb of Mylasa), was summoned by the god, for I was often falling into illnesses and suffering from indigestion. During my journey by boat he told me, in Aegina, not to be so irritable all the time. When I entered the sanctuary he told me to keep my head covered for two days; it was raining during this time. [He also told me] to eat bread and cheese and celery with lettuce, to bathe without any assistance, to run for exercise, to take lemon rind and soak it in water, to rub myself against the wall near the "Place Where Supernatural Voices Are Heard," to go for a walk on the "Upper Portico," to swing on a swing [or, to engage in passive exercise?], to smear myself with mud, to walk barefoot, to pour wine all over myself before climbing into the hot pool in the bathing establishment, to bathe all alone, to give an Attic drachma to the attendant, to offer a joint sacrifice to Asclepius, Epione, and the goddesses of Eleusis, and to drink milk with honey. One day when I drank only milk, the god said: "Put honey in your milk, so it can strike through [or, have the right effect, i.e., act as a laxative]." When I urged the god to heal me more quickly, I had a vision: I was walking out of the sanctuary toward the "Place Where Supernatural Voices are Heard," rubbed with salt and mustard all over, and a little boy was leading me, and the priest said to me: "You are cured; now pay the fee." I did what I had seen [i.e., acted out my vision]. When they rubbed me with salt and liquid mustard, it hurt, but after I had taken a bath, it hurt no longer. All this happened within nine days after my arrival. The god touched my left hand and my breast. On the following day, as I was offering a sacrifice, the flame leapt up and burned my hand so that blisters appeared. After awhile my hand healed. I stayed on, and the god told me to use anise with olive oil for my headache. Actually, I had no headache. But after I had done some studying it happened that I suffered from congestion of the brain. Taking olive oil, I got rid of my headache. [I was also told] to gargle with cold water for my swollen uvula—for I had asked the god for help with this problem, too—and the same for the tonsils. The god also told me to write all this down. I left, feeling grateful and restored to health.

43

Aelius Aristides was a prominent "sophist" (i.e., a professional lecturer and teacher) of the second century A.D. He was educated at Pergamon and Athens and later delivered lectures in Italy and Asia Minor. While staying in Smyrna he fell seriously ill, suffered for a long time, and finally went to the sanctuary of Asclepius at Pergamon, where he experienced a cure. His *Sacred Orations* (a series of six in a collection of fifty-five formal speeches that have survived) describes how a god appeared to him in dreams and gave him medical advice, which he always (or almost always) strictly followed, no matter how strange it appeared at first.

Two passages from the second of these orations are fairly typical. In the first passage, Aristides describes a dream that turned out to be very similar to a dream that one of the temple wardens had during the same night. The technique of incubation was practiced in Pergamon as it was in Epidaurus, and the patients and the temple wardens apparently got together to discuss their dreams; the fact that the two dreams were so similar obviously meant something.

To what should one attribute the coincidence? Partly, perhaps, to the long conversations the patients and wardens had during weeks and months of close proximity, but also to the fact that Aristides was a deeply religious person. His faith was strong, and mystic experiences, as we would call them today, were familiar to him. Among the priests and temple wardens serving the god, there must have been at least a few who were, like Aristides, firm believers; some of them may even have been "psychics," as we would say today, and could "tune in" to some congenial patients and "pick up" now and then one of their dreams. This probably did not happen regularly, but it happened.

This is only a tentative explanation in modern terms—the terms themselves actually explain nothing—but it is one that Aristides would have accepted, though he might have maintained that both dreams were sent by the god. At the same time it seems clear that long conversations between Aristides and the temple warden created a certain rapport. They obviously discussed his illness, and Aristides must have talked about his career, for he was a renowned figure, and public recognition meant a great deal to him. The situation in which he found himself in the dream— standing on a stage, addressing a festive crowd in white (corresponding to an audience in black today), delivering a grand ceremonial speech for a special occasion—must have been familiar to him.

We also learn from Aristides that physicians were available for consultations at Pergamon, that they made house calls at dawn, if necessary, and that they sometimes doubted the dream messages that came from the god. This doctor, for instance, worries about Aristides' weakened constitution. What the bad weather has to do with the drinking of wormwood in vinegar is not quite clear, unless the god also prescribed that it be taken out of doors. The solution for many patients may have been to compromise between the god's orders and the doctor's advice. It is typical of Aristides' attitude that he does not listen to the doctor in this instance.

Aelius Aristides, *Sacred Orations* 2
(= 24 [473–74] Dindorf)

One of the two temple wardens was called Philadelphus. One night he had the same dream vision that I had, though it was a little different. Philadelphus dreamed—this much I still remember—that there was, in the sacred theater, a crowd of people, all dressed in white and gathered together to worship the god. I was standing in their midst, delivering a speech and singing a hymn in praise of the god and saying, among many other things, how the god had changed the course of my life [or, saved my life?] on many occasions—just recently, when he told me to drink worm-wood diluted in vinegar, to relieve myself of my complaint. He also talked about a sacred stairway, I think, and about an epiphany of the god and the miracles that he performed. This was Philadelphus' dream.

And this was my own experience: I dreamed that I was standing in the entrance to the sanctuary and that other people were gathered there, too, as if they had come for the ceremony of purification, and that they were dressed in white and generally looked very festive. There I spoke about the god and addressed him as, among other things, "Dis-tributor of Destinies," because he does assign destinies to men. The ex-pression came to me from my own experience. I also mentioned the drink of wormwood, which had been some sort of revelation. It was an unmis-takable revelation, just as one feels unmistakably in thousands of cases the presence of the god. You can feel his touch, you can realize his coming with a kind of consciousness halfway between sleeping and waking. You want to look up to him and are deeply afraid that he might vanish too soon; you sharpen your ears and listen, half-dreaming, half-awake; your hair stands on end, you shed tears of joy, and humble pride fills your heart. Who could express this experience in words? Anyone who belongs to the initiated will know and recognize it.

After having had this vision, I called Theognotus, the physician, and when he came I told him my dream. Its divine character astonished him, but he did not know what to make of it, for I had been confined to bed for months. It seemed to us a good idea to call in Asclepiacus, the temple warden in whose house I stayed and to whom I had told my dreams. The temple warden came, but before we could say a word to him he began to tell us this:

"I have just come from my colleague"—he meant Phila-delphus—"for he called me about a wonderful dream he had last night concerning you."

And so Asclepiacus told us the vision of Philadelphus, and Phila-delphus himself, after we called him, confirmed it. Since our dreams agreed, we applied the remedy, and I drank more of it than anyone had ever drunk before, and the following day, at the god's direction, I drank an equal amount. It is impossible to describe the relief the potion brought me and how good it made me feel.

44

In this passage from the second of his *Sacred Orations* Aristides is still unwell, partly because he has followed bad advice instead of doing what the god told him to do. But he is now ready to obey the god uncondi- tionally. In the midst of winter Asclepius orders him to smear his body with mud and then to wash himself in the sacred spring. Such springs, incidentally, seem to have been radioactive, and the mud nearby may have had certain properties recognized by modern medicine.

Running three times around the temple in the midst of winter, smeared with mud, even wrapped in layers of clothing, seems rather outlandish, but this time Aristides did as the god ordered, without con- sulting the doctor, who would no doubt have advised against it. These were truly heroic measures, but apparently they worked.

Aelius Aristides, *Sacred Orations* 2 (= 24 [484–86] Dindorf)

It was during the spring equinox, when people smear mud on their bodies in honor of the god, but I was unable to do this, unless he would give me a sign to make a special effort. So I hesitated, although as far as I remember it was a warm day. A few days later a storm came up, the North Wind swept across the whole sky, and thick clouds gathered. It was winter once more. This was the kind of weather we had had when the god had ordered me to smear myself with mud near the sacred spring and to wash myself right there. People stared at me this time, too, and the air was so cold that I considered it a special treat to run to the spring; the water, more than anything else, was enough to warm me.

But this was only the beginning of the miracle. The following night, the god told me again to smear myself with mud, in the same way as before, and to run three times around the temple. The impact of the north wind was beyond words, and the frost was getting even more severe; there was no piece of clothing thick enough to protect yourself; the coldness went right through it and hit you in the side like a missile. Some of my companions, even though they did not have to do it, decided to join me and do what I did, because they wanted to give me moral support. I smeared myself and ran, giving the North Wind ample oppor- tunity to mangle me. Finally, I arrived at the spring and washed myself. One of my companions had turned around immediately; another fell into convulsions and had to be carried hurriedly into the bath building, where they revived him with great difficulty.

But then we had a real spring day. After that the winter temperatures returned, and we had very cold weather and icy winds again. And again the god told me to take mud, apply it to my body, sit down in the courtyard of the sanctuary, and invoke Zeus, the greatest and best of the gods. This, too, happened in the presence of many witnesses. But what was even more miraculous than anything I have ever told before is this: After the fever had lasted for forty days or more, and some of the meadows as well as the sea near the shore of Elaia where one descends from Pergamon were covered with ice, the god ordered me to put on a short tunic and nothing else, and to suffer through the whole ordeal in this garment, leave my bed, and wash myself in the spring outside.

45

This conversation concerns various kinds of folk medicine and the scientific medicine of the day. Someone states that the god Asclepius is actually on the side of scientific medicine, and then another person tells the story of a Babylonian miracle-worker who instantly healed a man who had been bitten by a snake. The Babylonian healer could also destroy all the snakes that infested the farm on which the accident had happened. Moreover, he was able to fly through the air and walk on water.

All this sounds impressive, but the way in which it is told suggests that the narrator doubts all the tales he relates. The old dragon who failed to obey the wizard's command is a built-in clue, and so are the heavy brogues that the wizard wore as he flew through the air. Lucian has a way of weaving together popular beliefs and giving them a twist that makes them look ridiculous.

Lucian, *The Lovers of Lies*, pars. 10–13

"It seems to me," Dinomachus said, "that when you talk like this you do not believe in the gods, at least not if you refuse to admit that such cures by invocation of holy names are possible."

"Don't say that, my dear friend," I replied. "Even if the gods exist, there is nothing to prevent that sort of thing from being untrue all the same. As far as I am concerned I worship the gods, and I notice the cures they effect and all the good that they do when they heal the sick by drugs and medical science. In fact, Asclepius himself and his sons cured their patients by applying beneficial drugs, not by wrapping them in lions' skins or weasels' skins."

"Never mind him," said Ion. "I will tell you a fantastic story. I was still a boy, about fourteen years old, when someone came and told my father that Midas the vine-dresser, normally a strong and hard-working farm hand, had been bitten by a snake around noon and was lying there, his leg already gangrenous. As he was tying up the twigs and twining them about the poles, the creature had crept close to him and bitten his big toe; then it had quickly slipped back into its hole as he was groaning in agony. While the story was still being told, we saw Midas being carried on a stretcher by his fellow slaves, all swollen and livid, his skin clammy, his breath very faint. Of course my father was distressed, but one of his friends who was there said to him: 'Don't worry; I will go at once and fetch the Babylonian, one of the Chaldeans, they say, and he will cure the fellow.' To make a long story short, the Babylonian came and brought Midas back to life: he drove the poison from his body by means of a spell and by tying to his foot a piece of stone that he had broken off the tombstone of a dead girl. Well, perhaps there is nothing extraordinary about that, even though Midas himself picked up the stretcher on which he had been carried and marched off to the fields, so powerful was the spell and the piece from the tombstone! But the Babylonian did other things which were truly supernatural. Early one morning he came to the farm, recited seven sacred names from an ancient book, purified the place by sulfur and torch, walked around it three times, and thus conjured forth all the reptiles that lived inside the boundaries. As if drawn toward the spell, large numbers of snakes, asps, vipers, horned snakes, darters, common toads, and puff toads arrived on the scene. Only an old dragon was left behind, perhaps because he was too old to drag himself out or because he had misunderstood the command. The magician noted that not all were present and so elected one of the youngest snakes to be sent as a messenger to the dragon, who presently appeared, too. When they were all assembled, the magician breathed on them, and they were immediately burned up by his breath. We were amazed."

"Tell me, Ion," I said, "did the messenger snake, I mean the young one, lead the dragon, who, as you say, was rather ancient, by the hand, or did the dragon have a stick and lean on it?"

"All right," said Cleodemus, "you make fun of this. But let me tell you that at one time I was even more of an unbeliever than you as far as these things are concerned, for I was convinced that they could not possibly happen. All the same, when I saw for the first time the stranger, the foreigner, you know—he said he came from the land of the Hyperboreans—fly through the air, I believed at once and surrendered, though I had resisted for a long time. What was there to do when I saw him flying through the air in broad daylight and walking on water and going through fire leisurely and on foot?"

"You actually saw this?" I asked. "The Hyperborean flying through the air and walking on water?"

"Yes, certainly," he answered, "and he wore heavy brogues on his feet, the kind that those people usually wear. . . ."

46

After having escaped Nero's secret police, Apollonius and his disciple, Damis, are in danger once more under the emperor Domitian, who twice (A.D. 89 and 95) banished "philosophers" from Italy, "philosophers" being a label that covered also practitioners of what we call the occult sciences.

Although the master and his disciple are imprisoned, in chains, Apollonius is calm, for he knows already that they will be freed by court order very soon, and even if that order of release should not come through, they would, in fact, be free—in the sense of the Stoic paradox that the wise man is always free. To emphasize this truth, Apollonius performs an instant miracle: he slips out of his shackles and then into them again.

Philostratus uses the story to discuss magic and miracles in general, and in doing so he applies Apollonius' own ideas. We are given a short account of how magic was thought to work in people's lives—in sport, in business, in love—wherever success depended on circumstances beyond the individual's control. Whenever people felt that they had failed, they often blamed themselves for not having used more potent magic.

But Apollonius, in spite of his performance of miraculous feats, in spite of the accusation that he was a powerful magician, declared that there was no such thing as magic. How, then, did he explain his own success? By the power of the mind? It is true that he usually did not perform an elaborate ritual, did not offer any sacrifice, and yet it would seem that he spoke with tongue in cheek, as if he wanted to say: "What is magic to you is some higher form of science to me, but you'll never understand the difference, so why bother to explain it?"

Philostratus, *Life of Apollonius of Tyana* 7.38–39

Damis said to Apollonius a little before noon: "Man from Tyana"—for Apollonius enjoyed being addressed in this way—"what is going to happen to us?" Apollonius replied: "What has happened to us already, of course, nothing more. No one is going to kill us." Damis asked: "But who could be as invulnerable as that? Will you ever be freed?" Apollonius answered: "As far as the court is concerned, today; as far as I am concerned, right now," and as he said this, he extricated his leg from the fetters and said to Damis: "Here, I have given you proof that I am free; now cheer up!"

It was then for the first time, Damis says, that he truly understood Philostratus' nature and realized that it was divine, superhuman. Without offering any sacrifice—and how could he have done this in prison?—and without saying a prayer, without even saying a word, he laughed at his fetters and then inserted his leg again, behaving like a prisoner in chains.

Naïve people attribute things like that to witchcraft, and they make the same mistake in judging many human actions. Athletes use magic, and so do all those who eagerly compete for victory, and although it contributes nothing to their success—they actually win by chance—the wretched creatures rob themselves of all credit and attribute it to witchcraft. Even if they lose, they still believe in it, saying: "If only I had offered that other sacrifice! If only I had used that other incense! I would have won!" That's what they say, and that's what they believe. Magic also comes to the doors of merchants, just like that, because it is easy to see how even they attribute their success in business to a wizard, but their failure to their own reluctance to spend money and to their not having offered enough sacrifices. Lovers especially are addicted to magic; they are sick anyway, and their disease makes them gullible, so they consult old hags about it and, not surprisingly, visit practitioners of this kind and listen to their nonsense. Some will give them a magic girdle to wear, some will give them stones from the depths of the earth or from the moon and the stars, and they are given all the spices that grow in India, and for this the impostors get splendid sums of money but don't give their customers any help at all. If men are successful in love, either because their darlings feel something for them or because their gifts make an impression on them, they sing hymns of praise to magic, as if it had produced this effect, but if the experiment does not work out, they blame it on some omission, saying they should have burned such and such an herb or offered such and such a sacrifice or melted such and such a substance, and that this was absolutely essential but hard to get. The various techniques by which they work signs from heaven and all sorts of other miracles have been recorded by certain authors who enjoyed a hearty laugh at the expense of this kind of art. Let me say only this: Young people should not be allowed to associate with such practitioners, lest they become accustomed to these things, even as a joke. But this digression has led me far enough from my topic; why should I attack any further a thing which is condemned by nature as well as by law?

47

In Philostratus' *Life of Apollonius* we find a parallel to the story of Asclepiades as Apuleius told it in his *Florida* [*no. 41*]. A grand funeral procession arouses Apollonius' curiosity. He asks permission to look at the body of a young woman who, he is told, died in the middle of her wedding, and he brings her back to life. The biographer asks the same question that has been asked before: Was the person actually alive, but in a state of coma? If so, the restoration of her life could not be called a miracle, properly speaking, even though the effect on the crowd would have been practically the same, because no one could possibly know the true reason, and the healer himself would not reveal what happened.

Philostratus, *Life of Apollonius of Tyana* 4.45

Here is another miracle that Apollonius performed. A young woman had died, it seemed, in the very hour of her wedding, and the bridegroom was following her bier, howling. This was only natural, since his marriage had been left unfulfilled, and all of Rome mourned with him, for the young woman belonged to a family of consular rank. Apollonius happened to witness this sad event and said: "Put down the bier; I shall stay the tears that you are shedding for this young woman." At the same time he wanted to know her name. The crowd thought that he was going to deliver the kind of oration that is appropriate in such a situation and that stirs up lamentations, but he did nothing of the kind; he simply touched the young woman and said something inaudible over her and woke her up from what had seemed death. The young woman spoke out loud and returned to her father's house, like Alecestis, after she had been brought back to life by Heracles. The relatives of the young woman offered him [Apollonius] 150,000 sesterces, but he said that he would be glad to give the money to the young woman as dowry. Now, did he detect in her body a spark of life which had not been noticed by those who had taken care of her? Apparently it had rained at the time, and yet a kind of vapor went up from her face. Or had life been totally extinguished and he brought her back to life with the warmth of his touch? This is an insoluble mystery, not only for me but for those who were present at the time.

48

Apollonius has a philosophical discussion with some other philosophers and is suddenly called upon to perform an exorcism, and he does it, at a distance, because the victim cannot be brought to him.

This story is different from most other accounts of exorcism because it has some bizarre, almost humorous, features. The way in which the mother describes the predicament of her son characterizes her as a naïve, uneducated woman. She believes that the daemon that possesses her son is in love with him; this is unusual. Finally, the daemon has a story of his own to tell: he hates women because his wife, a long time ago, disappointed him.

One might almost think that Philostratus—or his source—told this story with tongue in cheek.

Philostratus, *Life of Apollonius of Tyana* 3.38–39

The discussion was interrupted when among the wise men a messenger appeared. He brought with him some Indians who needed help. Among others, he presented a poor woman who implored them to do something for her son.

She said that he was sixteen years old and had been possessed by a daemon for two years, and that the daemon had a sarcastic and deceitful nature.

When one of the wise men asked her on what basis she made this claim, she answered: "My son is rather good-looking, and the daemon is in love with him and won't allow him to be normal, or go to school or to archery practice, or to stay at home, but drives him out to desert places. The boy does not even have his own voice, but speaks in a deep, hollow tone, the way grown-up men do, and when he looks at me, his eyes don't seem to be his own. All this makes me cry and scratch my cheeks. I try to talk sense into him, to a certain degree, but he doesn't even know me. As I was planning to come to you—in fact I have been planning it since last year—the daemon made himself known to me, using my son as a mouthpiece, and told me that he was the ghost of a man who had been killed in a war a long time ago, and the he had been very much in love with his wife at the time he was killed. But he had been dead for only three days when his wife married another man, thus mocking her previous marriage. Since then (the daemon said) he had begun to loathe the love of women and had transferred himself into this boy. He promised to give the boy many precious and useful gifts if I would not denounce him to you. This made an impression on me, but he has put me off again and again; he has complete control over my house, and his intentions are neither reasonable nor honorable."

Apollonius asked . . . if the boy was nearby. She said "No"; she had tried very hard to make him come here, "but the daemon," she said, "threatens to throw me into a crevice or a precipice and to kill my son if I bring him here for trial." "Be of good cheer," the wise man said, "for he will not kill him when he reads this," and he snatched a letter from his neckpiece and gave it to her. The letter, of course, was addressed to the daemon and contained the most appalling threats.

49

In later years Sosipatra became a famous philosopher and "psychic," as we would say today. The story of her early youth sounds like a fairy tale: Two old men arrive one day on her father's estate, are treated hospitably, and offer in exchange to educate the little girl, under certain conditions. The father agrees—he does not have much choice—and his daughter is then initiated by the two old men into the ancient mysteries. We are not told who the two old men are, but they are described as minor gods or benevolent daemons.

One might speculate that such stories were told in order to defend paganism against the increasing power of Christianity. Eunapius, like Julian the Apostate, is trying to say that the ancient gods are not dead, that they still walk the earth and take care of human beings, at least some chosen ones, as they had done in the days of the Golden Age. In this way they establish, as it were, a hidden elite, a secret aristocracy that will take over in the days to come, after Christianity has been defeated. Sosipatra represents the qualities that Julian wished to achieve, but according to this story she achieves them through divine grace as well as through years of training of some sort.

Eunapius, *Lives of the Philosophers and Sophists*, pp. 466–69 Boissonade

Eustathius, a man of great qualities, married Sosipatra, who actually made him look average and insignificant because of the abundance of her wisdom. Her reputation traveled so far that I must speak of her in this catalogue of wise men at some length. She was born in Asia Minor, near Ephesus, where the river Cayster flows through a plain, crosses it, and gives it its name. Her ancestors, her whole family, were wealthy and prosperous. When she was still a little child she seemed to bring a blessing to everything: such beauty and good manners brightened her early years.

She was five years old when two old men—both of them past their prime, but one even older than the other—carrying voluminous purses and dressed in leather garments, came to a country estate belonging to Sosipatra's parents. They persuaded the manager—this they were easily able to do—to entrust to them the care of the vineyards. When a harvest beyond expectation was the result—the owner was present, and little Sosipatra was with him—there was boundless amazement and a feeling that some divine influence might have been [involved]. The owner of the estate invited the two men to his table and treated them with great respect; at the same time, he took the other workers on the estate to task because they had not achieved the same results.

The two old men enjoyed the [typical] Greek hospitality and food but were also impressed and beguiled by the unusual beauty and charm of little Sosipatra and said [to her father]: "We usually keep our powers secret and unrevealed. This great vintage that you praise so much is only a joke, mere child's play, nothing compared to our supernatural abilities. But if you want from us a worthy compensation for this food and hospitality, not financially or in the form of perishable gifts, but something far above yourself and your way of life, a gift as high as heaven, reaching as far as the stars, then you should hand over your Sosipatra to us, because we are in a deeper sense [than you] her parents and her guardians. For the coming years you need fear neither illness nor death for your little girl, but remain calm and confident. But you must not set foot on this estate until, in the course of the annual revolutions of the sun, the fifth year has come. Riches will spring up and well up of their own accord from your estate, and your daughter will think unlike a woman or any average human being; in fact, you yourself will see something greater in your child. If you are a sensible man, you ought to accept our proposition with open arms, but if you are bothered by suspicions, let us assume that we have said nothing."

At this the father, although biting his tongue and cringing [with fear], put the child into their hands and gave her over to them. Then he called his manager and said to him: "Supply the old gentlemen with everything they want and ask no unnecessary questions." He said this, and even before the light of dawn began to appear, he left, as if he were running away from his daughter and his estate.

The old men—whether they were heroes or daemons or belonged to some race even more divine—took the girl. No one found out into what mysteries they initiated her, and even to those who were most eager to learn, it was not revealed into what rites they consecrated her.

Soon the time came, and the accounts of the estate's revenues were due. The girl's father came to the farm and found her so tall that he hardly recognized her; her beauty seemed to be of a different kind than before. It took her a while to recognize her father. He greeted her with great reverence, almost as if he were seeing another woman.

When her teachers came and the meal was served, they told him: "Ask the girl whatever you wish." Before he could say anything the girl told him: "Please ask me, father, what happened to you on your journey." He said: "All right, tell me." [The reader ought to know that] because he could well afford it, he traveled in a four-wheeled carriage, and a lot of accidents happen to that type of carriage, but she described every detail— what was said, the dangers, the fears he experienced—as if she had traveled along with him. The father was absolutely astonished; in fact, this was more than astonishment, it was a state of shock, and he was convinced that his daughter was a goddess. He fell on his knees before the men and implored them to tell him who they were. Slowly and reluctantly—but perhaps obeying the will of a god—they revealed to him that they had been initiated into the so-called Chaldean wisdom, and even that much they told in an enigmatic way, looking down to the ground. When Sosipatra's father clung to their knees in supplication, begging them to take over the estate, keep his daughter under their instruction, and initiate her into even higher mysteries they nodded their assent but did not say anything more. To him this seemed like a promise or an oracle, and he felt greatly encouraged, even though he could not understand the meaning of all this. In his heart he praised Homer pro-

fusely for having sung of a supernatural, of a divine, experience such
as that:

> Yes, and gods, looking like strangers from abroad,
> assuming all kinds of shapes, wander through the cities.
>
> (*Od.* 17.485–86)

For he certainly believed that he had met gods disguised as strangers.

While his mind was full of all this, he was overcome by sleep, but
the two men left the table, taking the girl along, and handed her very
affectionately and carefully the whole set of robes in which she had been
initiated, and added certain mystic symbols; they also put certain book-
lets into Sosipatra's chest, ordering her to seal it up. She was overjoyed by
the men, no less than her father had been. When dawn began to break
and the doors were opened and people went to their work, the [two] men
left along with the others, as was their custom. The girl ran to her father
with the good news, and one of the servants brought the chest. The father
asked for all the cash of his own that was available and from the estate
agents all that they had for their necessary expenses and sent for the men.
But they were nowhere to be seen. He said to Sosipatra: "What is this, my
child?" After a moment's thought she replied: "Now at last I understand
what they said. For when they handed me these things—and they wept
as they did it—they said to me: 'Child, take care [of them], for we shall
travel to the Western Ocean, but soon we shall return.'" This was absolutely positive evidence that those who had appeared [to them] were
daemons [blessed spirits]. So they had departed and went to whatever
place they went. The father took back the girl, who now was fully initiated
and filled with the divine spirit, though modest [about it], and allowed
her to live as she wished, never interfering with her affairs, though he
was sometimes a little annoyed at her silence.

As she reached full maturity, never having any other teachers, the
works of the [great] poets, philosophers, and orators were [constantly] on
her lips and texts that others who had spent a great deal of painstaking
trouble over [and] understood only dimly and with difficulty she could
interpret casually, effortlessly, and with ease, making their meaning clear
with her light, swift touch.

Well, she decided to get married, and beyond dispute Eustathius
of all men was the only one worthy to be her husband. . . .

·III·

DAEMONOLOGY

Introduction

Attested since Homer and used frequently in the *Corpus Hermeticum*, in the writings of Philo Judaeus, and in other ancient sources, the Greek word *daimon* originally meant "divine being." In fact, in the early texts the distinction between *daimon* 'divine being' and *theos* 'god' was not always clear. By the later Hellenistic period, however, the distinction between *theos* 'god' and *daimon* 'evil spirit' had become fairly common. "Evil spirit" is the meaning that *daimon* has in Matthew 8:31, the only passage in the New Testament where it is clearly attested. Sometimes the noun *daimon* is qualified by the adjective *kakos* or *ponēros*, both of which mean "bad," "evil" (e.g., Iambl., *Myst.* 3.31.15), but on the whole there seems to be a kind of dissociation between the terms *theos* and *daimon*, the former being applied to the highest divine beings, the latter to various lower species. Given the nature of Greek mythology or theology, these higher gods could not always be considered uniformly "good" or "kind," but they also could not be classified as persistently "evil."

A related word, *daimonion* (which is neuter; *daimon* is masculine or feminine), had a similar history. In classical Greek usage (e.g., Eur., *Bacch.* v. 894) it could simply designate "a divine being," but the tendency to differentiate it from *theos* is apparent in the charge made against Socrates that he introduced "strange [new] *daimonia*" in Athens (Xen., *Mem.* 1.1.1). Since Socrates himself explained his *daimonion* as an inner voice that warned him whenever he was about to do something wrong, it could not be considered simply an evil power, at least not within the Platonist tradition, for Plato states that "every *daimonion* is something in between a god and a mortal" (*Symp.* 202E). In fact, later Platonists such as Plutarch (*Dio* 2.3), and early Stoics as well (Chrysipp., *SVF* 2.338), felt it necessary to add the adjective *phaulos* 'bad' if they wanted to make it clear that they were speaking of an evil influence.

In popular usage such qualifications were apparently not necessary, for in the New Testament, as well as in the pagan texts, we hear of *daimonia* that entered into persons and caused illness, especially mental illness. If an exorcist was able to drive out the *daimonion*, he was thought to have cured that person. *Daimonia* were thought to live in deserted places (a ruined city is called a "habitation of daemons" in Revelation 18:2). The concept behind this phrase seems to be the following: After a city has been destroyed by an enemy, its inhabitants killed or dragged away as slaves, only the former gods of the community—degraded to the rank of daemons—remain in the ruins. They are organized under the leadership of Beelzebub, or Beelzebul (Luke 11:15, 18–19), whose name is probably derived from Baal, the main god of the Philistines. The name itself could mean either "lord of the flies" or "lord of filth," but the fact that Beelzebul (or Beelzebub) is the prince of daemons, from the Hebrew point of view, shows clearly that the supreme god of one culture has become the Satan of a hostile culture, and that his subordinate gods have been degraded.

Such beings were worshiped by other nations as well (e.g., by the Persians and Babylonians), and were thought to be capable of performing miracles like the pagan deities that were demoted by the Christians. But an ordinary ghost, an apparition without tangible body, also could be called a *daimonion* (Ignatius, *To the Smyrn.* 3.2).

Another term, originally neutral, but later charged with emotion, is *angelos* 'messenger'. In Homer, as well as in Luke 7:24, *angelos* is a human messenger sent out by a real person. But on Attic curse tablets,[1] "messengers" could be supernatural agents connected with the underworld, and the Neoplatonists associated them with gods and daemons: Porphyry, for example (*Marc.* 21), speaks of "divine angels and good daemons" when he means benign supernatural powers. At the same time, the term *messenger* was colorless enough in itself to allow all sorts of different interpretations. Depending on who it was who sent him, a spirit might be an "angel" or a "daemon." The complexity was such that Porphyry had to ask the question how one could distinguish among gods, archangels, angels, daemons, planetary rulers, and mere "souls,"[2] especially since the lower order of spirits occasionally posed as the higher ones. Iamblichus himself was reputed to have unmasked a bogus Apollo, conjured up by an Egyptian magician, but it turned out to be only the ghost of a gladiator.[3] Thus, cases of mistaken identity in the world of supernatural beings were possible, and only very advanced theurgists were thought to be able to distinguish clearly between a true theophany and the appearance of an ordinary ghost boosted temporarily to an exalted status by a fraudulent practitioner.

The Nature of Daemons and the Early History of the Belief in Spirits

The belief in daemons seems to have originated in Mesopotamia. We are fairly well informed on the daemonology of the Babylonians.[4] Apparently they organized daemons into armies, or hierarchies, and distinguished between different categories—for example, field daemons, graveyard daemons, and so on. Illness was caused by daemonic possession and could be healed by exorcism. There were ways of protecting one's house against evil spirits. Similar theories and practices are attested in Egypt.[5]

Evil spirits, called *daimones, alastores,* and *Erinyes,* are well documented in Aeschylus' *Oresteia.*[6] It seems pointless to ask whether the dramatist himself believed in their existence: the story, as he told it, required them. They can be generated by murder itself or by the curse of its victim, as in Horace's fifth epode. But, as in *Macbeth,* a murder that has not yet been committed sends *daimones* backward in time, as it were, to enter the heart of the murderer. There is a close connection between the belief in fate and the belief in daemons: the daemons know future events long before they happen, because they are fated to happen, long before human beings plan them or execute them. Hence, Plutarch associated daemons with oracles [see *nos. 87, 88, 89*]. We are dealing here with very ancient beliefs that the philosophers—Platonists and Stoics alike—tried to interpret "scientifically."

A wide range of unexplained pathological conditions—epilepsy, insanity, even sleepwalking or the delirium of high fever—were interpreted as the work of evil spirits.[7] Automatic speech, although perhaps not a "pathological" condition, made a much deeper impression on the observer than did most other paranormal phenomena: "A female automatist will suddenly begin to speak in a deep male voice; her bearing, her gestures, her facial expression are abruptly transformed; she speaks of matters quite outside her normal range of interests, and sometimes in a strange language or in a manner quite foreign to her normal character; and when her normal speech is restored, she frequently has no memory of what she said."[8] It is as if a power from above had taken over her body. Indeed, this is how ecstasy is described by Lucan [*no. 85*] and Seneca [*no. 83*].

The world of the ancients was populated by all sorts of spirits. Even if they did not take over a human body in order to express themselves or to work some mischief, contacts and communications could be established with them.[9] But on the whole, the ancients believed that only the "unquiet dead"—that is, those who had died before their time, met with a violent death (being murdered or killed in battle), or been deprived of proper burial—were earthbound and readily available.[10] Those were the spirits the magicians used, because they were thought to be angry about their fate and therefore ruthless and violent.

Daemons and the Spirits of the Dead

The ancients' belief in daemons was closely connected with their attitude toward the dead, and something ought to be said about that here.[11] The dead were divided into several classes. There were, for instance, the dead of the family. They had a kind of shadowy existence, as the custom of feeding them at certain times shows. A mixture of oil, honey, and water was poured onto the grave, or even through a tube that led into the grave, while the living were having a picnic nearby.

How could the dead be in Hades and in their graves at the same time? The ancients apparently believed that only their shades (two-dimensional images of their former selves) went down to Hades, while their bones or their ashes retained, magically, a particle of the extinguished life force, at least for a time. Hence the theme of the "grateful dead," as expressed, for instance, by the Hellenistic poet Leonidas of Tarentum, in a bucolic epitaph (*Anth. Pal.* 7.657.11–12): "There are ways, yes, there are ways, in which the dead, even though they are gone, can return your favors." And in an anonymous epigram (*Anth. Pal.* 7.330) that cannot be dated, we hear of a man who built a tomb for himself and for his wife, so that "even among the dead he might have her love."

Perhaps the Greeks of the classical age had inherited two different concepts of survival and tried to reconcile them as best they could. In the fifth century B.C. a third concept appeared, that of the soul, the *psychē*, which ascends to heaven, as witnessed in the epitaph for the Athenians who fell in the Battle of Potidaea (431 B.C.): "Heaven has received their souls, earth their bodies."[12] But *heaven* in Greek is *aither* 'the upper air', as distinguished from *āer* 'the air we breathe'; it is also the divine element in the human soul. Incidentally, the soldiers who had died for their country were treated like the family dead, because the *polis* was an extended family and owed a collective duty to those who had sacrificed their lives for the community. Their names were registered, their deeds honored.

In general, the ancients also believed in a nameless, unidentified multitude of ghosts who had to be taken care of at least once a year, in Athens during the *Anthesteria*, the festival of flowers in spring, when pots of cooked fruits were offered to them.

Necromancy[13] is defined as the art of predicting the future by means of communicating with the dead. The forms of communication vary, as the texts from Homer to Heliodorus show. As a technique, necromancy falls within the domain of magic (it is practiced by witches such as Erictho), but since it deals with the dead, it can also be discussed as part of daemonology, and since its aim is the revelation of future events, it is definitely a form of divination. This difficulty in classification shows once more how closely related the occult sciences were in antiquity. It is more or less an arbitrary decision to treat necromancy in this chapter.

The practice itself seems to be very old. We read in 1 Samuel 28:6ff. how King Saul in disguise consulted the "women of En-dor," although he himself had "made away with those who call up ghosts and spirits." At her visitor's request the woman conjured up the ghost of Samuel, and as soon as she saw him she knew the identity of her visitor, who apparently could only hear the ghost's voice, but did not actually see it. The ghost's gloomy prediction was fulfilled the next day, and that was the dramatic climax of the First Book of Samuel. Manasseh, one of the last kings of Judah, practiced soothsaying and divination and dealt with ghosts and spirits (2 Kings 21:6); this must be an allusion to necromancy, and it is made clear that the Lord, because of these "abominable things," brought disaster on Jerusalem and Judah. The Second Book of Kings ends soon afterward. From the references to necromancy in the Old Testament, one gains the impression that it was practiced commonly in other Near Eastern cultures, while it was anathema in Israel.

In Book 11 of the *Odyssey* [*no. 50*] Odysseus himself, instructed by Circe, plays the role of the necromancer, and the ceremony is performed with great dignity and compassion; there seems to be no stigma attached to it. It is perhaps significant, however, that Virgil transformed the theme in the *Aeneid*. Instead of conjuring up the dead, Aeneas descends into the underworld to visit them. His consultation with the Sibyl of Cumae and the rites he must perform contain magical elements.[14] The Sibyl herself is an ecstatic prophetess, comparable to the Pythia in Delphi; at the same time she acts as Aeneas' guide through the horrors of the underworld. More than a consultation, Aeneas' visit is the revelation of a whole philosophy of life; as such, it is comparable to initiation into the Eleusinian mysteries.[15]

In historical times, necromancy was condemned. Plato, both in his *Republic* (364B–E) and in his *Laws* (905D–907D), rejected the idea that gods or daemons could be influenced by spells and rituals, and he prescribed severe penalties for anyone who practiced necromancy; he himself considered it fraudulent, and he was concerned with its harmful results (*Laws* 909B; 933A–E).[16] During the years of Roman imperialism, there were heavy sanctions.[17] In Cicero's time a few Neo-Pythagoreans seem to have been attracted by necromancy, but in general it was considered a particularly loathsome form of magic. The dead themselves resented being disturbed, as we see from the writings of Lucan [*no. 58*] and Heliodorus [*no. 71*], and since necromancers were, almost by necessity, body snatchers, they came into conflict with the laws against desecrating tombs.[18]

The great necromantic scene in Aeschylus' *Persians* [*no. 52*] is quite different from the ritual in the *Odyssey*. Perhaps it reflects Greek notions of a Persian magical operation. Here, after the defeat of Salamis, the widow of King Darius, assisted by the Chorus (representing the

Persian nobility), conjures up the ghost of her husband to find out what caused the catastrophe and what course of action the Persians ought to take. Thus, necromancy, retrospective as well as divinatory, was practiced at the Persian court, presumably as a religious ritual, but Persia was a foreign country, and we have seen that, for the Greeks, the Persian *magi* were not only priests but also sorcerers,

Both Seneca and his nephew, Lucan, wrote under Nero, who was interested in magic, especially in necromancy.[19] It is difficult to reconstruct from their poetic accounts any historical reality, and it seems doubtful that either Seneca or Lucan ever saw a real necromancer in action. Both poets stress the sinister, shocking, revolting aspects of such ceremonies, Lucan even more than his uncle. In addition to the general atmosphere of horror, Lucan introduces some pseudoscientific speculation on how to revive a corpse. His superwitch, Erictho, pours boiling blood into the body of a soldier who had recently been killed, but she also injects many other substances. Here we may well have the prototype of Frankenstein, for Mary Shelley probably knew of this passage through her husband, a great admirer of the Roman poet.

Plutarch [*no. 63*] refers to a regular oracle of the dead (*psychomanteion*), probably near Cumae in southern Italy, but there is no elaborate ceremony: the procedure reminds one of the incubation rites in the temple of Asclepius at Epidaurus. The person who wished to get in touch with the dead fell asleep in the sanctuary and had a dream or vision. The element of shock and horror is absent, and yet, in a remote sense, this, too, is necromancy.[20]

In a necromantic scene from the *Aethiopica*, Heliodorus [*no. 71*] uses familiar elements, but adds several new twists: the Egyptian witch performs the ceremony on the body of her own son, who reproaches her for it; one of the involuntary eyewitnesses is a priest, who should never be exposed to such rites; the witch turns nasty and tries to kill the intruders, but ends up killing herself instead.

In necromantic ceremonies the dead are compelled by the magician to appear, but cases of spontaneous possession of a living person by a dead one are discussed by pagan theurgists and by Jewish and Christian writers.[21] The main controversy seems to be whether the "daemonic agents" are really the evil spirits of the dead or are actually daemons. Obviously, the distinction is difficult to draw, especially since the "agents" tended to veil their identity or even to lie about it until forced by the exorcist to confess their true name and origin.[22]

Heroes and Hero Worship

Heroes form a special class among the dead. Some heroes[23] were the ghosts of kings of old, who were considered powerful after death, at least for a time, because they had been powerful in life. Others, like Achilles or Odysseus, who had ruled over small kingdoms, were worshiped as heroes because of their glorious deeds. The distinction could easily become blurred. The fact is that there were many heroes' tombs, *heroa*, all over Greece and parts of Asia Minor. Some of them became objects of a cult that seems to have continued from the end of the heroic age down to classical times, but after a while the worship ceased, and finally even the location of the tombs was forgotten, until they were rediscovered in their ancient splendor, like the royal graves of Mycenae.

Historical persons could be heroized; Alexander the Great is an example,[24] and worship of the Roman emperors was a form of hero worship. But even philosophers after their death were sometimes worshiped as heroes by the members of their schools: Plato and Epicurus might be mentioned.

The hero belongs to the local community that he protects, but his power does not extend beyond those boundaries. Though usually benevolent to the people of the community, he could turn into a ghost or, like a daemon, cause epilepsy or mental illness.[25]

Ghosts and Related Phenomena

Tales about haunted houses seem to have been as popular in antiquity as they are today,[26] and the belief that spirits dwell at their place of death or burial is no doubt much older than Plato (*Phd.* 81C–D):[27]

> You know the stories about souls that, in their fear of the invisible, which is called "Hades," roam about tombs and burial grounds in the neighborhood of which, as they say, ghostly phantoms of souls have actually been seen; just the sort of apparition that souls like that might produce, souls which arc not pure when they are released [from the body] but still keep some of that visible substance, which explains why they can be seen . . . it is clearly not the souls of the good but those of the wicked that are compelled to wander about such places, as the penalty for a bad way of life in the past. They must continue to wander until they are once more chained up in a body.

This belief survived throughout antiquity and was accepted by the early Christians.

It is not easy to differentiate between ghosts, heroes, and daemons, for they all have something in common. Ghosts, though mostly evil, are associated with their tomb (or the place where they died), just as heroes are. Various Greek ghosts have names (Empusa, Gorgo, Lamia,

Mormo) that seem to underline their daemonic character; Ephialtes, for example, is a ghostlike nightmare daemon.

Vampires, a special kind of ghost, are not clearly attested in ancient literature. But it seems that Lamia, who will sooner or later eat her human lover, has vampirelike features, and the theme is common in Greek folklore. Herodotus says that Periander had sexual relations with his wife after he had killed her (accidentally, it seems), and the story is repeated by Nicolaus of Damascus (*FGrH* 90F58 Jacoby), probably following another early source, because Nicolaus adds "from love." But this is a case of necrophilia. Phlegon of Tralles (under Hadrian) tells the story of a vampire in a collection entitled *Strange Stories*, which was used by Goethe in his ballad *The Bride of Corinth*.

There is no pre-Christian evidence for the "poltergeist" phenomenon,[28] nor do we ever hear of the *âme en peine* 'the poor soul in pain' who is being punished for a crime committed in life and who usually can be redeemed by a prayer. The idea is certainly not alien to the Platonic concept of ghosts; in fact, it may be a Christian variation of it. The greatest collection of ghost stories which has come down to us from antiquity is the *Dialogues* of Gregory the Great (pope from 590 to 604).[29] The persons involved are all contemporaries, known to Gregory or his friends, and the ghosts often announce that they suffer in purgatory, or that they have been relieved by prayers or Masses.

The Greek word *phasma* is usually translated as "apparition" or "phantom" (see Hdt. 4.15: *phasma anthropou* 'spectral appearance of a man', etc.). Such apparitions have been reported over the centuries and they have taken on various forms: in Lucian's *Ship* one of the characters has seen Hecate at noon; in Philostratus' *Heroicus* (p. 130) someone has seen Protesilaus and his companions and (p. 140) the Giants on the Phlegrean fields.

The actual substance of such apparitions or phantoms was discussed by the Neoplatonists. To them, as Dodds points out, the "materialization" of immaterial beings presented a difficult problem.[30] Among the solutions offered, we may mention that of Proclus (Commentary on Plato's *Rep.* 1.39.1ff.): What we see is not the god himself but an emanation from him which is partly mortal, partly divine, and even this we do not see with our physical eyes but with the eyes of our astral body, according to the principle "like is perceived by like."

Some daemons are close to the gods themselves. They might be called "angels" in the Jewish or Christian sense. They can be associated with planets and fixed stars and, like those heavenly bodies, with plants and minerals on earth. Thus, the "sympathy" between stars and earthly organisms or objects which is part of the astrological doctrine could be combined with daemonology. The lower a daemon is placed in the hierarchy, the more malevolent he may be presumed to be, mischievous by nature, inclined to play nasty tricks. Some of these daemons like warm places but hate the light; hence, they look for human bodies to enter.

Black magic is essentially the technique of conjuring or summoning up one of these lower, nonincarnated daemons, arousing his or her anger, and channeling that anger in the direction of a victim. In ancient times this could be a risky business for the magician himself, and he usually had to take all sorts of precautions. Unlike the theurgist, the common magician did not attempt to influence the higher gods; he was satisfied with daemons of a lower rank; these may have been fallen deities who once had enjoyed great prestige, but who now were considered barely good enough for the everyday practical requirements of the magician.[31] We do hear, however, of the invocation of heroes such as Orpheus (*PGM* 7:451) or Homer (Apion of Alexandria, under Tiberius, claimed he had done this in order to ask the great poet about his real parents and birthplace).

Philosophers on Daemons

Daemonology became part of philosophy in the school of Plato, especially with Xenocrates, who succeeded Plato's direct successor, Speusippus, as head of the school (339–314 B.C.). There can be little doubt that the traditions concerning Socrates' *daimonion* had something to do with this great, absorbing interest, whether or not Socrates himself actually thought of that "inner voice" as a kind of being. "I seemed to hear a voice," Socrates is made to say in the *Phaedrus* (242B), but this voice never offered positive advice; it always stopped him from doing something wrong, as if it were an "inward sense of inhibition" (F. W. H. Myers). Nor was it a great flash, a spectacular vision of the kind that great religious leaders (Moses, Jesus) experienced; it was more like a small light that would appear and go away.

In later Platonism, Socrates' *daimonion* was interpreted as a kind of guardian angel or spiritual guide; according to the modern view, as expressed by Dodds but foreshadowed in Hermias,[32] the *daimonion* could be called the suprarational personality that controls the whole of our lives, including involuntary functions such as dreaming. Socrates' accusers certainly chose to interpret the *daimonion* as a strange god; hence the charge of "impiety" made against Socrates. What Plato thought about it is not quite clear. In the myths of the *Phaedo* (107D–E) and the *Republic* (617D, 620D–E) he speaks of guardian daemons who accompany a man through life, know his innermost thoughts, his most secret actions, and, after death, act as his advocates or accusers before the throne of judgment.[33] These guardian daemons are linked by Apuleius (*De Genio Socr.* 154) with Socrates' *daimonion*, but the connection may have been made long before Apuleius, and it is not inconceivable that Plato, in his "unwritten doctrine" (i.e., his oral teaching, which was reserved for his most advanced disciples), gave an interpretation along these lines.

Aristotle has been called "the father of scientific daemonology." His theory of the subordinate gods of the planetary spheres seems to anticipate the daemonology of Plutarch and Apuleius and even Iamblichus, but some of it may be part of the doctrine of the Academy to which Aristotle belonged for twenty years. Here, as in other areas, Aristotle may simply have formulated some ideas that had been discussed earlier by Plato and his most intimate disciples.

Guardian Spirits

In the Hellenistic period, the belief in a kind of guardian angel, a "good daemon" (*agathodaimon*), was fairly common. Some also believed in an "evil spirit" (*kakodaimon*), but Menander, in one of his plays (frag. 714 Sandbach [=550–51 Kock]), rejects this as a poor excuse for one's own mistakes:

> To each human being is assigned at the moment of his birth a good spirit, his guide through the mysteries of life. We must not believe that the spirit is evil and can harm our lives; he is good, and there is no evil in him. Every god must be good. But those who are bad themselves, who have bad characters and make a muddle out of their lives, managing everything badly through their own foolishness [text uncertain] . . . they make a divine being responsible and call it "bad," while they are actually bad themselves.

Pagans, Christians, and Skeptics on Daemons

Under the influence of Xenocrates, Plutarch developed a complex daemonology which, in many points, is close to that of Apuleius[34] and can be said to represent a kind of Platonic *koinē*. According to Plutarch (*De Genio Socr.* 589B), daemons are spiritual beings that think so intensely that they produce vibrations in the air which enable other spiritual beings (i.e., other daemons), as well as highly sensitive men and women, to "receive" their thoughts, as through antennae. Thus the phenomena of clairvoyance, prophecy, and the like can be explained.

Plutarch's tendency, especially in the treatise *On the Cessation of Oracles*, is to assign to daemons some of the functions traditionally assigned to the gods. Unlike the gods, daemons grow old and, after many centuries, die. Thus he explains the fact that the great oracles of the ancient world have declined: daemons, not gods, were in charge of them, and these daemons are now old and dying. In his essay *On the Cessation of Oracles* (419B) Plutarch tells the famous story of the death of the great Pan: Thamus, the Egyptian pilot of a ship, had been told by a mysterious voice to make the announcement, when passing a certain spot, that "the great

Pan is dead." He did this, and the most pitiful sounds of mourning were heard at once. The meaning of the story is fairly obvious: Now that the great daemon Pan was dead, the lesser daemons realized that their lives would soon come to an end.[35]

The "pagan theologians" (probably some Neoplatonist theurgists) quoted by Eusebius in *Preparation of the Gospel* 4.5 divide the world into four classes of higher beings: gods, daemons, heroes, and souls. The sublunar sphere is the region of the daemons. The gods generally control them, but there are spells by which an unnamed daemon can be used to threaten the gods themselves. Thus daemons can take the place of gods, and it is essentially up to the magician to decide who is more powerful than whom. In the end, as Eusebius points out, the fourfold division breaks down, and there is evidence of other classifications.

Daemons could become visible, but usually they manifested their presence by a sign. Philostratus, in *Life of Apollonius of Tyana* 6.27, tells the story of the ghost of an Ethiopian satyr who was very amorous and pursued the women of a village. Apollonius set up a trap—a trough full of wine—and though the ghost remained invisible, the wine was seen to disappear from the trough.

For centuries, Christians continued to believe in the reality, the power, of the pagan gods. They were not as powerful as God the Father and the Son, but they had to be reckoned with as the evil spirits they were now thought to be. Ideally, if you were a good Christian, Christ would protect you, just as good Jews might feel safe from magicians and the influence of the stars. Still, those powers were there, and under certain circumstances one might be at their mercy.

Wherever we discover the belief in daemons and daemonic possession, we also find the belief in the technique of exorcism. In antiquity, exorcism was practiced by Egyptians,[36] Jews,[37] and Greeks,[38] and the Christians took it over.[39]

Not everyone accepted these beliefs. Again, Lucian represents the voice of skepticism. In his *Lovers of Lies* (pars. 29ff.), a Pythagorean philosopher by the name of Arignotus is introduced. He has read a large number of Egyptian books on magic (corresponding to our Magical Papyri, no doubt), and he apparently is able to liberate a house from a daemon by talking to the daemon in Egyptian; elsewhere in *The Lovers of Lies* (par. 17) a Syrian exorcist drives daemons out of the bodies of "lunatics," and someone actually witnesses one coming out, all black and sooty. Needless to say, these stories are told tongue in cheek. But the fact that the Church accepted the reality of daemons, of daemonic possession and the efficacy of exorcism, shows how people's minds were literally in the clutches of fear, and how, in the absence of medical knowledge, a kind of psychotherapy, administered by the Church, had to be developed. Benedict (c. A.D. 480–543) was reputed to be the most successful *effugator daemonum*, and his medal is worn to this day as an amulet against evil spirits.

One may wonder whether daemonology ever existed as a "pure" science, without any application to magic. Daemons seem to have been destined for practical use, not for speculation alone. And yet, just like alchemy, daemonology seems to have had its mystic, contemplative side. There must have been a certain fascination in considering the ranks and hierarchies of daemons, in pronouncing their fantastic names. Platonists, such as Plutarch, who spent a great deal of their creative energies in thinking and writing about daemons, were certainly not magicians or exorcists; on the other hand, this part of their metaphysical doctrine was more than just an intellectual exercise; in a sense it helped them control the forces that were purported to control life.

Notes

1. E. Ziebarth, in *Nachr. Gesellsch. Wiss. Gött.*, 1899, pp. 105ff.
2. Iambl., *Myst.* 2.3; Dodds, *The Ancient Concept of Progress*, pp. 209–10.
3. Eunap., *Lives of the Philosophers and Sophists*, p. 473 Boissonade; Dodds, *The Ancient Concept of Progress*, p. 210.
4. Saggs, *The Greatness That Was Babylon*, pp. 302ff.
5. G. van der Leeuw, *La Religion dans son essence* (Paris: Payot, 1948), pp. 129ff., 236–37.
6. Dodds, *The Ancient Concept of Progress*, pp. 55–56.
7. Ibid.
8. Ibid., p. 195. Dodds refers to T. G. Oesterreich's important work *Possession, Demoniacal and Other*, trans. D. Ibbetson (New York: R. Smith, 1930).
9. Only the Epicureans and the Skeptics seem to have denied *ex cathedra* the possibility of communicating with the ghosts of the dead.
10. Dodds, *The Ancient Concept of Progress*, p. 206.
11. Dodds discusses the fairly ancient belief that some human souls might after death be promoted to the rank of daemons (ibid., p. 209, n. 1).
12. This epitaph was published by W. Peek in *Griechische Versinschriften* (Berlin: Akademie-Verlag, 1955), 1:8–9.
13. Cf. the account given by F. Cumont, *Lux Perpetua* (Paris: Geuthner, 1949), pp. 97ff.; and Dodds, *The Ancient Concept of Progress*, p. 207.
14. See F. L. Griffith, *Stories of the High Priests of Memphis* (Oxford: Clarendon Press, 1900), pp. 44–45. Virgil was considered a sorcerer in the Middle Ages; see Comparetti, *Virgilio nel medio evo*, passim.
15. G. Luck, in *American Journal of Philology* 94 (1973): 147ff. This was Bishop Warburton's theory, rejected by Gibbon but not at all improbable.
16. Dodds, *The Ancient Concept of Progress*, p. 117.
17. T. Mommsen, *Römisches Strafrecht* (Leipzig: Duncker und Humblot, 1899), p. 642; A. A. Barb, in *The Conflict between Paganism and Christianity in the Fourth*

Century, ed. Momigliano, pp. 102ff.; Dodds, *The Ancient Concept of Progress,* p. 207.

18. P. Brown, in *Witchcraft: Confessions and Accusations,* ed. Douglas; Dodds, *The Ancient Concept of Progress,* p. 207.

19. Suet., *Nero* 34.4.

20. Dodds, *The Greeks and the Irrational,* p. 111; idem, *The Ancient Concept of Progress,* p. 207, n. 3.

21. Dodds, *The Ancient Concept of Progress,* p. 157, n. 2, quotes Lactantius, *Div. Inst.* 2.2.6, and other testimonies.

22. Dodds, *The Ancient Concept of Progress,* pp. 208–9.

23. Not all heroes, as Dodds (ibid., p. 153) suggests; there seems to be a difference between Atreus, who was a powerful king, and Heracles, who earned the right to be worshiped.

24. See Luc., *Phars.* 10.20ff.

25. Some heroes have been considered "faded gods"—that is, powers who were originally divine but who, unlike the immortal gods, had died and were worshiped at their tombs rather than in temples, as the gods were. But the ritual surrounding the worship of these heroes seems to have been different from the normal worship of the dead.

26. Pliny, *Ep.* 7.27 and 4ff.; Lucian, *The Lovers of Lies,* pars. 30–31.

27. On the Babylonian belief in ghosts see Saggs, *The Greatness That Was Babylon,* pp. 309ff.

28. Dodds, *The Ancient Concept of Progress,* p. 158.

29. E. Bevan, *Sibyls and Seers* (London: Allen and Unwin, 1929), p. 95.

30. Dodds, *The Ancient Concept of Progress,* p. 205.

31. J. Leipoldt and S. Morenz, *Heilige Schriften* (Leipzig: Harassowitz, 1953), p. 187.

32. Dodds, *The Ancient Concept of Progress,* p. 192, n. 5, offers testimonies from the later Platonist tradition.

33. J. Dillon, The *Middle Platonists* (Ithaca, N.Y.: Cornell University Press, 1977), p. 320.

34. Ibid., pp. 216ff., 17ff.

35. See G. A. Gerhard, in *Sitzb. Heidelb. Akad.,* 1915; idem, in *Wien. Stud.* 37 (1915): 323ff. and 38 (1916): 343ff.

36. On exorcism in Hellenized Egypt see F. Cumont, *L'Egypte des astrologues* (Brussels: Fondation Egyptol. Reine Elizabeth, 1937), pp. 167ff.

37. See Joseph., *Jewish Antiquities* 8.5.2, on a case of exorcism performed in the presence of the emperor Vespasian.

38. Philostr., *Life of Apollonius of Tyana* 3.38, 4.30.

39. See K. Thraede, in *Reallexikon für Antike und Christentum* 7 (1969): 44ff. The *Rituale Romanum* is still the official handbook of the Roman Catholic Church for states of possession and the ritual of exorcism.

Texts

50

The earliest extant description of a necromantic ceremony is found in Book 11 of Homer's *Odyssey*. It is the model for Aeneas' descent to the underworld in Book 6 of Virgil's *Aeneid* and the magical operation of the witch Erictho in Book 6 of Lucan's *Pharsalia*. Unlike Erictho, Odysseus is not a professional, but he follows the instructions of a "witch" (actually a minor goddess), Circe, as Homer makes clear (*Od.* 10.487ff.).

The ditch that Odysseus must dig is apparently not very deep, but it seems to serve as an access to or exit from Hades. Around it the hero pours libations—milk, honey, wine, and later (not specifically mentioned) the blood of a ram. The sacrificial animal must be black in order to alert the heavenly gods that this offering is not intended for them, but rather for the deities of the underworld.

As might be expected, the ghost of the last person to die is the first to appear, presumably because it has not yet found its permanent place in Hades or may not yet have been admitted to Hades, because the body has not been properly buried.

The ghosts are eager to drink from the blood of the ram in the ditch, to regain, at least for a short time, some semblance of life, but Odysseus guards with his sword the precious substance and saves it for the ghost of the great seer Tiresias. As soon as Tiresias appears, Odysseus puts away his sword, and after the seer has delivered his prophecy, the other shades are allowed to drink a little of the blood, Odysseus' mother, Anticleia, first. What she says helps us understand how Homer and his contemporaries viewed death: as the separation of body and soul.

Both Anticleia and Tiresias speak as if Odysseus has actually descended into Hades. This is strange, for he has been standing all the time right there, near the pit, but perhaps, by magical substitution, the pit symbolizes the underworld. Homer is showing us two "truths" that seem to contradict each other: How can Odysseus at the same time go to the underworld and remain above ground? Because, through magic, he descends symbolically, or because a part of him actually descends while his body remains above.

In the end, Homer's Odysseus, like Dr. Faustus in Goethe's drama, is granted visions of the beautiful heroines of Greek myth whom he could not have known before because they had died long ago. Here we detect Homer's sense of humor: his hero, who was so strongly attracted to living women, is allowed to enjoy, as a special privilege, at least a glimpse of some famous beauties of the past.

Homer, *Odyssey* 11.12–224

The sun went down, and all the paths across the sea were in darkness. Our ship had reached the limits of the deep Ocean; the nation of the Cimmerians lives there, and they have a city, all wrapped in mist and clouds. Never does the Sun shine upon them and look at them with his beams, not [in the morning,] when he climbs up the starry sky, nor [in the evening,] when he turns back from heaven toward the earth. Gloomy night is spread over these poor people.

After we had landed we beached the ship and took out our sheep. We walked along the Ocean shore until we came to the spot that Circe had described. There Perimedes and Eurylochus held the victims while I drew my sharp sword from my hip to dig a ditch about a cubit long and a cubit deep. Around it I poured libations for all the dead, first of milk and honey, then of sweet wine, and finally of water; on top I sprinkled shiny barley. On my knees I then prayed to the dead, those insubstantial beings, and promised them after my return to Ithaca the sacrifice of a heifer, the best to be found on my estate, and a funeral pyre full of precious things. Especially for Tiresias I promised to sacrifice a ram, all black, a choice male from my flocks.

After praying to the nation of the dead and making my vows to them, I took the sheep and cut off their heads over the ditch in such a way that the dark blood dripped into it. From the depths of Erebus flocked the souls of the dead, the deceased: young women and adolescents, old men who had suffered a great deal, delicate maidens who never got over their first sad experience, many soldiers who had been wounded by bronze spears and still held their bloodstained weapons. They all crowded around the trench, coming from different directions, and their wailing was weird. The fear that makes one pale overwhelmed me. I ordered my companions to hurry up and skin the sheep that lay there, slaughtered by my merciless sword, and burn them, praying to the gods [of the underworld], great Hades and terrible Persephone. I myself sat there, holding my sharp sword that I had drawn from the hip, to prevent the dead, those insubstantial beings, from coming any closer to the blood until I had my answer from Tiresias.

The first that came was the soul of my companion Elpenor, for he had not yet been buried deep in the wide earth. We had to leave his body, unlamented and unburied, in the house of Circe. When I saw him I felt sorry for him and began to cry and said to him quickly:

"Elpenor, how did you get into the gloomy darkness? You were faster on foot than I on my dark ship."

I said this, and he answered in a wailing voice:

"Divine son of Laertes, resourceful Odysseus: the harsh verdict of a god and far too much wine were my downfall. I had stretched out on Circe's roof, and it did not occur to me to step on the long ladder to climb down again. Instead, I fell headlong from the housetop and broke one of the vertebrae in my neck. My soul went down to Hades. But now, on my knees before you, I beg you—in the name of those who are not here, your wife, your father who cared for you when you were a baby, and in the name of Telemachus, whom you had to leave behind in your house all by himself—I beg you, my lord, to remember me. I know that once you leave from here, from the house of Hades, you will steer your well-built ship to the island Aeaea. Please do not leave me behind, unlamented and un-buried, forsaking me, lest I become for you a tool of divine retribution, but cremate me with all the weapons that I still have, and heap over me, at the edge of the foaming sea, a mound, so that future generations may re-member an unhappy man. Please do this for me, and fix on my tomb the oar that in life I pulled among my companions."

Thus he spoke, and I said to him in reply:

"Yes, my poor friend, I shall take care that this is done."

So the two of us sat there, carrying on a sad conversation, I with my sword held away from me, over the blood, while the phantom of my friend, on the other side [of the ditch], had a great deal to say.

Then came the soul of my dead mother, Anticleia, daughter of noble Autolycus; when I had left for sacred Ilion she had been alive. I felt sorry when I saw her and began to cry. Nevertheless, even though it hurt very much, I would not let her come closer to the blood; first I had to consult Tiresias.

And the soul of Tiresias of Thebes came, holding a scepter of gold. He recognized me and said:

"Divine son of Laertes, resourceful Odysseus, what made you leave the sunlight, my poor friend, and come here to visit the dead in their joyless place? Please get up from that pit and turn away your sharp sword so that I may drink the blood and tell the truth."

So he spoke. I drew back and pushed my sword with the silver hilt into its scabbard. The great seer drank the dark blood and then said to me:

"You have come, Odysseus, in order to be told about a pleasant way home? A god will make it hard for you. I do not think that you will escape the attention of the Earth-Shaker, who still holds a grudge against you and hates you because you blinded his son. Yet in spite of this, though suffering great hardship, you may get there, if you and your companions choose to control yourselves when your well-made ship first comes to the island Thrinacria, finding a refuge from the dark-blue sea. You will find there at pasture the oxen and the fat sheep of Helios, who sees everything and hears everything. Now, if you think of your safe return and leave those alone, you may very well get back to Ithaca, though under great hardships, but if you harm them, I would predict ruin to your ship and your companions. And even if you escape, you will come home after a delay and in sad shape, in someone else's ship, having lost all your companions. You will find trouble in your house, arrogant men who eat up your livelihood, suitors of your godlike wife who try to win her with gifts. You will surely punish them for their violence when you come home, but once you have killed these pretenders in your house, either by deceit or openly with your sharp sword of bronze, you must take up your well-made oar and go away until you come to men who know nothing of the sea, who eat food that is not spiced with salt, who know nothing of ships whose cheeks are painted red and nothing of well-made oars that act as wings for ships. I shall give you an obvious clue that you cannot possibly miss: When you meet another traveler who says that you carry a winnow fan on your handsome shoulder, then you must stick your well-made oar into the ground and offer a splendid sacrifice to the lord Poseidon: a ram, a bull, and a boar who covers sows. And then you can go home again and offer splendid hecatombs to the immortal gods who rule over the wide heaven, to all of them in order. Death will come to you from the sea, and it will not be violent at all, but it will end your life when comfortable old age has worn you out. You will be surrounded by your prosperous people. I am telling you the truth."

This he said, and I spoke to him in reply:

"Tiresias, clearly the gods themselves have spun this [destiny of mine]. But come now, tell me something, and give me a true answer: I see here the soul of my dead mother, but she sits in silence near the blood, and she has not yet deigned to look at her son or to speak to him. Tell me, sir, what will make her recognize my presence?"

This I said, and he gave me this reply:

"It is easy for me to tell you this and make you understand: If you allow any of the dead, the deceased, to come near the blood, he will give you a true answer; but if you begrudge it to him, he will go back to the place where he came from."

Having said this and delivered his prophecy, the soul of the lord Tiresias went back into the palace of Hades. I waited patiently right there until my mother had come and drunk the dark-colored blood. At once she recognized me, and with sad laments she quickly said to me:

"My child, how did you get here, under the fog and the darkness, still alive? This is a hard experience for the living. Large rivers and frightful waters lie in between: first of all the Ocean, which cannot be crossed on foot; one needs a well-made ship. Have you come here from Troy, with your companions and your ship, after wandering for a long time? Have you not yet been in Ithaca and seen your wife in your palace?"

[*Odysseus then asks his mother how she died; she answers that it was her longing for him that shortened her life.*]

So she spoke, but I debated within myself and wanted to take the soul of my dead mother in my arms. Three times I started out because I had this urge to take her in my arms, and three times she slipped out of my hands like a shadow or a dream, and the pain in my heart grew even sharper. I said to her quickly:

"Mother, why do you not wait for me when I want to embrace you, so that even in Hades we can hold each other and share the sad pleasure of mourning? Or has noble Persephone sent me a shadow to make me grieve and lament even more?"

So I spoke. My queenly mother answered at once:

"No, no, my child, unfortunate beyond all other mortals! Persephone, the daughter of Zeus, is not deceiving you; this is the law for all mortals when they die: the sinews no longer hold the flesh and the bones together, but the force, the violence, of the fire consumes all that as soon as the spirit has left the white bones, and like a dream the soul flutters and flies away. You must work your way back to the light as soon as possible."

[*Before he leaves, Odysseus is allowed to see the ghosts of many beautiful heroines of Greek myth.*]

51

In his survey of myths concerning the early history of the world, Hesiod (c. 800 B.C.) describes five successive generations or races: the golden, the silver, the bronze, the heroic, and the iron. He knows that he lives in the last of these, and that the one before, the heroic age, is but a distant memory. The golden race did not completely disappear but lived on in the form of "kind spirits" or "benevolent daemons," a privilege granted to them by Zeus, who also assigned to them certain functions and areas; thus they act as his invisible agents or ambassadors.

Zeus in his wrath wiped out the silver race because it refused to worship the Olympian gods. If we may judge from Near Eastern parallels, it would appear that these people, like the people of Israel at times, worshiped foreign gods, perhaps those of the Egyptians, and neglected their own. Yet, for some obscure reason, the "spirits" of the people of the silver age were worshiped by subsequent generations of Greeks, though they occupied a lower level than did the "kind spirits" mentioned above.

Thus Hesiod seems to establish a hierarchy: (1) the Olympian gods; (2) the spirits of the upper order, who are good; and (3) the spirits of a lower order, who are basically bad. The fact that the Greeks worshiped the spirits of the lower order, too, should not surprise us. They could blame these spirits for all the bad things that happened in the world and so exonerate the gods and the daemons of the upper order. Thus, even at this early stage of Greek religion and folklore, a simple system of theodicy was developed. It is also clear that the phrase "blessed spirits of the second rank" is something of a euphemism. People were afraid of calling them by their real name, that is, "evil spirits," just as they were afraid of calling the Furies by their real name, substituting the term *Eumenides* ("the kind ones") instead and paying them due tribute in order to appease them.

At any rate, these are the two classes of daemons that Hesiod reckons with in the following text, and his authority was such that the distinction was accepted by subsequent generations and became the basis of philosophical systems. Hesiod is quite firm when he declares that the heroes of the age of myth did not survive into his own time as "spirits." Some of them, he claims, did not survive at all; others were removed to the isles of the blessed, somewhere at the end of the world. These isles (or one of them, at least) are ruled by Kronos, who once headed a pre-Olympian dynasty of gods.

This passage is an important example of early Greek theology. Whatever daemons you honor, good ones or bad, Hesiod seems to say, do not believe that they are the spirits of the heroes of old (i.e., the men and women of the heroic age). Yet we know that in classical and postclassical times hero worship was very common in Greece. Since hero worship is not attested in Homer, and Hesiod is close to him in time, we may speculate that the practice began to become popular in this period. Hesiod's version influenced later philosophical thought, but hero worship flourished as well.

Hesiod, *Works and Days*, vv. 109–93

First the immortal gods who live on Olympus created a golden race of mortal men. This was in the time of Cronus, when he was king in heaven. They lived like gods, without any sorrow in their hearts, free of cares and pain, and they were not subject to wretched old age, but, always youthful of limbs, they enjoyed festive days, far from all evil. When they died it was as if they were overcome by sleep. All good things were theirs. The bountiful earth produced willingly all kinds of food, and plenty of it. In peace and quiet they gladly lived on their land, blessed with all the goods.

After the earth hid this race of men in darkness, they became kind spirits (literally: "good daemons") on earth by the will of great Zeus, guardians of mortal men; they watched over retribution and crimes, clothed in mist, walking over the whole earth, giving wealth. This was one of their royal privileges.

Next, the Olympian gods created a far inferior race, the silver race, quite unlike the golden one in body and mind. For a hundred years a child grew up by his loving mother's side and played in a completely childlike state in his home. But when these people were fully grown and had reached maturity, they lived only for a very short while, and they were unhappy because of their foolishness. They could not refrain from hurting each other badly, nor did they want to honor the immortal gods and offer sacrifice at the holy altars of the blessed ones, as it was right for men, according to their own rites. Zeus in anger put them away because they would not offer honor to the blessed gods who live on Olympus. After this race of men, too, was hidden in the earth, they were called "blessed mortals of the second rank," but they certainly had their honor, too.

Then Zeus the father made a third race of mortal men, the bronze race, totally unlike the silver race. They came from ash trees and were terrible and violent and constantly engaged in tragic wars and crimes. They never ate bread, and their stubborn souls were as hard as steel; they were unapproachable. Terrible arms of great strength grew out of the shoulders on their solid frames. Their armor was of bronze, of bronze were their houses, and they worked with bronze tools. There was no black iron. They killed each other with their own hands and went down, nameless, into the moldy house of cold Hades. Formidable as they were, black death took them away, and they left the sun's shiny light.

When this race also was hidden in the earth, Zeus, the son of Cronus, made another one, the fourth, on the bountiful earth. It was more just and better, a godlike race of heroes who are called demigods, the one just before us in the wide world. Terrible wars and savage battles destroyed them, some before Thebes, the city of Cadmus with the seven gates, fighting over the flocks of the descendants of Oedipus; others before Troy, where ships had taken them across the great gulf of the sea, for the sake of Helen with the lovely hair. For some of them this was the end of their lives, and death covered them; others were given by Zeus, the son of Cronus, an existence, a way of life far from men, at the end of the world, far from the immortal gods; and Cronus is their king. There they live, their hearts free of sorrow, on the Islands of the Blessed, near the Ocean with the deep whirlpools, happy heroes for whom the bountiful earth bears ripe honey-sweet fruit three times a year.

And then . . . I wish I did not have to live among the men of the fifth race; if only I had died before or could have been born later! For this now is truly a race of iron. Neither by day nor by night will they ever cease from toil and misery. The gods will always send them painful sorrows. Zeus will destroy this race of mortal men, too, when their babies are born with gray hair. The father will not resemble his own children, nor the children their father; the guest will not be welcomed by his host, the friend by his friend, the brother by his brother, the way it used to be. Soon they will not honor their aging parents but will blame them and hurt them with poisonous words, sinful men who have no respect for the gods! They might even refuse to give their old parents the payment for their nurture, putting might before right. . . .

52

In his tragedy *The Persians*, Aeschylus presents a necromantic ceremony in the Persian capital, after the news of the defeat at Salamis (480 B.C.) has arrived. The Queen Mother, Atossa, comes out of the royal palace in black robes, carrying the gifts of milk, honey, holy water, wine, and olive oil, along with a wreath. At the tomb of her husband, Darius I, she deposits the wreath and pours out libations.

While she performs this ritual, the chorus sings hymns of praise to the dead, and some of these may have been sung in Persian or what sounded like Persian to a Greek audience, for the chorus says in Greek, at one point: "Does our blessed, godlike king hear me, as I utter, in my unintelligible foreign language mournful laments of all sorts?" Since Persian was not a foreign language for a Persian audience, it would appear that the poet, at least for the first performance of his play, added laments in Persian or what could have passed for Persian. If these songs ever existed in the written text of the play, they must have been deleted soon thereafter, for the Greek scribes were reluctant to copy what seemed to them to be sheer nonsense. But on stage the effect may have been tremendous, and the use of foreign words or phrases in magical ceremonies is well attested in the Magical Papyri.

Darius is deified in death, like the Egyptian Pharaohs, like the rulers of Mycenae, like Alexander the Great, like the Roman emperors. Even in Hades he has certain powers and privileges (unlike, e.g., Homer's Achilles). He is willing to appear and is granted a brief leave of absence from Hades in order to give advice to his people in an emergency. Darius wears the crown, the robes, and the saffron-colored sandals in which he was buried.

The scene has certain comical undertones—the reference to Persian as an unintelligible language (in Persia!), and the royal ghost's complaint that it is much easier to go down to Hades than to come back.

The ceremony itself is best described as a poetic and dramatic rendering of an authentic ceremony, though it was probably more Greek than Persian.

Aeschylus, *Persians*, vv. 607–99

ATOSSA (*Queen Mother of Persia*): So I have come out of the palace once more, without my chariot, without my splendid robes, bringing to the father of my son propitiatory libations, gifts that soothe the dead: white milk, sweet to drink, from an unblemished cow; golden honey, the distillation of the bees that work on blossoms; holy water from a pure spring; this refreshing, unmixed drink from an ancient vine, its mother in the fields; and here is the fragrant fruit of the pale green olive that lives its abundant life among the leaves; there are flowers woven into a garland, the children of the generous earth.

But come, my friends; sing hymns of praise to the dead, while I offer them these libations, and conjure up the spirit of Darius; I shall pour these offerings, for the earth to drink, to the gods of the underworld.

CHORUS: Royal lady, venerable to the Persians! Let the libations flow down into the chambers of the earth, and we, in our hymns, will pray to the guides of the dead beneath the earth to be gracious to us.

Yes, holy gods of the underworld, Earth and Hermes and you, king of the dead, send up to the light a soul from below, for if he knows any new remedy for our distress, he alone among mortals might tell us what to do.

Does our blessed, godlike king hear me, as I utter, in my unintelligible foreign language, doleful laments of all sorts? Or must I shout my wretched misery? Does he hear me down below?

Earth and all you other rulers of the shades, allow the glorious spirit, the god of the Persians who was born in Susa, to leave your palace. No one like him was ever buried in Persian earth; please let him come.

Dear is that man, dear is his tomb; dear are the qualities that are buried there. Aidoneus, you guide the shades to the upper world, let him come, Aidoneus, the divine lord Darius! Ah!

He has never sent his people into death by waging ruinous, senseless wars; so the Persians called him "divine counselor," and he was a divine counselor indeed, for he led his armies well.

Our king, our ancient king, come here, come back! Rise to the top of your tomb! Lift the saffron-colored sandals on your feet! Show us the crest of your royal crown! Approach, merciful father Darian! Oh!

Lord of our lord, appear and listen to our pitiful, unheard-of sorrows! The darkness of Styx is hovering in the air; the whole youth of your nation has perished. Approach, merciful father Darius! Oh!

Alas! Alas! Your friends wept many tears when you died . . . [the text of the following two verses is uncertain] Our country has lost all its triremes; we have no more ships, no more ships!

GHOST OF DARIUS (*rising from the tomb*): Faithful of the faithful, companions of my youth, old men of Persia! What is this pain that afflicts our nation? The earth groans: it is beaten and torn. As I look at my wife standing near my tomb, I am alarmed, though I have accepted her libations gladly. But you, standing close to my tomb, are chanting laments, and in shrill songs that bring back souls you call me most pitifully. There is no easy exit from the underworld, you know—mainly because the gods down there are better at seizing than at letting go! But since I have certain powers even among them, here I am. Go ahead; I must account for my time. What is this sudden tragedy that has hit the Persians so hard?

CHORUS: I am afraid to look at you; I am afraid to speak to you; I still feel that ancient awe of you.

DARIUS: I know, but since I have listened to your laments and have come back from the world below, put aside your awe of me, make a long story short, and tell me everything in brief from the beginning to the end.

[*The Chorus is still afraid to speak; so the ghost now addresses Atossa, who tells him the news of the Persian defeat. Darius puts the blame on his son Xerxes alone, while Atossa also holds his counselors responsible. The Chorus then asks the ghost for a word of advice, and he gives it to them: never attack Greece again. After having urged Atossa to be kind and compassionate to her defeated son, he* "departs to the darkness beneath the earth" (*v. 839*).]

53

What Socrates himself said about his *daimonion*, the "inner voice" that gave him advice, we do not know, but in the *Apology*, which his disciple Plato wrote, there is a memorable passage. Socrates was sentenced to death by his fellow citizens because two accusations made against him were considered proven: (1) that he had corrupted the youth; (2) that he had introduced new gods.

History shows that unpopular figures have often been attacked on moral and religious grounds. In a sense, the campaign against Socrates may be called a witch hunt. In the speech that Plato makes him deliver in court, he explains how his *daimonion* worked, but he does not actually say what he thought it was. The experience, to him, was very real; he is not using poetic language to describe something fairly trivial that might happen to any of us. According to Xenophon, another disciple who also wrote an *Apology* for his master, Socrates used to call his *daimonion* "the voice of god" (Xen., *Apol.* 12). Since the great oracles of the ancient world were considered the mouthpieces of gods, Socrates' *daimonion* might be called his "private oracle."

The true nature of Socrates' experience has often been discussed by Platonists—for example, by Apuleius in *On Socrates' Genius* and by Plutarch in *On Socrates' Sign*. Modern psychologists have written about it. Obviously even his contemporaries did not understand the phenomenon, and some chose to misunderstand it. To call it *daimonion* would, indeed, arouse the suspicion that Socrates was worshiping a secret, nameless deity. If this deity (or daemon or spirit) worked for him, it gave him special powers that were inaccessible to others—hence the accusation of atheism and the implication of witchcraft. Only sorcerers paid tribute to nameless deities in private. Similar maneuvers were used centuries later to convict Apuleius, as we know from his *Apologia* (c. A.D. 160).

Plato, *Apology of Socrates* 33B8–E8, 39C1–40C3

Now why is it that some people enjoy spending a good deal of time in my company? Citizens of Athens, you have heard the reason; I have told you the whole truth. The reason is this: people enjoy hearing me cross-examine those who think they are wise but are not. This, of course, is not unpleasant. I maintain that I have been told by the god to do this—in oracles, in dreams, and in any other way in which any divine power has ever told a human being to do anything. This is true, citizens of Athens, and it can easily be proved. For if I really have corrupted some of the young and am now corrupting some, surely when they were grown up and realized that I gave them some bad advice when they were young they would come forward by themselves and accuse me and wish to see me punished. Or else, if they were unwilling to do anything about it themselves, some of their relatives—their fathers, their brothers, or anyone else close to them—would now remember and demand punishment. At any rate, I see many of them right here in court—first of all Crito, who is about my age and belongs to the same tribe, father of Critobulus over there; then Lysanias of Sphettus, father of Aeschines over there; also Antiphon of Cephisus, father of Epigenes. And there are others whose brothers have been my companions in that pursuit: Nicostratus, son of Theozotides, brother of Theodotus—Theodotus, by the way, is dead, so he could not beg his brother—and Paralius there, son of Demodocus, whose brother was Theages. . . .

[*Socrates maintains his innocence, and he knows that his defense is strong, but he is willing to accept the death sentence, though the charges against him are malicious and unfair.*]

Now I wish to make a prophecy to you, my fellow citizens who have sentenced me to death, for I have now reached the point where human beings are particularly apt to deliver prophecies—shortly before they die. I tell you, my friends, my murderers, that very soon after my execution a punishment much worse than the sentence of death which you passed on me will catch up with you, God knows! Now you think you have accomplished something by removing the danger of having to give an account of your lives, but I tell you, the very opposite will happen to you. For you will meet many more critics than before; I have tried to restrain them until now—you did not notice it—and they will be even more obnoxious, because they are so much younger, and you will be even more upset. If you think that by executing people you can prevent others from criticizing your unnatural way of life, you are mistaken. . . .

To me, my judges—for I am sure it is right for me to call you "judges"—a wonderful thing has happened. The familiar prophetic voice of my "spiritual guide" has manifested itself very frequently all my life and has opposed me, even in trivial matters, whenever I was about to do something wrong. What has happened to me now, as you can see for yourselves, might well be thought and is generally held to be the ultimate evil. And yet, when I left my house early this morning, the sign of the god did not oppose me, nor [did it manifest itself] on my way here to the court, nor at any moment during my speech when I was about to say something. On many other occasions it made me stop short in the middle of a speech, but in this matter it opposed nothing I did or said. What should I assume to be the reason for this? I will tell you: What is happening to me must be good, and those of us who consider death an evil must be wrong. . . .

54

Ancient ghost stories attest the popular belief in some form of survival of the person after death. Ghosts are, in fact, visible daemons, as Pausanias' description of "Cemetery Hill," near Marathon, shows. Just as invisible daemons were worshiped throughout Greece, visible ones also might have their cult, though they were usually considered a nuisance. People shunned haunted places then as now because they often indicated the presence of evil—murder, for instance, or violent death.

It is obvious that an ancient battlefield on which thousands of men had been killed in the prime of their lives would yield a certain number of permanent ghosts (even ghost horses!), apparitions that were still reported in the time of Pausanias, who wrote a travel guide to Greece c. A.D. 150.

The English word *ghost* itself shows how ancient beliefs sometimes survive. It can mean "soul" or "spirit," as opposed to the body, but it can also mean "a spectral apparition," and the Third Person of the Trinity is called either "the Holy Spirit" or "the Holy Ghost." Similarly, the German word *Geist* has a fairly wide range of meaning, with "spirit" in one sense or another fitting most of them.

Pausanias traveled all over Greece in the second century A.D. and visited the famous sites. He listened to the stories of the tourist guides as he looked at the monuments, but he also did some research on his own.

In the battle of Marathon (490 B.C.) many men lost their lives, and their bodies were buried there. Such an ancient battlefield—ancient even in the days of Pausanias—is no ordinary place. Every now and then the battle is reenacted at night, but it is dangerous to go there and wait for it to happen. The ghosts do not like idle curiosity.

All of the fallen soldiers are considered "heroes," but three divine or semidivine beings are singled out for special worship: Marathon, the eponymous hero of the site; Heracles, who was believed to have helped the Greeks; and a mysterious apparition called Echetlaeus, who used his plow share as a weapon.

Pausanias, *Description of Greece* 1.32.3–4 .

There is a county called Marathon, halfway between Athens and Carystus in Euboea. It was in this part of Attica that the foreign army [i.e., the Persians] landed, was defeated in battle, and lost some ships as it took off again. In the plain there is a grave for the Athenians, and on it there are slabs with the names of the fallen, arranged according to their tribes. There is another grave for the Boeotians, one for the Plataeans, and one for the slaves, because slaves had fought there for the first time [along with the free].

There is also a separate monument for one man, Miltiades, the son of Cimon, though his end came later, after he had failed to take Parus and had been brought to trial by the Athenians because of this.

At this place you can hear all night horses whinnying and men fighting. No one who stays there just to have this experience gets any good out of it, but the ghosts [or daemons] do not get angry with anyone who happens to be there against his will.

The people of Marathon worship both those who died in the fighting, calling them "heroes," and [a semidivine being called] "Marathon," from whom the county derives its name, but also Heracles, saying that they were the first among the Greeks to acknowledge him as a god. They say also that a man took part in the battle who looked and was dressed like a farmer. He slaughtered many of the Persians with his plowshare, and when everything was over he disappeared. But when the Athenians consulted the oracle, the god would not tell them anything except to honor "Echetlaeus" [i.e., the man with the plowshare] as a hero.

55

Pausanias' description of a famous painting that could be seen in Delphi in ancient times gives us the common Greek view of Hades. Part of it served as an illustration of Odysseus' consultation of the seer Tiresias [*no. 50*]. It was clearly represented as a real *katabasis* 'descent', either because the painter, Polygnotus, understood the text in this way, or perhaps because he could not represent the seeming contradiction between descent and nondescent that we have noticed above.

The way in which he made visible the topography of the underworld, with all its inhabitants known from myth, literature, and earlier works of art, was much admired in antiquity. In a sense, the painting was monumental and encyclopedic, and the wealth of detail must have been astonishing. In another sense it worked on the emotions of those who still believed that this was life after death, at least for those who had sinned or committed a crime on earth. The mystery religions and the characteristic ethical doctrine preached at Delphi, where the painting stood, held out hope for those who put themselves under the gods and began a new life.

The artist included some characters that seem to belong to the realm of folklore rather than literature—for example, the daemon Eurynomus, who eats the flesh of corpses (i.e., causes their decaying). Pausanias tried to look him up in the *Odyssey* as well as in other early epics that are no longer extant, but he could not find this particular daemon. Guides were no doubt available to explain the details, and thus, perhaps, they created a new mythology for the benefit of the tourists.

Pausanias, *Description of Greece* 10.28.1–10.29.1

[*One part of the large painting of Polygnotus in the Lounge at Delphi shows the fall of Troy and the departure of the Greeks.*] The other part of the painting, the one on the left, shows Odysseus, who has descended into the so-called Hades to consult the soul of Tiresias about his safe return home. The details of the painting are as follows: There is water that looks like a river, obviously the Acheron, with reeds growing in it and fish swimming in it whose forms appear so dim that one would take them to be shadows rather than fish. There is a boat on the river, with the ferryman [Charon] at the oars. Polygnotus has followed, it seems to me, the *Minyad*, for there is a passage in the *Minyad* which refers to Theseus and Pirithoous:

"But then they could not find the boat upon which the dead embark, the one that Charon, the old ferryman, steers, within its anchoring-place."

For this reason Polygnotus painted Charon as a man well advanced in years. The passengers in the boat are not altogether clearly visible. Tellis seems to be a young adolescent, Cleobaea still a young woman; she holds on her knees a chest of the kind they usually make for Demeter. As far as Tellis is concerned, I have only heard that the poet Archilochus was his grandson, and of Cleobaea it is said that she brought the mysteries of Demeter from Parus to Thasus.

On the bank of the Acheron there is a remarkable group, under Charon's boat. There is a man who treated his father unjustly, and he is now being strangled by his father. In those days people honored their parents above anything else. . . . [*A digression follows.*] Next to the man who abused his father, and who for this suffers his full share of punishment in Hades, there is a man who pays the penalty for sacrilege. The woman punishing him is skilled in drugs, especially harmful ones. Clearly in those days people were very religious.

Higher up than the figures just mentioned is Eurynomus. The guides at Delphi say that he is one of the daemons in Hades and that he eats the flesh off the corpses, leaving them only their bones. Homer's *Odyssey* and the epic entitled *Minyad* and the *Nostoi*—they do refer to Hades and its horrors—know nothing of a daemon called Eurynomus. But let me describe at least what he is like and how he is represented in the painting. His color is black-blue, like flies that buzz around meat, and he is showing his teeth, and he sits on the skin of a vulture. . . .

Even higher up than the figures just mentioned are two companions of Odysseus, Perimedes and Eurylochus, carrying victims for sacrifice; the victims are black rams. . . .

56

This is an exorcist's ritual from the Great Magical Papyrus in Paris. It is far more complicated than the exorcisms described in the Bible. Certain substances have to be cooked in olive oil, certain words written on a tin tablet, certain formulas recited. In the main formula the daemon possessing the patient is threatened by divine names from different cultures: Egypt, Israel, Greco-Roman paganism, Christianity, and some others that cannot be clearly identified. The whole adds up to a massive attack on the daemon. If the god of one culture is powerless, the combination of many gods will certainly help. In some cases the powers of the gods to whom the daemon must eventually yield are emphasized by striking examples.

The food taboo prescribed at the end is interesting. It does not necessarily mean that the magician who designed this ritual was Jewish. He may simply have used Hebrew words (or what he thought were Hebrew words) and assumed that ritual purity, according to the Jewish custom, made the words more effective. An exorcist of this type probably did not belong to any of the great religions of the time, one would assume; but this did not prevent him from borrowing from them in order to reinforce his magic.

The Great Magical Papyrus in Paris (=*PGM* 1:170–73)

For those possessed by daemons a well-tested charm by Pibêchês. Take oil from unripe olives together with the plant mastigia and lotus pith and cook it with colorless marjoram, saying: "[magic words; among others, IOEL, HARI, PHTHA], come out of X." [Common formulas.] The protective charm you must write on a tin tablet: "[magic words], "and hang it on the patient. This is an object of fear for every daemon and frightens him. Stand facing him and exorcise him. The formula of exorcism is the following: "I conjure you by the god of the Hebrews, Jesus [magic words], you who appear in fire, you who are in the midst of land and snow and fog, Tannetis, let your angel descend, the pitiless one, and let him arrest the daemon that flies around this creature shaped by God in his holy paradise, for I pray to the holy god through Ammon [magic words]. I conjure you [magic words], I conjure you by him who appeared to Osrael [=Israel] in a pillar of light and a cloud by night and who has saved his people from Pharaoh and has brought upon Pharaoh the ten plagues because he would not listen. I conjure you, every daemonic spirit, to tell me who you are; I conjure you by the seal that Solomon put upon the tongue of Jeremiah, and he spoke. So you speak, too, and tell me what kind of a daemon you are, one in heaven or one in the air or one on the ground or one underground or one in the underworld, or a Ebusaen or a Chersaeon or a Pharisee. Speak, whatever you are, for I conjure you by God the light-bringer, the invincible one, the one who knows what is in the heart of every living creature, the one who created the race of men from dust, who brings [them] out of uncertain [places], who gathers the clouds, sending down rain upon the earth, and blesses its fruit and is blessed by every heavenly power of angels and archangels. I conjure you by the great god Sabaôth, who stopped the river Jordan and divided the Red Sea through which Israel marched, making it passable. For I conjure you by him who revealed the hundred and forty tongues and distributed them according to his own command. I conjure you by him who burned down the stiff-necked giants with his beams of fire, who praises the heaven of heavens. I conjure you by him who put mountains around the sea [or?] a wall of sand and told it not to overflow, and the deep obeyed. Thus must you also obey, every daemonic spirit, for I conjure you by him who has moved the four winds together from holy eternities, by the heavenlike, sealike, cloudlike [god], the fire-bringer, the invincible. I conjure you by him who is in Jerusalem, the pure [city], for whom and near whom the unextinguishable fire burns forever and ever, with his holy name [magic words], before whom trembles the hellfire, and flames leap up all around, and iron explodes, and whom every mountain fears from the depth of its foundations. I conjure you, every daemonic spirit, by him who looks down on earth and makes its foundations tremble and has created the universe from a state of nonbeing into a state of being."

But I urge you who use this exorcism not to eat any pork, and every spirit and daemon will be subject unto you, whoever he may be. As you exorcise, breathe once [at the patient], beginning at the toes, blowing all the way up to his face, and he [the daemon] will be arrested. Be pure and keep this. For the spell is in Hebrew, and it is kept among pure men.

57

Whether Seneca's tragedies were actually performed on stage or were merely recited is still the subject of controversy. This necromantic scene from one of his dramas (written during the first half of the first century A.D.) was narrated, perhaps because it would have been difficult to show the action on stage. As a Stoic philosopher, Seneca was interested in contemporary science (he wrote a scientific work, *Quaestiones Naturales* [*Scientific Problems*] in prose); he also condemned superstitions and wrote a work (now lost) on that subject. In one of his *Moral Essays* (*De Beneficiis* [*On Good Deeds*]) he writes: "No normal human being is afraid of a god. It is insane to fear what is good for you, and no one can love what he fears" (4.19.1).

Since fear—fear of unknown powers—is such an important element in magic, it is puzzling that Seneca paid any attention to magic at all, and yet he did, not only here, but also in his *Medea*. Perhaps, like authors before him, he looked upon magic as a literary theme that offered great possibilities. Descriptions of magical ceremonies were apt to shock the reader and the audience, and ever since Aristotle, the "shock effect" had been considered one of the functions of drama. As a philosopher, Seneca wanted to help his readers overcome fear; as a playwright, he thought it necessary to terrify them, in order to achieve a *kátharsis*, a kind of purification of the nervous system. The magical scene is not necessary for the plot of the play; Sophocles and other dramatists did not use it. One suspects, then, that Seneca threw it in for the sake of its "shock effect."

Did Seneca or his nephew, Lucan [see *no. 58*], ever witness a necromantic ceremony? We do not know, but since Nero himself was interested in this sort of thing, it is quite possible. We know from the Magical Papyri that such rituals were performed, but to reconstruct them from this dramatic text would be a mistake. On the other hand, the theme already had a long history, and Seneca may have borrowed from literature rather than from life—for example, from the "daemonic personifications" in Book 6 of Virgil's *Aeneid*—adding some touches of his own.

Seneca, *Oedipus*, vv. 530–626

CREON: Far from the city, near the valley through which the Dirce flows, there is a grove, dark with oak trees. Cypresses, lifting up their heads from the deep woods, dominate the forest with their evergreen masses. Ancient oak trees stretch out their twisted branches, rotting from decay. The ravages of age have broken the side of this tree; that one, about to fall because its roots have grown weak, leans precariously against another trunk. There are laurel trees with bitter berries, basswood trees with light leaves, myrtle from Paphus, elms that will someday move their oars through the wide sea, the fir tree that grows toward the sun and exposes its knotless sides to the Zephyrs. In the middle of the woods there is an enormous tree whose heavy shade weighs on the smaller plants and which guards the grove all by itself, spreading out its branches in a wide perimeter. At its foot there is a sinister pool which never sees the sunlight, still and stagnant in eternal frost; a brackish swamp surrounds the sluggish spring.

When the old priest had entered this place he acted quickly. The place itself offered night. The earth was dug up, and a fire, snatched from a pyre, was thrown on top. The seer drapes himself in a funereal robe and waves a branch. The black garment reaches down to his feet. The old man in his sinister apparel draws nearer, gloomily. Yew, the plant of death, crowns his head. Black sheep and black oxen are dragged to the ditch. The flame consumes the sacrificial meal, and the cattle, still alive, struggle in the deadly fire. The priest now calls the shades and him who rules over the shades and him who guards the entrance to the pool of death. He lets the magic spells roll and sings in ecstasy threatening words that either appease or force the frail shades. He pours an offering of blood on the altar and lets the animals burn whole. He floods the ditch with blood and pours the white milky liquid on top; with his left hand he sprinkles wine. Once more he sings, looks down on the ground, and calls the shades with an even louder, more ecstatic voice.

The pack of Hecate barks. Three times the hollow valley echoes with a mournful sound. The ground trembles, the earth quakes.

"They have heard me!" cries the seer. "The spells that I have poured out are working! The dark chaos is breaking open, and the peoples of Dis are allowed to come to the world above!"

The whole forest sinks into the ground. The whole grove quivers in horror. The earth gives way and groans deep inside. (Is it because she resents the fact that Acheron's hidden depths are opened up? Or is it because the earth herself has thunderously ripped her structure to let the dead pass through? Or is it because three-headed Cerberus, mad with rage, has pulled on his heavy chain?) Suddenly the earth splits and opens up an enormous chasm.

I saw with my own eyes the stagnant pools among the shades; with my own eyes I saw the bloodless gods and the night that is truly night. My blood turned cold, stopped, and froze in my veins.

A wild cohort jumped forth. The whole offspring of the dragon stood there in arms, the armies of the two brothers born from the teeth sown near Dirce, the merciless destruction of the people of Thebes! There was a yell coming from the black Furies, blind Madness and Horror, and all the other creatures that eternal Darkness produces and hides. There was Bereavement tearing at her hair, Disease barely holding up her weary head, Old Age, a burden to herself, and halting Fear. My courage fell. Even the old priest's daughter, who was familiar with his sacred rites and

magic arts, was shocked. But he, fearless and bold, conjured up the
bloodless folk of savage Dis.

At once they appeared, flying through the air like delicate mist,
breathing the air under the open sky. The crowds attracted by the seer's
voice were more numerous than the leaves that grow on Mount Eryx,
more numerous than the flowers that come out on Mount Hybla in the
middle of spring when swarming bees form a tight ball in the air, more
numerous than the waves that break on the Ionian Sea, more numerous
than the birds that escape from the winter and from the threats of icy
Strymon and cut through the sky to exchange arctic snow for the mild
climate of the Nile. Nervously the trembling souls seek hiding places in
the shady grove. . . .

[*A series of apparitions from the underworld follows.*]

Often was Laius conjured up, and finally he lifted his disgraceful
head, but he sat down at a distance from the crowd, hiding his face. The
priest insisted and doubled his incantations until Laius showed the features he had concealed so far. I shudder as I describe him: there he stood,
his body horribly covered with gore, his hair dirty, disgusting, and covered with filth. In ecstasy he yelled. . . .

[*Laius' ghost now reveals that his son Oedipus, king of Thebes, is responsible for the plague that has befallen the city; Oedipus has killed him and married
his own mother; Oedipus must be punished.*]

58

From this text it would appear that Lucan tried to surpass his uncle Seneca
in the description of horror. He has created in this unfinished epic on the
civil war between Caesar and Pompey a kind of superwitch, Erictho, who
is consulted by the "worthless" son of Pompey on the eve of the decisive
battle of Pharsalus (48 B.C.). Since Lucan wished to compete with Virgil as
an epic poet, it is safe to say that this necromantic scene in Book 6 of his
work was designed to invite comparison with Book 6 of the *Aeneid*, the
hero's visit to the underworld.

Lucan first enumerates various methods of divination, but adds
that for Pompey's son necromancy is the only reliable way of exploring
the future. The rites involved are presented as monstrous and disgusting,
but the poet goes on and on, as if he enjoys all the gruesome details. It is a
neat literary trick: Lucan professes to be shocked by the magical practices
he describes, and yet they seem to give him a certain thrill.

Erictho has enormous power and no scruples whatsoever about
using it. The central idea of the whole passage—the revival of a corpse—
may have been discussed as a scientific problem at the time. Shelley, who
admired Lucan and placed him above Virgil as a poet, must have read this
passage with his wife, Mary, for it is almost certainly the nucleus of
Frankenstein's experiment.

Lucan, *Pharsalia* 6.413–830

When the rival leaders had pitched their camps in the doomed part of the world, everyone was disturbed by a feeling that the battle was near. Obviously the grim hour of decision was approaching, and destiny was moving in. Worthless characters trembled and feared the worst, but a few, anticipating an uncertain outcome, built up morale and coped with hope and fear alike.

Among [them] . . . was Sextus, the unworthy son of the great Pompey. Later, in exile, he was to become a pirate, haunting the sea around Sicily, disgracing the glory that his father had won in naval battles. Goaded by fear, he wanted to know the course of fate. He could stand no delay and was tormented by all the events that the future held, and so he did not consult the tripods of Delus or the Pythian caverns, and he cared not to find out what the sound made by the bronze cauldron of Jupiter at Dodona means—Dodona, which produced the first human food—nor did he ask for someone to read the future in the entrails, to interpret the signs of birds, watch the lightnings of heaven, investigate the stars by means of the Assyrian science, or practice any other science which is secret but not unlawful. He was familiar with the occult knowledge of the cruel sorcerers that are an abomination to the gods, the gloomy altars where funeral rites are performed; he knew that Pluto and the shades below can be relied upon, and he was perverse enough to believe that the gods above have little knowledge. The very region [of Thessaly] supported his vicious, insane delusion: the camp was close to the habitation of Thessalian witches, whose bold criminal acts surpass your imagination and whose specialty is the impossible.

Moreover, the earth of Thessaly produces poisonous herbs in the mountains, and the rocks feel it when magicians sing their deadly spells. Many plants grow there that may compel the gods, and the woman who came from Colchis [Medea] picked in Thessalian country many herbs that she did not bring along. The impious incantations of a horrible race attract the attention of the gods, who turn a deaf ear to so many nations, so many peoples. The witches' voice alone reaches through the remote regions of heaven and conveys compelling words even to a reluctant deity, a deity not distracted by care for the sky and the revolving firmament. When her hideous mumbo-jumbo has reached the stars, a Thessalian witch can call away the gods from every altar except her own, even though Persian Babylon and Memphis, full of mysteries, may open every shrine of their ancient magicians. Through the song of a Thessalian witch a love that is not willed by destiny enters an insensible heart, and strict old men burn with forbidden passions. Not only are their poisonous potions or the tumor full of juice which they snatch from the forehead of a foal—the indication that its mother will love it—powerful: no, men's minds are destroyed by magic spells, even if they have not been poisoned by any dangerous drug. Men and women who are not joined in marriage and not attracted to each other by charm or beauty can be drawn together by the magic power of a thread that is being twirled. The decrees of nature cease to operate; nights grow longer and delay the days; the heavenly sphere does not obey the law; the swift firmament slows down, as soon as it has heard a magic spell; and Jupiter is amazed that heaven does not rotate on its swift axis, although he keeps pushing it hard. At one time [the witches] fill everything with rain and hide the warm sun behind a veil of clouds; there is thunder in the sky, and Jupiter knows nothing about it; by the same kind of spell they disperse the large expanses of wet mist and the disheveled locks of the clouds. There are no winds, but the sea swells, and then again it is forbidden to feel the power of a storm and lies silent, even though the South Wind tries to stir it up and the sails that carry a ship against the wind belly out. The waterfall on the face of a steep cliff hangs suspended in midair, and rivers do not run in their natural directions.

The Nile does not rise in the summer; the Maeander straightens out its course, and the Arar rushes the sluggish Rhone. The mountains lower their peaks and flatten out their ridges; Olympus looks up at the clouds, and the snows of Scythia thaw without any sun, even in the midst of a harsh winter. When the tide is moved by the moon, Thessalian charms defend the shore and drive back the tide. The earth, too, shakes off the axis of her solid mass, and her gravity stumbles and tends toward the center of the universe. Struck by the voice [of a witch] the mass of this enormous structure splits and offers a view of the sky that rotates around it. Every animal that has the ability to kill and is equipped by nature to do harm fears the Thessalian witches and provides them with murderous techniques. The greedy tiger and the lion, noble in his wrath, show their best manners and fawn upon the witches; the snake unfolds his frosty coils just to please them and stretches at full length on ground that is covered with dew; the bodies of knotted vipers break apart and get joined together again, and serpents collapse, because man-made poison is blown at them.

Why do the gods trouble to obey these spells? Why are they afraid of ignoring them? What mutual agreement puts pressure on the gods? Must they obey, or does it give them pleasure to obey? Is this allegiance caused by some obscure religion, or do the witches enforce it with silent threats? Do witches have power over all the gods, or are their incantations effective against only one particular god, who can inflict the compulsion inflicted upon him on the whole world?

These witches first brought down the stars from the fast-moving sky, and by their techniques the clear moon, attacked by dreadful, poisonous incantations, grew dim and burned with a dark and earthly light, just as if the earth had cut off the moon from the reflections of her brother, the sun, and projected its own shadows into the light from heaven. The moon is so strongly affected by magic spells and pulled down so hard that she finally drops her foam from a close distance on the plants below.

These criminal rites, these wicked practices of a horrible race, were scorned by savage Erictho as being too pious, and she degraded a science that was already tainted with rites before unknown. To her, it was taboo to seek shelter for her abominable person in a city or in a normal house; she lived in deserted tombs and inhabited graves from which the ghosts had been driven, and the deities of hell loved her. Neither the heavenly gods nor the fact that she was still living prevented her from visiting [reading *ambire* for *audire*] the assemblies of the dead or from knowing the dwellings beyond the Styx and the mysteries of Dis in hell. The face of the loathsome witch is haggard, hideous, and decomposed; her features inspire fear because of their hellish pallor; they are covered with disheveled hair and are never seen on a bright sky: only if rain and black clouds conceal the stars does the witch emerge from the tombs she has stripped and try to catch the lightning of the night. As she stomps over a fertile cornfield, she burns the seeds, and her breath poisons air that was wholesome before.

She never prays to the heavenly gods, never invokes divine aid by a suppliant hymn, knows nothing about the entrails of a sacrificial victim. She only enjoys placing upon an altar the burning logs and the incense that she has stolen from a kindled pyre.

As soon as they hear her voice uttering a magic prayer, the gods grant her every kind of horror; they are afraid to hear the second spell. She buries alive those whose souls are still in control of their bodies, and Death catches up with them against his own will, because years of life are still due them. Or else she brings back dead bodies from the grave, by turning around the funeral procession; corpses actually escape death. This witch snatches the smoking ashes, the burning bones of the young, from the midst of the pyre and grabs the very torch the parents were holding, collects the pieces of the bier that are fluttering in black smoke, the burial garments that crumble into ashes and the cinders that smell of the corpse. But when the bodies have been put into stone sarcophagi, which drain off the body fluids and absorb the liquid marrow, drying out the corpse, she feasts greedily, savagely, on all the limbs, thrusts her fingers into the eye sockets, scoops out gleefully the frozen eyeballs, and gnaws the yellow nails on the withered hand. With her teeth she bites through the fatal noose on the rope and plucks the corpse dangling from the gallows; she scrapes criminals off the cross, tearing away the rain-beaten flesh and the bones baked in the glaring sun. She takes off the nails that pierce the hands, the black juices of corruption that drip all over the corpse, and the clotted fluids, and when a tendon resists her bite, she pulls it down with her weight. Wherever any corpse lies unburied on the ground, she sits near it, before any birds or beasts arrive, but she has no intention of dissecting the body with a knife or with her nails; she waits for the wolves to tear it apart and then snatches the prey from their hungry throats.

She is ready to commit a murder whenever she needs the fresh blood that gushes forth when a throat is slit and whenever her ghoulish repasts require flesh that still throbs. She also slits women's wombs and delivers babies by an unnatural method, in order to offer them on a burning altar. And whenever she needs evil spirits as her henchmen, she creates them herself [by killing someone]. Every human casualty serves her in some way. She rips off the bloom on the face of a child's body, and when an adolescent dies, her left hand cuts off a lock of his hair. Quite often, when a dear relative dies, the horrible witch bends over his body, and as she kisses him, she mutilates his face and opens his closed mouth with her teeth; then she bites the tip of the tongue that lies in the dry throat, pours whispered sounds between the cold lips, and sends a secret message of horror down to the shades of Styx.

Her reputation in the country made her known to Pompey [the son], and he picked his way across deserted fields, when night occupied the high heaven, and the sun beneath our earth marked the hour of noon. Faithful, trusted creatures who assisted her in her crimes went to and fro among the ruined tombs and graves till they saw her far away, sitting on a steep rock where the Balkan mountains slope down and extend their ridges toward Pharsalia. She was experimenting with a spell unknown to other sorcerers and to the gods of witchcraft, and she composed an incantation for an unheard-of purpose. She was worried that the Civil War might wander off to some other part of the world and that Thessaly might miss this tremendous slaughter, and so the witch poisoned the countryside near Philippi [i.e., Pharsalus] with her spells and sprinkled it with her horrible drugs, to stop it from letting the War move elsewhere, because she wanted to have all those dead to herself and make use of the blood of the whole world. She was hoping to mutilate the bodies of slaughtered kings, to sweep off [reading *auerrere* for *auertere*] the ashes of the whole Roman people, and to get hold of the bones of the aristocracy, in order to control its shades. She had only one passionate concern: what part of Pompey's stretched-out corpse she might snatch, or on what limb of Caesar's she might pounce.

The worthless son of Pompey spoke first and said to her: "You are the pride of Thessalian witches. You have the power to reveal to mankind its future and the power to change the course of events. Please tell me exactly what turn the hazard of war is going to take. I am not just a Roman plebeian—I am the son of Pompey, and everyone knows me—and I shall either rule the world or inherit disaster. I am worried because my heart is struck with doubts; on the other hand, I can deal with dangers that are spelled out to me. Chance hits us unexpectedly and unforeseen—take this power away from it! Torture the gods—or leave them alone and extort the truth from the dead! Open up the seat of Elysium, summon Death himself, and force him to tell us which one of us will be his prey. It is a difficult task, I know, but it might be of interest, even to you, to find out which way the hazard of this enormous issue is going to go."

The ruthless witch is glad that her reputation is so widespread and answers: "Young man, if you wanted to change a minor decree of fate, it would be easy to force the gods into any course of action, even against their will. When the planets with their beams commit one single soul to death, witchcraft has the power to delay the event. Even if all the stars promise to people a ripe old age, we can cut short their lives by our magic herbs. But if the chain of causes goes back to the origin of the world and the universal fate suffers and you want to make a minor change, then the whole of mankind must expect one single blow, and Fortuna has more power than the Thessalian witches—we admit it. If you just want to know what will happen to you, there are many easy ways that lead to the truth: earth and sky, the seas, the plains, and the rocks of Rhodope will speak to us. But the obvious method—since there is such an abundance of men who were recently killed—would be to pick one body from the Thessalian fields; then the mouth of a corpse that is still warm because death occurred only a short time ago will speak clearly [to us], and it will not be a dismal shade, with limbs dried in the sun, hissing sounds that our ears cannot make out."

Thus the witch spoke and by her magic made the night twice as dark as before. She wrapped her sinister head in a veil of smog and moved among the bodies of the slain that had been cast out and denied burial. At once the wolves fled and the vultures pulled out their talons and flew away, still hungry; meanwhile, the witch picked out her "prophet"; she inspected the innermost organs, cold in death, and found that the tissue of the hardened lung was undamaged, and she looked for the power of speech in the dead body. Now the destiny of many men killed in battle is hanging in the balance: who is the one she might want to call back to the upper world? Had she attempted to raise a whole army of dead from the plain and make them fight again, the laws of the underworld would have yielded to her, and an entire host, brought up from Stygian Avernus by the power of a monstrous witch, would have joined the ranks.

At last she chose a corpse, inserted a hook into its throat, and attached the hook to a rope taken from the gallows [text and translation uncertain]; with this contraption she dragged the wretched corpse over rocks and stones, to bring it back to life, and placed it beneath a high rock of a hollow mountain that savage Erictho had condemned to witness her rites.

The ground there descended abruptly and led down almost as far as the dark caverns of the underworld. A gloomy wood with drooping leaves borders it, and it is shaded by yew trees that the sun cannot penetrate and that never turn their tops toward the sky. Inside the caves there is darkness and gray mold caused by eternal night; only magic can produce light. Even in the gorge of Taenarus the air is less sluggish and stagnant—it is the gloomy zone between the hidden world and our own, and the rulers of Tartarus are not afraid of letting the shades go that far. Although the Thessalian witch imposes her will on destiny, it is doubtful whether she actually sees the shades of the underworld because she has dragged them there [i.e., to her cave] or because she has descended [into the underworld] herself.

She wrapped herself in a dark, hellish robe of various shades, threw back her hair, revealed her face, and tied her shaggy locks with vipers serving as ribbons.

When she saw that young Pompey's companions grew pale and he himself trembled, she turned her lifeless face toward him, stared at him with her evil eyes, and said:

"Drop your fears! Let not your hearts flutter any more! Right now a new life, a true life, from its looks, will be given to him, so that you can hear him speak, no matter how much you are afraid. And even if I were to show you the pools of Styx, the shore that consists of hissing flames, and you could see, by my magic, the Furies, Cerberus shaking his mane of snakes, and the chained bodies of the Giants, you would have no reason to fear the shades that are afraid of me, cowards!"

Now first of all she pierced the breast of the corpse, opening new wounds in it which she filled with boiling blood. The inner organs she washed clean of gore and poured in a generous portion of moonjuice. With this she mixed everything that nature conceives and brings forth under evil stars: foam from the mouth of dogs that have rabies; the inner organs of a lynx; the lump of a frightful hyena; the marrow of a stag that had lived on a diet of snakes; the Echeneis, which holds a ship motionless in the middle of the ocean, even though the South Wind stretches her ropes; eyes of dragons; stones that produce a sound when warmed under a breeding eagle; the flying serpent of Arabia; the viper born from the Red Sea which guards the precious shell; the skin that the Libyan horn snake peels off when it is still alive; the ashes of the Phoenix, which places its body on an altar in the East. All this was there in abundance.

After she had thrown in ordinary poisons that are known by their names, she added leaves soaked in unutterable spells and herbs on which her own disgusting mouth had spat when they first appeared and all the poisons that she herself had given to the world.

Finally her voice, more capable than any herb of invoking the powers of hell, first uttered inarticulate sounds that seemed completely different from human speech. You could hear the barking of dogs in that voice, the howling of wolves, the moaning of the restless owl and of the screech owl that flies by night, the shrieking and roaring of a wild beast, the hiss of a serpent, the sound of waves beating against rocks, of forests in the wind, the thunder that detonates from a cloud—all these noises were in her voice. Then she wrapped the rest in a Thessalian spell, and her voice reached as far as the Tartarus:

"Furies! Horrors of hell! Sinners that are tortured! Chaos, eager to destroy countless worlds! Ruler of the underworld, who suffers for endless centuries because the death of the [heavenly] gods does not come soon enough! Styx! Elysium, where no Thessalian witch is allowed to enter! Persephone, who hates her mother in heaven! Hecate, third personification of my own goddess, who enables me to communicate with the dead without speaking! Custodian of the vast domain, who feeds the savage Dog with bits of human flesh! Sisters who must now spin a second thread of life! Ancient Ferryman of the burning waves, who is exhausted from rowing back the shades to me! Listen to my prayer!

"If these lips of mine that call you have been tainted sufficiently with crime, if I have always eaten human flesh before chanting such spells, if I have often cut open human breasts still full of life divine and washed them out with warm brains, if any baby could have lived, once his head and inner organs were placed on your dishes—grant me my prayer!

"I am not asking for a shade lurking in the depths of Tartarus, a shade that has become accustomed to darkness long ago; no, I am asking for one that has just left the light and was on his way down; he still lingers at the very entrance of the chasm that leads down to gloomy Orcus, and even though he obeys my spell, he will join the Manes just once. Let a shade who was just recently one of Pompey's soldiers tell his son the whole future; and remember that you ought to be grateful for the Civil War!"

When she had spoken these words, she raised her head, her mouth foaming, and saw beside her the ghost of the unburied corpse. It was afraid of the lifeless body, the hated confinement of its former prison, and it shrank from entering the wound in the breast, the inner organs, and the tissue split open by the fatal wound. Poor wretch! You are cruelly deprived of death's last gift: the inability to die [a second time].

Erictho wonders that the Fates had the power to cause this delay. Angry at Death, she whips the motionless corpse with a live snake, and through the chinks in the ground which she had opened up with her spells, she barks at the shades and breaks the silence of their realm:

"Tisiphone and Megara! Are you listening to me? Will you not use your savage whips to drive his wretched soul through the wasteland of Erebus? Just wait, I shall conjure you up by your real names and abandon you, hounds of hell, in the light of the upper world. Over graves and burial grounds I shall follow you and watch you and drive you away from every tomb and every urn! And you, Hecate, with your pale and morbid aspect, whose face is usually different, made-up, when you visit the gods [above], I shall show you to them as you really are and forbid you to change your hellish face! Shall I tell what kind of food it is that keeps you there, Persephone, under the huge mass of earth, what bond of love unites you with the gloomy king of night, what defilement you suffered to make your mother not want to call you back? On you, lowest of the rulers of the world, I shall focus the sun breaking open your caves, and suddenly daylight will hit you. Will you obey? Or must I recruit him who always makes the earth tremble when his name is invoked, who can look at the Gorgon's head unveiled, who lashes a frightened Fury with her own whip, who dwells in the part of Tartarus that is hidden from your view, for whom you are the 'gods above,' who commits perjury in the name of Styx?"

At once the clotted blood began to boil, heated the blackish wounds, circulated in the body, and reached the extremities of the limbs. Struck by it, the vital tissues in the cold breast began to vibrate, new life stole into organs unaccustomed to it and struggled with death. Every limb began to shake, the sinews stretched, and the corpse, far from rising slowly, limb by limb, from the ground, jumped up as if rebounding from the earth and stood at once erect. His eyelids were wide open, his eyeballs bare. His face was not yet that of a living person; it looked as if he were already dead. He remained pale and stiff and in a daze, thrust upon the world as he was. His lips were locked and produced no sound; voice and utterance were only given to him in order that he might deliver an oracle.

The witch said: "Tell me what I want to know, and your reward will be great, for if you speak the truth, I shall make you safe from witchcraft as long as the world lasts. On such a pyre, with such fuel, shall I cremate your corpse, chanting at the same time a Stygian spell, so that your shade will never have to respond to the incantations of any witch. This privilege should make it worth your while to have lived twice: neither spells nor herbs will venture to interrupt your long sleep of oblivion, once I have given you death. From the tripod [of Delphi] and the prophets of the gods one expects an ambiguous answer, but whoever seeks the truth from the shades and has the nerve to approach the oracles of grim death must leave with clear information. Please do not hold back anything: tell me what will happen and where; provide the voice through which Fate may speak to me."

She added a spell which furnished to the ghost the knowledge of all she was asking.

The dead man, looking sad and shedding many tears, spoke. "You have called me back from the high shore of the silent river; there I did not see the Fates spinning their gloomy threads, but I learned from all the dead that a terrible strife divides the dead Romans and that our Civil War has shattered the peace of the underworld. Some great Romans have left the Elysian fields; others come from gloomy Tartarus [reading *Elysias alii sedes, at Tartara maesta / diuersi liquere duces*]. They revealed (to me) what the Fates have in store. The blessed shades looked sad; I saw the Decii, father and son, who had devoted their lives to the gods in battle; Camillus and the Curii were crying; and Sulla protested against Rome's fortune. Scipio was mourning because an unlucky descendant of his was destined to perish on Libyan soil; and Cato, an even fiercer enemy of Carthage [than Scipio], lamented the death that his descendant prefers to slavery. Only one of the blessed shades did I see rejoicing: the first consul after the expulsion of the kings, Brutus.

"But dangerous Catiline had torn and broken his fetters and was exulting, and so were fierce Marius and Cethegus with the naked arm. I saw the delight of Drusus, that famous demagogue who had proposed unreasonable laws; I saw the delight of the Gracchi, who had tried the impossible. Their hands were chained by everlasting links of steel, and they [themselves] were locked in the prison of Hades, but they applauded, and the whole bunch of criminals demanded the fields of the blessed. The king of the stagnant realm opened wide his gloomy residence; he sharpened steep rocks and hard steel for fetters and prepared tortures for the victor. But take this consolation with you, son of Pompey: the dead are looking forward to welcoming your father and his family in a quiet retreat, and they are reserving a place for the house of Pompey in the brighter region of their kingdom. Let not the glory of a short life trouble you; the hour will come that wipes out the distinction between the leaders. Hurry up and die, be proud of your great soul when you descend from graves, however small, and trample on the shades of the gods of Rome. Whose grave will be near the Nile, and whose near the Tiber? That is the question, and [in the end] the [whole] battle between the two rivals is merely about their place of burial. Do not ask about your own destiny: the Fates will reveal it to you, and I shall be silent; your father himself, a more reliable prophet, will tell you everything [when he appears to you] on Sicilian soil, and even he will not know where to summon you and whence to keep you away. . . . [*A spurious line follows in the text.*] Beware of Europe, Africa, and Asia Minor, poor wretches; Fortune will divide [reading *distribuet*] your tombs among the lands over which you once triumphed, and in all the world you will find no safer place than Pharsalus."

Having delivered his prophecy he stood there in silence and sorrow and pleaded to die once more. Magic spells and herbs were needed before the corpse could die, and death, having used up its powers already, could not claim his life again. The witch now built an enormous pyre of wood. The dead man walked to the fire, and Erictho left him there, stretched out on the lighted pile, and allowed him finally to die. She then walked back with Sextus to his father's camp. The sky was now taking on the color of dawn, but she ordered night to hold back day and give them thick darkness, until they set foot safely within the encampment.

59

When the great oracles of the ancient world—Delphi, for example—began to lose their prestige, a good deal of concern arose among pagan theologians and philosophers. Plutarch, the Platonist, who had held a priesthood for life at Delphi since A.D. 95, devoted one of his treatises to the problem. The theory he seemed to favor is this: Not the gods themselves—the Apollo of Delphi, for instance—but some minor deities, are responsible for the maintenance, the continuity, of the oracular spirits at the famous shrines. Unlike the Olympian gods, these daemons grow old and finally, after many centuries, die. It is an interesting theory, for it implies the belief in a cosmic force that is more concentrated or more intense at certain points on the globe than at others. When this force is detected at a certain place, that place becomes "holy." But if the force gradually vanishes, the holy place will be deserted.

To illustrate his point, Plutarch tells the famous story of the death of "the Great Pan," who was clearly a powerful daemon; the lesser daemons knew at once their time had come when they heard of his death.

Substituting mere daemons for the Olympians helped uphold the prestige of the ancient gods against the skepticism of some philosophical schools and the attacks of the Christians. In the end, the Christians claimed that no valid distinction could be drawn between such gods and daemons.

Plutarch, *On the Cessation of Oracles*, pp. 418E–419E

[*Cleombrotus, one of the participants in the dialogue, has just proposed a theory that daemons or minor gods, not any of the major divinities, are responsible for the oracles. This theory does not appeal to Heracleon, another participant in the dialogue.*]

"That it is not the gods," said Heracleon, "who are in charge of the oracles, since the gods ought to be free of earthly concerns, but that daemons, the servants of the gods, are in charge does not seem such a bad idea to me, but to take, by the handful, so to speak, lines from Empedocles and impose on these daemons sins and delusions and errors sent by the gods, and to assume that they finally die, as if they were men—this seems to me a little too rash and uncivilized."

At this point Cleombrotus asked Philip who this young man [i.e., Heracleon] was and whence he came, and after learning his name and his city, he said: "Heracleon, we have become involved in strange discussions, but we know what we are doing. When you discuss important ideas, you need important principles if you want to come anywhere near the truth. But you are inconsistent, because you take back something that you just granted: you agree that daemons exist, but by denying that they can be bad and mortal, you no longer admit that they are daemons. For in what respect are they different from the gods if, as regards their substance, they possess immortality and, as regards their qualities, freedom from emotion and sin?"

As Heracleon was silently thinking about this, Philip said: "No, Heracleon, we have inherited bad daemons not only from Empedocles but also from Platon, Xenocrates and Chrysippus, and Democritus, too, who by his prayer to meet 'propitious daemons' clearly acknowledged the existence of another class—tricky and full of evil intentions and urges. As to the question whether daemons can die, I have heard a story from a man who was neither a fool nor an impostor. The father of Aemilianus, the professor of rhetoric whose students some of you have been, was called Epiterses; he was a school teacher and lived in the same town I did. He told me that he once made a trip to Italy and embarked on a ship that carried commercial goods and a large number of passengers. It was already evening; they were near the Echinades Islands. The wind dropped, and the ship drifted near Paxi.

"Many of the passengers were awake, and some were still drinking after having finished their dinner. Suddenly a voice was heard from Paxi loudly calling 'Thamus! Thamus!' Everybody was astonished. Thamus happened to be our pilot, an Egyptian, but he was not known by name even to many of us on board. The voice called twice, and he remained silent, but the third time, he answered. The caller, raising his voice, now said: 'When you get across to Palodes, announce that the Great Pan is dead.' On hearing this, Epitherses said, everybody was amazed, and they argued among themselves whether it might be better to do what they were told or not to get involved in something and let the matter go. So Thamus decided that if there should be a breeze he would sail past and say nothing, but with no wind and a smooth sea all around he would announce what he had been told. When he came near Palodes, and there was no wind, no wave, Thamus looked from the stern toward the land and said the words as he had heard them: 'The Great Pan is dead.' He had not yet finished when there was much wailing, not just from one person, but from many, mingled with shouts of amazement. Since there were many persons on board, the story soon spread in all of Rome, and Thamus was sent for by the emperor Tiberius. Tiberius became so convinced that the story was true that he ordered a thorough investigation concerning Pan; the scholars at his court—and there were many of them—guessed that he was the son of Hermes and Penelope."

But Philip also had several witnesses among those present; they had heard the story from Aemilianus when he was an old man.

Demetrius said that among the islands near the coast of Britain many were isolated and deserted, and some had the names of daemons and heroes. He himself, by order of the emperor, had made a voyage of exploration and observation to the nearest of these islands. It had only a few inhabitants: holy men who are all considered inviolate by the Britons. Soon after his arrival there was great tumult in the air and many portents were observed: thunder exploded and lightning hit the earth. When things had quieted down, the people on the island said that one of the more powerful spirits had passed away. . . .

60

In the dialogue *On the Cessation of Oracles* Plutarch also discusses daemons in general. He tends to dissociate the gods from any direct contact with human beings and to introduce daemons as intermediaries. In referring to Hesiod [*no. 51*], he interprets—correctly, it would seem—Hesiod's distinction between good and bad daemons. His attempt to compute the average life expectancy of a daemon seems a little far-fetched, but his description of the transformation of bodies and souls is beautiful, for it asserts the reality of a higher, spiritual order of existence.

Plutarch, *On the Cessation of Oracles*, pp. 414E–415D

[*Lamprias says:*] It is really naïve and childish to believe that the god himself . . . enters the body of the prophet and speaks forth, using his lips and his voice as an instrument. For if you mix up a god with human functions, you violate his majesty and you disregard his dignity and the excellence of his nature.

[*Cleombrotus answers:*] You are right, but since it is difficult to grasp and define how Providence enters and to what point one should let it enter, some maintain that the god has absolutely nothing to do with it, while others see in him the cause of everything. Both positions are equally far from a balanced and responsible view. I agree with those who say that Plato, when he discovered the element which underlies all created qualities—the element which is now called "matter" and "nature"—relieved philosophers of many serious problems. But there are those who have discovered that the race of daemons, halfway between gods and men, communicates between the gods and mankind and establishes a relationship between them and us. It is irrelevant whether this theory goes back to the *magi* who followed Zoroaster or is Thracian and belongs to Orpheus, or is Egyptian or Phrygian, as we may guess from seeing how the ritual of both [of the latter] countries includes many themes relating to death and mourning, and that these form part of their ceremonies and liturgies.

Among the Greeks, Homer seems to use both terms indifferently. He sometimes calls the gods "daemons." Hesiod was the first to distinguish clearly and explicitly between three different classes of rational beings: the gods, the heroes, and mankind. This means that he believed in a transformation by which the men of the Golden Age became good daemons in great numbers, and by which some of the demigods were admitted to the ranks of the heroes.

Others assume a transformation of bodies as well as of souls. Just as one sees water generated from earth, air from water, fire from air, as matter moves upward, thus the superior souls undergo a transformation from men to heroes and from heroes to daemons, but from the rank of daemons only a few are purified over a long period of time because of their excellence and come to partake altogether in divine nature. But it also happens that some of them cannot gain control over themselves and are degraded and clothed once more in mortal bodies and have a dark, dim life, like mist.

Hesiod also thinks that death comes to daemons at the end of certain periods of time. . . .

The sum total of a daemon's life span is nine thousand seven hundred and twenty years. . . .

61

In this passage from his dialogue *On the Cessation of Oracles*, Plutarch makes the point that the gods do not operate directly; rather, they communicate through daemons, their servants, messengers, assistants, or secretaries. Daemons, for example, supervise sacrifices and mystery rites; they punish the guilty and sustain the oracles.

Plutarch, *On the Cessation of Oracles*, pp. 418C–D

Allow me to bring this preliminary discussion to a suitable conclusion, for we now have reached that point. Let us venture to say, too, after so many others have said it, that when daemons in charge of divination vanish, the oracles vanish along with them and are gone. When daemons go into exile or emigrate, the oracles lose their power, but when the daemons come back, even after a long time, the oracles speak again, like musical instruments when there are players to use them.

62

In his treatise *On Isis and Osiris*, Plutarch offers further speculations on the nature of daemons. He quotes from Hesiod, Empedocles, Plato, and

Plato's disciple Xenocrates, who has been called "the father of scientific daemonology." The emphasis here is on evil daemons. Some of them are what we would call the "fallen angels" of pagan antiquity. Others seem to be evil by nature—for example, Typhon, who in the myth and ritual of Isis and Osiris, represents the eternal villain, the permanent antagonist in a kind of cosmic drama between benevolent and malevolent deities.

To Plutarch, who witnessed the rapid growth of the Isis cult during his lifetime, these Egyptian deities, even the good ones, looked like daemons that had been promoted to higher ranks in return for exceptionally good behavior. In other words, Plutarch was pragmatic enough to recognize a measure of success even in the religious sphere. Isis and Osiris were definitely not part of the Greek Pantheon, but the appeal of their cult in the late Hellenistic and early Imperial periods is a fact. According to Plutarch, their success as deities was based on a kind of advancement within a divine hierarchy which, of course, required the approval of all the highest authorities and was, therefore, acceptable. This spiritual advancement reflects the hierarchies that we already know on earth, and thus our search for the highest powers must go on.

Plutarch, *On Isis and Osiris*, pp. 361A–E

It would seem that daemons have a complex and abnormal nature and purpose; hence Plato assigns to the Olympian gods that which is on the right side and odd numbers, and to the daemons the opposite of these. Xenocrates believes that unlucky days and all holidays that are characterized by beatings or lamentations or fasting or bad language or obscene jokes are not proper occasions for honoring gods and good daemons. He believes that there are in the atmosphere great, powerful presences that are also ill-tempered and unpleasant and enjoy the sort of thing just mentioned and, if they get it, cause no further trouble.

Hesiod calls the good, kindly daemons "holy daemons" and "guardians of mankind," and he says that "they give wealth, which is their royal privilege."

Plato calls this category "interpreting" and "ministering," halfway between gods and men, carrying upward the prayers and wishes of men and bringing to us from the realm of the gods oracles and welcome gifts.

Empedocles says that daemons get punished for the bad things they do and the duties they neglect: "The power of aether drives them into the sea; / the sea spits them out onto the soil of the earth; / the earth sends them to the rays of the tireless sun; / and the sun throws them into the whirlpool of aether: / one region takes them from another, and they all hate them." The daemons are punished and purified up to the point when they take back the nature and rank that are naturally theirs.

Stories like these and similar ones are told, they say, about Typhon. His jealousy and vicious temper made him do terrible things: he stirred up everything and flooded the whole earth and the sea with evils. Later, he had to pay the penalty. The avenger was Isis, the sister-wife of Osiris: she quenched the insane fury of Typhon and put an end to it. But then she did not simply forget the struggles and trials that she had been through, or her wanderings and the many brave and wise things that she had done. She would not accept silence and oblivion, but into the holiest ritual [=the initiation rites of the Isis mysteries?] she introduced symbols and representations of her former sufferings. She sanctified these as a lesson in piety and an encouragement for men and women who are the victims of similar predicaments. She and Osiris were promoted to the rank of gods from that of benevolent daemons because of their admirable conduct. This happened later to Heracles and Dionysus. It seems appropriate that they receive joint honors as gods and daemons. Their power is everywhere, but especially in the regions above the earth and beneath the earth. . . .

63

Many ancient philosophers wrote "Consolations" to their friends and patrons and even to themselves to give help and comfort in times of bereavement. Two essays or addresses of this kind are attributed to Plutarch: one to his wife on the death of their child; the other to Apollonius, a friend. The following text probably was not written by Plutarch, but it represents the genre quite well.

One of the arguments used in this kind of literature goes as follows: Death is not the evil which most people consider it to be; it is, in fact, a blessing. A few stories are then told to illustrate this truth. In the present text the third story is particularly important, for it documents the existence, in antiquity, of "oracles of the dead" (*psychomanteia* 'soul oracles'). In this case the oracle is consulted not about the future but about the past: A father has suddenly lost his only child and suspects foul play. He visits a *psychomanteion*, probably the one at Cumae, near Naples, which is associated with the famous sibyl (see Virg., *Aen.* 6). There he offers a sacrifice, falls asleep, and has a vision. The procedure is a form of incubation, although in this case the vision is sought not for the sake of finding a cure for a disease but in order to establish a fact in the past. It might be said, however, that the father's anxieties and suspicions about his son's death could easily have become an obsession and manifested itself in a nervous disorder. At the same time, he simply wants to know the truth, and the truth is revealed to him by two *psychai* 'souls', that of his father and that of his son. The message that the "soul," or "daemon," of his son delivers to Elysius (the name sounds as if it had been invented for the occasion) is simply that we do not know what death really is and that people die because their natural time has come, even if we do not understand it.

The story may be unhistorical, but it shows that the Greeks and Romans believed in various means of communicating with the dead. Dreams were one of them. The special function of the *psychomanteion* was to set up the conditions under which such dreams would occur. The technique or techniques used were probably similar to those employed for incubations.

Plutarch, *Consolation Addressed to Apollonius,* pp. 109A–D

Pindar tells us that Agamedes and Trophonius, after having built the temple of Delphi, demanded their pay from Apollo. The god answered that he would pay them seven days later and urged them, in the meantime, to enjoy themselves. They did as they were told, and on the seventh night they died in their sleep.

The delegates of the Boeotians went to Delphi to consult the god, and Pindar is supposed to have told them to ask the question, "What is best for man?" The priestess answered that he ought to know the answer, if he really was the author of the story about Trophonius and Agamedes. On the other hand, if he wanted to find out by himself, it would become clear to him in the near future. From this response Pindar concluded that he should prepare himself for death, and in fact he died shortly afterward.

And here is the story about the Italian [i.e., South-Italian Greek] Euthynous. He was the son of Elysius of Terina, a prominent man in that community because of his qualities, his wealth, and his reputation. Euthynous died suddenly, and no one knew why. It occurred to Elysius—as it might have occurred to anyone—that perhaps his son had died of poisoning, for he was his only child, destined to inherit a substantial fortune. Because he did not know how to verify this suspicion, he went to an oracle of the dead [*psychomanteion*]. After he had offered the prescribed sacrifices, he fell asleep and had a vision. His father appeared to him, coming toward him. When Elysius saw his father, he told him in detail everything that had happened to his son and urged and implored him to find the cause of death. His father answered: "This is exactly why I came. Take from this person here the object that he brings to you. From this you will find out everything that distresses you." The person he pointed out was a young man who followed him and resembled Euthynous [the son], both in age and in stature. When he asked him who he was, the young man replied: "I am the soul [literally, the daemon] of your son." And as he said this, he gave the father a little scroll. Elysius unrolled it and saw written on it three lines:

Truly, the minds of men are lost in ignorance.
Euthynous died a natural death, in accordance with fate.
It was not right for him to live, nor for his parents.

This is what you can read in the accounts of ancient writers.

64

Here we have a piece of folklore that was not included in the *Odyssey*,
though it may be quite old. One of Odysseus' companions keeps plagu-
ing the inhabitants of a Sicilian town who had stoned him to death for
raping a local girl. The Delphic oracle is consulted and supports the
daemon, because he was a hero, after all, and a cult is established in his
honor. Every year the most beautiful girl in the whole community must be
given to the daemon-hero as his wife. What is meant by the word *given* is
not quite clear, but the context seems to suggest a human sacrifice, not
just a *hieros gamos* 'sacred wedding', or a ritual rape. The girl either died or
disappeared, it would seem. The real hero of the story, a famous boxer,
Euthymus, falls in love with the intended victim and wrestles with the
daemon, just as Heracles wrestled with Death in Euripides' *Alcestis*, driving him "out of the land." Euthymus then marries the girl, and they live
happily thereafter: in fact, he never dies, but becomes a daemon (a good
one, no doubt) himself. Pausanias saw a painting, a copy of a much older
original, which illustrated this quaint story. In it the evil daemon, Lycas
by name, appears as an "awfully black" figure, terrifying in appearance,
dressed in a wolf's skin (*lykos* means "wolf" in Greek). Perhaps this is the
origin of the story of Dracula and the wolf-man. It should be noted that
throughout the story the terms *hero* and *daemon* are used interchangeably.

Pausanias, *Description of Greece* 6.6

[*Euthymus was a famous boxer; he was born in Southern Italy and returned there
after one of his Olympic victories.*]

When Euthymus had returned to Italy he fought the Hero. This is the
story. During Odysseus' wanderings after the fall of Troy, they say that he
was carried by winds to some of the cities of Italy and Sicily. He landed
with his ships at Temesa. One of the sailors got drunk and raped a young
woman, and for this crime he was stoned to death by the villagers. Odysseus paid no attention whatsoever to the death of this man and sailed
away, but the daemon of the man who had been stoned to death by the
people never missed an opportunity to murder someone in Temesa, attacking all age groups. Finally the whole population was ready to leave
Temesa and Italy altogether, but the Pythia would not let them. She told
them to appease the Hero by measuring out for him a holy precinct,

building him a temple, and giving him as his wife every year the most beautiful young woman to be found in Temesa. They did, of course, what the god had ordered, and the daemon did not terrorize them any further.

Euthymus happened to come to Temesa at the time when the customary tribute was paid to the daemon. When he found out about their problem he expressed the wish to enter the temple and have a look at the girl. When he saw her, his first reaction was to feel sorry for her, but his second was to fall in love. The girl swore to marry him if he saved her. Euthymus prepared himself and waited for the entrance of the daemon. He fought him and won, and the Hero—since he had been driven out of the land—dived into the sea and disappeared. Euthymus had a splendid wedding, and the people there were free forever from the daemon.

I also heard another story about Euthymus: he reached a ripe old age and managed to escape death, leaving human life in some different way. . . . This is what I have heard, but I also know the following from a painting that I happened to see. It was a copy of an older painting. There is young Sybaris and the river Calabrus and the spring Lyca, and a hero's sanctuary nearby and the city of Temesa. Among these figures there is also the daemon whom Euthymus drove out: his color is terribly dark, and he is really terrifying to look at; a wolf's skin serves as his dress, and according to an inscription on the painting his name was "Wolf-Man."

65

The story of Thelyphron is a tragicomic episode in Apuleius' novel, *Metamorphoses*. Apuleius was interested in witchcraft himself, and the novel undoubtedly has autobiographical elements. This particular episode reflects the popular belief that witches needed corpses or parts of them for their magical operations; therefore, corpses had to be guarded carefully until they were cremated. People who could afford it hired a guard. Here, a young man who desperately needs money takes on a job that turns out not to be as easy as it appeared. In the course of the story the corpse is called back to life twice, once in secret by the witches and once in front of a crowd by a famous Egyptian "prophet"—that is, a necromancer—dressed in linen robes, with palm-leaf sandals on his feet and a shaven head. As in *no. 63*, the circumstances of his death are cleared up by the dead man himself.

Apuleius, *Metamorphoses*, or *The Golden Ass*, 2.21–30

When I was still a minor under the care of a ward, I traveled from Miletus to the games in Olympia, and since I also wanted to visit this famous province, I wandered through all of Thessaly and arrived in Larissa under an unlucky star. My travel funds were quite low, and I felt so poor that I walked all over the place looking for help. In the middle of the mar-

ketplace I saw a tall, elderly man. He was standing on a stone and announced in a loud voice that he was hiring someone to guard a corpse. I
said to a passer-by: "What is this I hear? Are the corpses in this country in
the habit of running away?" He answered: "Hush! You are obviously very
young and very much a stranger, and so of course you don't know that
you are in Thessaly, where the witches generally gnaw the flesh off dead
men's faces and use it as an ingredient in their magic." I said: "Could you
please tell me what it involves to stand guard over a corpse?" He replied:
"Well, first one has to remain completely awake all night, the eyes wide
open, never closed for a second, and always concentrated on the corpse;
one must never take them off [it], not even glance sideways, because the
evil witches can transform themselves into any animal they like and
approach so stealthily that they can even deceive the eyes of the Sun and
of Justice with great ease. They take on the shape of birds or dogs or mice
or even that of flies. By their horrible spells they manage to put the guards
to sleep. No one can say for sure what tricks these vicious women invent
to satisfy their lust. And yet for this wretched job the pay is usually not
higher than four or six ducats. Oh—I almost forgot to tell you: if the
corpse is not delivered intact in the morning, the guard must furnish from
his own face that part that has been eaten off the corpse and is missing."

When I heard this I mustered up my courage, approached the
crier at once, and said to him: "You need not shout any more. Here is your
guard, ready. Let me have the pay." He answered: "A thousand drachmas
will be deposited in your name. But listen, young man: you must be very
careful if you want to watch this corpse and guard it properly against
those awful harpies; he is the son of one of the chief men in the city." I
said: "Don't be ridiculous. Save your worry. You see before you a man of
iron who never sleeps and has sharper eyesight than Lynceus or Argus—
who is, in fact, all eyes." I had hardly finished speaking when he quickly
led me to a house whose main entrance was locked. He took me through a
small back door and opened a dark room with closed windows. Then he
showed me a weeping lady all in black, walked up to her and said to her:
"Here is the man I hired; he has taken the responsibility of guarding your
husband." She pushed back the hair that hung into her face on both sides,
showed a face that was impressive even in mourning, and said, looking at
me: "I beg you, make sure you do a really good job." I said: "Don't worry,
just add a good tip."

She agreed, got up, and led me into another room. There she
showed me a body covered with a shiny linen shroud, which she herself
removed in the presence of seven witnesses. She wept over him for a long
time and then appealed to the conscience of all those present as she
pointed out the parts of the body while someone carefully took an inventory in legal language: "Look," she said, "the nose is there, the eyes
are unhurt, the ears in good shape, the lips not damaged, the chin in one

piece. You are witnesses to this, fellow citizens." When the inventory was signed and sealed, and she was about to leave, I said to her: "Madam, will you arrange for me to have everything I need?" She asked: "Well, what do you need?" I answered: "A fairly large lamp and enough oil to last till daybreak, warm water with a few flasks of wine, a cup, and a plate full of leftovers." But she shook her head and said: "Leave me alone, you fool. You want to dine and have a good time in a house of mourning in which for days and days not even a smoke was seen? Do you think you have come here for a party? Don't you think it would be more appropriate to the occasion to mourn and weep?" As she said this she looked at a maid and said: "Quick, Myrrhine, give him a lamp and oil, lock him in the room to do his job, and leave at once."

Thus left alone, I rubbed my eyes to comfort the corpse and to keep myself awake during the vigil, and I sang to amuse myself. Twilight fell and turned into night, and night grew deeper, and it was really time to go to sleep, and it was probably past midnight. I was scared to death, especially when all of a sudden a weasel slipped in and stood there looking at me intently. The nerve of the tiny animal annoyed me. I said: "Move on, you filthy creature, and get back to the likes of you in the garden before I let you have it. What are you waiting for?" It turned around and disappeared from the room at once. Almost immediately I fell into a deep sleep—it was like sinking into a bottomless pit—and even the Delphic oracle could not have determined which of the two of us lying there was more dead than the other. I was practically lifeless, nonexistent, and needed a guard myself.

The peace—or truce—of the night was broken by the crowing of the "crested watch." I finally woke up in a state of terror and ran over to the corpse. I held the lamp close to see his face clearly and checked all the details. Everything seemed to be in order. At this moment the poor widow, still weeping, burst into the room, accompanied by the witnesses of the evening before. She threw herself on the body, kissed it again and again for a long time, and then, guided by the lamp, registered everything. She turned around and called for her steward Philodespotus and told him: "Give this fine guard his pay at once." It was handed out to me and she said: "I thank you very much, young man. You have done me a tremendous service, and you will be a friend of the family from now on." I was absolutely overjoyed at this unexpected benefit and at the bright gold coins I was tossing up in my hand, and I said to her: "But madam, please consider me one of your servants, and whenever you need my help be sure to call on me." I had hardly said this when all her people jumped on me, called me a scoundrel, cursed me, and attacked me with all kinds of improvised weapons: one of them boxed me in the face, another dug his elbows into my back, a third hit me in the ribs hard; they kicked me, pulled my hair, tore my clothes. I was almost torn to pieces, just like

Adonis [text uncertain], that arrogant youth, or Musaeus or Orpheus [?], and kicked out of the house in terrible shape.

I stopped in the next street and recovered somewhat, and as I remembered my tactless and ill-omened remark, I had to admit to myself that I deserved even more beatings than I had received. Meanwhile, the dead body had been mourned and saluted for the last time and was now being carried according to ancient tradition (he belonged, after all, to the aristocracy) in a solemn funeral procession across the marketplace.

An older man in black, looking sad and crying as he tore his fine white hair, approached the bier, clutched it with both hands, and cried, his voice tense and choking with sobs: "Fellow citizens! I appeal to your sense of honor and your love for our city! This man has been murdered! Help! A shocking deed has been done, and you must punish this evil, wicked woman drastically. She and no one else has poisoned this poor young man, my nephew, to oblige her lover and to inherit her husband's estate!" Thus the old man continued to appeal to one person after another with pitiful complaints. The crowd went wild, and since such a crime seemed plausible, they were ready to believe it. People shouted for fire, demanded stones, and incited a bunch of young men to kill the woman. She produced well-rehearsed tears and, calling on all the gods, swore in the language of true religion that she could never have committed such a horrible crime.

The old man said: "Let us leave the judgment of truth to divine providence. Here is Zatchlas, an outstanding Egyptian necromancer who has made an agreement with me some time ago to bring back briefly, for a considerable fee, the spirit of the young man from the underworld and to revive his body by restoring it back to life from death." As he said this he brought forward a young man dressed in linen robes, with palm-leaf sandals on his feet, his head completely shaven. The old man kissed his hands repeatedly and touched his knees; then he said: "Reverend sir, have mercy, have mercy! I implore you by the stars of heaven, by the gods of the underworld, by the elements of nature, by the silence of the night and the hidden things of Coptus and the flooding of the Nile and the mysteries of Memphis and the sacred rattles of Pharus! Grant him the brief enjoyment of sunshine! Pour a little light into eyes that are shut forever! I am not quarreling with fate, nor am I denying the earth what belongs to it: I only ask for a few spare moments of life to have at least the consolation of revenge." The necromancer, favorably impressed by these words, placed a magic herb on the lips of the dead man and another on his breast. Then he turned to the east and prayed in silence to the glorious Sun for success. The whole scenario looked so impressive that all those present could hardly wait to see a tremendous miracle happen.

I managed to push my way into the crowd and to climb up on a slightly raised stone directly behind the bier, and I watched everything with great interest. Soon the breast of the corpse began to heave as breath returned to it; the vein of life began to pulsate; the whole body was filled with spirit. The corpse sat up, and it was the young man who spoke: "Why did you have to call me back briefly to the business of life when I had already my drink of Lethe and was floating on the Stygian swamp? Leave me alone, I beg you, leave me alone, and allow me to have my peace." This was the voice we heard coming from the body. The prophet sounded a little more excited as he cried: "Why don't you reveal and relate to the people all the hidden details of your death? Don't you realize that I am able to invoke the Furies with my incantations and have your weary limbs tormented?" The one on the bier understood this and with a deep sigh addressed the people: "I have been finished off by the evil practices of my young bride; she sentenced me to drink poison; the bed I had to vacate for her adulterous lover was still warm." That fine wife of his showed great presence of mind and without any regard for the gods argued stubbornly with her husband, who argued back. The crowd got all heated up, but people disagreed violently: some wanted to see that wicked woman buried alive at once with the body of her husband; others insisted that the false testimony of a corpse ought not to be accepted.

The whole disagreement was settled by the following words of the young husband. With another deep sigh he said: "I will give you clear proof of the truth and nothing but the truth, and I will tell you something that absolutely no one else can know." He pointed his finger at me and continued: "This is the man who guarded my corpse throughout the whole night most conscientiously and carefully while the witches were waiting to attack my remains. To this purpose they had taken on various shapes, but in vain, for they were unable to fool his vigilance and dedication. Finally they enveloped him in a cloud of sleep, and when he was buried in deep slumber they kept calling my name again and again, until my lifeless limbs and my cold body clumsily and reluctantly obeyed their magic commands. Now this man was alive, of course, but he slept like a corpse, and since he had no idea that his name was the same as mine, he stood up and walked around without resisting, exactly like a ghost. Even though the doors of the room had been carefully locked, through a tiny hole in the wall they cut off first his nose and then his ears. So he suffered mutilation in my place. To improve on their deceit they glued on his head a pair of wax ears shaped exactly like the ones they had cut off, and they also gave him a fake nose. And now, there he is, poor fellow. He thinks he was rewarded for his dedication, but he was rewarded for his mutilation!"

I was horrified as he said this, and tried to touch my face. I grabbed my nose: it came off. I felt my ears: they just dropped. Everyone pointed at me and wagged their heads, and there was thunderous laughter. Bursting into a cold sweat, I tried to escape between the legs of the people standing there. And I was never able to go home again, mutilated and ridiculous as I was, but I let my hair grow on both sides to cover the place where my ears had been, and for cosmetic reasons I glued a compact bandage on my face to make up for the lack of my nose.

66

According to his biographer, Philostratus, Apollonius of Tyana, the philosopher and miracle-worker, was successful as an exorcist. The young man he healed is described as a "playboy" who belonged to an ancient family and whose problem had not been recognized until Apollonius came to town. The reference to "singers on wheels" is curious; apparently these were ambulant satirists who used their carriages as platforms. The practice seems to have survived in the context of the carnival along the Rhine, from Basel to Cologne.

    The exorcism worked by Apollonius is different from Jesus' miracles. The way this daemon responds to the philosopher, and the feat he performs for the benefit of the crowd—to prove that he really is a daemon—seem unique. After he is healed, the young man naturally becomes a disciple of Apollonius.

    The act of exorcism is quite simple: an angry look and a stern admonition from the master are enough to drive the daemon out.

Philostratus, *Life of Apollonius of Tyana* 4.20

Apollonius was discussing the problem of libations, and a young playboy happened to be present at his lecture. The young man had such a terrible reputation that he had once been the target of songs from "cabarets-on-wheels." He was from Corcyra and traced his pedigree back to Alcinous the Phaeacian, the host of Odysseus. Apollonius went on about libations and urged his audience not to drink from one particular cup but to keep it for the gods without touching it or drinking from it. At one point he urged them to have handles attached to the cup and to pour the libation over the handle, this being the part from which men practically never drink. The young man burst into loud, vulgar laughter. Apollonius looked at him and said: "It is not you who behave in an insulting manner, but the daemon who drives you to do this, and you don't know it." The young man actually had no idea that he was possessed. He used to laugh at things that made no one else laugh, and then fall to weeping without any reason, and he used to talk and sing to himself. Now, most people thought it was the exuberance of youth that led him into these moods, but actually he was the mouthpiece of the daemon, and he seemed to be drunk when he was not [text uncertain]. When Apollonius looked at him, the ghost [in him] began to cry in fear and anger—it sounded like people being burned and racked—and swore to leave the young man alone and never possess any person again. Apollonius spoke angrily to him, the way a master speaks to a shifty, scheming, shameless slave, and ordered him to leave the young man alone and show by a sign that he had done so. The daemon said: "Yes, I will throw down that statue over there," and he pointed at one of the statues in the King's Portico, for this is where all this took place. Now, it would be impossible to describe the commotion of the crowd and the way they clapped their hands in wonder when the statue first began to sway gently and then crashed down! The young man rubbed his eyes, as if he had just woken up, and looked toward the radiant sun. He was very embarrassed when he saw everyone staring at him. He no longer seemed dissolute, nor did he have that crazy look: he had returned to his own true self, just as if he had been cured by a drug. He gave up his fancy clothes and elegant apparel and all the other requisites of his Sybaritic way of life and fell in love with [philosophical] austerity, put on the [philosopher's] cloak, and modeled his character after that of Apollonius.

67

Plotinus (c. A.D. 205–270) was the last great creative thinker of pagan antiquity. He thought of himself as a Platonist, but in fact he transformed Platonism into a new synthesis which also contained Pythagorean and Stoic elements. This new philosophical school—Neoplatonism—appealed to the educated classes because it seemed to explain in rational or near-rational terms some of the mysteries of life while at the same time salvaging traditions cherished by pagan culture.

Since Plotinus was born in Egypt, a theurgic ceremony performed by an Egyptian priest in a temple of Isis may have had special meaning for him. The priest offers to grant Plotinus a vision of his own "familiar spirit." This is a Greek interpretation of the Latin word *genius*, for which the Greeks had no exact equivalent. There were many spirits or daemons in the universe, but according to ancient Roman belief, only one "belonged" to an individual.

The priest, who has expected an ordinary "familiar spirit," is amazed that Plotinus' *genius* belongs to a different species of daemons altogether. We learn that at these ceremonies an attendant is needed to hold a couple of sacred chickens. The chickens will be strangled at once if the spirit that appears turns out to be threatening. This sacrifice was probably conceived as an instant peace offering, after which the spirit would leave without harming any of the participants. In this case the attendant panics, strangles the chickens, and the daemon leaves, but before he leaves, Plotinus gets a good look at him.

A monograph entitled *On the Spirit That Allotted Us to Himself* is preserved among Plotinus' writings (*Enn.* 3.4 [= tract 15 Harder]), but no mention is made of this incident there; it may be an anecdote that Plotinus told some of his students. In fact, the tract is little more than an interpretation of some Platonic passages (from the *Phaedo*, the *Timaeus*, the *Republic*, etc.) dealing with daemons.

The belief in the existence of daemons seems to have been an essential part of Neoplatonism, but the ability to actually see one's own guardian spirit was a privilege granted to only a few. Those who, like Plotinus, were granted the gift, apparently encouraged their disciples to study hard, work on themselves, and achieve the spiritual progress that would lead them to a higher level of awareness.

Porphyry, *Life of Plotinus*, pars. 56–60

From the time of his birth Plotinus had some very special gifts. An Egyptian priest came to Rome and became acquainted with him through a friend. This priest wanted to give Plotinus a demonstration of his [occult] science and invited him to be present at an appearance of his familiar spirit. Plotinus accepted willingly. The conjuring took place in the temple of Isis because this was, as the Egyptian said, the only "pure place" that he could find in all of Rome. But when the spirit was conjured and was asked to show himself, a god appeared that did not belong to that category of spirits. At this point the Egyptian cried: "Blessed are you who have a god as a familiar and not a spirit of the lower class!" But there was no opportunity to ask the apparition any questions or even to look at it any longer, because the friend who shared the experience strangled the chickens that he held as a safeguard, either because he was jealous or because he was afraid of something. Since Plotinus had a higher divine being as a familiar, he concentrated his divine eye for a while on that being. This experience prompted him to write a monograph, *On the Spirit That Allotted Us to Himself*, wherein he tried to give reasons for the differences between familiars.

68

Iamblichus (c. A.D. 250–325), a student of Plotinus' disciple Porphyry, discusses daemonology from a Neoplatonist point of view, probably using *Enn.* 3.4 (= tract 15 Harder) as a starting point. The text is difficult and probably corrupt in several places, but the message seems clear: the true philosopher must be able to distinguish the different classes of daemons from each other as well as from the higher gods.

Iamblichus, *On the Mysteries of Egypt* 1.20

You discuss the problem of "what distinguishes the daemons from the visible and the invisible gods"—the ones that are invisible but connected with the visible ones. Taking this as a starting point, I will show what the difference is. The visible gods are joined to the intelligible gods and have the same form as far as they are concerned. The daemons are quite different as far as their substance is concerned, and they barely look like them. This is how the daemons are different from the visible gods. They differ from the invisible gods in regard to their invisibility, for the daemons are invisible and cannot be perceived in any way by the senses. But the gods even transcend rational knowledge and perception tied to matter [or, reading *anylou* for *enylou* in the Greek, "immaterial perception"]. Because the gods are unknown and invisible they are named, for they are invisible in a completely different manner than are the daemons. Well now, being invisible, are they superior to the visible gods in respect of their being invisible? Not at all. The divine, no matter where it is and how far it extends, has the same power and domination over everything that is subordinate. Therefore, even if it is visible, it rules over the daemons of the air, for neither the environment nor the part of the universe affects in any way the authority of the gods; their total substance remains the same everywhere, indivisible, unchangeable, and all the lower orders worship it in the same way, according to the law of nature.

69

Iamblichus continues to discuss disembodied spirits here. It may seem strange that a distinguished theologian and philosopher would spend so much time and ingenuity on the subject of daemonology, but once the existence of such beings was admitted—and we have the testimony of Plotinus as well as the long Platonist tradition to document this belief—they had to be defined, distinguished, classified. Daemonology had become a science, and it was developed according to scientific principles. As we saw in *no. 67*, it was important to recognize the true character of a vision. It could be dangerous, or at least embarrassing, to mistake a god for a mere guardian spirit, or vice versa. Hence the subject also had a practical value.

Iamblichus, *On the Mysteries of Egypt* 2.1

I must also explain to you how a daemon is different from a hero and from a soul, and whether the difference is in the substance, the potential, or the activity.

I maintain that daemons are produced according to the generative and creative powers of the gods in the most remote termination of the progression and its ultimate division. Heroes are produced according to the vital principles in divine beings. The first and perfect degrees of the souls are their final product, and they begin their division at this point.

Since their substance is generated in this way from different causes, the substance itself must vary. That of the daemons is productive: it fashions the cosmic organisms and completes the authority of every single creature. The substance of the heroes is life-giving, rational, and consists in control over the souls. To the daemons one must attribute the generative powers that control the organism and the connection of soul and body. It seems right to assign to the heroes the life-producing powers that rule over men and are detached from creation.

Following this we must also define their activities. We must assume that those of the daemons are cosmic in a higher sense and have a wider extension as far as their effects are concerned, while those of the heroes are not as far-reaching and are oriented toward the disposition of the souls.

After these classes have been defined we come to the next one [the soul]. It descends to the end of the divine orders and has been allotted from these two [upper] orders certain measured shares of powers. It also grows from other, special, additions that come from itself. At different times it projects different images and principles and ever-different lives. It uses a variety of lives and ideas, according to the individual regions of the universe. It joins whatever organism it wants to join and withdraws from it whenever it wants to. It presents thoughts that are related to things that exist and will exist. It attaches itself to the gods in virtue of essential or potential harmonies other than those which associate daemons and heroes with them [the gods]. It has less of the eternity of the similar life and potential, but because of the good will of the gods and the radiation of light given out by them, it often rises to the higher order of the angels. This happens when it no longer remains within the boundaries of the soul but perfects itself completely into an angelic soul and an immaculate life. Hence the soul seems to present in itself all sorts of substances and activities and a variety of thoughts and all kinds of ideas. But if the truth must be told, the soul is always defined according to one specific criterion, but when it associates itself with leading causes, it joins different causes at different times.

70

In his work *The Preparation of the Gospel*, Eusebius of Caesarea (c. A.D. 260–340) wanted to show that pagan history and pagan civilization played a role in God's plan to save the world. In the course of the work he gives a summary of that part of pagan theology which dealt with daemons and their relationship with gods and heroes. That evil daemons had been worshiped from time immemorial has been noted already [*no. 50*]. The main edge of Eusebius' polemic against the pagan theologians (mostly the Neoplatonists) is what he sees as their exclusive worship of evil powers; he accuses them of offering only a kind of lip service to their benign deities.

This oversimplification may have been made in the interests of Christian propaganda. Moreover, from a strict Christian point of view, all pagan deities were evil, and to worship any of them was a sin. To a pagan believer it may have seemed safe to honor, above all, the evil powers, since the benevolent ones were good anyway, although this reasoning does not seem to be sound theology.

Eusebius points to an important aspect of ancient religion: ever since heroic times, certain powers had been worshiped because they were powerful and fearsome, not because they were considered loving or good. Hence the world was ready to embrace the new religion, with its message of divine love.

Eusebius, *The Preparation of the Gospel* 4.5

Those who have a thorough knowledge of pagan theology . . . divide the whole doctrine into four parts: first of all they distinguish the supreme god; they say they know that he rules over everything and that he is the father and the king of all the gods. After him there is a second category of gods; then comes the category of daemons; and as number four they list the heroes. All these, they say, share in the idea of the Good, and thus in a sense lead and in another sense are led, and every substance of this kind, they say, can be called light because it participates in light. But they also say that Evil is in control of what is bad; this is the category of the evil daemons; there is no friendship between them and the Good; they certainly have an enormous power in the sphere that is totally opposed to the Good; and everything of this kind they call "darkness." Having distinguished these categories, they say that heaven and the ether as far down as the moon are assigned to the gods; to the daemons, the region around the moon and the atmosphere; to the souls [of the dead], the terrestrial regions and the subterranean spaces. Having established these distinctions, they say that one must first of all worship the gods of heaven and of the ether; then the good daemons; in the third place the souls of the heroes; and in the fourth place one must soothe the evil and malevolent daemons. After they have made these distinctions in theory, they confuse everything in practice, and instead of worshiping all the powers mentioned, they worship only the evil powers and serve them exclusively, as I will show. . . .

71

Heliodorus, author of the novel *Ethiopian Tales*, or *The Story of Theagenes and Charicleia*, probably lived in the third century A.D. Like Apollonius of Tyana, whose biography by Philostratus apparently made some impression on him, he seems to have been, at least for part of his life, a Neo-

Pythagorean. Later, according to tradition, he converted to Christianity and became Bishop of Tricca in Thessaly.

In this episode of his novel the heroine, Charicleia, accompanied by Calasiris, an elderly Egyptian priest, witnesses—much against her will—a necromantic scene. An old woman, obviously a witch, revives the dead body of her son. The ditch she digs, the libation she pours, and the sword she manipulates remind us of the Homeric *Nekyia* in the *Odyssey* [*no. 50*], but there is also a doll made of dough mixed with fennel and laurel. The whole operation is successful up to a point, but we are told by the dead man himself that it is a sinful endeavor because it violates the Fates, and that death (actually provided by law) would be an appropriate punishment. Moreover [see *no. 58*], the dead resent being called back to life.

All this is made even worse by the fact that a priest, a holy man beloved by the gods, is forced to be a witness to the horrible scene. We learn from this that certain pagan priests were not even allowed to watch magical rites, much less perform them. Nevertheless, Calasiris is able to gather some helpful information from the dead man.

Heliodorus, *Aethiopica*, or *Ethiopian Tales*, 6.14–15

[*Calasiris, an elderly priest of Isis, and Charicleia, the beautiful young heroine of the novel, are traveling together through Egypt and come across a large number of dead bodies. It looks as though, not long ago, Persians and Egyptians had fought a fierce battle. The only living being there is an old Egyptian woman who is mourning the loss of her son. She tells the two travelers to spend the night there and promises to escort them to the next village in the morning.*]

Calasiris told Charicleia everything the old woman had said to him [in Egyptian] by translating it faithfully. They walked away from the slain bodies for a short distance and came to a little hill. There Calasiris stretched himself out, using his quiver as a pillow, while Charicleia sat down, using her purse as a cushion.

The moon rose and illuminated everything with her bright light; it happened to be the third night after the full moon. Calasiris felt his age and was tired from the journey, so he fell asleep. Charicleia, however, kept awake by her worries, became the eyewitness to a gruesome spectacle, but one that was not unfamiliar to Egyptian women.

The old woman, feeling undisturbed and unobserved, first dug a ditch and then lit a pyre that had been built on either side of it. After placing the body of her son in between, she lifted from a tripod that was standing there an earthenware jug of honey, one of milk, and another one of wine, and poured their contents into the ditch, one after another. Then she took a male figure made of dough, adorned with laurel and fennel, and threw it into the ditch. Finally she grabbed a sword, began to shake, as if in a trance, addressed the moon in many prayers that sounded wild and exotic, cut herself in the arm, wiped off the blood with a laurel branch, and sprinkled it over the pyre.

After performing more magic of this kind, she bent down to the body of her son, chanted something into his ear, and forced him, by her spells, to stand up straight.

Charicleia had already observed the first part of the ceremony with growing fear, but now she really began to shudder, and because of the horror she felt at this unusual spectacle she woke up Calasiris and made him, too, watch what was going on.

Thus the two sat in the dark without being seen, but they could easily observe what was happening in the light coming from the pyre. Since they were not too far away, they could also hear what the old woman said, for she now began to ask the dead man questions in a fairly loud voice.

She wanted to know whether his brother, her surviving son, would return safe and sound.

The dead man did not say anything in reply; he just nodded, without giving a clear indication to the old woman whether she might expect to see her wish fulfilled or not. Suddenly he collapsed and lay with his face on the ground. She turned the body on its back, continued relentlessly with her questions, and whispered, or so it seemed, even stronger incantations into his ears. Holding the sword in her hand, she jumped back and forth between the ditch and the pyre, aroused him once more, and, as he stood up, renewed her questions and forced him to make his prediction not just by nodding but in clear language.

While the old woman was occupied with this, Charicleia kept urging Calasiris to move closer to the action and to ask questions about Theagenes. He refused, saying that it was a sin even to watch this spectacle, and that they were excused only by the fact that they had no choice. He added that priests were not allowed to enjoy such sights or even to be present; their predictions were the result of the correct kind of sacrifice and a prayer coming from a pure heart, whereas impure outsiders were operating, in fact, with earth and bodies, just like the Egyptian woman whom, by chance, they were able to observe.

Before he could finish his sentence, the dead man began to mumble in a dull, deep voice that sounded as if it came from a closed vault or a cave.

"Mother, so far I have been very patient with you, and I have tolerated the fact that you are sinning against human nature, that you violate the law of the Fates, and that you try to move by your magic what may never be moved. For even the dead respect their parents, at least up to a certain point. But by your behavior you undermine and destroy this respect: you have not only applied ruthless methods to begin with, but you have now pushed your ruthlessness to the extreme by forcing a dead body not only to get up but also to nod and talk, without taking care of my burial, but preventing me from joining the other souls, only thinking of your own needs. Listen to what I wanted to tell you before but did not, out of respect for you: Neither will your [other] son return alive, nor will you yourself escape death by the sword. Since you have always devoted your life to unlawful practices such as these, you shall very soon meet the violent end that is destined for all people like you. In addition, not only have you had the nerve to perform such mysteries, mysteries veiled in silence and darkness, all by yourself, but you have just now betrayed the fates of the dead in front of witnesses. One of them happens to be a priest, but that is not the worst, for he is wise enough to keep such things under the seal of secrecy and never to mention them; he is also, by the way, beloved by the gods. This is why he will be able to stop his two sons from fighting each other and reconcile them instead—they are getting ready for a duel to the death with swords—if only he will hurry up. What is more serious is this: a girl sees and hears everything that is happening to me; a young woman overwhelmed by love, she has wandered through practically the whole world for the sake of her beloved, but after a thousand troubles, a thousand dangers that will lead her to the limits of the earth, she will live happily and in royal style with him ever after."

Having said this, he collapsed and lay still.

The old woman understood at once that the two strangers were the spectators. She grabbed the sword and, mad with fury—you could tell from her expression—she wanted to attack them and looked for them everywhere, suspecting that they were hiding among the bodies. She was determined to kill them, if only she could find them, because they had maliciously, or so she thought, disturbed her magic by watching her. As she was searching in blind fury among the corpses, she did not see the end of a spear sticking up. It pierced her body, and she fell to the ground, dead.

Thus, as she deserved, she at once fulfilled her son's prediction.

·IV·

DIVINATION

Introduction

Foretelling the future, interpreting the past, and, in general, discovering hidden truth (by way of clairvoyance, precognition, telepathy, and other such phenomena) was called *divinatio* by the Romans. The noun *divinatio* is derived from the verb *divinare* 'to predict', which is no doubt related to *divinus* 'divine' in the sense of "pertaining to a god or to the gods." The linguistic evidence in antiquity shows that the gift of predicting future events or grasping things by extrasensory perception was something that came from the gods, and this is confirmed by myth. According to Aeschylus (*Ag.* 1203ff.), Cassandra had been given her prophetic powers by Apollo to win her love. Similarly, Tiresias was endowed with the gift of prophecy, either by Zeus or by Athena, to compensate him for the curse that had made him blind.

The Greek word for "prophetic power" or "gift of divination" is *manteia;* the word for "prophet" or "prophetess" is *mantis.* The Greeks were probably right in connecting these two words with *mainomai* 'to be mad' and *mania* 'madness', but of course they were not thinking of permanent insanity; rather, they meant an abnormal state of mind which lasted for a short time. The word *ekstasis* also is used to describe this abnormal state; it means "stepping out of one's self" and is best understood today as "trance," though in antiquity it could mean a form of "possession." The association of prophetic powers with "madness" seems to be a very old idea among the Indo-European tribes, as the etymology shows,[1] and the descriptions of prophetic trance [*nos. 82* and *85*] stress this aspect. It should be said, however, that this is only one form of divination; there are forms (for example, the interpretation of dreams, or astrological forecasts) that do not require—in fact, they preclude—abnormal behavior.

Something should be said about the original meaning of the

words *prophet, prophecy,* and the like. In Greek, *prophetes* literally means "a person who speaks for someone else," and that someone else is usually a god, though in Delphi the priests who interpreted the obscure utterances of the Pythia were also called *prophetai*. The Pythia was the *mantis,* directly inspired by Apollo, but her message from the god had to be put into comprehensible form, into verse, for those who consulted the oracle. These *prophetai* were not directly in touch with the god; they were one step removed. Plato (*Ti.* 72A) says that the term *prophetes* should be reserved for those priestly interpreters who translated the frenzied utterances of the ecstatic seer (*mantis*) into intelligible Greek. But, in general, *prophetes* is a person who speaks for a god, or through whom a god speaks and reveals his plans. This is true for the prophets of the Old Testament, for John the Baptist, for Jesus, for anyone who proclaims a divine message with a special sense of mission.

Divination had its roots in Mesopotamia. The gift of prophecy and the status it confers were taken for granted in the Old Testament. Prophets were men of God who had the privilege of seeing him in a vision or hearing his voice, but then it became their duty to bring his message to the community. The prophetic books of the Old Testament, with their magnificent poetry, show that this was by no means an easy job; he who had to spread God's message usually encountered indifference or downright hostility, especially if he denounced heresy and vice and prophesied doom. The Greek myths of Cassandra and Tiresias mentioned above also show that the gift of prophecy was a blessing and a curse in one.[2]

The Babylonians believed that the decisions of their gods, like those of their kings, were arbitrary, but that mankind could at least guess their will. Any event on earth, even a trivial one, could reflect or foreshadow the intentions of the gods because the universe is a living organism, a whole, and what happens in one part of it might be caused by a happening in some distant part. Here we see a germ of the theory of "cosmic sympathy" formulated by Posidonius. Lists of unusual happenings were kept in Babylonia, and later (perhaps through Etruscan influence) in Rome. These observations were later matched with events that affected the whole country: the death of a king, a famine, a war. Among the techniques practiced we find astrology, liver divination, and the interpretation of dreams; the birth of freaks and the strange behavior of animals also were thought to have special meaning.

Cicero's work *On Divination* (*De Divinatione*) is the most important ancient text we have. It should be read in conjunction with his treatises *On the Gods* (*De Natura Deorum*) and *On Fate* (*De Fato*), because certain forms of divination were part of ancient religion, and the doctrine that all things are determined or decreed by fate naturally favored the belief that divination was possible. Cicero's three treatises give us a fairly full picture of Hellenistic theology as it was taught in the various philosophical schools.

As far as divination is concerned, Cicero himself remains skeptical, but he borrows a good deal from philosophers who firmly believed in the various methods of predicting the future. One of the leading minds of what is now called Middle Stoicism, Posidonius of Apamea (c. 135–50 B.C.), seems to have written a book in which he tried to show, from the many cases he had collected, that divination actually works. In order to find a philosophical reason for the phenomenon, he established the principle of "cosmic sympathy," which is at the basis of all occult sciences. Thus we know from Cicero (*Div.* 1.64) how Posidonius explained dreams that came true: in sleep the human soul communicates either with the gods directly or with an "immortal soul" (i.e., one of the many daemons that throng the air beneath the moon). These divine beings know the future, and they often share their knowledge with human souls when they are not encumbered by the body.

Natural and Artificial Types of Divination Dreams

According to Cicero (*Div.* 1.11; 2.26), who seems to follow Posidonius, there are two main types of divination: natural and artificial.[3] The most obvious form of natural divination is by dreams; we have just seen how Posidonius accounted for dreams that anticipated future events. Dreams are called "the oldest oracle" by Plutarch (*Conv. Sept. Sap.* 15). Often the dreamer himself understood the meaning of his dream; but sometimes he would consult a professional interpreter. Their lore is preserved in dream books such as Artemidorus' *Oneirocritica* (*The Art of Judging Dreams*).[4]

A special way of inducing meaningful dreams is known as incubation (Gk. *enkoimesis* 'sleeping in a temple'). In certain sanctuaries— for instance, in the temple of Asclepius at Epidaurus—the visitor had to follow an established ritual (fasting, praying, bathing, sacrificing) and then spend the night in the temple. In his sleep he would see the god and receive from him advice about the problem that had brought him there, usually a grave illness. By following the god's advice, many patients whose doctors had given up on them recovered miraculously, and many of their cures are recorded in inscriptions and in literary works—for example, in the *Speeches* of Aelius Aristides (second century A.D.), who had been healed himself. Hence, this special kind of divination is also called *iatromancy*.

The dream experience seems to have been fairly predictable. The prescribed ritual no doubt conditioned those who sought help; the holy place, the presence of kindly priests, and the records of earlier cures inscribed on the walls to document the reality of divine healing must have heightened their expectations; quite possibly they were also given a drug. For many patients these ancient sanctuaries were a kind of last resort, like Lourdes today.

Physical and mental sickness may be considered a borderline condition which allows the body to release certain powers that it does not normally possess. Aristotle (frag. 12a Ross) tells a story about his friend Eudemus, who during a serious illness had instant knowledge of his recovery and was at the same time able to predict the imminent death of Alexander, king of Pherae. Similarly, Augustine (*De Gen. ad Litt.* 12.17) reports the case of a mentally disturbed person who was regularly visited by a priest and "saw" him during all the phases of his journey between his own house, twelve miles away, and that of the patient.[5]

Like other forms of divination, the interpretation of dreams was practiced at an early date in Mesopotamia.[6] In Egypt this art was in the hands of priests and was so highly regarded that King Esarhaddon of Assyria, when he conquered Egypt in 671 B.C., took a number of these priests back to Assyria with him. The *Papyrus Chester Beatty* 3 (c. 1800 B.C.) contains an elaborate dream book that is similar to the dream book of Artemidorus, which was written two thousand years later: eating donkey meat in a dream is good (it means a promotion); making love to one's mother is good ("he will be supported by his fellow citizens"); diving into a river is good ("his sins will be taken away from him"); having intercourse with a pig is bad ("he will lose his possessions"). The Egyptians believed that man, in his sleep, had access to a universe which is different from the one we normally inhabit and that, though the body is asleep, the soul is somehow awakened to a new life.

In the Old Testament, dreams are one way in which man communicates with God, though it is admitted that some night visions are meaningless or even misleading. The dreams experienced by kings, priests, and prophets are naturally more significant than those had by others, and kings sleep in holy places if they need help from God: Solomon's dream at Gibeon (1 Kings 3:4–15; 2 Chronicles 1:3–12) is an incubation dream; Joseph's dream (Genesis 37:5–11) is one of the oldest dreams of prediction on record; and Pharaoh's dream (Genesis 41:1–45), which none of the Egyptian "magicians and sages" could interpret, is explained to him by Joseph, because he "has the spirit of God in him." Since dreams come from God—or from a god—only he who has the divine spirit in him will be able to understand them. Curiously, Pharaoh does not have the authority to interpret his own dream.

The Talmudic tradition also recognizes the value of dreams. According to Rabbi Jochanan, "Three kinds of dreams come true: the dream in the morning, the dream which someone [else] has about you, and the dream which is interpreted by another dream." Clearly, if a dream needs interpretation, the best interpretation comes from God, in the form of another dream.

The earliest dream in Greek literature is found in Homer's *Iliad* (2.5ff.). It is a deceitful dream sent by Zeus to Agamemnon, the commander in chief of the Greeks before Troy, "in order to destroy many Achaeans in their camp," as Homer says, and eventually make the Greeks realize how valuable a fighter Achilles, who has just been insulted by Agamemnon, will prove to be. The dream vision urges Agamemnon to attack the Trojans at once. Clearly the gods can send false dreams, and Nestor, the wisest of the Greeks, says in the assembly of elders in which the dream is discussed: "If any other man had told us about this dream, we would declare it false and turn away from it; but now it was he who claims to be by far the greatest among the Achaeans who had the vision." The fact that the supreme commander experienced the dream and was ready to take it as a good omen seems to exclude any doubt.

In the *Odyssey* (19.562ff.) Penelope develops a kind of theory of misleading and trustworthy dreams.. She uses the image of two gates, one made of ivory, one of horn. The deceptive dreams fly through the gates of ivory, and those that accurately predict the future fly through the gates of horn. But it is difficult to distinguish one from the other, and in this particular instance, Penelope's instinct tells her that the dream is not true, although she would like to believe in it.

According to Hesiod (*Theog.* 211–13), dreams are creatures of the Night, along with Sleep, Doom, Death, and other sinister personifications. It is strange that Hesiod, in the seventh century B.C., seems to ignore pleasant dreams, of which there is no lack in early epic poetry; he thinks only of frightening visions, deceptive dreams, and nightmares.

A powerful religious movement that originated in Greece in the seventh century B.C. is known as Orphism. Some Orphic theories concerning the soul impressed later poets and thinkers such as Pindar, Aeschylus, Sophocles, and Plato. They taught that, during sleep, the soul was freed and could leave the body in order to communicate with higher beings. While the body is awake, the soul (or "the subconscious," as we might say) is asleep, but when the body is asleep, the soul is wide awake and acquires what we today would call extrasensory perception. The soul, as Aeschylus says (*Ag.* 178; cf. 975 and Fraenkel's notes),[7] sits in the heart like a prophetess in her chair and interprets the visions of the blood. This striking image anticipates later philosophical theories.

Similarly, Euripides (*Iphigenia Taurica* 1261ff.) says that dreams are creatures of the Earth. The text and interpretation of this choral passage are controversial, but the playwright seems to compare the dreams to the visions of the Pythia, who also received her insights from the Earth. The Chorus, consisting of Greek women, takes it for granted that dreams "tell what happened first, what happened later, and what will happen in the future."

In Plato's *Phaedo* (60C–61C) Socrates reminisces in prison about a recurring dream vision in which the dream figure—always the same—urges him to "make music." The expression is ambiguous in Greek; it could refer to any of the arts and crafts sacred to the Muses, including what we call "music," but it might also refer to poetry or philosophy, for Socrates felt that, for many years, he had been "making music" through philosophical discussions. Perhaps we ought to translate the order of the dream figure as "Be creative!" To Socrates the highest form of creativity was philosophical (or scientific) investigation. But after his trial, awaiting execution, he realizes that some supernatural power wants him to write poetry while he still has time, and he does this by versifying some of Aesop's fables that he knows by heart.

This is obviously the type of dream called *chrematismos* 'oracular response' by Macrobius (fifth century A.D.) and *admonitio* 'command' by Chalcidius (also fifth century). This type, Macrobius writes, "occurs when in sleep the dreamer's parent, or some other respected or impressive person, perhaps a priest, or even a god, reveals without symbolism what will or will not happen, what should be done or avoided."[8]

That Socrates paid attention to the messages delivered by dreams and that he placed them on the same level as the responses given by the established oracles and the "inner voice" that he listened to is clear from a passage in his *Apology* (33C): "God has ordered me to do this, both through oracles and dreams and in all the other ways used by divine providence for giving its commands."

Xenophon, like Plato a disciple of Socrates, believed that divination through dreams was possible and should not be neglected (*Cyr.* 8.7.21): "It is in sleep that the soul really shows its divine nature; it is in sleep that it enjoys a kind of insight into the future; and this apparently happens, because it is completely free in sleep."

Plato went one step further when he claimed that we can control our dreams and that such control is, in fact, essential (*Rep.* 571C). Before going to sleep we must awaken our rational powers and concentrate on noble thoughts. If we do not indulge our baser appetites too much and if we are able to free ourselves from passions, we shall see in our dreams the truth; otherwise we will be the victims of absurd visions.[9]

In one of his early dialogues, when he was still under the influence of Plato, his teacher, Aristotle said: "The mind recovers its true nature during sleep" (*On Philosophy,* frag. 12a Ross). In his later writings (*On Sleep, On Dreams, On Divination in Sleep,* all parts of the *Parva Naturalia* [*Short Scientific Treatises*]) he is more cautious when dealing with dreams. He denies, for instance, that they are sent by a god, for if the gods wished to communicate with men, they could do so in the daytime, and they would show more discrimination in choosing the dreamers.[10] To him, dreams are affections of the central organ of consciousness. The dreamer is sensitive to the slightest disturbances in his organism, and these will affect his dreams. While asleep, he may hear a faint noise and dream of a thunderstorm. `

Dreams certainly have their meaning, and physicians should tell their patients to pay attention to dreams. The best dream interpreter, according to Aristotle, is the man who spots analogies and recognizes the true image behind the dream image, for the true image is often broken or distorted or changed through the dream process, just as an image reflected in water is distorted by ripples on the surface.

Aristotle recognizes the common origin of the following three phenomena: dreams, the hallucinations of the sick, and the optic illusions of the sane. Though dreams are not divine, they are daemonic, "for Nature is daemonic"[11] (a profound remark). If a dream comes true, it may just be coincidence, but there are two types of dreams that can be taken as predictions: those that disclose foreknowledge of the dreamer's state of health, and those that initiate their own fulfillment by strongly suggesting to the dreamer a course of action.[12] We can take it for granted that most of Aristotle's contemporaries believed in dreams, for we hear of various practices of averting an outcome threatened by bad dreams. People either "told it to the sun" or prayed or took ablutions or offered sacrifices.[13] This was a form of psychotherapy, and even for the fatalist the law of predetermination was not broken, for the prevention of catastrophe, once the warning had been issued in a dream, could easily be predetermined.

The Stoic philosophers were busy collecting case histories of predictions (in dreams, oracles, etc.) that came true, mainly in order to provide an empirical base for their theory of predetermination. Cicero, in his treatise *On Divination*, uses these collections, along with some personal reminiscences, mainly to show that they were open to doubt. Posidonius, a Stoic thinker who had considerable influence on later philosophers, was convinced that divine powers communicate with human beings through dreams, and that they do this in three different ways: (1) the soul, being divine, is allowed to see the future as only gods or daemons see it; (2) the air is full of disembodied souls (daemons), which enter the organism of the dreamer; (3) the gods speak directly to the dreamer. Posidonius' belief in the reality of occult experiences must have been so strong that he formulated his theory of "cosmic sympathy" to account for them.

We have already seen how the Stoics dealt with an argument that was designed to weaken their doctrine of fate. If dreams effectively warn human beings of impending dangers, the whole irrevocable chain of events becomes problematic. A man dreams of being shipwrecked and consequently cancels the passage on a ship which he has reserved. The ship, indeed, goes down with every soul on board, but the man who stayed at home is safe. How does this agree with the Stoic doctrine that no one can escape his fate? Seneca (*Scientific Problems* 2.37–38), probably following Posidonius, offers an answer: "Certain events have been left suspended, as it were, by the immortal gods, so that they may end happily if one addresses prayers to the gods, and makes vows. Therefore this [happy outcome] is not against fate: it is, in itself, part of fate."

Seneca's reply to the skeptic's objection looks deceptively simple, but it breaks the wholly impersonal chain of events ruled by fate by introducing a personal power that can be influenced—the power of the gods. The Stoics, however, seem to have been satisfied by this reply. Their need to believe was probably greater than their urge to doubt.

A Greek novel written in the second century A.D. by Achilles Tatius, who, according to tradition, became a Christian and rose to become a bishop, gives a different explanation:

> The divine power often wishes to show the future to human beings in the night, not in order to protect them from a tragic event (because fate cannot be controlled), but to help them accept such an event when it occurs. For when disasters come in a row, unexpectedly, they produce a sudden shock and overwhelm people totally, but if people are prepared for them and can think about them beforehand, it averts a little the sharp edge of pain.[14]

Lucretius (*De Rerum Natura* 4.749–822, 961–1036) puts the doctrine of Epicurus into Latin verse, and from his poem, written in the first century B.C., we can see that the Epicurean theory of dreams owes more to Aristotle than to Plato. According to Lucretius (i.e., Epicurus), we see in our dreams the things with which we are concerned during our waking hours: lawyers dream of their cases, generals of their battles, Lucretius himself of the book that he is planning to write. In short, we dream of the activity that absorbs our main energies, our hopes, and our ambitions. But we also dream of things that give us pleasure, such as music, dancing, plays, and entertainment in general, for sleep is a period of relaxation.

Since Lucretius, following Epicurus, wants the gods to be entirely carefree and blissful, he cannot admit that they are the least bit concerned about human affairs; therefore, they cannot send dreams warning of impending disaster. A purely rational explanation of dreams appealed to the Epicureans, and Aristotle, perhaps following Democritus, had given one, at least tentatively.

But the vast majority continued to believe in the meaning of dreams, as we can see from the existence of dream books. The oldest preserved dream book dates from the second century A.D. Its author, Artemidorus of Daldi, was a professional interpreter of dreams with scientific and didactic interests. Not only did he collect over three thousand dreams from those who consulted him, but he also took a good look at the people themselves. Thus, though bizarre in many ways, his book is a document of human psychology.

Artemidorus attempts to establish various levels of classification in his dream book. He distinguishes between dreams proper, visions, oracles, fantasies, and apparitions; then again, he separates dreams that forecast events from dreams that are concerned with the present.

Symbolism is the key to understanding the dream mechanism, according to Artemidorus. Some of the symbols are fairly obvious. An abyss means impending danger; a blossoming tree, happiness and prosperity. Bathing in clear water symbolizes good fortune; in muddy water, the opposite. A candle being lighted announces a birth in the family; one already lit hints at success; one burning dimly indicates distress of some kind. In a sense, Artemidorus already anticipates the Freudian concepts of wish fulfillment and wish substitution; thus he says that the dreamer, if he is in love with a woman, will not see the object of his passion in his dreams, but he will see, for example, a horse, a mirror, a ship, the sea, or a woman's garment (Artem., *Oneirocr.*, preface to Book 4). It is up to the dream interpreter to find out whether his client is in love, and then he will understand the nature of the symbolism. In general, the client's personality, his habits, his profession, his recurrent dreams, have to be considered, for all of these might affect the symbolism of his dreams. Being struck by lightning, for instance, has at least fifteen different meanings, and only a long interview can bring out the specific nuance.

The most famous passage in Artemidorus' *Oneirocritica* is 1.79, which concerns the "dream of Oedipus" [*no. 92*] and its variations. Calmly and in an almost clinical manner, Artemidorus discusses various types of dreams involving sexual intercourse with one's mother. The theme of incest is compounded by bizarre practices (even necrophilia, it seems), and each variation of the theme has a specific meaning.

Sometimes Artemidorus' approach is empirical. Among the thousands of dreams he must have listened to in his professional career, he matches some with the experiences the dreamers had afterward, and he draws certain conclusions. The ancient astrologers worked in the same manner, and they, too, used symbolism. Perhaps it is characteristic of all occult sciences that they have a "scientific" or "empirical" basis, but that they also resort to images, symbols, and analogies that no modern scientist would accept.

Marcus Aurelius, a Stoic who became emperor of Rome in A.D. 161, records in his *Meditations* that he received medical advice in dreams (1.17.20). In a remarkable passage (9.27) he urges the reader, in almost

Biblical terms, to feel kindly toward those who hate him, and reminds him that even his enemies benefit from dreams and oracles, although for their own, presumably crooked, purposes. But though Marcus Aurelius believes in various forms of divination, he rejects magic, exorcism, and "such things" (1.6). This shows how selective a highly educated Greek or Roman could be: he might accept one of the "occult" sciences but be hostile toward others.

In the first century A.D., mainly in Rome and Alexandria, a new version of the Pythagorean school appeared. Its doctrine was a blend of (presumably) genuine Pythagorean tradition, Platonism, Stoicism, and other philosophies that had been formulated since Pythagoras' death. Among other things, these late disciples had inherited from Pythagoras an interest in occult phenomena. Apollonius of Tyana, who is usually labeled a Neo-Pythagorean (he is discussed in Chapter 1 above), was a healer, exorcist, and miracle-worker. A later philosopher, Iamblichus, actually a Neoplatonist, wrote a *Life of Pythagoras* (c. A.D. 300) in which he claimed (65.114) that Pythagoras, like Plato, taught that sleep and dreams could be controlled. To fall asleep while listening to soft, soothing music would create a mood in which light, pleasant, and meaningful dreams might be expected. From this point of view, dreaming was considered to be a creative activity that demanded a certain technique and training that one might compare to biofeedback today. The emphasis was definitely on spiritual discipline; any kind of food, drink, or drug that would stupefy body and soul was strictly forbidden. The Neo-Pythagoreans were especially interested in the "admonition" type of dream, called *admonitio* by Chalcidius and *chrematismos* by Artemidorus (*Oneirocr.* 1.2). (The Greek noun is derived from the verb *chrematizo*, which means "to give a revelation, in a dream or an oracle," and which also occurs in the New Testament.)

This new version of Pythagoreanism had a strong influence on Neoplatonism. Indeed, it was a Neoplatonist, Synesius (c. A.D. 373–410; he became a Christian bishop in 409 or 410), who theorized in his book, *On Dreams*, that dreams are preludes to real events and put us in the right mood for what is to come. Synesius argued that since no two people are completely alike, there can be no rules for all dreams; we have to find our own interpretation. This theory seems to have been directed against Artemidorus' style of dreambooks, with their vague symbolism and even vaguer empiricism. Synesius himself found that his dreams helped him in his work: they gave him ideas. Once, when he went hunting, a dream suggested to him a new kind of trap.

To Synesius, dreams could be both revealing and obscure, but even in their obscurity some revelation might abide. He knew people who had no education but who dreamed that they were talking with the Muses and woke up as great poets. "Make your bed on a Delphic tripod,"

Synesius says, "and you will lead a nobler life. Everyone, woman or man, can do it, because sleep is the most readily available oracle of all. The soul is lucid and mobile only when the body is asleep" (*De Insomniis* 144B).

Christians and pagans alike believed in the meaning of dreams, and dream books continued to be written throughout Byzantine times. Several of them have been preserved, the best-known, perhaps, under the name of Achmes.

What has been written on dreams in modern times often seems to echo ancient theories.[15] In his *Interpretation of Dreams,* Freud quotes Aristotle and Artemidorus and follows their clues. C. G. Jung and others, in *Man and His Symbols,* writes: "Many crises in our lives have a long unconscious history. We move toward them step by step, unaware of the dangers that are accumulating."[16] And E. R. Dodds, who has tried to combine psychoanalysis and anthropology with the more traditional methods of classical scholarship, writes that certain dreams (he calls them culture-pattern dreams) are closely related to myth,[17] because, as Jane Harrison once put it, myth is the dream-thinking of the people, just as the dream is the myth of the individual. In other words, we create in dreams our own mythology, but only part of it comes from personal experience, distant or near; some images flow from the "collective unconscious" we have inherited from our ancestors.

It is almost impossible to understand a culture without knowing about its typical dreams and the typical interpretations of them. But the material we have is scanty, and much of it may have been edited or manipulated in some way. Still, since we are all dreamers, we can probably sense the hidden mechanisms that produced certain dreams in ancient times, for more than likely they also give rise to dreams today.

Oracles as Institutions

Dreams were called "the oldest oracle" by Plutarch, and everyone could have prophetic powers in dreams. But there existed, throughout the ancient world, establishments where predictions were regularly delivered by prophets. Not every prophet was associated with such a sanctuary, however; diviners practiced everywhere, and most did not enjoy the status of the Delphic Pythia or the Sibyl of Cumae. In fact, these free-lancing diviners were "shrunken" medicine men who had only one gift left, the gift of prophecy, unlike Orpheus or Pythagoras, who controlled a whole range of secret powers.[18]

As early as Homer, divination came under the control of religion and was concentrated in a few shrines that soon became prominent and wealthy. At a very early date, Apollo seems to have been in charge of trance mediumship, while Asclepius, his son, guaranteed true dreams. Some of the ancient divinities, such as Hecate, were still invoked to grant a glimpse into the future.

What is an oracle? The word has three basic meanings: (1) a response given by a priest or priestess at the shrine of a deity; (2) the shrine itself (thus we speak of the Delphic oracle as a sanctuary where oracles were delivered to those who consulted it); and (3) the "real" oracle, the power that inspired the messages that emanated, as it were, from another world and had to be interpreted.[19]

The techniques used to obtain predictions varied from shrine to shrine, and it is difficult to understand them at this distance in time. To dismiss them as fraud, as the philosophers of the Age of Enlightenment did, hardly seems possible, however. Bernard de Fontenelle (1657–1757) compared the ancients' belief in oracles with their belief in the gods, one which he assumed was not very deep: "Act like the others and believe whatever you like." It was essential to conform publicly, to offer the right sacrifice in the right way; if one did this, one could make fun of it in private. Thus, "You might or might not believe in oracles, but they continued to be consulted for centuries, because custom has a hold on people which need not be reinforced by reason."[20]

An Egyptian oracle in the oasis of Siwa in the Libyan Desert, that of Ammon, or Amen ("The Hidden One"), may have had some influence on the organization of the sanctuaries at Delphi and Dodona in Greece.[21] Statesmen from Athens and Sparta went there in the fifth and fourth centuries B.C., and Alexander the Great consulted it too. We know very little about the method of divination that was practiced there.

Since the Delphic oracle is the most famous institution of its kind in Greece, it might be useful to discuss it first. Phenomena such as prophecy, ecstasy, enthusiasm, clairvoyance, trance, and talking in tongues can perhaps be best illustrated by our knowledge—inadequate as it is—of what happened at Delphi, for at least part of the collective experience of thousands of visitors has been recorded.

Before we discuss the oracles as institutions where prophecy was practiced, we should say something about prophecy as a form of divination.[22] The foretelling of events as the result of a vision or hearing the voice of a divine being or entering a state of inspiration is well documented in the ancient Near East. We know of prophets (1 Samuel 10:5ff.; 19:24) who are even older than the "canonical" prophets Isaiah and Jeremiah, for instance. The nature of Old Testament prophecy has often been studied[23] and is, strictly speaking, outside the limits of this book. In the New Testament John the Baptist and Jesus are called "prophets" in the Gospels; Jesus was even taken to be one of the ancient prophets come to life again (Mark 8:28, etc.). In the early Church, people who had the special gift of uttering words in trance were called "prophets" (the word is sometimes translated as "charismatists"), for example, in Jerusalem (Acts 11:27; 15:32) and in Antioch (Acts 13:1). In a very old Christian text, *The Teaching of the Twelve Apostles* (*Didache*, probably composed c. A.D. 150, but some sections of which are older), we find references to these "charismatists." They are distinguished from the "apostles" (or "missioners") and from the "teachers" (see 1 Corinthians 12:28). Unlike the teachers, the "charismatists" were inspired, and unlike the "speakers in tongues," their message was intelligible, though they might forget immediately afterward what they had said. The genuine "prophets" were highly regarded by the community, but apparently there were also impostors who faked their gift as an easy way to make a living (*Didache* 11–12).

"Speaking in tongues" (*glossolalia*), a form of inspired ecstatic utterance, is not exclusively a Christian phenomenon; it occurred in various religious contexts of the Hellenistic period,[24] and it is described in an old testimony concerning the Delphic Pythia (Heraclitus, quoted by Plutarch, *De Pyth. Or.*, p. 24): "She is in trance [*mania* 'madness'], does not smile, speaks in inarticulate, harsh sounds, but she is in touch with the god." A much later witness, Lucian (*Alex.*, par. 23), writes that the sibyl's speech sounds like Hebrew or Phoenician, and that those who do not understand her are amazed. The point, of course, is that it is neither Hebrew nor Phoenician nor any other language known to man (the use of Semitic words in magical Greek formulas is something else), but just a broken, inarticulate, incoherent outpouring of sounds.

In the early Church, being "filled with the spirit" created three spectacular gifts: (1) prophecy; (2) "speaking in tongues"; (3) the power of healing. "Speaking in tongues," as distinguished from "prophesying," referred to the unintelligible sounds of ecstatic speech.[25]

Speaking a "foreign" (i.e., unintelligible) language and predicting future events was also taken to be a symptom of possession.[26] This is not surprising, for the trance of the Pythia has also been described as a form of possession. Apollo takes over, fills her, controls her. The difference lies in the nature of the divine power that "takes over" a human being: the Holy Spirit on the one hand, a malevolent daemon on the other.

Prophetic ecstasy is usually explained as "trance," a state of consciousness induced by a divine power in which the normal mind is suspended and normal language is often replaced by unintelligible utterances. Galen, a medical authority of the second century A.D., describes it as "a madness that lasts only a short time," and, indeed, the Greek language itself reflects the connection of *mania* 'madness' with *mantis* 'seer'. The phenomenon has been studied many times,[27] but like related phenomena such as hypnosis, it is not fully understood today. Prophetic ecstasy is a characteristic of the *shaman*.[28] It can be brought about by a kind of self-hypnosis—for example, by the monotonous murmuring of prayers or magical formulas, by taking drugs (herbs, mushrooms, toxic substances such as ergot) and inhaling aromatic vapors, or by dancing or engaging in other forms of exercise (the whirling dervishes). A strict ritual

preceding the actual trance (fasting, bathing, lack of sleep), the presence
of the priests in their robes, the awesome surroundings—all this could
prepare (or "program," as we would say today) the medium. The trance
could also be faked, as we know from Lucan (*Phars.* 5.124–61), because
the real experience of divine possession could be traumatic and was
thought to shorten the medium's life. But judging from Lucan's episode,
there were signs that gave a faked ecstasy away.

Prophetic visions or insights are described in Homer more than
once. Helenus, the Trojan seer (*Il.* 7.44–45), "understood in his mind the
decision that the gods in their deliberations had made." Toward the end
of the *Odyssey* (20.345ff.) the suitors who are doomed to die so soon at the
hands of Odysseus, the hero who has already returned, eat and drink,
laugh and scoff, as usual, but "their laughing jaws are no longer their
own, and the meat they eat is defiled with blood, and their minds foretell
grief." They continue to laugh and eat, but somehow they sense that
disaster is near. The soothsayer Theoclymenus interprets it for them
when he shouts:

> Poor wretches! Do you realize what terrible fate will befall you?
> Your heads, your faces, your knees are wrapped in darkness;
> the sound of wailing has broken out like fire; your cheeks are
> running with tears! The walls and the beautiful pillars are
> splashed with blood! The entrance to the court and the court
> itself are full of ghosts headed toward the underworld, the
> darkness! The sun has completely gone from the sky, and the
> mist of evil has spread across it!

The suitors respond with more merry laughter.

It is a remarkable scene: a sense of disaster hangs in the air, and
even the suitors feel it, benighted as they are, but the seer Theoclymenus
actually sees it all in a flash. This kind of sudden vision, which can be
excruciating[29] for the seer himself and usually is not fully realized by
those who are about to suffer, seems typical, and Homer's audience must
have recognized it at once as a case of clairvoyance, an authentic phenomenon, not just a literary device.

The ancients believed that in a state of trance, the soul leaves the
body and is granted visions. Such a state can be induced by a ritual.[30] The
highest form of ecstasy is the union of the soul with the divinity or the
One (Plot., *Enn.* 6.9.11), not as the gift of the One, but as the result of
human effort or discipline. This does not appear to be a purely Neoplatonist concept; it is probably connected with the much older Greek
idea that man alone—without the help of the gods, and even, like Prometheus, against the gods—can achieve great things. It also seems related to
the idea that magic or theurgy can practically compel divine powers to

become accessible, in other words, to make trance possible in the first place. But trance does not always lead to this ultimate experience, though it does open up another world.

It is difficult to understand trance, because the "psychics" who have it are not always articulate. In his *Autobiography*, John Cowper Powys comes close to a description that seems meaningful even to those who have never had such an experience. One day, in San Francisco, he felt stirring within him

> that formidable daimon which . . . can be reached somewhere
> in my nature, and which when it is reached has the Devil's
> own force. . . . I became aware, more vividly than I had ever
> been, that the secret of life consists in sharing the madness of
> God, I mean the power of rousing a peculiar exultation in
> yourself as you confront the Inanimate, an exultation which is
> really a cosmic eroticism.[31]

Ecstasy is sometimes distinguished from *enthusiasm*, which means, literally, "being full of God," but it can also be translated as "possession" or "inspiration." In their own language the ancients tried to describe an experience that was very real to them, but since they could not find a scientific explanation for it, they had to create an image—that of having a god inside (*enthusiasmos*) or being touched (or filled) by the spirit (*inspiratio*).[32]

Naturally, prophetic ecstasy could occur anywhere, at any time, even outside the great sanctuaries such as Delphi, but the ancients tried to control these irrational phenomena, to keep them under the strict supervision of a body of priests. Perhaps we should substitute the term *clairvoyance* for *prophecy*, for, according to F. W. H. Myers, clairvoyance is "the faculty or art of perceiving, as though visually, with some coincidental truth, some distant scene," and such distance could be in time as well as in space. Some ancient seers were no doubt true visionaries.[33] The terms *premonition* and *precognition* also have been used, but they do not explain why and how these experiences occur.[34] The Pythia, the entranced woman at Delphi, can be described as a "medium" or an "automatist," but these are just labels; at most, they allow comparisons to be drawn with experiments conducted in more recent times.

One distinction should perhaps be made. A prophetic vision may occur spontaneously and out of context, so to speak, like the vision of the seer Theoclymenus in the *Odyssey*, or the vision of Cassandra shortly before she and Agamemnon are murdered. In these cases it almost seems that a certain location is already charged or filled by the vibrations of a terrible event that is about to happen, and a "psychic" picks up these vibrations. Similarly, a "psychic" may pick up from a certain location

vibrations of dramatic events that happened in the past: Cassandra had
this ability, too (Aesch., *Ag.* 1194ff.).[35] Precognition, retrocognition, and
telepathy may be different aspects of the same gift. On the other hand,
one wonders whether the Delphic Pythia and her *prophetai*, who dealt
with the questions of visitor after visitor, day after day, can be called
"psychic" in the same sense. The inarticulate response of the Pythia
meant only one thing to the visitor: the oracle was working; the priestess
was in touch with the god. But her answer also had to be interpreted, and
at this point all kinds of rational considerations may have entered: politics, economics, diplomacy. The oracle, as delivered to the visitor, was a
finished product. At best, it contained a genuine vision, but one that
had been filtered through some of the shrewdest minds in all of Greece.
An oracular response of this kind clearly differs from the apocalyptic visions of John.

Revelation means the "disclosure" or "uncovering" (*apocalypsis*) of
God's will through visions and dreams, but primarily through the initiative of God, not through a special technique or concerning one particular religion as a whole or, more narrowly, its mystic doctrine of the Last
Things. In one sense Judaism and Christianity are revealed religions; in
another sense their eschatology concerns an apocalypse, because it predicts the ultimate conflict between the supreme powers of good
and the supreme powers of evil, with the good prevailing. This type of
religious thought may have been taken over by some Jews from
Zoroastrianism, the ancient Persian state religion (see Porph., *Plot.*, ch.
16), and the tradition was continued by the early Christian Church. Hermeticism, on the other hand, is a philosophy that was revealed to mankind by the Egyptian god Thoth, the equivalent of Hermes, and such
occult sciences as alchemy and astrology [see *no. 92*] were considered by
their practitioners to be the gift of some god. Thus, in later antiquity, the
element of revelation distinguished religion from philosophy, occult science from science.[36]

Sanctuaries where divination was exercised regularly, as part of
the cult of a god, are known as oracles (L. *oracula*, Gk. *manteia* or
chresteria).[37] But as noted earlier, an oracle is also the response of the god
to a question asked by a visitor to the shrine.

The method of divination varied from shrine to shrine.[38] Sometimes the will of the god was explored by the casting or drawing of lots
(*klēroi, sortes*)—for example, dice or sticks or bones. The word *sortilegus*
originally designated a soothsayer who practiced this particular method
of divination (*sortes legere* 'to pick up lots'); later, by extension, it referred
to any type of prophecy or sorcery. It must be a very old technique, for it
was practiced at Clarus, Praeneste, Antium, and elsewhere. A later vari-
ant is the consultation of scrolls or books (bibliomancy) by opening them
at random or pricking them with a needle: Homer, Virgil, and the Bible

(*sortes Homericae, sortes Virgilianae*, and *sortes Biblicae*) were the obvious texts chosen.[39] This do-it-yourself method could easily be carried out at home, but when important decisions were at stake, the great shrines were still visited. One suspects that traveling to a famous oracle—Delphi, for instance, or Antium—was a way of life, like a pilgrimage in the time of Chaucer, and that the actual consultation was only part of a rather complex religious and social experience. Of course, there were certain methods that could not be duplicated anywhere else—the genuine trance of the Pythia at Delphi, for instance, or the rustling of the leaves of the sacred oak at Dodona.

Two collections of oracles might be mentioned here: the *Sibylline Oracles* and the *Chaldean Oracles*. Sibyls were women who, like Cassandra or the Delphic Pythia, prophesied in trance. Ten places in the Mediterranean world are known as residences of Sibyls, although originally there seems to have been only one. The Sibyl of Cumae is known from Book 6 of Virgil's *Aeneid*, and the ecstatic character of her prophecy is made clear by the poet (vv. 77–102); later she becomes the hero's guide through the underworld. A collection of prophecies written in Greek hexameters and attributed to various Sibyls was kept in Rome, in the temple of Apollo on the Palatine, for consultation by a special committee at the command of the Senate in times of crisis. This original collection was destroyed in a fire in 83 B.C.; a second collection, drawn from different sources, was destroyed in A.D. 405. What still exists today under the title *Sibylline Oracles*[40] is a forgery, although some genuine Greek oracles are interspersed through it. Part of it is Jewish propaganda against pagan culture and the beginnings of Roman imperialism (from the second century B.C. on); these texts were later rewritten, interpolated, and enlarged to suit the Christian polemic against paganism and the empire as well.[41]

The *Chaldean Oracles* appear to have been the work of one Julianus, who lived under Marcus Aurelius and is considered the founder of theurgy. Proclus and Iamblichus, the Neoplatonists, wrote commentaries on them. Where these "oracles" originally came from, no one knows. Dodds does not think that Julianus forged them; they remind him more of the trance utterances of modern "spirit guides."[42] Thus Julianus may have listened to the "revelations" of a visionary or a medium, transcribed them into verse, and supplied explanations. They contain guidelines for a cult of the sun and fire, but they also give instructions on how to conduct theurgical operations—for instance, how to conjure up a god.[43]

The most famous oracle of the ancient world was in Delphi.[44] Its origins probably go back to Minoan times, and for many centuries it must have been a sanctuary of the great earth goddess *Gā*, or *Gaia*. The Greek name *Delphoi* may be connected with *delphys* 'womb', since the Pythia in a sense did receive her inspiration from the womb, the inside of the earth. Another clue is given by the *omphalos*, a very old stone that once stood in the adytum of the temple of Apollo and marked or represented the "navel" of the earth, as the inscription *Gās* 'of the earth' indicates. The fact that at the oracle the most important function is performed by a woman implies that this was originally the sanctuary of a goddess, not a god. The very nature of the Pythia's trance suggests the influence of the earth, and her name recalls the ancient Python snake, which was thought to be female and presumably was the cult image under which the great goddess was worshiped.

Moreover, as is often the case, Greek mythology seems to have preserved part of the historical truth by making Apollo kill the Python. The oldest version of the myth appears in the *Homeric Hymn to the Pythian Apollo* (perhaps sixth century B.C.). It suggests that toward the end of the second millennium B.C., when Greek-speaking Dorians invaded the Pre-Greek world of what is now called Greece, they took over some of the great sanctuaries and changed their character, at least to a certain extent. Apollo replaced Gaia, and her cult image, the snake, was smashed, but the prophetic ecstasy of the priestess was, with great foresight, preserved as an institution.

How the Pythia's trance was induced is still a mystery. The archaeologists have shown that there was no chasm from which she could breathe any kind of natural gas.[45] Scholars who chewed large numbers of laurel leaves felt no special effect. Drinking the holy water or bathing in it can no longer be tested; these may have played a certain role, along with fasting, praying, and staying awake—essentially magical operations—in inducing the trance that led up to the ultimate vision.[46] For many Greeks and Romans it was a case of possession, of a god or daemon taking over. In modern terms the Pythia can be described as a "medium" or a "vocal automatist."[47] Telepathy and clairvoyance cannot be excluded: Tacitus (*Ann.* 2.54) says that the priest at Clarus, another famous oracle, would merely ask for the names of the clients present, then retire to a sacred grotto, drink the sacred water, and give the appropriate answers to questions he had not even heard. Plutarch (*De Garr.*, ch. 20) reports that the Pythia did this in certain cases; this means, perhaps, that certain Pythias did have the gift of clairvoyance, while others did not.

Another oracle of Apollo was located at Clarus, near Colophon.[48] The sanctuary seems to have been very old, but the oracle became especially famous during the imperial period. The "prophet," assisted by a priest and a "thespiode" (i.e., a "singer of prophecies"), followed the procedure described above. Dodds is inclined to attribute this feat to thought-reading, though he also points out that the utterances of the prophet (who was generally uneducated, like the Pythia) were enigmatic and therefore had to be interpreted; this interpretative step appears to have been the function of the "thespiode," whose contribution to the psychic process is difficult to estimate.[49]

At each of the other oracles on which we have information, divination seems to have been practiced in a special way. Trophonius, a hero,
had a famous oracle at Lebadea; its archaic ritual is described by Pausanias
(9.37.4ff.). At many oracles the behavior of animals was observed. At
Dodona not only was the rustling of the leaves of the sacred oak of Zeus
considered meaningful, but so, too, was the flight and cooing of the
sacred doves on and around that tree. At the oracle of Apollo at Sura, in
Lycia, omens were read from the movements of sacred fish that were kept
in a tank. At Epirus, tame snakes were kept in a grove of Apollo, and
when the priestess fed them, and their appetite was good, a good harvest
could be predicted. The behavior of the underground snake of Lanuvium
(an ancient city in the Alban hills where Juno was worshiped as Sospita)
was interpreted in a similar way. According to Propertius (*Eleg.* 4.8.5ff.),
once a year, when the giant snake was heard whistling for food, girls were
sent down the "sacred way" into a dark cave. They could see nothing, but
they felt the head of the snake as it snatched the food from a basket. If the
snake accepted the food, it was a sign that the girls were chaste (though
Propertius does not say this explicitly), and the farmers shouted: "The
year will be fruitful!"

All these customs reflected a form of animal worship which pre-
dated by centuries the arrival of the Olympian gods in Greece. It is interesting to note that animals representing three realms—earth, water,
and air—played a role in divination. Snakes were associated with chtho-
nian deities and with heroes, as we see in Delphi, where the Python
represented the earth goddess herself. Birds were even more important.
The interpretation of their flight, their cries, and other behavioral patterns
was the subject of a special art, augury, a topic we will turn to later in this
chapter.

The Rise and Fall of the Oracles

Two questions about the oracles have often been asked but have never
been answered conclusively: (1) How did oracles, some more than others,
gain their enormous prestige and influence in the ancient world? (2) Why
did they eventually decline?

To deal with the first question, we ought to consider, as Dodds
did, the religion, culture, and social life of Greece in the archaic and
classical periods.[50] It is a historical fact that the belief in the authority of
the oracle of Delphi was deeply rooted in the minds of the educated and
the uneducated, and that this belief could not be shaken by striking proof
that the oracle was fallible and downright subversive—for instance,
when it discouraged the Greeks from resisting the might of the Persian
Empire in the early fifth century B.C. The Greeks won, but they soon
forgot that the oracle had given them bad advice. This can only mean that

the Greeks believed in oracles because they needed them. They had neither the divine legacy of Scripture nor an established church, and their feelings of guilt and fear could only be controlled, it seems, by faith in a constantly renewable and more-or-less dependable divine revelation. The Delphic oracle gave them this and more.

The Delphic priests seem to have developed over the centuries a theology and a moral philosophy which stressed purity in ritual as well as in everyday life. Those who entered the temple were greeted by two large inscriptions: "Know thyself" (i.e., realize how unimportant you are, compared to the gods) and "Nothing in excess" (no idle admonition, for the Greeks, far from being the rational beings they are thought to have been, tended to do things in excess).

Socrates believed in the Delphic oracle, as he believed in his own *daimonion,* and so did his disciples Xenophon[51] and Plato[52] (the latter, perhaps, with certain reservations).

The importance of Delphi in world religion, politics, and economics has been compared to that of the Vatican today, and the comparison, taken with a grain of salt, is helpful. News of anything that happened in that *piccolo mondo antico* must have reached Delphi—which no doubt had a large network of agents and consultants—in record time. Delphi was also a financial center where gifts from kings and city-states to the god Apollo were kept and displayed. In addition, Delphi offered banking facilities: currency could be exchanged, and certain gifts were actually treated as investments. In the period of colonization, which expanded Greek influence beyond the Mediterranean, the advice of the oracle determined the choice of new sites.[53]

Finally, for many Greeks and Romans, a visit to the sanctuary was almost a way of life, an experience comparable to the pilgrimages of the Middle Ages. Delphi was a place where Greeks from many isolated cities and islands could meet each other, pay the god their reverence, receive guidance from him, and enjoy the plays and athletic contests that were offered for the entertainment of visitors.

Before the Roman period few doubts concerning the good faith of the priests serving at the oracles were expressed, though the possibility of fraud in certain instances was not rejected. In the Age of Enlightenment, oracles were regarded as a triumph of charlatanism and deceit and as evidence of the strange superstitions of the ancient world. The best-known attempt to discredit all oracles is Bernard de Fontenelle's *Histoire critique des oracles,* which was first published in 1687. Fontenelle, who was neither a historian nor a classical scholar, made two points: (1) oracles could not possibly have been inspired by divine powers; (2) they did not cease with the birth of Christ. The critique stirred up a lively controversy because it was felt to be an attack on the *fable convenue,* superstitions and bigotry that had been tolerated and encouraged by powerful institutions in all ages, not just in antiquity. Among other things, Fontenelle maintained that "custom, which need not be reinforced by reason, has enormous influence on people." It was, according to him, perfectly possible for a Greek or a Roman to ridicule the Delphic oracle in private, but to go through the motions of traveling there, offering the right kind of sacrifice in the customary way, and consulting the god just for show: "Act like the others, believe whatever you like." This was certainly true for many educated Greeks and Romans of the Hellenistic and imperial periods, but probably not for earlier centuries.

The second question—why did the oracles decline and finally disappear—is discussed by Plutarch in his essay *On the Cessation of Oracles*.[54] Some of the reasons he offers are social and economic. Oracles can flourish only if they are visited regularly by large crowds that spend large amounts of money or leave splendid gifts behind. As a result of wars, and, later, as a result of Roman rule, the population and prosperity of central Greece had declined in the Hellenistic period. An impoverished Greece could no longer support the oracles. The fact that the ancient city-states had lost their independence was an additional factor. Their rivalry, both political and economic, had no doubt been manipulated and exploited by the great oracles. Under Roman rule this was no longer possible, and Rome herself had no interest in supporting the oracles, though distinguished Romans, out of curiosity, still visited the shrines.

To these explanations, other scholars have added the following: the expanding belief in astrology and similar types of do-it-yourself oracles; the publication of the *Sibylline Oracles* and similar collections; and, above all, the growth of Christianity.

Plutarch's main argument, however, is theological. Defending the supreme authority of the gods, he claims that they are not responsible for the operation of the oracles dedicated to them. Instead, he says, some very powerful daemons are in charge, but since daemons are mortal, they grow old and eventually die. To illustrate this he tells the haunting story of the death of Great Pan (which supposedly occurred under Tiberius). As Plutarch interprets it, Great Pan was an important daemon, and the news of his death frightened away all the minor daemons because they knew at once that the time of their own deaths had come. There is also a Christian explanation: Christ chased these daemons from the world.[55]

Speculation about the death of Pan continued in the Renaissance and afterward. Rabelais thought that Pan was Christ, for *pan* means "all," and Christ is mankind's all.[56] This idea was taken up by Fontenelle in his *Histoire critique des oracles*. The fact that Christ was crucified at about the same time that Great Pan died suggested to him that it was Jesus' death and resurrection that upset the daemons so much, because they realized they could no longer control mankind. But Fontenelle also considered the possibility that Jesus and Great Pan might be "daemons" of approximately the same rank, and that the death of one would affect the other.

Even if the story of Great Pan has no foundation whatsoever, it seems to sum up the mood of an entire era and its historical truth is that of a myth, albeit a late myth. The lifetime of Plutarch (c. A.D. 45–125), who took the myth seriously, coincides with the time in which almost all the books of the New Testament were written.

Augury

An important form of divination in Greece and Rome was augury (augurium), the interpretation of the flight, sound, and manner of feeding of birds. This technique was practiced so commonly that augur became the word for any soothsayer, diviner, or prophet. Cicero, who was an augur himself, though he did not take the office very seriously, states that this craft was practiced in the ancient Near East in different cultures.[57] From Greek mythology we know that in the heroic age there were seers who understood the "language of the birds"—Calchas, Melampus, and Tiresias, among others. Moreover, it should be noted that these seers could interpret other phenomena as well. According to Homer (Il. 2.308ff.), Calchas understood at once an event that involved a dragon (a huge snake) and nine sparrows. Melampus understood the speech of all creatures, including birds, because snakes had licked his ears (Schol. Hom., Od. 11.290). Tiresias, who once observed two snakes coupling (Hyg., Fab., nr. 75), was blind when he received his prophetic gift, and thus would have been unable to observe birds flying; yet he, too, is labeled an augur. Strangely enough, we find the same association with birds and snakes in this list of great seers that we noted earlier. This should not be surprising, however, for snakes represent the divine powers of the earth, while birds might be envisaged as being in closer contact with the Olympian gods. The fact that Calchas, Melampus, and Tiresias were not committed to augury alone indicates that the oracles coming from the ancient earth goddess through her messengers, the snakes, had not been completely superseded by the oracles coming from the heavenly gods through their messengers, the birds. As might be expected, Greek mythology describes an age of transition.

In Greek, a bird of omen or augury is called an oionos, and a person who "foretells from the flight and cries of birds" is known as an oionistes, oionethetes, or oionoskopos. A whole family of words was built up around this ancient custom. No important decision affecting a country or an army was made without first consulting the birds.

According to Cicero (Div. 1.92), this divination technique was known in Asia Minor as well as in Greece. In Rome it was entrusted to a college of *augures*. This college, one of the most distinguished in Rome, originally consisted of three members, but was gradually increased to sixteen. The etymology of *augur* is uncertain, but the traditional derivation *avis* 'bird' and *gero* 'to carry' seems impossible; it may be an Etruscan word. Strictly speaking, the augurs were not diviners; it was their function to find out, by observing certain signs, whether or not the gods approved of a certain plan of action. The signs were divided into *oblativa* 'casual ones'[58] and *impetrativa* 'those one watches for'. In observing wild birds, the augur defined (in words) a specific area of the sky or the land, called *templum*, and only what happened within this area was considered significant.

Alectryomancy was another method by which the Romans explored the will of the gods. It consisted in consulting the sacred chickens that were carried along on military campaigns. If, before a battle, the chickens ate their food so greedily that some of it fell from their beaks, this was considered an excellent omen.

Auguria were taken before any important public event, such as elections, a governor's entrance into a province, and the like, and this naturally gave the augurs great power, a power they occasionally misused for political reasons. A synonym or near-synonym for *augurium* (the difference in meaning, if any, is not clear) is *auspicium* (probably from *avis* 'bird' and an old verb, *specio* 'to watch'). This term was extended to cover many types of divination, from "the observation of things in heaven" to "frightening portents." Only certain magistrates had the right to take *auspicia*, and only consuls, praetors, and censors were allowed to perform the more elaborate ritual of the "major auspices."

The "Etruscan Art"

The inspection of the entrails of a sacrificial victim, especially of the liver (hepatoscopy) was thought to give a clue to the future. This technique was called *Etrusca disciplina* 'Etruscan art', or *haruspicina* (sc. *ars*), or *haruspicium* (analogous to *auspicium*), and its practitioners were known as *haruspices*.[59] The first part of the word, *haru-*, is compared by linguists to Gk. *chorde* 'guts', and the second part seems to be derived from the verb *specio* 'to watch,' which we have already encountered. The Romans learned this technique from the Etruscans, but the Etruscans apparently brought it with them from the Near East, for we know that it was practiced by the Babylonians and the Hittites.[60]

In Rome, a body of sixty *haruspices*, headed by a chief *haruspex*, became a threat to the *augures*, but the two techniques were practiced side by side for centuries.

The Etruscans apparently created a myth to explain the origin of this form of divination.[61] Cicero tells the story irreverently (*Div.* 2.50). An Etruscan farmer was plowing his field near the town of Tarquinii, about sixty miles from Rome, when a childlike creature suddenly emerged from one of the deeper furrows. That creature introduced himself as Tages and proceeded to reveal the secrets of *haruspicina* to all the Etruscans who had, in the meantime, assembled around him and were eagerly writing down every word. This marked the beginning of a doctrine that was later expanded, but as Cicero adds, rather sarcastically, "This is what we hear from them [the Etruscans]; this is what *their* writings [the priestly books] preserve; this is the origin of *their* science." Cicero talks about the Etruscan diviners the way a Victorian Englishman might talk about the Welsh Druids: they represent a different culture, and he is puzzled (and amused) that this foreign ritual could still have such a hold on the Roman imagination. Elsewhere (*Div.* 2.51) he quotes with approval something that Cato the Elder (c. 200 B.C.) once said: "How can two *haruspices,* upon meeting, not laugh at each other?"[62]

The *haruspices* observed and interpreted three kinds of phenomena: the entrails of animals; unnatural things or events in nature; and lightning (Cic., *Div.* 1.12; 2.26). The Etruscan *haruspex* Arruns, as described by Lucan (*Phars.* 1.584ff.), is probably not historical, but his qualifications would fit any practitioner of the craft: "He knows thoroughly the course of the thunderbolt, the marks on entrails still warm and the messages of winged creatures that fly through the air. He orders . . . the destruction of monsters which nature had produced, as abnormal births [reading *dissors,* with Oudendorp, for ms. *discors*] from mixed [reading *mixto,* with Grotius, for ms. *nullo*] seed and gives instructions to burn the abominable offspring of a barren womb with wood from a tree of bad omen." He performs a sacrifice (1.609ff.) and observes one horrifying omen after another; the liver, for instance, has two lobes, one of which is limp and flabby, while the other throbs with a hectic rhythm. When he sees this, the *haruspex* knows that a catastrophe is imminent, but he does not have the courage to tell the truth—that a civil war between Caesar and Pompey is unavoidable. The passage from Lucan also shows how we ought to understand "unnatural things or events in nature" (*monstra*). These include teratological, that is, abnormal or monstrous, formations in animals or plants, misshapen organisms of any kind, and strange meterological phenomena. Such events were reported from all parts of Italy, to be analyzed by the experts, and if they occurred more frequently in one particular year, rumors of an impending crisis began to circulate.

The interpretation of lightning was also part of the "Etruscan science." It was important to note from which of sixteen sections of the sky the lightning came and what spot or object on earth it hit.

Other Methods of Divination

There are so many other methods of divination that it is almost impossible to list them, except, perhaps, those that are labeled with a specific name. Most of them did not require any apparatus or technical expertise and could be practiced almost anywhere. The catalogues compiled by scholars are rather tedious to read, but since this is a chapter of cultural history—and one that provides some curious insights into human psychology—a brief survey seems appropriate. The information we have comes from various sources, many of them late and inexplicit, but it seems that much of the material was compiled by Marcus Terentius Varro (116–27 B.C.) in Book 41 of his monumental work, *The History of Rome and Its Religion* (*Antiquitates Rerum Humanarum et Divinarum*). Varro was one of the greatest scholars of his time and an authority on Roman religion, and later writers—the Church fathers for example—used him extensively, but the work as a whole is lost.

The body movements of human beings, especially their involuntary behavior (twitching, sneezing, etc.), provided omens. A visible part of someone's body might suddenly move spasmodically and give, to the observer, some indication of the future.

The various methods of divining from inanimate objects were divided by Varro into four classes that corresponded to the four elements: geomancy, aeromancy, pyromancy, hydromancy (*Schol. Dan. Virg. Aen.* 3.359; Isid., *Etym.* 8.9.13). Actually, the phrase *inanimate objects* is misleading, because to the ancient Greeks and Romans, especially to Platonists and Stoics, nothing was wholly inanimate. Divination was possible because there was at least part of a cosmic soul in everything.

Geomancy was the art of divining by means of lines formed by throwing earth on a surface. *Aeromancy* consisted in casting sand or dirt into the wind and studying the shape of the resulting dust cloud; or in throwing seeds into the wind, allowing them to settle on the ground, and interpreting their pattern (though this is also considered a form of *aleuromancy*).[63] The modern method of teacup reading might be compared, even though the element is water rather than air. *Pyromancy* (or *empyromancy*) is divination by fire or signs derived from fire: if incense is placed on fire, we speak of *libanomancy*; if flour is thrown on the flames, this is a form of *aleuromancy*; if an egg is broken over the fire, the term is *oöscopy.*[64] When the shoulder blade of a sheep is heated over the coals, one uses the term *omoplatoscopy* or *scapulomancy.*

All these methods were obviously practiced at some time in one or more parts of the ancient world. The fire and the materials preferred strongly suggest a sacrifice offered to a god—Apollo for example—because incense and grain were used as offerings, either along with a slaughtered animal or instead of it, from time immemorial. Since the deity was thought to be present at such a ceremony, it was he or she who conveyed the omen, but it may have been the duty of a priest to interpret it. Any sacrifice of this kind could be performed in private, but the more solemn the occasion, the greater the likelihood that more people were present.

The various subdivisions of *hydromancy* 'divination by water'[65] are not always clearly defined. The term *scrying* is used for "crystal gazing," but strictly speaking, water or any other translucent or shiny surface could have been substituted for the crystal, which is not attested before Byzantine times.[66] This technique allows the "medium" to see a series of hallucinatory moving pictures "within" the shining object.[67] Not everyone, at least not in modern times, can be a "medium": F. W. H. Myers, who was a classical scholar and a psychic, estimated that perhaps one man or woman in twenty can experience hallucinations of this kind.[68]

At least two methods of scrying were used in antiquity. In one the translucent object was a mirror—not necessarily in the modern sense of the word, but a highly polished metal surface, a soldier's shield for instance. This method is called *catoptromancy*. In the other a glass or bowl of water was used, and for this the terms *lecanomancy* 'divination by bowl' and *hydromancy* 'divination by water' are attested.

Hydromancy,[69] like many other methods of divination, seems to have originated in Babylonia and reached the Greco-Roman world via Egypt, in the first century B.C. or earlier.[70] It was fairly popular throughout antiquity and in Byzantine times. In Europe, during the Middle Ages and later, it was associated with witchcraft, and in some countries severe penalties prohibited this seemingly harmless practice.

One ancient method is described by M. P. Nilsson:

> Scrying was done by gazing at the surface of water, a method . . . which reminds us of modern crystal-gazing. A medium, an innocent boy, was chosen after he had been tested and found suitable. . . . The medium, with his eyes shut or bandaged, lay on his belly, with his face over a vessel containing water. Thereupon certain ceremonies were gone through which led up to the trance into which the medium passed by staring at the surface of the water, wherein he saw the beings summoned up by the magician, and then gave answers to the questions asked.[71]

The methods varied according to the nature of the shiny object used and the medium employed; sometimes a pregnant woman was substituted for the "innocent" boy (*innocent* here meaning "lacking sexual experience"). Sometimes the term *gastromancy* ('divination by the belly' was used, because the vessel filled with water was called *gastra* 'belly-shaped vessel'.[72]

Other requisites mentioned are: a small altar, a statue of a god, a lantern (Apul., *Apol.*, ch. 42). A magical papyrus in London (*PGM* 5) describes how to obtain an oracle from Serapis. One needs a bowl, a lamp, a bench, and a young boy. The prescribed ritual involves the following: the invocation of Serapis, pouring the water into the bowl, lighting the lamp (at this point the boy probably stretches out on the bench so that he can look down into the bowl), waiting for visions in the water, a prayer to dismiss the god, a charm to protect the boy.

In ancient terms this is a magical ceremony. We would call the boy a medium. When the boy sees certain things in the water (a throne carried by four men crowned with olive branches, preceded by a censer bearer, is mentioned), the priest knows that the medium is now in trance. These images can vary from cult to cult, from age to age. In this case we are probably glimpsing a ritual procession in honor of the god Serapis in the late Hellenistic period. In theory, other images could be substituted, but this particular vision has survived for centuries, for we have a remarkably similar account of the same kind of ceremony from an English traveler, E. W. Lane, who visited Egypt in the nineteenth century.[73] The images that the boy-medium sees at the beginning of his trance are also certainly scenes of temple life in Egypt two thousand or more years ago. One possible explanation is that this technique was taught by one generation of magicians to the next for centuries, and that along with the technique a certain way of "programming" the medium was inherited. This programming could have been done when the boy was hypnotized. The long survival of these ancient practices, at least under certain circumstances, is truly astonishing.

Crystal gazing (*crystallomancy*) is not referred to by this name before Byzantine times, but the practice itself seems to be older.[74] The favorite mineral used by the ancient diviners was the beryl, a transparent stone pale green in color and passing into light blue, yellow, and white; the green variety of the transparent beryl is the emerald, while the pale bluish-green variety is the aquamarine. All these stones were used in antiquity, but in modern times "crystal balls" made of clear glass have been substituted.[75]

No doubt many other techniques of divination were known to the ancients but were never described in detail. The term *rhabdomancy* appears in a gloss without further explanation. Translated as "divination by means of a rod or wand," it is connected with a passage from Herodotus (4.67) in which we are told that the Medes, the Persians, and the Scythians used a stick or rod for divining. How they used it is not known, but it is reasonable to assume that Herodotus was speaking of the "divining rod" used for dowsing or "water witching" to this day.[76] No clear reference is found in any ancient author, though on the strength of Numbers 20:7–11 Moses is sometimes called the first dowser, assuming that the staff with which he struck the rock twice, after speaking to it, was a divining rod, not a magic wand.

According to the historian Ammianus Marcellinus (29.1.25ff.), participants in magical operations involving a kind of Ouija board were brought to trial for high treason.[77] Their instrument, produced as evidence, was a tripod of olive wood which supported a circular metal dish. On the rim of the dish were engraved the twenty-four letters of the Greek alphabet. A ring hanging from a thin linen thread began to swing from letter to letter, spelling out words and arranging the words into hexameters. Then someone asked the crucial question: "Who will be our next emperor?" Slowly the ring began to spell: first a *theta*, then an *epsilon*, then an *omikron*—it could only mean Theodorus, or so they thought. Unfortunately, they were wrong. One of them informed a so-called friend, and soon afterward they were all arrested, tried, and put to death, and Theodorus, though he insisted to the end that he knew nothing of the whole experiment, was put to death also. Had they only been a little more patient, the divination board would have told them the truth. Seven years later the reigning emperor, Valens, was killed, and his successor was Theodosius.

A board similar to the one described above was excavated at Pergamon,[78] but it is not really a member of the Ouija board family; it is more like a roulette table, for the answers it provides seem to be determined by chance alone.

Chiromancy, or palmistry, is mentioned in the second century A.D. by Pollux (2.152), but apparently it was practiced in the Far East at least two thousand years before that. Originally it was based on intuition combined with symbolism, and some of the symbolism was derived from astrology. Lines in the hand forming a triangle (trine, 120° in astrology) were considered a good sign, while lines resembling a square (90° in astrology) were interpreted as a bad omen.

Tarot cards, as popular today as they were in the Middle Ages, were possibly created in Egypt as part of the Cabalistic tradition. When they were brought to Spain by Jewish scholars, they were adapted to Medieval society; for example, the medieval clergy was symbolized by cups or chalices, the nobility by swords, merchants by pentacles, and peasants by wands. In subsequent centuries these class distinctions lost their meaning, and the cards were filled with new magical significance as practitioners interpreted the changing social scene. Basically, tarot is a variation of the sortilege technique, for each card represents the elaboration of one symbol.

The preceding survey of the methods used in ancient divination, incomplete as it is, shows that almost anything could be used to predict the future—the human body, the organs of an animal, minerals, artifacts, the four elements, even the stars. Almost anything that could be experienced or observed, anything that attracted attention, anything that could be manipulated—in a simple way or in an elaborate ritual—had some meaning for the individual or the community. Certain techniques were confined to certain places. Some required highly skilled practitioners, but many were devised for the use of the ordinary person. In a universe where supernatural powers were thought to influence every act and thought, ancient divination was essentially a form of psychotherapy. It helped people cope with their worries about the future, and it forced them to reach decisions after all the rational angles had been explored.

Notes

1. See Dodds, *The Greeks and the Irrational*, p. 70.
2. See H. Gunkel, *Die Propheten* (Tübingen: Mohr, 1917).
3. All the essential information is given in A. St. Pease's article in the *Oxford Classical Dictionary* (2nd ed.), s.v. "Divination."
4. There is a French translation of Artemidorus' *Oneirocritica*, with valuable notes, by A.-J. Festugière (Paris: Vrin, 1975) and an English one by R. J. White (Park Ridge, N.J.: Noyes, 1975). Dodds, *The Greeks and the Irrational*, ch. 4, is devoted to dreams. See also G. E. V. Grunebaum and R. Caillois, eds., *The Dream and Human Societies* (Berkeley and Los Angeles: University of California Press, 1966). On incubation see L. Deubner, *De Incubatione* (Giessen: Töpelmann, 1900).
5. Dodds, *The Ancient Concept of Progress*, p. 174.
6. The dream book of Ashurbanipal has been published and translated by A. L. Oppenheim in *Transactions and Proceedings of the American Philosophical Society*, n.s., 46 (1956). The dreams sent by the gods to kings, priests, or wise men were considered self-explanatory, so to speak, because these persons had the authority to interpret them.
7. Aeschylus' *Agamemnon* is a tragedy about a Greek ruler who won a war and returned with a prophetess, Cassandra, as his captive; she foresaw his and her own doom.
8. Dodds, *The Greeks and the Irrational*, p. 120.
9. According to Plato, prophetic dreams originate in the rational soul but are seen by the irrational soul as images reflected on the smooth surface of the human liver; see the reference to the *Timaeus* in Dodds, *The Greeks and the Irrational*, p. 120.
10. Dodds, *The Greeks and the Irrational*, p. 120.
11. Ibid.
12. Ibid.
13. Dodds, *The Ancient Concept of Progress*, p. 183.
14. Achilles Tatius, *The Adventures of Leucippe and Clitophon* 1.3.2.
15. See W. O. Stevens, *The Mystery of Dreams* (New York: Dodd, Mead, 1949); and E. Fromm, *The Forgotten Language* (New York: Holt, Rinehart, 1959), esp. pp.

47ff. on Freud and Jung. See also A. Faraday, *Dream Power* (New York: Coward, McCann, and Gheoghegan, 1972).

16. C. G. Jung et al., eds., *Man and His Symbols* (Garden City, N.Y.: Doubleday, 1964), p. 51.
17. Dodds, *The Greeks and the Irrational*, p. 104.
18. W. R. Halliday, *Greek Divination* (London: Macmillan, 1913), ch. 3. "Bacis" may have been the name given to a whole group of inspired prophets who were active in the seventh and sixth centuries B.C. Another legendary figure, "Musaeus," seems to be related to "Orpheus"; he is a healer as well as a diviner.
19. R. Flacelière, *Greek Oracles*, trans. D. Garman (New York: Norton, 1963). F. W. H. Myers' *Essays Classical* (London: Macmillan, 1904) and M. P. Nilsson's *Cults, Myths, Oracles, and Politics in the Ancient World* (Lund: Gleerup, 1951) also are important.
20. Bernard de Fontenelle, *Histoire critique des oracles*, ed. L. Maigron (Paris: Cornély, 1908), p. 70.
21. See S. A. B. Mercer, *Religion of Ancient Egypt* (London: Luzac, 1949), pp. 157ff.
22. See A. Guillaume, *Prophecy and Divination* (London: Hodder and Stoughton, 1938).
23. See, e.g., H. H. Rowley, *The Servant of the Lord* (Oxford: Blackwell, 1965).
24. See E. Rohde, *Psyche*, 3rd ed. (Tübingen: Mohr, 1903), 2:18ff.; R. Reitzenstein, *Hellenistische Mysterienreligionen*, 3rd ed. (Leipzig: Teubner, 1910), pp. 236ff.
25. See *Dictionary of the Bible*, 2nd ed., s.v. "Tongues, gift of"; A. Mackie, *The Gift of Tongues* (New York: Doran, 1922).
26. Dodds, *The Ancient Concept of Progress*, p. 174, quotes from a Byzantine author, Psellus, *How Daemons Operate*, ch. 14, and points out that the *Rituale Romanum*, still the official Roman Catholic handbook for exorcists, cites as criteria of possession "the ability to speak or understand an unknown language and to reveal things distant or hidden."
27. Rohde, *Psyche*, 2:18ff.; Dodds, *The Greeks and the Irrational*, pp. 77ff.
28. See I. M. Lewis, *Ecstatic Religion: An Anthropological Study of Spirit Possession and Shamanism* (1971; reprint, Harmondsworth: Penguin Books, 1975).
29. This anguish of prophetic revelation is well attested and may be compared to Jung's "painful process of individuation."
30. See A. Dieterich, *Eine Mithrasliturgie*, 2nd ed. (Leipzig: Teubner, 1903), pp. 2ff.
31. John Cowper Powys, *Autobiography* (New York: Simon and Schuster, 1934), p. 531.
32. See R. A. Knox, *Enthusiasm: A Chapter in the History of Religion* (New York: Oxford University Press, 1950).
33. See E. Bevan, *Sibyls and Seers* (London: Allen and Unwin, 1929).
34. Dodds, *The Ancient Concept of Progress*, pp. 176ff., gives a very instructive survey of possible explanations; he distinguishes clairvoyance from precognition, for apparently only the latter is explained by "divine images" (pp. 162, 202). One cannot help feeling that occult phenomena, like religious experiences, may be labeled and classified, but that the labels in themselves are no explanation.

35. On "retrocognition" see ibid., p. 160, n. 3. Sir Wallis Budge, in *By Nile and Tigris* (London: Murray, 1922), p. 122, tells us that he once relived in a room a horrible event that had actually taken place a long time ago. He goes on to explain that places can be like phonograph records, and that the psychic is like the needle that brings out the sound (i.e., the experience that is engraved in the place).

36. See S. Morenz, *Aegyptische Religion* (Ithaca, N.Y.: Cornell University Press, 1973), pp. 32ff.

37. See note 19 above.

38. Since the Egyptian oracle Amun, or Ammon ("the Hidden One"), was famous in Greece, one may assume that the Greeks inherited this form of divination from an older culture; see Mercer, *Religion of Ancient Egypt,* pp. 157ff.

39. Verses from Homer were written on papyrus, and then one particular verse was selected by throwing dice or pricking the papyrus with a needle; that verse was then interpreted as a response to one's question; see A. Vogliano, *ACME* 1 (1948): 226ff.

40. An English translation is found in R. H. Charles, *Apocrypha and Pseudepigrapha of the Old Testament* (Oxford: Clarendon Press, 1913), vol. 2.

41. See P. Fraser, *Ptolemaic Egypt,* 3 vols. (Oxford: Clarendon Press, 1968), 1:708ff.

42. Fragments of the *Chaldean Oracles* were compiled and edited by W. Kroll (Leipzig: Teubner, 1894). For Dodds' comments on them, see *The Greeks and the Irrational,* pp. 283ff.

43. See H. Lewy, *Chaldaean Oracles and Theurgy;* and the new edition by H. Tardieu (Paris: Etudes Augustiniennes, 1978).

44. See H. W. Parke, *Greek Oracles* (London: Hutchinson, 1967).

45. Plutarch himself seems to have believed in "prophetic exhalations from the earth"; see *On the Cessation of Oracles,* ch. 44.

46. Cf. G. Luck, in *Gnomon* 25 (1953): 364.

47. Dodds, *The Greeks and the Irrational,* pp. 70ff., 87ff.

48. K. Buresch, *Klaros* (Leipzig: Teubner, 1899); C. Picard, *Ephèse et Claros* (Paris: Boccard, 1922).

49. Dodds, *The Ancient Concept of Progress,* pp. 168, 198–99.

50. Dodds, *The Greeks and the Irrational,* pp. 74–75, 93.

51. M. P. Nilsson, *Greek Popular Religion* (New York: Columbia University Press, 1940), pp. 123–24.

52. Dodds, *The Greeks and the Irrational,* pp. 217–18, 222–23.

53. Nilsson, *Cults, Myths, Oracles, and Politics in the Ancient World,* pp. 95ff.

54. Plutarch, *De Defectu Oraculorum,* ed. R. Flacelière (Paris: Les Belles Lettres, 1947).

55. Euseb., *Praep. Evang.* 5.17; see also D. A. Russell, *Plutarch* (New York: Scribner, 1973), p. 145.

56. Rabelais, *Pantagruel* 4.28, quoted by Flacelière, in his edition of Plutarch's *De Defectu Oraculorum,* p. 79; see also Russell, *Plutarch,* p. 145.

57. Cic., *Div.* 1.92.

58. *Oblativa* were comparable to *enodia,* chance appearances of animals during a

walk or a journey. In German folklore, a black cat that crosses one's path means bad luck.

59. See Sir James Frazer's translation of Pausanias' *Description of Greece* (London: Macmillan, 1898), vol. 4; and G. Dumézil, *Archaic Roman Religion*, trans. P. Krapp (Chicago: University of Chicago Press, 1970), vol. 2.

60. Models of the liver of a sacrificial animal—no doubt used for teaching purposes—have been found in Boghazköi (Hittite territory) and in Piacenza (Etruscan territory). This would support the hypothesis that the Etruscans learned this particular technique of prediction from the Babylonians and taught it to the Romans.

61. See Cic., *Div.* 2.50, and Pease's note in his edition.

62. The answer, Cicero implied, is that they know only too well that the ritual is all a fraud.

63. See *The World Almanac Book of the Strange* (New York: New American Library, 1977), p. 402.

64. The egg could also be broken over water, and the shape that it formed would then be interpreted.

65. The *Shorter Oxford Dictionary of the English Language* (Oxford: Clarendon Press, 1975) adds: "or the pretended appearance of spirits therein."

66. *To scry* is apparently a shortened form of *to descry*, i.e., "to discover by observation."

67. Dodds, *The Ancient Concept of Progress*, pp. 186ff.

68. F. W. H. Myers, *Human Personality and Its Survival of Bodily Death* (London: Longmans Green, 1906), 1:237, quoted in Dodds, *The Ancient Concept of Progress*, pp. 186ff. In ancient times, young boys and girls were used, and their success rate seems to have been rather high.

69. A. Bouché-Leclerq, *Histoire de la divination dans l'antiquité*, 4 vols. (Paris, 1879–82), 1:185ff., 339–40.

70. Dodds, *The Ancient Concept of Progress*, p. 188.

71. M. P. Nilsson, *Greek Piety*, trans. H. J. Rose (New York: Norton, 1969), pp. 146ff. On modern methods see T. Besterman, *Crystal Gazing* (London: Rider, 1924); J. Melville, *Crystal Gazing and Clairvoyance* (Wellingsborough: Aquarius Press, 1970).

72. The term *gastromancy* is ambiguous, for it may also refer to ventriloquism.

73. See E. W. Lane, *An Account of the Manners and Customs of the Modern Egyptians*, 3 vols. (London: Nattal, 1846), quoted in Hull, *Hellenistic Magic*, pp. 21–22.

74. Dodds, *The Ancient Concept of Progress*, p. 186, n. 2.

75. For more information on scrying, see ibid., pp. 186ff.; there Dodds tells the story of a conjurer who used a device in order to fake a vision.

76. See W. Barrett and T. Besterman, *The Divining Rod* (New Hyde Park, N.J.: University Books, 1968). Minerals, ores, oil, and water have been located by this method. It does not always seem to work, but its success, on the whole, is undisputed; the phenomenon itself remains unexplained.

77. Dodds, *The Ancient Concept of Progress*, pp. 193–94, tells the story as described by Marcellinus and others.

78. See R. Wünsch, *Antikes Zaubergerät* (Berlin: Reimer, 1905).

Texts

The divination techniques described in the following texts are different, but the principle is the same: the participants in these rituals assumed that the future was somehow present, either visible in trance or written in the sky (astrology will be treated in Chapter 5) or understandable through dreams. Some of these techniques were more elaborate than others. The professional dream interpreter needed his dream books; the professional astrologer, his astrolabe, his ephemerids, and other tools. Although a medium apparently needed no requisites to enter a state of trance, the Delphic oracle, where ecstatic mediumship was the mode of divination, was a large institution composed of many buildings and a sizable staff of priests and attendants.

Essentially, ancient divination was a form of communication between gods and men. The oracles were sanctuaries where gods were thought to reside and be willing to talk to men and women under certain conditions, sometimes through an intermediary (the prophet), sometimes directly (in a dream).

72

Heraclitus, the "obscure philosopher," lived around 500 B.C., a time when the Delphic oracle enjoyed its full prestige and prosperity. In this statement he tries to define the "obscurity" of the oracle, which must have perplexed those who wanted clear-cut answers to their questions or explicit guidance in difficult situations. It has often been suspected that the oracle's ambiguity was deliberate: because several possibilities could be read into a prediction, the god would be right, no matter what happened.

Heraclitus prefers a different explanation. He distinguishes between two different ways of communicating (besides not communicating), "to speak out" and "to signify." The first way is the one we use in everyday conversation; the second is that of the poets, but also of some philosophers, notably Heraclitus himself. The relatively few fragments that are preserved from Heraclitus' works suggest that he modeled his style on that of the Delphic oracle, always saying too little rather than too much. Perhaps this has been the guiding principle of all great diviners throughout the ages; Nostradamus' predictions, published in the sixteenth century and still not fully understood today, are a good example of this cryptic style.

Heraclitus, quoted by Plutarch in *The Oracles of the Pythia*, p. 404

The Delphic oracle does not speak out; it does not hide: it signifies.

73

This excerpt from Xenophon's *Memorabilia* (*Recollections of Socrates*) could be discussed under "Daemonology" as well as under "Divination." It is an attempt, after Socrates' execution, to absolve him from the charge of having "introduced strange gods." Such a charge was indeed serious, for the gods might punish a whole community for the wrongs of one person. Xenophon, a disciple of Socrates', testifies that Socrates honored all the gods an Athenian was expected to honor, but that he also believed in a "spiritual force" that was, in a way, his own private oracle. It gave him "clues"; like the Delphic oracle, it did not spell things out. Apparently Socrates always knew what this inner voice meant, but when he was asked to give advice to his friends, he did not always want to take full responsibility for it, and so he would send them to one of the established oracles.

In speaking of his teacher, Xenophon also discusses divination in general. Socrates, like most Greeks of his time, including such eminently sensible men as Xenophon himself, firmly believed in divination, not only as a possibility, but as a practical necessity. The methods used (augury, prophetic voices, secret tokens, sacrifices) did not matter so much, though Socrates clearly preferred his own method. Divination worked because the gods made it work.

According to Socrates, in order to be successful in life, man needs all the expertise in his field that he can acquire, but he also needs knowledge of the future. Without this knowledge, he cannot prosper. It is curious that Socrates, who is so often labeled a rationalist, believed in the influence of irrational forces in our lives.

Xenophon, *Memorabilia*, or *Recollections of Socrates*, 1.1

I have often wondered by what arguments Socrates' prosecutors were able to persuade the Athenians that he deserved to die, according to [the laws of] the city. The indictment against him said in effect: "Socrates is guilty of rejecting the gods that the city worships and of introducing strange new deities of a different kind; he is also guilty of corrupting the youth."

First of all, what proof did they offer for his rejecting the gods that the city worshiped? He could often be seen performing sacrifices both at home and at the public altars of the city; he never practiced divination in secret. It was common knowledge that Socrates claimed to be guided by a "spiritual force" [*daimonion*], and this was probably the main reason for the charge that he was introducing new deities. But what he introduced was in no way more strange than the beliefs of other people in divination by augury, prophetic voices, secret tokens, and sacrifices. For they do not believe that the birds or the people they meet by coincidence actually know something that might help the diviner; [they believe] that the gods give us clues through them, and this is what Socrates believed, too. Only, while most people say that they have been dissuaded or encouraged by the birds or those they met by chance, Socrates said exactly what he meant: he said that the "spiritual force" gave him clues. Many of his companions were advised by him to do this and not to do that, just as the "spiritual force" guided him. Those who followed his advice were successful, those who did not, had cause for regret. . . . Obviously, Socrates would not have given this advice if he had not been confident that what he said would come true. And who else could have given him that confidence but a god? And since he had confidence in the gods, how could he possibly not believe in them?

Another way he had of dealing with close friends was this: the things that had to be done he told them to do as best they could. But if the outcome of something was doubtful, he sent his friends to the oracle to find out whether or not this ought to be done. Those who wanted to take good care of their household or of the state, he said, needed divination in addition [to their expertise]. For the carpenter's craft or that of the smith or the farmer or the ruler of men or the knowledge of dialectics or logic or economics or tactics . . . all these subjects he thought could be acquired by the human mind, but the most important part of these sciences had been reserved by the gods to themselves, and it was not accessible to men. You may plant a field well, but you do not know who will reap the harvest; you may build a house well, but you do not know who will live in it; you may be a good commander, but you do not know whether you will be successful in your command; you may be a good politician, but you do not know whether your politics will be good for the state; you may marry a beautiful woman, but you do not know whether she will bring you grief; you may gain powerful connections in the state through your marriage, but you do not know whether you will be exiled because of them. If any man thinks that none of these pursuits is controlled by a divine force and that all of them depend on human reason, he must be mad [in the Greek text here there is a play on the words of *daimonion* 'divine force' and *daimonān* 'to be possessed']. But it would also be mad to seek by divination something which men are allowed by the gods to learn by using their reason, to ask, for example: Is it better to hire an experienced coachman to drive my carriage or one who has no experience? Is it better to hire an experienced sailor to steer my ship or one who has no experience? This applies to everything that can be determined by counting, measuring, or weighing. To put such questions to the gods he considered an act of impiety. He said that we must learn what the gods have allowed us to achieve by learning, and that we must try to find out from them by means of divination what we, as human beings, cannot know for certain; the gods would give a clue to those who were in their favor.

74

The questions people asked the oracle at Dodona were written on thin lead tablets and apparently stored in the archives of the sanctuary. Many of them have been excavated and published. The responses of the oracle seem to have perished. As this selection (mostly from the third century B.C.) indicates, some questions were rather trivial in nature.

Dodona, an oracle of Zeus, was situated in the mountains of Epirus in northwestern Greece. We know that it was established in remote antiquity, for Homer writes of it (*Il.* 16.233–35; *Od.* 14.327–28, 19.296–97). A gigantic oak, the tree of Zeus, formed the center of the cult, and the rustling of its leaves was thought to reveal the will of the god. Zeus was worshiped at Dodona as Zeus Naios, and his consort was not Hera but Dione—actually a feminine form of Zeus, although Homer knows her as one of Zeus' many mistresses. The priests were called *Selloi* and are described by Homer as "those who do not wash their feet and sleep on the ground" (*Il.* 16.255); the priestesses were called "the Old Ladies" or "the Pigeons." These designations seem to document the long history of the sanctuary, for washing one's feet and sleeping on beds were relatively modern customs, and the name "Pigeons" reminded visitors of the ancient cult legend according to which a pigeon flying from Thebes in Egypt had lighted on the oak tree and, speaking with a human voice, ordered the institution of the oracle.

The questions asked represent various concerns and worries of individuals and communities:

793: It is difficult for the modern-day reader to understand why a city-state like the Mondaiatai would send a special delegation to Dodona just to find out whether a loan to a certain lady would be a safe investment or not. The city fathers probably let a number of similar requests pile up and sent them to the oracle in a batch, and from such a batch only this tablet has survived.

794. This man, Heracleidas, must have been married before, but

in his previous marriage(s) he had remained childless. His new wife is not yet pregnant, and he is getting impatient.

797. A man whose wife is pregnant worries whether he is the father or not. It is difficult to see how the oracle would answer such a question. Surely the priests were aware of the tragedy they would cause by confirming the husband's suspicions. An ambiguous answer in the true "oracular" style would not have helped, either.

799. Another business venture. It seems to involve a switch from one type of farming to another or, possibly, the expansion of a farm operation. On the reverse side of the tablet we read a note that was obviously added by the priest in charge or his clerk; it consists of (1) a brief rubric; (2) the abbreviated name of the petitioner; (3) a number. Since the name is abbreviated almost beyond recognition, we may assume that everyone was given a number and that the combination of rubric and name was meant to exclude any possible error.

Questions Asked at Dodona (= Dittenberger, *Sylloge*[2] 793–95, 797–99)

793. The state of the Mondaiatai consults Zeus Naios and Dione about the money of Themisto, whether she can afford it and whether it is all right to lend it.

794. Heraclides asks Zeus and Dione for good fortune and wants to know from the god about a child, if he will have one from his wife Aegle, the one he has now.

795. Nicocrateia would like to know to what god she ought to offer sacrifice in order to get well and feel better and make her illness go away.

797. Lysanius wants to know from Zeus Naios and Dione whether the child Annyla is expecting is his or not.

798. Is it more profitable for me and of much greater advantage to buy the house in the city and the piece of land?

799. Cleotas asks Zeus and Dione whether it is profitable and to his advantage to keep cattle. [On the reverse: About keeping cattle. K⟨LE⟩⟨OYTAS⟩. Nr. 5].

75

This inscription from the late first century B.C. records a decree of the Senate of the city-state of Anaphe, but it also includes the question that one citizen, Timotheus, submitted to an oracle, as well as the oracle's response.

Timotheus must have been a wealthy man. He was willing to build, for his city, a temple to Aphrodite. Such a gift, seemingly spontaneous, was often a form of taxation, but it also lent a certain amount of prestige to the donor. Officially, this oracle had to be consulted about the whole project and about the specific location of the temple. There is no need for Timotheus to describe the location—the god will know [see *no.* 74, par. 798]. In the end, the god approves the project and states his preference for one location over the other; he also gives further instructions, which ultimately lead to this record.

Timotheus Wants to Build a Temple (= Dittenberger, *Sylloge*[2] 555)

Timotheus asked the god whether it would be all right and appropriate for him to ask the city to build a temple of Aphrodite in the place he has in mind, in the precinct of Apollo of Asgelata, and let it be public property, or [build] it in the sanctuary of Asclepius, in the place he has in mind.

The god answered that he should ask [the city to have it built] in the precinct of Apollo and, after the completion of the temple, have the decree, the oracle, and the request inscribed on a stone slab. The Senate made a decision on these matters and granted him his request, provided the Assembly would approve of it, too.

76

This fragmentary inscription in three pieces was found on a hill near the Pergamene Gulf on the site of the ancient city of Demetrias. According to scholars, it dates from the first century B.C.

The text of the inscription shows that even minor cities (not well known in history) could have an oracle of their own. In this instance the oracle of Apollo of Corope is called an ancient institution, which in this context probably means "pre-Hellenistic." In the first century B.C. the great oracles were declining, and an effort was begun in Demetrias to reorganize the whole procedure of oracular consultation and to establish stricter rules. It is clear from the inscription that the secular authorities of the city, including the chief of police, were responsible for parts of the operation. Presumably they had neglected their duties in previous years, and the implication is that complaints had been made against them. But the visitors themselves had not always behaved properly either: they had not always worn their best garments, or they had been drunk and disorderly. Some of them may even have tried to bribe the officials in order to get preferential treatment. The strict rules prescribed represent an effort at reform, an attempt to restore the oracle to its former prestige. About the method of divination employed at the oracle the text says nothing.

Procedure at an Oracle (= Dittenberger, *Sylloge*[2] 790)

During the priesthood of Crino, son of Parmenio, on the tenth of the Areius month, a motion was presented by:

Crino, son of Parmenio of Homolion, priest of Zeus Acraeus; Dionysidorus, son of Euphraeus of Aeolia, commander of the Magnesians; by the commanders Aetolion, son of Demetrius of Pagasae; Cleogenes, son of Amyntas of Halae [more names] . . .

Whereas our city devoutly worships all gods, especially Apollo of Corope, and honors him with the most signal honors because of the blessings it has received from the god who gives, through his oracle, clear instructions, both in general and individually, concerning health and welfare,

It is right and appropriate, since the oracle is ancient and has been held in high esteem by our forefathers, and since many foreigners visit the seat of the oracle, that the city should take very careful measures for the proper maintenance of the oracle.

Let the Council and the People decree that whenever an oracular consultation has been completed, the priest of Apollo appointed by the city who happens to be in charge at the time, and one representative of the commanders, the guardians of the law, one delegate from both ruling bodies and one from the prytanies, the treasurer and the secretary of the god, and the keeper of the oracle [or, the interpreter?] must go [or, attend?].

If any one of those mentioned above is sick or abroad, he must send someone else. The commanders and the guardians of the law must enroll staff-bearers from among the citizens, namely, three men under thirty who shall have the authority to punish unruly elements. The staff-beater shall be paid from the collected contributions an allowance for two days, a drachma a day. If one of the enrolled [staff-bearers] fails to show up, he shall pay a fine of fifty drachmas to the city, after the commanders and the guardians of the law have established his culpability. When those mentioned above are present at the oracle and perform the sacrifice according to tradition, with a favorable result, the secretary of the god shall collect, immediately after the sacrifice, the petitions of those who wish to consult the oracle, write all their names on a white tablet, and exhibit the white tablet at once in front of the temple and lead them in, calling them up according to the order of their names, unless someone may have the privilege of being called ahead of the others. If the person called up is not present, the secretary shall lead in the following one, until the one called up [before] happens to arrive. In the sanctuary, the persons entered on the lists shall sit properly, in shining [i.e., festive] garments, crowned with laurel wreaths, clean and sober, and they shall receive the tablets from those who deliver the oracle. When the consultation has been completed, they shall throw the tablets into a vessel and seal [them?] with the seal of the commanders and the guardians of the law and also with that of the priest, and they shall let it [the vessel?] remain in the sanctuary. At dawn the secretary of the god shall bring in the vessel, show the seals to those mentioned before, open them, read from the list the names in their order, and give back to each one the tablet . . . [with] the oracle.

The staff-bearer shall take precautions about maintaining order if necessary. In the Assembly of the people, in the month of Aphrodision, before everything else, the examiners shall, in the presence of the people, administer to all persons mentioned before the following oath: "I swear by Zeus of Acra and by Apollo of Corope and by Artemis of Iolcus and by all the other gods and goddesses that I have performed all my duties as specified in the decree which was authorized concerning the oracle in the year of the priesthood of Crino, son of Parmenio."

After they have sworn this they shall be declared guiltless [or, they shall be released from their responsibility?]. If anyone does not take this oath, the examiners and any one of the citizens who wishes [to shall be] free to bring a complaint against him on the grounds of every single offense [that he may have committed]. If the examiners do not take any of the actions mentioned before, they will be responsible to their successors in office and to anyone else who wishes [to bring a charge against them]. To make sure that this decree is enforced forever, the ten annually chosen commanders and the guardians of the law shall hand over this decree to the officials who will be elected in the future. Furthermore, a copy of the decree shall be inscribed on a stone slab at the expense of the "Wall Builders" [officials responsible for repairs to the city walls] and is to be set up in the sanctuary of Apollo of Corope. . . .

77

Cicero's treatise *On Divination* is essentially an attack on the Stoic doctrine of divination as it was presented by Posidonius. In this passage, Cicero deals with oracles. He argues that oracles flourished only as long as people were naïve and credulous; as soon as the skepticism of the New Academy (i.e., the nondogmatic Platonists with whom Cicero had studied in Athens) had undermined the Stoic position, the oracles began to decline.

Cicero quotes two famous responses of the Delphic oracle. One had been given to Croesus, the last king of Lydia (sixth century B.C.); the other, to Pyrrhus, the last strong king of Epirus (fourth/third century B.C.). In both cases, an ambitious king was planning to attack a foreign power—Croesus, the Persians; Pyrrhus, the Romans. In both cases the god of Delphi was consulted. And in both cases the answer given was ambiguous: Croesus was defeated and thus destroyed his own kingdom; Pyrrhus, although "able" to defeat the Romans, achieved only a "Pyrrhic victory" and had to retire to Greece with about one-third of his army and without the strength needed to strike once more.

Even though the oracle had the last word, Cicero argues that it was misleading in both cases and did not keep its part of the bargain. The truth of the matter was that the oracle was a paid consultant who did not always give the best advice to clients.

Cicero also questions whether the oracular responses are historical. Had not, perhaps, Herodotus made up one, Ennius the other? The second response, not preserved in Greek, sounds especially suspicious: we have only this poetic version in Latin, yet at that time the oracle no longer went to the trouble of putting its responses in verse, and certainly not in Latin verse.

That the prestige of the oracles had declined in Cicero's time is well attested, and the philosophers of the era came up with various explanations. The Stoic theory that Cicero quotes appears in a slightly modified form in Lucan [*no. 85*] and also in Plutarch [*no. 87*]. The historical or economic reasons are difficult to assess, but there seem to have been three major ones: (1) in the first centuries of our era there was a tendency to move away from the great religious centers, to find a more personal relationship with the deity, a relationship that needed no elaborate apparatus; (2) Greece, like Judea, was incorporated into the Roman Empire, and the Romans did not do a great deal to support the famous old sanctuaries; (3) the countries occupied by the Roman legions were soon impoverished, for through the Roman tax system any wealth that might have gone to Delphi or Dodona went to Rome instead.

Cicero, *On Divination* 2.115–17

A famous oracle was given to the wealthiest ruler of Asia Minor:

> When Croesus crosses the Halys, he will destroy a
> mighty empire.

He thought that he was going to destroy his powerful enemy; [in fact] he lost his own. No matter which of the two events happened, the oracle would have been right. But why should I believe that this oracle was ever given to Croesus? Why should I believe that Herodotus is more reliable than Ennius? Was Herodotus less likely to make up something about Croesus than Ennius about Pyrrhus? For who ever believed that the oracle of Apollo made the following response to Pyrrhus?

> I tell you, descendant of Aeacus, that you are able to
> conquer Rome.

First of all, Apollo never answered in Latin. Second, the Greeks never heard of this particular oracle. Moreover, in the time of Pyrrhus, Apollo no longer spoke in verse. . . .

But the main point is this: Why are oracles of this kind [text and sense uncertain] no longer issued at Delphi, not only in our own time, but

for some time [text uncertain], so that the oracle has fallen into total
neglect [sense uncertain]? When the Stoics are pressed by this argument,
they answer that age has caused the evaporation of the power of the place
in the earth from which the breath came that aroused the mind of the
Pythia and made her utter oracles. . . . But when did this power evapo-
rate? Perhaps after people became less credulous?

78

In *On divination*, Cicero deals with various aspects of Stoic doctrine as
presented by Chrysippus (c. 280–207 B.C.), who defended it vigorously
against the doubts of the skeptics (2.130). Cicero is also familiar with
Posidonius (c. 135–50 B.C.), who, it seems, had collected a substantial
body of evidence to support his thesis that divination worked. But the
Stoics, as Cicero shows (1.82), also used purely logical arguments. If, as
the Stoics maintained, the gods are omniscient, all-powerful, and concerned for the welfare of mankind, it follows that they know what the
future will bring and are willing to share their knowledge with us because
it may help us.

In another excerpt (1.72) Cicero distinguishes between "natural"
and "technical" divination. Interpreting one's own dream is an instance
of natural divination, but various other techniques of predicting the future have to be learned.

Divination as a science may be based on statistics (1.109–10).
Cicero uses the words "frequency of records," but that is what we mean
by "statistics"; such statistics were probably kept over centuries by the
Babylonians and Egyptians, but possibly also by the Greeks and Romans.
The augurs, for instance, might note the behavior of birds at a certain
moment and tie their observations to striking events that followed soon
afterward. Even respectable historians like Livy listed unusual phenomena that were reported during a given year and worried the people,
but he leaves it up to the reader to match these "warnings" with actual
events. In a sense, this method is scientific, and it does not require the
intervention of a god or a daemon, though practitioners may claim that it
was a god who originally revealed these secrets to mankind. An ancient
legend may serve as an example: Tages, a divine being who looked like a
child, was unearthed by a farmer in a field near Tarquinia and there
revealed the secrets of the "Etruscan discipline" of divination to a committee of twelve Etruscans.

In the last excerpt (2.33) Cicero reluctantly admits the validity of
the Stoic concept that the universe is a living organism and that all its
parts are connected by "cosmic sympathy," but he rejects the practical
application of these principles. A haruspex looks at the liver of a freshly

slaughtered sheep and tells a person where to dig to find a buried treasure. How does the universe enter into all this?

Cicero, *On Divination*, excerpts

2.130. Chrysippus defined divination as the power to see, to understand, to interpret the signs that are given to men by the gods.

1.82. That divination really works is shown by the following Stoic argument: If the gods exist but do not reveal to men the future, either they do not love men, or they do not know what will happen, or they think that men have no interest in knowing the future, or they consider it beneath their majesty to warn men about the future, or even the gods are unable to warn us of what lies ahead. But they certainly love us, for they mean well and are friendly to mankind; they certainly know what they themselves have planned and established; it is definitely in our interest to know what will happen, for knowing it will make us more careful; it is entirely consistent with their majesty, for nothing is more important [to them] than to do good deeds; and of course they are able to predict the future.

1.72. Everything that is interpreted by guesses or observed and recorded in specific events belongs to the kind of divination . . . that is called "technical," not "natural." The *haruspices* [interpreters of internal organs of sacrificial animals, prodigies, lightning], the *coniectores* [soothsayers], and the *augures* [bird watchers] belong to this [category]. This sort of thing is rejected by the Peripatetics but is accepted by the Stoics.

1.109–10. Could there be a relatively easy science of technical predictions, but a more hidden one of divine predictions? For events that are foreshadowed in internal organs, in lightning, and in the stars [are interpreted] by a science based on long observation, and a long tradition adds in every subject, through accumulated observations, an incredible amount of knowledge. This kind of knowledge is possible, even without any influence, any impulse from the gods, because statistics [literally, "the frequency of records"] indicate what happens as a result of something else and what it means.

The other type of divination is "natural" and must be, as I have said before, and, as the greatest philosophers thought, theologically speaking, seen in relation to the gods, for we have sipped, we have imbibed our souls from the gods. Since the universe is filled to the brim with a sense that lasts forever, with a mind that is divine, it follows logically that the spirits of men are directed by the contact with spirits divine.

1.118. The Stoics do not believe that a god is actually present in the dividing lines of livers or in the sounds that birds make, for this is unsuitable for gods, unworthy of them, and simply cannot be imagined. They believe that from the beginning the world was designed in such a way that certain events would follow certain signs—signs in internal organs, in birds, in lightning, in portents, in stars, in dream visions, in the utterances of madmen. Those who really understand these things do not often go wrong; bad guesses and bad interpretations are wrong not because the facts mislead them but because the interpreters are incompetent.

2.33. What relationship do these things [i.e., the entrails from which the seers predict the future] have to the nature [of the universe]? Let us admit that it is held together by one common feeling and that it forms a unit—I see that this is the opinion of the physicists and especially of those who think that the whole universe is one—but what can the world have in common with the discovery of a treasure?

79

Cicero's treatise *On Divination* is not systematic; he returns to the same questions in different parts of the work.

The argument he makes in 2.41 is directed against the Stoic doctrine that the gods care for us and therefore want us to know the future [see *no. 78*]. Cicero (or his skeptic source) turns this around and says that there can be no knowledge of the future; hence there are no gods. Whether Cicero himself was an agnostic is a different matter; here he simply wants to show that the Stoic argument does not prove what it is supposed to prove.

Another argument the Stoics were fond of using is the concept of a universal consensus of mankind (2.81): All nations worship gods; therefore, all nations practice divination. Cicero reduces this argument *ad absurdum* by saying (1) that the Stoics themselves ignore the universal consensus when it does not serve their cause, and (2) that nothing is as universal as stupidity.

Cicero makes another point by asking these questions: Why should the gods give us any clues concerning the future, and, conceding that they actually give them, why are they usually so vague? The gods are supposed to help us because they love us. Why, then, do they make things needlessly difficult for us? Warning us of a disaster is not an act of kindness unless they also tell us how to avoid the disaster. Cicero also mentions catastrophes that occur without warning, noting that *post factum* a seer could always claim that he had foretold them.

Finally, he reports a few typical *omina* or *portenta* that to the average Roman could only be interpreted as signs of impending disaster. Here Cicero argues from a strictly philosophical point of view, and it is interesting to see that, for him, philosophy (or science) begins with Thales of Miletus (sixth century B.C.). Science (or philosophy), Thales contends, ought to liberate the human mind from irrational fears and superstitions by showing that everything has a natural cause and that there is no need to invoke supernatural powers. To understand the natural causes did not mean to control them, however, and in a sense, man was just as helpless as before.

Cicero, *On Divination,* excerpts

2.41. The Stoics actually argue when they are particularly eager [to make their point]: "If there are gods, there is divination; the gods are; therefore, there is divination." It would make much more sense to say: "There is no divination; therefore, there are no gods."

2.81. [*The defender of divination objects:*] But all kings, peoples, nations, make use of auspices. [*Cicero retorts:*] As if anything were as universal as the fact that people are stupid! As if you yourself would agree with the majority whenever you form a judgment! How many are there who deny that pleasure is a good? Most people even call it the highest good. Do their numbers shake the Stoics in their conviction? Or do the masses bow before the Stoics' authority in most matters? . . .

What is this premonition sent by the gods, this so-called warning of impending disasters? What do the immortal gods have in mind when they give us clues that we cannot understand without interpreters and—this is my second point—against which we are defenseless anyway? No decent human being would do that: predict to a friend an imminent disaster from which there is no way of escape. Physicians often realize the truth, but they never tell the patient that he will die of a certain illness. For the prediction of misfortune is [only] accepted when advice on how to avoid it is joined to the prediction. In what way did portents or their interpreters help the Spartans in the past or, more recently, the Romans? If they are to be considered signs of the gods, why are they so obscure? If the gods really wanted us to know the future, they should have stated it clearly; if they did not want us to know it, they should not even have hinted at it.

[*Prodigies and portents have no special significance; they can be explained by natural causes:*]

2.58. It has been reported that bloody rain fell, that the river Atratus was flowing with blood, that the statues of the gods had been sweating. Do you think that Thales or Anaxagoras or any other scientist would have believed these reports? There is no blood, no sweat, except from a body. . . .

2.60. Or does it frighten you when some monstrous birth from a beast or a human being is described? To make it short: all these things have a natural explanation. Whatever is born, no matter what it may be like, must have its origin from nature; therefore, even if it turns out to be abnormal, it cannot exist outside of nature. So by all means investigate the cause of a strange phenomenon, if you can; if you cannot find any, you may take it for granted that nothing could have happened without a cause, and whatever terror the strangeness of the phenomenon may have given you, the principles of science will drive it away.

80

Cicero here reports the doctrine of "natural divination" as formulated by Posidonius. This great Stoic philosopher believed that the air around us is full of invisible souls or spirits. Some of them are on the way to being incarnated, some have just left a dead body, some are absenting themselves temporarily from a sleeping person. There must be a certain intercourse, an exchange of ideas, between these spirits and the gods.

It seems that Posidonius had recorded a number of case histories that, to him, proved beyond a doubt that divination was possible, and he had developed this theory to explain the phenomenon. He was also convinced that the dying develop special powers of precognition or have some sort of remote control, and as an explanation he offered the theory that the soul, the divine part of the human personality, leaves the dying body and thereafter is able to use its full powers.

Many such stories were told and believed. One of the reasons why Stoicism was such a popular philosophy in the Late Republic and Early Empire was its appeal to popular beliefs and the use it made of them.

Cicero, *On Divination* 1.63–64

When, in sleep, the mind is separated from the companionship of the body and is not in touch with it, it remembers the past, sees the present, foresees the future. The body of the sleeper lies as if he were dead, but his mind is alert and alive. This is true to a much higher degree after death, when the mind has left the body altogether; therefore, when death approaches, the mind is much more divine. For those who are seriously, critically ill see the very approach of death; therefore, they have visions of the dead, and at this point they are anxious to be worthy of praise; but those who have not led the kind of life that one should lead regret their sins deeply. To show that the dying foresee the future, Posidonius quotes the following example: A man on Rhodes was dying and named six of his contemporaries in the order in which they were going to die [after him]. Posidonius thinks that there are three ways in which the gods cause dreams in men: first, because the mind foresees the future all by itself; second, because the air is full of immortal spirits on which the seal of truth appears as if it had been imprinted on them; third, because the gods themselves talk with those who are asleep.

81

Cicero now criticizes Posidonius' theory of dreams. Experience tells us that not all of our dreams come true; in fact, in a lifetime the vast majority of dreams offer no clues about the future. To this the Stoic might reply that we seldom remember all the details of a dream, and even if we did remember most of them, we would be unable to interpret all of them properly. It is true that the serious interpreters of dreams—Artemidorus for instance—insisted on being told all the details of a dream and claimed to know their true meaning.

     Cicero dismisses this argument. If this were true, why would the gods, caring and benevolent as they are supposed to be, not spell out the meaning for us? The Stoic might answer: Not everyone has the same kind of dreams. Most people have senseless, incomplete, confusing dreams; only the wise man dreams in a clear, consistent, and meaningful manner.

     Cicero's sarcasm aside, the Stoics were not totally wrong. There are dreamers and there are dreamers, and in ancient times there was even a technique that taught people how to prepare themselves for veridic dreams, through diet, exercise, prayers, meditation, and the like.

Cicero, *On Divination* 2.127–28

Well, who would be bold enough to say that all dreams are true? "Some dreams are true," says Ennius, "but not necessarily all." But what kind of distinction is this, anyway? Which does he consider true, which false? And if the true ones are sent by a god, where do the false ones come from? For if they, too, are divine, what could be more inconsistent than god? And what is sillier than to vex the minds of men with false, deceitful visions? If true visions are divine, and false ones are human, what kind of arbitrary distinction are you proposing? Does this mean that god makes this, nature that? Should one not rather assume that god made every-thing—but this you deny—or nature made everything? But since you deny the former, one must necessarily admit the latter. . . . When the mind cannot make use of the limbs and the sense because the body is tired, it encounters vague visions of different kinds from residual impres-sions, as Aristotle says, of things that it did or thought while awake; when those get out of control, strange kinds of dreams result.

82

This scene from Seneca's *Agamemnon* only remotely resembles Aeschylus' tragedy of the same title, but the story is roughly the same: Agamemnon, king of Mycenae and supreme commander of the Greeks during the

Trojan War, returns in triumph to Mycenae after an absence of more than ten years. He brings with him his captive Cassandra, the most beautiful of King Priam's daughters. Apollo, who had fallen in love with her at one time, had bestowed on her the gift of prophecy, but when she disappointed him, he put a curse on her: though her visions of doom would inevitably come true, no one would believe her. This curse plagues her during her whole career as a prophetess: When her brother Paris is born, she predicts that he will some day ruin Troy, but no one believes her; she also warns the people against the Wooden Horse, but no one listens.

During the sack of Troy, Ajax, the son of Oileus, had dragged her away from the altar of Athena, where she was seeking refuge. Later, Agamemnon claimed her as his personal property. Now that he has returned, his wife, Clytemnestra, and her lover, Aegisthus, are planning to murder him as well as his mistress, and that is what Cassandra foresees.

The Chorus observes Cassandra entering into a state of trance. For the description, Seneca uses a few details from Virgil's *Aeneid* 6.77–82 and 6.98–102 (the trance of the Sibyl of Cumae). A theme that sometimes occurs in such descriptions [see also *no. 85*] is that of a prophetess who is unwilling to abandon herself to the god who is taking over and controls her. This act of taking possession of the prophetess is often described in almost sexual terms, as a kind of rape. In Seneca's text, part of Cassandra's eccentric behavior is explained as her desperate struggle against the overpowering presence of the god. Also, to have vivid premonitions of disaster without being able to do anything about them was surely a painful experience. In addition, the physical shock of trance was considered traumatic and health-damaging.

With bitter irony Cassandra calls herself a "false prophet," because this is what people have always called her. Now nature seems to change around her: the sun disappears from the sky, darkness descends, there are two suns, two royal palaces of Mycenae. This double vision seems to be characteristic of trance. Then Cassandra sees the queen, ax in hand, and her victim, Agamemnon, in the shape of a lion, about to be killed. She also hears the voices of members of her family, the royal family of Troy, all dead—Priam, Hector, Troilus, Deiphobus. She sees the Furies and other Monsters of the underworld, and realizes they are ready to receive new shades, including herself. Although she is doomed, the brutal, humiliating end of the Greek conqueror is a triumph for the conquered Trojans, and Cassandra does not fail to make this point.

Seneca, *Agamemnon*, vv. 710–78

CHORUS: Suddenly the priestess of Phoebus is silent. Her cheeks are pale, and her whole body shakes. Her fillets stiffen; her soft hair stands on end; her heart hisses frantically with a choking sound. Her glance wanders unsteadily in different directions; her eyes seem to twist and turn inward and then again just to stare motionless. Now she lifts her head up into the air, higher than usual, and walks erect. Now she is getting ready to unseal her vocal chords against their will; now she tries to close her lips but cannot keep her words inside. Here is a priestess in ecstasy who fights against her god!

CASSANDRA: Sacred heights of Parnassus! Why do you prick me with the goad of an unfamiliar madness? I have lost my mind; why do you sweep me away? Leave me, Phoebus! I am no longer yours. Extinguish the flame that you have kindled deep in my breast! What good does it do if I rush around like mad? Who needs my bacchantic frenzy? Troy has fallen: What is left for me, a "false" prophet, to do? Where am I? The kindly light is gone; deep darkness blinds my sight; heaven, covered with gloom, hides itself from me. But look! There are two bright suns in the sky; there is a double Argus with two towering palaces!—I can see the groves of Ida where the fateful shepherd sits, appointed to judge between the mighty goddesses.—Kings, beware of incestuous offspring! That country boy shall overturn a royal house!—Who is that madwoman? Why does she carry a naked sword in her hand? She is dressed like a Spartan but carries the ax of the Amazons. Who is the hero she attacks? Now my eyes are focussing on another face—whose? An African lion, the king of beasts, his neck formerly so proud, lies there, bitten by a vicious tooth, bloodied by the bite of a bold lioness.—Shades of my dead ones, why do you call me? I am the only one still alive. I shall follow you, father, I, the witness of Troy's funeral. Brother, help of the Trojans, terror of the Greeks, I see you. But I do not see you in your former splendor, your hands still hot from the burning ships! Your body is mangled, your arms bruised by heavy bonds. Troilus, you met Achilles too soon; I shall follow you. Your face, Deiphobus, is unrecognizable—a gift from your new wife. I am glad to wade through the depth of the Stygian pool, to see the savage dog of Tartarus and the realms of gloomy Dis. Today the ferry of black Phlegethon will carry over two royal souls—one of a conqueror and one of the conquered. Shades, hear my prayer. Water by which the gods swear, hear my prayer. For a short while open the cover from the world of darkness, that the ghostly crowd of Trojans may look at Mycenae. Look, wretched souls: the Fates have made a full turn!

The squalid sisters are threatening. They brandish their bloody whips; they hold half-burned torches in their left hands; their pale cheeks are bloated; black funereal robes gird their emaciated loins. The fearful noises of night come alive. The bones of a huge body, rotten and decayed long ago, lie there in a slimy swamp. Look! Old Tantalus forgets his thirst and no longer tries to drink that water that eludes his lips; he is sad because someone will die very soon. But father Dardanus rejoices and walks around in majestic manner.

CHORUS: Her ecstatic rambling has collapsed. She has fallen on her knees in front of the altar like a bull that received a badly aimed stroke on his neck. Let us lift her up. . . .

83

In this later scene from Seneca's *Agamemnon*, one of Cassandra's predictions [see *no. 82*] comes true: the assassination of Agamemnon. Since the playwright has already dealt with the phenomenon of trance (or ecstasy), he pays little attention to it here, but the words *madness, ecstasy,* and *vision* indicate to the audience what is going on. The sun's standing still has nothing to do with Cassandra's vision, however; the sun stops in its course because it is shocked and indignant at what it has seen.

This monologue is more rhetorical than the earlier one and less informative, but it serves an important dramatic function: the violent action does not have to be shown on stage; the audience experiences it not through a messenger's report, not "from the top of the walls" (*teichoskopia*), but literally through the walls of the royal palace, thanks to Cassandra's special gift.

Seneca, *Agamemnon*, vv. 867–908

CASSANDRA: Something monstrous is happening within, something comparable to the Ten Years [of the Trojan War]. Ah, ah, what is this? Rise, my soul, and take the prize of your madness. We, the conquered Trojans, are now victorious. All is well: Troy has risen again. When you fell, father, you dragged Mycenae with you. Your conqueror turns to flight. Never before has the ecstasy of my prophetic mind given me such a clear vision. I see it, I am in the midst of it, am enjoying it! No blurred picture deceives my sight. Let us look at it:

A banquet for many guests is being held in the royal palace, just like that last one we had at Troy. The couches are shining with Trojan purple. They drink their wine from the golden cups that once belonged to ancient Assaracus. In his embroidered robes Agamemnon himself lies on a raised couch, his body draped in the magnificent spoils of Priam. His wife is urging him to take off the garments that belonged to the enemy; she wants him to put on the robes that her faithful hands have woven.

I shudder. My soul trembles. Shall an exile kill a king, an adulterer kill the husband? Yes, the fateful day has come. The end of the banquet will see the murder of my lord. Blood will drip into the wine. The deadly robe, thrown treacherously over him, will tie him up and deliver him to his assassins: the large, impenetrable folds envelop his head and leave no way to his arms. With a shaking head the weakling there stabs at Agamemnon's side but does not manage to thrust the sword in all the way; he stops, dumfounded, in the midst of the act of wounding him.

Agamemnon is like a bristling boar deep in the woods, entangled in a net and trying to escape from it, but the more he struggles, the tighter he draws his bonds, and his rage is in vain. So the king struggles to throw off the folds that move around him on all sides and rob him of his sight, and though he is enmeshed, he still seeks his assailant. But now Clytemnestra, enraged, snatches a double ax. Like a priest at the altar who marks with his eyes the oxen's neck before he strikes with his ax, the ruthless woman aims now this way, now that. He is hit! The deed is done! His head, not yet wholly severed, hangs by a slender thread; blood streams from his trunk; his lips quiver. And yet they will not leave him alone: Aegisthus still attacks the lifeless victim and keeps hacking at the corpse, and Clytemnestra helps him as he stabs. In committing this enormous crime, the two of them keep up their family tradition: after all, he is Thyestes' son, and she is Helen's sister. The sun stands still. . . .

84

From another of Seneca's dramas, *Heracles on Mount Oeta*, comes this brief reference to a prediction the oracles of Delphi and Dodona had made to the hero years ago. Now that he lies dying, Heracles realizes that the prediction is about to be fulfilled. He had killed the Centaur, Nessus, when he tried to rape Heracles' wife, Deianira, as he carried her through a stream. Heracles killed the Centaur with one of his poisoned arrows from the shore, but before he died, Nessus persuaded Deianira to keep some of his blood as a love potion. A few years later, when Heracles fell in love with another woman, Iole, his jealous wife smeared the drug on a garment and gave it to him. As soon as the hero put it on, the poison from his own arrow began to destroy him slowly.

The same story was dramatized by Sophocles in the *Women of Trachis,* and it has a parallel in the myth of Medea.

Heracles, as befitted his stature, consulted two of the most famous oracles of Greece about his death, and their predictions agreed. They were also enigmatic: how could Heracles, the great conqueror who had even come back from the underworld, die at the hands of a man he had already killed?

Seneca, *Heracles on Mount Oeta*, vv. 1472–78

HERACLES: Very well; it is fulfilled. My fate becomes clear: this is my last day. The oracular oak and the grove that shook the temples of Cirrha with a rumbling that came from Parnassus once predicted this destiny to me: "Heracles! You, the conqueror, will fall some day by the hand of a man you have killed. This is the end destined to you after you have traveled all over the earth, the seas, and through the realm of the shades."

85

In his *Pharsalia,* an unfinished epic on the civil war between Caesar and Pompey, Lucan describes a consultation of the Delphic oracle by a distinguished Roman, Appius, who wishes to know the outcome of the war. This consultation is supposed to have taken place in 49 or 48 B.C., shortly before Caesar's decisive victory at Pharsalus. The scene has a counterpart in a later book of the epic, in which one of Pompey's sons, immediately before the battle, approaches a famous Thessalian witch, Erictho, and asks her the same question. The poet's interest in various methods of divination is evident. He addresses himself to a question that was much debated at the time: why the prestige of the great oracles had declined. At the same time, he reintroduces an old theme: Odysseus had conjured up the dead in Book 11 of the *Odyssey;* Aeneas had descended into the underworld in Book 6 of the *Aeneid;* the aim of both had been to be told of future events.

First, Lucan attempts to explore the secret behind the Delphic oracle. As a Stoic, he believes in a divine power that may manifest itself in different forms in different parts of the universe. An earlier age had called this power "Apollo." Lucan does not reject the ancient myth, but he offers a more "modern" explanation. He assumes that there is a divine power above and a divine power beneath, and that they are the same power.

Lucan's theory is that the Delphic oracle had declined for political reasons. The Roman emperors (and possibly even the Senate during the Late Republic) had done their best to undermine the authority of the oracle. Any non-Roman methods of predicting the future had, in principle, become suspect because of the power they gave to the practitioner or the institution involved. This is one of the reasons why astrologers (along with philosophers!) were periodically expelled from Italy. But the very fear of this power shows how firmly rooted the belief in divination was. On this question Lucan probably reflected the views of his uncle, Seneca, who had had a good deal of political experience and knew one emperor, Nero, intimately.

According to Lucan, the Delphic priestesses were not unhappy when fewer and fewer visitors came, because they knew that their health was overtaxed by their duties; to produce one genuine trance after another was hard work. In this instance, the Pythia, who had been recruited in a great hurry and almost at random, it seems, because the priests were not prepared for the visit of such an illustrious Roman, tries to fake an ecstasy but does not get away with it. By telling us what she did not do, Lucan lists the characteristics of a real trance: inarticulate cries that fill the temple, quivering sounds, whispers, hair standing on end, and, as a sort of subterranean accompaniment, a small earthquake that is felt in the temple. (How this last effect was produced we do not know.) If any of these signs were not in evidence, the visitor, feeling cheated, would insist on the real thing.

Scared into submission, the young woman in Lucan's story goes into a real trance, her very first. The god takes over, fills her with his presence, and literally drives her mad, for a while at least. Apollo "rapes" her and rides her and remains in total control.

The poet makes an effort to understand the nature of the Pythia's vision, and he approaches the problem in terms of the Stoic concept of time. Somehow, in this one moment, the whole past and the whole future of mankind are concentrated, for they are part of a colossal scheme that transcends the human mind. The Pythia is allowed to pick from her grandiose vision only one detail—one that is important to the visitor. Her ecstasy then reaches a new climax and she collapses.

Following this, Lucan inserts a brief diatribe. Why do the gods not reveal such essential information to mankind more willingly? It is the same argument that Cicero used in his treatise *On Divination*. Have the gods not yet decided who is to win the war? Or do they have an ulterior plan: let Caesar win now in Thessaly, but have him assassinated dramatically four years later in the Senate.

Then there is another description of the visible aspects of trance: rolling eyes, constantly changing expression, flushed face, sighing and moaning.

When the Pythia returns to her normal state of consciousness, she has forgotten everything she saw.

Lucan, *Pharsalia* 5.86–224

Which one of the gods is hidden here? What divine power, exiled from heaven, agrees to live here, locked up in dark caves? What heavenly god supports the weight of the earth, holding all the secrets of the eternal course of events, sharing with the sky knowledge of the future, willing to manifest himself to the nations, suffering the contact of men? He must be great and powerful, no matter whether he merely predicts fate or if everything he proclaims becomes fate. Perhaps a large portion of the main god is embedded in the earth and rules it, supporting the globe that is suspended in empty space, and it may be this part which comes out of the cave of Delphi and can be breathed in, though it belongs to Jupiter in heaven. When this divine power has been received in the heart of the virgin [the priestess], it strikes the human soul of the prophetess with a sound and opens her lips, as the top of Mount Etna in Sicily boils over from the pressure of the flames and as Typhoeus, trembling under the timeless mass of Inarime where he lies, breathes smoke out of the rocks of Campania.

. . . The Delphic oracle fell silent when rulers became afraid of the

future and stopped the gods from speaking. Our age misses this gift of
the gods more than any others. But the priestesses of Delphi are not
unhappy that they may no longer speak; in fact they are glad that the
oracle has ceased. For if the god enters someone's heart, premature death
is the penalty or the reward for having received him; the human organism
is battered by the sting and the surge of that ecstasy, and the pounding of
the gods shakes up the fragile souls. . . .

[*Much against her will, the priestess is led into the temple and forced to
make the necessary preparations so that an oracle can be given to a distinguished
Roman visitor, Appius.*]

. . . A twisted fillet binds her hair in front, and a white headband
with a laurel branch from Phocis holds the locks that flow down her back.
She still hesitates and pauses, but the priest pushes her by force into the
temple.

Afraid of entering the oracle-giving recess of the inner sanctuary,
she stops near the entrance of the temple, pretends that she is possessed
by the god, and utters words that she makes up, but her heart remains
unmoved. No inarticulate cries or whispers indicate that divine ecstasy
inspires her mind. She could do more harm this way to the oracle and to
Apollo's reputation than to the important gentleman to whom she gave a
false prophecy. Her words do not rush forth with a quivering sound; her
voice is unable to fill the expanse of the huge temple; her hair does not
bristle and shake off the laurel wreath; the temple floor does not tremble,
the trees do not move. These are all signs that she is afraid of entrusting
herself to Apollo.

Appius notices that the oracle does not work and cries out in fury:
"The gods whom you fake and I will punish you as you deserve, wicked
woman, unless you descend at once into the cave! I have come to consult
you about a world torn by a great war. Stop giving me your own words!"

Scared at last, the young woman takes refuge by the tripod. She
stands near the vast chasm, and there she remains, and now her soul,
which has never had this experience before, draws in the divine power
that the spirit of the rock, still active after so many centuries, conveys to
her. At last Apollo takes over the soul of the Delphic priestess. Never
before has he forced his way so fully into the body of a prophetess,
driving out her normal consciousness and taking the place of everything
that is human in her heart. Frantically, out of her mind, she runs through
the sanctuary. Her neck no longer belongs to her; her bristling hair shakes
off the fillets and garlands of Apollo as she whirls, tossing her head,
through the empty space of the temple. As she runs she kicks over the
tripods that are in her way. She boils over with a tremendous fire, because
she is full of your wrath, Apollo! You do not only use your whip on her
and inject fire into her vitals as you goad her; she also feels your curb and

as a prophetess she may not reveal as much as she is allowed to know. All time concentrates in one complex; all the centuries descend on her heart—poor woman!—and the great chain of events lies open; the whole future struggles to come into the light; destinies fight destinies to be expressed in her voice. She sees everything; the first day and the last day of the world, the dimensions of the Ocean, the sum of the sands! As the Sibyl of Cumae in her cave on Euboea resents the fact that her trance should be of service to many nations and out of this great heap of destinies picks haughtily only the ones affecting Rome, thus Phemonoe, possessed by Phoebus, is troubled and has to search for a long time before she finds the fate of Appius—the man who has come to consult the god who is hidden in the land of Castalia—concealed among the fates of more important men. When she finds it, madness and ecstasy begin to flow in earnest from her foaming lips. She moans and utters loud, inarticulate cries. Then her wailing rises in the huge temple. Finally, when she is completely overpowered, she shouts these words:

"Roman, you will not take part in this crucial battle, but you will escape the horrible dangers of war. You alone will dwell in peace in a broad hollow of the coast of Euboea."

Apollo closes her throat and cuts short any further words.

Oracles! Guardians of destinies! Secrets of the universe! Apollo, master of truth! The [other] gods have not hidden a single day in the future from you. Why are you afraid to reveal the final act in the tragedy of a great nation, the massacre of captains, the death of kings, and the destruction of so many other countries dragged along by the bloodbath, the catastrophe of Rome? Have the gods not yet decided to perpetrate this horrible crime? Are the stars still hesitant to sentence Pompey to death? Are the fates of thousands still held in suspense? Or are you silent so that you can permit Fortune to wield the avenging sword, punish mad ambition, and have a tyrant undergo once more the punishment at the hands of a Brutus?

The priestess throws herself against the temple doors. They open and she rushes out, driven from the sanctuary. But her frenzy continues, and the god, who has not left her body, is still in control. After all, she has not told the whole truth. Her eyes roll wildly, and her glance roams over the whole sky. The expressions on her face change constantly: now she looks frightened, now fierce and menacing. A fiery flush spreads over her features and colors her pale cheeks, but her pallor does not seem to indicate fear; rather it inspires it. Her heart is overtired but cannot relax; voiceless sighs that sound like the moaning of a turbulent sea after the North Wind has ceased to blow still heave her breast.

As she returns to the ordinary light of day from the sacred light that has showed her the future, she is enveloped by darkness. Apollo sends Lethe from Styx into her innermost being to snatch away the secrets of the gods. Truth flees from her heart. Knowledge of the future returns to Apollo's tripod. She falls to the ground and barely recovers. . . .

86

In chapter 14 of his First Letter to the Corinthians, Paul writes of spiritual gifts. Speaking in tongues is one gift, delivering prophecies is another. The two are not the same, according to Paul, though they might seem to be closely related.

The Pythia did not always make sense when she uttered prophecies, and what she uttered had to be translated into normal Greek by the priests.

The early Christian communities were composed of Jews and Gentiles, two groups which had different cultural and religious traditions. The Jews had inherited the tradition of the Old Testament prophets, who spoke in a highly poetic but quite understandable idiom. The Greeks were accustomed to ecstatic outpourings that had to be translated into intelligible Greek by trained interpreters.

Paul seems to try to reconcile both traditions. He concedes that they are both legitimate, but he expresses a preference for the prophetic style of the Old Testament. He is rather diplomatic, but he has not much use for the ecstatic type of utterance unless it is kept under control and translated for the congregation at once.

It required true genius to reconcile such different traditions within a new religious group, and Paul, though he prefers one, recognizes the validity of the other. Apparently the Corinthians still liked to hear someone speak "in tongues" now and then, for the very fact that the language was unintelligible proved that it emanated from another world.

Paul, First Letter to the Corinthians 14:1–33

Seek love, but strive also after other spiritual gifts, especially prophecy. For he who speaks in tongues [i.e., uses the language of ecstasy] is talking with God, not with people, for no one understands him: he speaks mysteries in a state of inspiration. But when someone prophesies, he speaks to people and gives them spiritual strength, encouragement, and comfort. The person who speaks in tongues gives spiritual strength to himself, but the prophet gives spiritual strength to the community. I want all of you to speak in tongues, but I am even more anxious for you to prophesy. The prophet is greater than the one who speaks in tongues—unless he can interpret [himself], so that the congregation may receive spiritual strength.

Now, brothers, if I come to you speaking in tongues, what good shall I do you, unless what I say to you is revelation or knowledge or prophecy or instruction? Inanimate things produce voices, too—a flute, for instance, or a kithara—but all the same, if I do not give their sounds [regular] intervals, how can you recognize the melody on the flute or the kithara? Or again, if I blow an indistinct signal on the trumpet, who will prepare for battle? In the same way, if you speak in tongues without giving a clear message, how can anyone understand the meaning of your speech? You will be talking to the wind. It happens that there are many kinds of sound in the world—nothing is soundless—but if I do not understand the meaning of something that is said, I will be a foreigner [i.e., talking gibberish] in the eyes of the speaker, and he will be a foreigner [i.e., talking gibberish] as far as I am concerned. Since you are eager for the gifts of the Spirit, you, too, must work toward the spiritual strengthening of the congregation, in order to excel.

Therefore, the person who speaks in tongues must pray for the gift of interpretation. If I pray in ecstatic language, the spirit in me prays, but my mind is unproductive. What does this mean? I shall have to pray as the Spirit moves me, but I shall also have to pray with my mind [i.e., in a meaningful way]; I shall sing hymns as the Spirit moves me, but I shall also have to pray with my mind [i.e., in a meaningful way]. For if you praise God in ecstatic language, how can the person who occupies the place of the "outsider" know when to say "Amen" to your prayer of thanksgiving, if he does not understand what you are saying? Your prayer of thanksgiving is fine, but the "other person" does not feel uplifted spiritually. Thank God, I speak in tongues more often [or, better] than you, but in the congregation I would rather say five words through my mind [i.e., in a meaningful, articulate way] than thousands of words in ecstatic [i.e., unintelligible] language.

Brothers, do not become children in your minds; be childlike, as far as evil is concerned, but be mature in your minds. It is written in the Law: "Through men of foreign tongues and on the lips of foreigners will I speak to this nation, and even so they will not listen to me" [Isaiah 28:11–12; Deuteronomy 28:49], says the Lord. Hence the [strange] tongues are meant as a sign not for the believers but for the unbelievers. If the whole congregation is assembled and all are speaking in tongues and some "outsider" or unbeliever walks in, will he not say that you are crazy? But if the whole congregation utters prophecies and some unbeliever or "outsider" walks in, he will feel convinced by everyone, search his soul because of everyone. The secrets of his heart are laid bare, and so he will fall on his face and worship God and announce: "Truly God is among you!"

What does all this mean, brothers? When you get together, each of you has a hymn, has a piece of instruction, has a revelation, has a message in ecstatic language, has an interpretation [of the message]. All of this must be directed toward spiritual strengthening. If it is a matter of speaking in tongues, let two speak, or at most three, and only one at a time, and one person should interpret. If no interpreter happens to be there, the [ecstatic] speaker should not address the congregation at all, but talk to himself and to God. Only two or three prophets should speak, and the rest should examine [what they say]. If someone else, being seated, has a vision, let the first speaker stop. For all of you can utter prophecies, one by one, so that the whole congregation may receive instruction and comfort. The prophetic spirit is controlled by the prophets [themselves], for God is the author of peace, not of disorder.

87

Plutarch deals with the Delphic oracle in several of his philosophical treatises and dialogues. His interest may be explained by the fact that he held a priesthood there for life, from A.D. 95. His *Pythian Dialogues* seem to be late works; the group includes *On the Cessation of Oracles*, *On the E in Delphi*, and *On the Oracles of the Pythia*. In them he discusses various problems of daemonology and divination. The explanation of clairvoyance he proposes would have been acceptable to Platonists as well as Stoics; this shows what a strong influence Posidonius had on Middle Platonism. Plutarch states that every soul has the gift of clairvoyance, whether it is embodied or not, but as long as it coexists with the body, this faculty is relatively weak, though it is there nonetheless, more evident in sleep or in trance ("inspiration") than in our normal state of consciousness.

Plutarch also believes that certain forces are transmitted through the air, or in water, and that these forces somehow enter a body and produce a change in the soul. Plutarch must have spoken to informants who had actually experienced trance and who tried to describe to him what had happened to them, how they felt, and so on. Not surprisingly, he has to resort to images in the end.

Plutarch, *On the Cessation of Oracles*, pp. 431E–432E

If the souls that have been separated from a body or never shared existence with one at all are daemons according to you [i.e., the Platonists] and the divine Hesiod [*Works and Days*, v. 123], "holy dwellers on earth, guardians of mortal men," why should we deprive embodied souls of that power, that natural gift, by which daemons foresee and predict the future? It is not likely that any faculty, any dimension, is added to the souls after they leave the body, beyond those that they had before, but they have them always; they are merely weaker as long as the soul is joined to a body. Some are completely imperceptible and hidden, others weak and dim, just as ineffective and slow as people who try to see in a fog or move in water, and they need a great deal of care in restoring their proper function and a cleansing to remove that which hides it. The sun does not become bright the moment it bursts through the clouds; it is always bright, but to us it appears somber and dim when we see it through mist. In the same way the soul does not acquire the power to prophesy when it has left the body—as if it were emerging from a cloud—but it has that power right now, though it is blinded by its association and cohesion with the body. We should not be surprised or skeptical; all we need to do is look at the faculty of the soul which is the reverse of prophecy, the one called "memory": what an achievement it shows by keeping and preserving the past, or rather the present! Nothing that is past has any kind of existence or reality, but as soon as it happens, it is gone, all of it—actions, words, and experiences—for time, like a stream, bears everything away. But this faculty of the soul [i.e., memory] somehow gets hold of things that are not real and invests them with shape and substance. . . .

Therefore, all souls have this power [of prophecy]; it is innate, though dim and hardly real, and yet it often fully blossoms and radiates in dreams and sometimes in the hour of death, when the body becomes purified or acquires a disposition suitable for that purpose, a disposition through which the reasoning faculty, the ability to think, is relaxed and released from the present and can turn [reading *epistrephomenon*] to the irrational imaginary range of the future. It is not true, as Euripides says [frag. 973 Nauck²], "the best seer is he who makes the best guess"; no, it is the intelligent man who follows the rational part of his soul, the part that leads the way by making reasonable guesses. The prophetic gift is like a writing tablet without writing, both irrational and indeterminate in itself, but capable of images, impressions [reading *kai pathesi*], and presentiments, and it paradoxically grasps the future when the future seems as remote as possible from the present. This remoteness is brought about by a condition, a disposition, of the body that is affected by a change known as "inspiration." Often the body all by itself attains this condition, but the earth sends up to human beings the sources of many faculties other than this, some of which produce trance, illness, even death, but others that are helpful, pleasant, and beneficial, as can be seen from the accounts of those who have experienced them. But the current, the spirit, of prophecy is the most divine, the most sacred, whether it approaches all by itself through the air or together with running water, for when it enters the body, it produces in the soul a strange, unusual disposition. It is difficult to describe its character accurately, but a number of analogies offer themselves. . . . [A few images are listed: it is like wine when its fumes rise to the head, or like a hot steel knife dipped into water.]

88

Once more, Plutarch asserts the universal validity of divination. It is a natural activity of the human soul, and one should not be surprised that it exists. Even the term *foretelling* is misleading; one should simply use the word *telling*.

The distinction he makes between an event that happens after having been foretold, and the foretelling of an event that will happen, is hard to grasp, and it looks like one of the subtleties of Stoic logic that Cicero struggled with in his treatise *On Fate*. It also seems strange that Plutarch calls certain predictions "lies," even though they are confirmed by events. Perhaps what he is saying is this: In the "ocean of time"—that is, during a period of millions of years—all predictions that have ever been made will come true. This may be similar to the modern paradox according to which a million monkeys working at a million typewriters during a million years will eventually produce the works of Shakespeare. But for Plutarch, it seems, the prediction of an event in the very distant future is not a valid prediction. To be useful in human terms it has to be fulfilled within a reasonably short time.

Plutarch, *On the Oracles of the Pythia*, pp. 398–99

. . . What kind of event can there be that is not a debt owed by time to nature? Is there anything so strange, so unexpected, on land, on sea, in cities, among men, that it cannot be predicted before it actually happens? And this can hardly even be called "foretelling," just "telling," or even better: throwing and scattering words that have no basis into infinite space. Occasionally chance meets them as they wander around, and of its own accord coincides with them. There is a difference, I think, between an event that happens after having been told, and the telling of an event that will happen. For an account concerning things that do not [yet] exist contains in itself an element of error, and it is not fair [to have] to wait for a confirmation that comes by accident, nor should one use as compelling proof of having foretold the event with [accurate] knowledge the fact that the event happened after having been foretold; infinity brings everything around. No, the "good guesser" whom the proverb recommends as the "best seer" [Eur., frag. 973 Nauck[2]] is more like a man who looks for clues on the ground and explores the future by means of reasonable forecasts. Prophets of the type of the Sibyl or Bacis have tossed and scattered their predictions at random into the ocean of time—words and phrases referring to experiences and events of all kinds—and although some of them actually come true as a result of chance, what is told now is nevertheless a lie, even if it turns out to be true, should the event happen.

89

The appearance of the Pythia and the sound of her voice clearly showed how ancient an institution the oracle was. She did not wear fashionable robes, nor was she perfumed, nor did she sing melodiously like a popular music hall entertainer of the period. In some shrines aromatic essences such as incense were burned on the altar, but the Pythia used only the archaic ingredients, laurel leaves and barley groats (the same ingredients, incidentally, that were used in magical ceremonies [see *no. 4*]). Prophesying was a harsh, demanding business, and any frills would have been considered inappropriate. In the end, however, when she was in a state of trance, the Pythia's gift was the secret knowledge of the centuries.

Plutarch, *On the E at Delphi*, pp. 396–97

Sarapion said: "Yes, Boethus, we are sick, as far as our ears and eyes are concerned, for as a result of our soft, luxurious life style we are accustomed to considering that which is [merely] pleasant as [truly] beautiful and to saying so. Before long we shall criticize the Pythia because she does not chant as melodiously as Glauce, who sings to the kithara, and because she does not wear perfume and purple robes when she descends into the inner shrine, and because she does not burn on the altar cassia or ladanum or frankincense, but only laurel leaves and barley groats. Do you not feel the charm of Sappho's songs—how they soothe and bewitch those who listen to them? But the Sibyl, "with her ecstatic mouth," as Heraclitus says, even though her words are unsmiling, unadorned, unperfumed, yet she reaches through the space of a thousand years because of the god."

90

Again Plutarch attempts to show, by means of logic rather than empirically, that divination works. This kind of argument often sounds more plausible in Greek than in any translation. Here, as elsewhere, Plutarch operates with the categories of time: past, present, future. He believes in a chain of causes and effects which stretches from the beginnings of time to infinity. What the Pythia sees in one glance, the scientific mind—if not the individual, at least the collective mind—ought to discover in due time. Hence the need for statistics as a basis for predictions.

Plutarch, *On the E at Delphi*, p. 387

The god is a prophet, and the art of prophecy concerns the future as it results from the present and the past. There is nothing that comes into being without a cause, nothing that could not reasonably be predicted. Since the present follows the past and the future follows the present very closely, according to a constant process that leads from the beginning to the end, he who understands the natural connections and interrelations of the causes with one another can also declare [Hom., *Il.* 1.70] "the present, the future, and the past." Homer was right to place the present first, then the future, and then the past, for the syllogism based on a hypothetical proposition has as its base that which is; for instance, "if this is, then this [other thing] has preceded it" or "if this is, then this [other thing] will be." The technical and rational part of this, as has been said, is the understanding of the [necessary] consequence, and the argument derives its premises from sense perception. So, even if it is not much of a statement to make, I shall not hesitate to make it: The tripod of truth is the argument that establishes the relationship between a later and an earlier event and then, taking the existence [of something] as a premise, brings the syllogism to its conclusion.

91

One of Apollonius' famous predictions concerned the year A.D. 69, the year during which Rome saw three successive emperors (Galba, Otho, and Vitellius), each of whom was in power for only a short time. Apollonius' admiring biographer, Philostratus, tries to defend him from any suspicion of witchcraft. He argues that Apollonius did not claim to be able to change the course of fate by means of magic. Like Apuleius, who also was accused of practicing magic, Apollonius claimed to be a philosopher, a scientist who simply interpreted certain signs that were there for all to see.

Philostratus, *Life of Apollonius of Tyana* 5.12

I have given sufficient proof that Apollonius' foreknowledge of these events was due to supernatural inspiration, and that it would not be reasonable to consider him a magician, but let me add some further arguments. Magicians—and in my opinion they are the most wretched of men—claim to be able to change the course of destiny either by tormenting daemons or by using weird rites, charms, or plasters. Many of those who have been brought to justice have admitted that this was the nature of their science. Apollonius, on the other hand, accepted the decrees of destiny and openly stated that they must, by necessity, take their course; hence his clairvoyance was divine revelation, not magic.

92

Artemidorus lived in the second century A.D., mostly in Daldis, Lydia, but he traveled widely in order to collect interpretations of dreams and books on dreams. In addition to his treatise *The Art of Judging Dreams*, he wrote works on augury and palmistry.

    In the dedication of his book on dreams he tells us that he learned a great deal from talking to professional dream interpreters in many cities. Although they were despised by most respectable citizens, these men had some valuable information to give. We learn, incidentally, that in any ancient city one could expect to find such dream interpreters in the marketplace; perhaps they had their booths there, like the fortunetellers of our age. They also traveled around to festivals, hoping to find more customers among the large crowds that these events attracted. Their fees cannot have been excessive. Artemidorus does not put himself in the same class as these practitioners, but he respects their experience and their knowledge of human nature. He sounds like a man who is passionately interested in his subject but who also wishes to be of help to his fellow-man.

At the beginning of his work, Artemidorus establishes a fundamental distinction between "theorematic" and "allegorical" dreams. The former are self-evident, so to speak: they foreshadow an event more or less correctly. The latter need interpretation.

Artemidorus emphasizes how important it is to remember a dream from beginning to end. More often than not, the interpreter will be tempted to analyze an incomplete dream sequence, but when he does that, he only deceives his client and ultimately hurts his own reputation.

Artemidorus then interprets a few dreams, not in any systematic order, it seems, but perhaps to cite examples of those he considers typical. Many of the dreams seem strange to us; many are about incest, sexual perversions, violence. Perhaps only an interpreter who belonged to the same culture could make sense of them.

From the examples that Artemidorus gives (1.2) we see that then, as now, people were "programmed," as it were, by certain experiences, and later—sometimes much later—translated their hopes and fears into dreams by means of these experiences, creating thereby a vocabulary for their own dream language.

The dream about being back in school (1.53) does not have a happy meaning, because most people's school years seem to be unhappy and frustrating.

Dramatic performances had an immediate emotional impact on ancient audiences and a delayed impact in dreams. Since drama was a representation of human experience compressed within a few hours, it served as a symbolic language for emotions that could not be expressed in any other way.

In 1.78 Artemidorus has something to say about sexual dreams. It seems that people in antiquity often dreamed of sexual intercourse of one kind or another. According to Suetonius' *Life of Julius Caesar* (ch. 7), Caesar dreamt that he slept with his mother, and though he was disturbed by this, the interpreters assured him that he would rule the world, for one's mother is a symbol of the earth.

What Artemidorus writes helps us to understand ancient civilization. Husbands were supposed to have control over their wives and expected obedience from them. To be seen entering or leaving a brothel was slightly embarrassing but not a disgrace. The various interpretations of the brothel as symbol are very curious.

As far as the "Oedipus dream" is concerned (1.79), Artemidorus fully agrees with the interpreters of Caesar's dream almost two centuries earlier.

Crucifixion was widely used in the Greek world as a means of execution, not just in the days of the Roman emperors. To dream of death on the cross is not necessarily bad, Artemidorus points out (2.53), and he advises consideration of the particular person's circumstances.

In the preface to Book 4 he offers some general advice. He is convinced that people who lead healthy, normal, decent lives will not be troubled by strange, disturbing dreams. To that extent we have control over our dreams. Dream interpreters, because of their peculiar profession, tend to have dreams that are quite different from those of the average person.

According to Artemidorus, there are six criteria that ought to be applied to any dream: (1) is it in accordance with nature? (2) with law? (3) with custom? (4) with art? (5) with the person's name? (6) with time? The distinction between "nature" and "law" seems to correspond roughly to the one between "unwritten" and "written" law, while "custom" somehow belongs to both areas. "Art" means the profession of the dreamer, whose "name" also plays a certain role in the interpretation. "Time" apparently designates the period in the dreamer's life; it is not normal, for instance, for middle-aged men to dream that they are going to school again.

In 4.3 Artemidorus briefly deals with magical practices. He compares magic to blackmail, which, in a sense, it is. To try to blackmail a god into doing us a favor would be as absurd as putting pressure on some influential person. On the other hand, to pray for a dream is not magic, and to thank the gods for a favor is simply good manners.

Once more—in 4.59—Artemidorus emphasizes the need for full information about the dreamer and his dream. He rejects astrology as a supporting science. Essentially, the dream itself tells the story.

Artemidorus, *Oneirocritica*, or *On the Art of Judging Dreams*, excerpts

Book 1, dedication

There is no book on the interpretation of dreams that I have not acquired, making this my main ambition. The seers of the marketplace are generally despised, and the respectable-looking citizens, raising their eyebrows, call them charlatans, impostors, clowns. I paid no attention to this slander, but associated with them for many years, in the cities of Greece, at the great festivals, in Asia Minor, in Italy, on the major and more densely populated islands, and I was willing to listen to ancient dreams and the events that followed them; for there is no other way to master this discipline.

Book 1, ch. 2

Some dreams are theorematic, some allegorical. Theorematic are those whose fulfillment resembles the vision they offer. A traveler dreamed that he was shipwrecked, and this is what happened. As soon as sleep left him, the ship was sucked down and wrecked, and he, with a few others, saved his life with difficulty. Another man dreamed that he was wounded by a man with whom he had agreed to go hunting the next day. As they left together, he was wounded on the shoulder, just as it had happened in the dream. Someone dreamed that he received money from a friend; the next morning he accepted ten mines from the friend and kept them as a deposit. There are many other examples of this kind.

Allegorical dreams, on the other hand, signify something through something else; in these dreams the soul, according to certain laws, hints at something in the manner of a riddle. . . .

A dream is a motion or a formation of the soul with many aspects, hinting at good or bad things to come. . . .

Let me tell you that dreams which are not remembered completely cannot be interpreted, no matter whether the dreamer has forgotten the middle or the end. For if you want to make sense of a dream [text uncertain] you must explore the point to which the vision leads: only what is remembered from beginning to end can be interpreted.

Just as the seers who offer a sacrifice do not call ambiguous signs untrue—they say only that they do not understand the signs that accompany their sacrifice—thus the interpreter of dreams must not give his opinion nor improvise a response concerning things he cannot fully comprehend, for he will lose his prestige, and the dreamer will get hurt.

Book 1, ch. 53

Learning to read and write [in a dream], not having learned it before, predicts something good for the dreamer, but it will be preceded by pain and fear, for students are afraid and suffer pain, even though they learn for their own good. If someone who has already learned to read and write learns it again, this must mean something painful and strange, for one gets elementary education in childhood. Therefore, this indicates incompetence as well as fear and pain. Such a dream promises something good only to him who wants a child, for then not he himself but the child that will be born to him will learn to read and write.

If a Roman learns Greek or a Greek learns Latin, it means that the former will associate with Greeks, the latter with Romans. Having had this kind of dream, many Romans married Greek women or Greeks married Roman women. I know a man who dreamed that he was learning Latin: he was condemned to slavery; it never happens that a slave learns Greek.

Book 1, ch. 56

To perform in a tragedy or have tragic roles or masks or listen to tragic actors or recite iambic lines: if one remembers the words, the events will be according to the context; if one does not remember them, there will be wretchedness, slavery, battles, violence, dangers, and even more terrible and cruel things than those; for tragedies are full of them.

To perform in a comedy or listen to comic actors or have comic masks or roles: if they represent the Old Comedy, they indicate ribald jokes and verbal fights; if they represent Modern Comedy, they anticipate the same things as tragedy but promise a satisfactory, happy ending; for such are the plots of comic pieces.

Book 1, ch. 76

To dance in a theater with a made-up face [or, wearing a mask] and the rest of the traditional costume means success and praise; for a poor man it means riches, but they will not last until he is old, for on the stage the actor represents a royal personage and has many servants, but when the play is over, he is left alone. . . .

Book 1, ch. 78

In the chapter on sexual intercourse the best division might be the following: (a) intercourse that is both lawful and natural; (b) unlawful intercourse; (c) unnatural intercourse.

First, concerning lawful intercourse, I have this to say. If you make love with your own wife, and she is willing and agreeable and does not offer any resistance, this is fine for everyone; for one's wife means either one's craft or one's profession—an area from which we derive pleasure, over which we command and have control, as we have over a wife. The dream therefore indicates the profit from such things. People enjoy sex, but they also enjoy profit. If the wife resists and does not surrender her body, it means the opposite. The same interpretation applies to one's mistress.

To have intercourse with prostitutes who are established in brothels indicates a moderate embarrassment and a small expense. For to approach such women means both embarrassment and expense. This dream is favorable to all kinds of enterprises, for these women are called "working women" by some; they are most accommodating and never say no. It would also seem to be a good sign to enter a brothel and be able to leave it; not being able to get out is bad. I knew someone who dreamed that he went into a brothel and could not leave it; a few days later he was dead. What happened to him corresponded to the dream, for a brothel, like a cemetery, is called a "public place": the cemetery receives the dead, and in the brothel there is a great waste of human sperm. So it makes sense that the brothel would be assimilated to death. . . .

Book 1, ch. 79 (the Oedipus dream)

The chapter on the mother has many different aspects, parts, and subdivisions unnoticed by many interpreters of dreams so far. It is like this. Sexual intercourse in itself is not sufficient to show the meaning, but the different kinds of embraces and positions of the bodies predict different events. First of all we must talk about the position "body to body," when the mother is still alive, for it does not mean the same thing if she is dead. If someone has intercourse [in a dream] with his mother, "body to body"—in the position which some call "natural"—and she is still alive, and his father is in good health, it means that his father will hate him, because of the jealousy that exists among men in general. If the father is in poor health, he will die [soon], for the son who has the dream will be in charge of his mother both as her son and as [if he were] her husband. It is a propitious dream for any craftsman and artisan, for it is customary to call one's trade one's "mother," and to have intercourse with one's mother could not possibly mean anything else but to work full time and to make a living from one's trade. It is also a good dream for political leaders and politicians, for the mother symbolizes the fatherland. Just as he who has intercourse "according to the rule of Aphrodite" [i.e., in the normal position] has control over the whole body of the woman if she is willing and consents, thus the dreamer will control the politics of his city-state. . . .

Book 1, ch. 80

To have intercourse with a god or a goddess or to be penetrated by a god means death for one who is ill, for the soul, at this point, when it is about to leave the body in which it dwells, foresees that it will meet and associate with the gods; for the others [i.e., those who are not ill], if they enjoy the experience, it means help from those above; if not, fear and trouble. . . .

Book 2, ch. 53 (dreams about different kinds of death)

To be crucified is good for all seafarers, for the cross is made of beams and nails, just like a ship, and the mast of a ship looks like a cross. It is good for a poor man, for the victim of crucifixion is high up and feeds many birds. It brings hidden things into the open, for the crucified person is plainly visible. It is bad for the rich, for those who are crucified are naked, and their flesh wastes away. . . . To be crucified in a city means [to hold] an office in that city, corresponding to the place of the cross. . . .

Book 2, ch. 55

To descend into Hades and to see all the things down there—the things
that people believe to be there—means loss of work and loss of income to
those who are prosperous and successful, for the inhabitants of Hades are
inactive, cold, without motion. For those who are in fear, sorrow, or grief,
it means deliverance from cares and worries, for the inhabitants of Hades
do not worry and are free from cares. For the others, it means travels—or
at any rate it drives them away from the place where they live. Not only
did the ancients say of one who went on a long trip that he "went to
Hades"—the story itself shows that the inhabitants of Hades are not all in
the same place. . . .

Book 3, ch. 56

Dreaming of a chef in your house is a good sign if you want to get married;
you need a chef for a wedding. It is a good sign for the poor as well, for
only people who have plenty of food hire cooks. For those who are ill, it
predicts irritations and inflammations and a general imbalance in the
body juices which can lead to acidity, according to the experts in these
matters. But it also predicts tears, because of the smoke the chef produces. It also brings hidden things and things that were done in secret
into the open, for the creations of the chef are brought out into the open
and served to the guests and they appear as what they are [i.e., they are as
good as they look].

Book 4, preface

Remember that those who lead a good and useful life never have any
ordinary dreams or any irrational fantasies but always dream visions and
mostly theorematic ones. For their soul is not, at the surface, troubled by
fear or hope, and they are in control of the pleasures of the body. In short,
a good person never has an ordinary dream or an irrational fantasy. Do
not deceive yourself: The average person and the competent interpreter
of dreams do not have the same dreams, for the average person dreams of
the same things that he wants or fears [during the day], but the wise and
the experts in these matters signify only the sort of things they want. If
someone who is not an expert has a dream, that dream should be interpreted as an ordinary one, not as a dream vision [text uncertain]. Let us
assume that someone who is competent in these matters—either because
he has consulted books on the interpretation of dreams, or because he has
associated with interpreters of dreams, or because he has a natural talent
in this direction—is in love with a woman: he will dream not of the
beloved one but of a horse or a mirror or a ship or the sea or a female
animal or a feminine garment or anything else that signifies a
woman. . . .

To make this less confusing for you, let me tell you that many people—in fact, most people . . . —have only ordinary dreams; there are altogether very few, in fact only the interpreters of dreams, who have the other kind of dreams, the one I just mentioned.

Book 4, ch. 2

It is a general principle that all dreams that are in accordance with nature or law or custom or art or name or time mean something good, and that all dreams contrary to those [six points] are bad and unprofitable. But remember that this theory is not absolute and universal; it only works most of the time. For many dreams have a good outcome, though they go against the reality of everyday life and are not in accordance with nature or those other points. For example, someone dreamed that he was beating his mother. This is certainly a crime, and yet it brought him success, for he happened to be a potter; we call the earth "mother," and the potter works with the earth that he beats. So he worked with great success. . . .

Book 4, ch. 3

The dreams people have when they worry about some business or other, or when they are moved by some irrational urge or desire, you may consider "worrying dreams." We also call them "asked-for dreams," because one asks a god to send a dream concerning some business at hand. But remember: when you ask for a dream, do not burn any incense, and do not say unspeakable names. In short, do not demand anything from the gods which involves magic practices. It would be ridiculous for gods to obey those who demand something with threats, for men of influence refuse the petitions of those who threaten and blackmail them, but grant favors to those who approach them politely. After having had the dream you should sacrifice and give thanks. Those who impose laws on the gods, you should not take seriously; they say, for example: "Should I do this?" or "Will this be granted to me?" or "May I now see the fruit of Demeter? Or, if not, that of Dionysus?" or "If this is good for me and profitable, may I have it? If not, should I give it?" There is a fundamental error in all of this. . . . You must pray to the god about the things that worry you, but the way in which you phrase your request beforehand you must leave to the god or to your soul.

Book 4, ch. 59

You should also first find out about the way of life of the person [who consults you]; I mean, you should inform yourself carefully. And if you cannot get any reliable information from the dreamer, postpone your advice for the moment and ask someone else, lest you make a mistake. . . . Stay away from those who think that dreams must be interpreted according to the horoscope of the dreamer, the good ones as well as the bad ones. They say that the beneficent planets, when they are unable to do something good for you, at least make you feel good in your dreams, and that the maleficent planets, when they are unable to hurt you, at least disturb and frighten you in your dreams. If this were true, no dream would ever be realized; but in fact the good ones and the bad ones are realized, each according to its meaning.

93

As a starting point for his discussion of trance Iamblichus uses the profound changes that can be observed in the personality of the "medium." The body no longer has the sensations, the reflexes, that it has in a normal state of consciousness. If the body is not subjected to its usual limitations and affections (i.e., feeling pain), then the mind, Iamblichus argues, also must reach a new level. He notes that no trance is exactly like another, and though his explanation is purely speculative, the observation itself may well be valid. Among other things, he mentions levitation and the manifestation of fire. At the same time he seems to feel that not every "medium" is able to experience the fullness of the vision or share it with others.

Iamblichus, *On the Mysteries of Egypt* 3.4–6

You state that there are many who grasp the future by means of divine possession and divine inspiration and that they are awake as far as their ability to act and their sense perceptions are concerned, but not really conscious or not as conscious as before. I also want to show, in this context, the characteristics of those who are truly possessed by the gods. For if they submit their whole life as a vehicle, as a tool, to the gods who inspire them, they either exchange their human life for a divine life or else they adjust their life to the god and do not act according to their own sense perceptions, nor are they awake like those whose senses are completely awake. They do not perceive the future by themselves, nor do they move like those who act on an impulse. They are not conscious in the way they were before, nor do they concentrate their native intelligence on themselves or manifest any special knowledge.

And here is important proof: Many [of those who are in trance] do not get burned, even if they are close to a fire, for because of the divine inspiration fire does not touch them. When they are actually burned, many do not react, because at this moment they do not live the life of a [normal] creature. Some are pierced by daggers and do not feel [the pain]; others have their backs cut open with hatchets; still others are wounded with knives about their arms and are totally unaware of it. Whatever they do is out of the human sphere. The inaccessible becomes accessible to those who are divinely inspired: they jump into fire and walk through fire; they cross over streams like the priestess in Cataballa. All this goes to show that in their state of divine possession they are no longer in their normal state of consciousness and that they no longer lead the normal life of a person, of a creature, as far as sense perception and volition are concerned. They exchange these for another, more divine kind of life which inspires and possesses them completely.

There are different kinds of divine trance, and divine inspiration operates in many different ways. It manifests itself through a number of different signs. For one thing, the various gods from whom we receive inspiration produce different kinds of inspiration. For another, the particular kind of divine possession, as it changes, also modifies the nature of the divine inspiration. For either the god takes possession of us, or we become totally part of the god, or else we coordinate our activity with his own. At times we participate in the lowest power of the god, at other times in his intermediate power, and then again in his highest power. Sometimes it is simple participation, sometimes a sharing, sometimes a combination of these types. Either the soul alone enjoys it, or it shares it with the body, or it is the whole person that enjoys it.

As a result, the outward signs of divine possession are manifold: movement of the body or of some of its parts, or total lack of any kind of movement; harmonious tunes, dances, melodious voices, or the opposites of these. Bodies have been seen to rise up or grow larger or float in the air, and the opposites of these phenomena also have been observed. The voice [of the person in trance] seemed to be completely even in volume and in the intervals between sound and silence, and then again there was unevenness. In other instances the sounds swelled and diminished, but occasionally something else happened.

But most importantly: The medium who draws down a divine being sees the spirit descending, sees how great it is, what it is like, and is able to persuade and control it in mysterious ways. The one received sees the shape of the fire before receiving it. Sometimes the fire becomes visible to all who are watching, either as the god descends or as he ascends. Therefore, those who know are able to grasp the real truth, the real power, the real order, that he represents, and they understand in what respect he is qualified to communicate the truth and grant power or maintain it. Those who draw down the spirits without these wonderful experiences are stumbling in the dark, so to speak, and do not know what they are doing, except for certain quite unimportant signs on the body of the person possessed and other trivial manifestations; the full reality of divine inspiration remains hidden to them, and they are without knowledge.

94

Like Plutarch and others before him, Iamblichus attempts to explain how oracles function. He singles out three famous ones: Clarus, near Colophon; Didyma (Branchidae), near Miletus; and Delphi. All of them were oracles of Apollo. A prophetess transmitted the message from the god at Delphi and Didyma, while Clarus had a male priest. At Clarus, water from a sacred spring underneath the temple played a role which Iamblichus tries to elucidate. According to him, water only induces a certain disposition in the priest; the real illumination must still come from above. Other rituals have to be observed by the priest-prophet, and they also help to prepare him, but they do not, by themselves, produce the vision.

Similarly, the firelike substance that the Pythia inhales serves only as a preparation. The god is not in that substance; he has to come from somewhere else. The ritual at Didyma is different, but it, too, is a kind of prelude—necessary, it would seem, but not the inspiration itself.

Perhaps all these practices were reproduced elsewhere faithfully, but unsuccessfully, by certain theurgists. Hence Iamblichus comes to the conclusion that oracular prophecy is impossible without the divine presence. In fact, he argues, whatever natural conditions there are have to be created by the god at one time, and the god inspires the ritual that surrounds them. Everything thus comes from the god; he is the ultimate source of prophecy.

Iamblichus, *On the Mysteries of Egypt* 3.11

There is a . . . kind of divination, well known and impressive. It has many components and is inspired by a god. It is the oracle.

You have this to say concerning it: "There are some who drink water, like the priest of Apollo Clarius at Colophon. Others are sitting near the mouth of a cave, like the priestesses who prophesy at Delphi. Others inhale steam, like the prophetesses of the Branchidae." You mention these three famous oracles, not because they were the only ones (for there were many more that you did not mention), but because they were more important than the others and because you were able to point out the problem with sufficient clarity. I am thinking of the way in which divination is sent by the gods to mankind. For these reasons you were satisfied with those examples. So I, too, shall discuss only these three, omitting the vast majority of oracles.

First, the oracle at Colophon. Everyone agrees that water is used to prophesy. They say that there is a spring in a subterranean structure and that the priest on certain prescribed nights drinks from it after many preliminary ceremonies have been performed. After having drunk he begins to prophesy; but he remains invisible to the spectators present. This shows clearly that the water must be prophetic, but in what way it is prophetic is not, according to the proverb, "for everyone to know." It would appear that a kind of prophetic spirit comes through it, but this is actually not true. For the divine does not spread in such a partitioned and disjointed way among its partakers but, offering itself from the outside, it illuminates the spring, filling it with its own prophetic power. And yet not the whole inspiration which the god offers comes from the water; [the water] only produces an aptitude and a purification of the luminous spirit in us through which we become capable of receiving the god. There is another presence of the god which precedes this one and shines from on high. This one is not far from anyone who, by his affinity, is in touch with it. It comes all of a sudden and uses the prophet as an instrument. He is no longer himself and has no idea of what he says or where he is. As a result, even after having delivered the prophecy, he recovers with difficulty. Before drinking from the water he has fasted for a whole day and a whole night and, going into trance, has withdrawn all by himself into a part of the sanctuary inaccessible to the crowd. By keeping aloof and distant from human preoccupations, he renders himself pure and ready to receive the god. Therefore, he possesses the inspiration of the god that shines into the pure sanctuary of his soul; the inspiration can take possession without hindrance, and the perfect presence finds no obstacle.

The prophetess at Delphi gives oracles to people from a thin, firelike spirit that rises from somewhere through a crevice, or she makes predictions sitting in the sanctuary on a bronze tripod or on a four-footed stool that is sacred to the god. In any case she gives herself entirely to a divine spirit, and she shines with a ray from the divine fire. An intense, concentrated fire comes up through the crevice and surrounds her on all sides, filling her with divine radiance. When she takes her place on the seat of the god, she adapts and conforms herself to his firm divinatory power. As a result of both preliminaries she becomes completely the possession of the god. He then appears to her and illuminates her as a separate entity, because he is different from the fire, the spirit, his own seat, and from all the normal and sacred apparatuses that are visible.

The prophetess of the Branchidae also receives the god in herself, whether she is filled with divine radiance as she holds the wand originally handed down by the god, or whether she is seated on an axle, or whether she dips her feet or the border of her garment into water, or whether she breathes in the vapor of the water; by all these [external] things she is prepared to receive the god from the outside and take part in him.

This is also shown by the large number of sacrifices and by the ritual of the whole ceremony and by all the other acts performed religiously before the delivery of an oracle: the bathing of the prophetess, her fasting for three whole days, her stay in the inner sanctuary, and the fact that she already participates in the light and enjoys it for a long time. All this goes to show that the god is called in prayer to be present and that he comes from outside, and that a marvelous inspiration takes place even before she comes to her accustomed place. It also shows that the god in the spirit rising from the source is separate from the place and more ancient than its present use; that he is in fact the cause of this use and the source of the whole practice of divination.

95

In Porphyry's biography of Plotinus the "psychic" gifts of the master are briefly mentioned: he identified the slave who had stolen a necklace from a lady who lived in his house; he also predicted the future of some children. When Porphyry lapsed into a state of depression (he called it "melancholy") and contemplated suicide, the master sensed it and counseled him.

It is curious to see that the last great philosopher and theologian of paganism, like the early *shamans,* was credited with supernatural abilities. A man like Plotinus, whose life is reasonably well documented and whose writings—at least most of them—have survived, is not a shadowy figure like Orpheus. It would not do to dismiss him as a fraud who impressed his naïve disciples with a few occult tricks. If asked whether this was magic, he might have answered, like Apollonius of Tyana: "No, it is something philosophers know about."

Porphyry, *Life of Plotinus,* par. 61

Plotinus also had an almost supernatural knowledge of human nature. Chione, a highly respectable widow, lived with her children in his house. One day her precious necklace was stolen. The servants were assembled, and Plotinus looked each of them in the eyes. "This is the thief," he said, and pointed at one of them. The man was whipped but denied persistently at first; later he confessed, went to get the stolen object, and brought it back. Plotinus also predicted how each of the children who lived with him would turn out. He described what sort of a person Polemon was and said that he would be amorous and not live long, and this is what actually happened. Once he sensed that I, Porphyry, was planning to commit suicide. I happened to be in his house, and all of a sudden he approached me and said that my intention did not have its roots in my mind but in a certain type of gall disease [literally, "melancholy disease"], and he told me to leave the country. I took his advice and went to Sicily, to a well-known man called Probus; I had heard that he lived in Lilybaeum.

This is how I dropped my intention and why I was prevented from staying with Plotinus until his death.

96

Eunapius (fourth/fifth century A.D.) had studied rhetoric, philosophy, and apparently also medicine and earned his living as a "sophist"—a professional lecturer and teacher. He seems to have enjoyed a great reputation, for at one time he exercised a high priestly function, that of "hiero-phant," at the mystery cult of Eleusis. His *Lives of the Philosophers and Sophists* is full of curious anecdotes like this one concerning Sosipatra, a lady of great prestige who was roughly his contemporary. She represents the curious symbiosis of superior philosophical reasoning and astonish-ing psychic abilities. In the middle of a serious philosophical discussion she has a telepathic experience involving her lover ("cousin" is a term of endearment), Philometor.

One of her three sons, Antoninus, inherited her gifts and became a famous teacher and visionary himself. Among other things, he pre-dicted the destruction of the great temple of Serapis in Alexandria by the Christians. Antoninus died in A.D. 390, and the temple was destroyed in the following year.

That such a man abstained from theurgy is remarkable, but he may have been afraid, as Eunapius implies, of the strict laws that prohib-ited the practice of all forms of sorcery. He even refused to discuss the-ological questions in public.

Eunapius is hostile to the Christians and their cult of martyrs and relics. This, to him, looks suspiciously like witchcraft, for magicians tradi-tionally used parts of corpses and operated with "envoys" from the gods (i.e., daemons). To worship dead bodies in the ancient temple that now served as a church was to desecrate the former pagan sanctuary; to a pagan, death was a pollution, and the presence of a corpse in a temple was unthinkable.

Eunapius, *Lives of the Philosophers and Sophists*, p. 470 Boissonade

Once all her friends met in Sosipatra's house. Philometor was not pres-ent; he stayed in the country. The problem they discussed was the soul. Several theories were suggested, but then Sosipatra began to speak, and soon her proofs disposed of the arguments that had been proposed. Then she entered into a discussion of the descent of the soul and what part of it is subject to punishment, what part immortal. In the midst of her ecstatic, enthusiastic discourse, she fell silent, as though her voice had been cut off, and after a short while she cried out to the whole group: "What is this? There is cousin Philometor, riding in a carriage! The carriage has just been overturned in a rough spot in the road, and both his legs are in danger! But his servants have dragged him out, and he is all right; his elbows and hands are hurt, but even those wounds are harmless. They are carrying him on a stretcher, moaning!" This is what she said, and it was the truth. Everyone realized that Sosipatra was omnipresent, and whenever any-thing happened, she was there, which is what the philosophers say about the gods.

She died leaving three sons. The names of two of them do not
have to be mentioned, but [the third], Antoninus, was worthy of his
parents, for he established himself at the Canobic mouth of the Nile and
devoted himself completely to the religious rites as they were practiced
there and did his best to live up to his mother's prediction. All the young
men who were healthy in mind and thirsted for philosophy studied with
him, and the temple was full of candidates for the priesthood. Although
he still seemed to be human and spent his time with human beings, he
predicted to all his disciples that after his death the sanctuary would no
longer exist, that the great, holy temple of Serapis would become a dark,
shapeless thing and be transformed into something else, and that a fantastic, unattractive gloom would gain control over the most beautiful
things on earth. Time confirmed all these prophecies, and the event
finally gave him the authority of an oracle. . . .

Antoninus [as I have said before] went to Alexandria and was
impressed by the mouth of the Nile at Canobus and just loved being
there; and so he dedicated himself completely to the gods that are worshiped there.

Very soon he reached affinity with the divine, despised his body,
freed himself from the pleasures of the body, and applied himself to the
wisdom that is unknown to the crowd. Perhaps I ought to say a little more
about this. He showed no desire to practice theurgy or anything else that
is supernatural, possibly because he was afraid of the imperial policy that
was opposed to such practices. But everyone admired his discipline and
his strong, inflexible character, and all the students in Alexandria used to
see him on the seashore. For Alexandria, because of the sanctuary of
Serapis, was a world of religion all by itself. Those who came there from
all parts of the world were equal in number to the local population. After
having worshiped the god, they hurried on to Antoninus, some—the
ones who were in a real hurry—by land, while some were happy to use
the river boats that carried them leisurely toward their studies. When
they were given an interview, some would propose a scientific problem
and would at once be nourished by Plato's philosophy, but those who
asked about things divine would "encounter a statue": he would not say a
word to any of them, but, fixing his eyes and looking up at the sky, he
would sit there without speaking, and he would not give in. No one ever
saw him entering easily into a discussion of these things with anyone.

Not so long afterward there was a clear sign that he had some
divine element in him. No sooner had he left the community of men than
the cults of Alexandria and the sanctuary of Serapis in particular were
completely destroyed—not only the cults, but the buildings as well. . . .

So-called monks were imported into the sacred places . . . , they
collected the bones and skulls of criminals . . . and made them out to be

gods . . . , calling them "martyrs" and some sort of "ministers" and "ambassadors" sent from the gods to receive men's prayers . . . , but of course this only enhanced Antoninus' reputation as a clairvoyant, because he had told everyone that the temples would become tombs. . . .

·V·

ASTROLOGY

Introduction

Astrology, one of the oldest of the occult sciences, is no doubt older than astronomy, but it cannot be entirely separated from it. In fact, the Latin words *astrologia* and *astronomia* both designate what is today called "astrology." Even in English, the term *astronomy* had both meanings until the beginning of the Age of Enlightenment. The Greek word *mathesis* 'learning' can mean specifically "astrology," while *mathematikos* is not so much a "mathematician" as an "astrologer." In the ancient world, as today, astrology was based on mathematics and astronomy. The interest in astronomy and its development as a science in the modern sense can be explained in part by its practical value to the astrologer. And even though astrology may appear to be nonsensical to a modern scientist, it has been called the most "scientific" of all the occult sciences.[1]

Astrology had its beginnings in Mesopotamia, among the Chaldeans, who seem to have been a caste of Babylonian priests, though the name was originally used for the inhabitants of Kaldu in southeastern Babylonia. They probably used their astronomical knowledge to establish calendars and determine the dates of religious festivals. In later antiquity, every astrologer, whether he came from Mesopotamia or not, was called a "Chaldean."[2] In the interim, the Assyrians had conquered Babylonia and developed astrological techniques. Their king, Ashurbanipal, compiled an enormous archive in which astrological charts were kept on clay tablets, probably matching predictions with events, but also, it seems, establishing reliable ephemerides—that is, tables showing the computed or observed place of a heavenly body from day to day over many centuries—so that errors could be corrected. Although some lenses made of rock crystal have been found, neither the Babylonians nor the Assyrians had precision instruments with which to observe the stars. Perhaps the clear skies of the region made telescopes less necessary than they are today. In any event, the mathematical techniques and the methods of teamwork that were developed during this period were quite advanced.[3]

There are two main types of ancient astrology: (1) "judicial" astrology (first used in Chaucer), which predicts from celestial or meteorological phenomena the future of the king or the country (whether there will be wars, famines, and floods, or good harvests, peace, and prosperity); and (2) horoscopic astrology, which relates to the character and fortune of an individual. The first type seems to be older than the second; for a long time astrology was apparently a privilege of kings.[4] But both types are based on the belief that the position of the planets in the zodiac determines the future of an individual and, if this individual happens to be a king, that of his country as well.

The horoscope of a child born on April 29, 263 B.C., may be quoted as an example of Babylonian astrology: "At the time [of birth] the Sun was in 13:30° Aries, the Moon in 10° Aquarius, Jupiter at the beginning of Leo, Venus with the Sun, Saturn in Cancer, Mars at the end of Cancer. . . . He will be lacking in wealth. . . . His food will not satisfy his hunger. The wealth that he has in youth will not remain [?]. For thirty-six years he will have wealth. His days will be long." (The rest of the text is obscure.)[5]

In this Babylonian nativity, the Sun is very strong in Aries, after its natural place in Leo, and so the prediction mentions longevity and health. But if a planet was in a sign opposed to its natural rulership, only evil could come; thus, in the Babylonian chart, Saturn in Cancer is unfavorable (Cancer is opposite to Capricorn, where Saturn has his home), and so loss of money and possessions, a wasting away of material things, is predicted.

From Babylonia, astrological lore traveled to the other Hellenized parts of the Middle East, especially Egypt, but also to Greece. In the early decades of the third century B.C., a Babylonian priest, Berossus, dedicated a work on Babylonian history (now lost) to King Antiochus I (324–261 B.C.), the second ruler of the Seleucid Empire, an important outpost of Greek civilization in the East. This work, which included astrological doctrine, probably made its way to Egypt, where an ambitious astrological text ascribed to "Nechepso" and "Petosiris" was composed in the second half of the second century B.C. Nechepso and Petosiris claimed to have derived their knowledge from the god Hermes, but it seems reasonable to assume that they were familiar with Babylonian traditions.

The new doctrine then spread through the Greek world and was eagerly discussed by different philosophical schools. Aristotle had already described the stars as beings with supernatural intelligence, incorporeal deities, and ascribed to them a rational sort of influence on life on earth. Most Stoic philosophers accepted astrology because of their belief in fate and their acceptance of the law of cosmic sympathy. Astrology was rejected, however, by skeptics within the Platonic Academy (e.g., by Carneades) and outside it (e.g., by Sextus Empiricus).

Something ought also be said about the way astrology was treated in Old Testament times. The people of Israel knew, of course, that it was a prestigious art among their neighbors, the Babylonians and the Assyrians, and there is some evidence that, at times, even in Israel, the powers of the stars were recognized, though these powers were considered subordinate to Yahweh, not independent of him. In one of the oldest surviving pieces of Hebrew literature, the Song of Deborah, written after Barak's victory over Sisera, we read (Judges 5:20): "The stars have fought from heaven above; the stars in their courses have fought against Sisera." But the Song of Deborah is a hymn of thanksgiving to Yahweh.

Isaiah (or rather the "Second Isaiah," a later prophet) scorns the Chaldean astrologers (Isaiah 47:13): "Let your astrologers, your star-gazers who predict your future month by month, stand up and save you." He groups these astrologers with the magicians as "advisers" of the king and the people of Babylon: they claim to be able to save their nation, but they are all doomed. This attitude seems more typical of the Old Testament.

In the Book of Daniel, which, according to tradition, was composed in the sixth century B.C. at the court of Babylon, Daniel is made chief of the "wise men" of Babylon, that is, the astrologers and magicians (Daniel 2:48), and yet he remains faithful to the laws of his religion (Daniel 1). Hence, it may have been thought permissible for a Jew to practice astrology under certain circumstances. The Book of Daniel is believed by many scholars to have been written in the second century B.C., however, and if that is true, it reflects the ideas of the Hellenistic period.

It was, in fact, in Egypt that astrology found fertile soil, as magic had. Here the precepts formulated by the Chaldeans were organized into a system.[6] Astrologers were now available to ordinary people, and they were consulted on all kinds of matters—business, politics, love. Some astrologers, like the one in Propertius 4.1.7–20, might even claim for themselves the status of a seer or hierophant,[7] thus sharing with the magician a kind of occult knowledge that gave him power and impressed his clients. But there is also a genuine 'astral mysticism', corresponding to the religious feelings which alchemists sometimes experienced: see Ptolemy's epigram [no. 113] and Vettius Valens' testimony [no. 115] that astrology has freed him from fear and desire.

The earliest Greek horoscopes are preserved on papyri or graffiti from the first century B.C., but the practice itself must be much older. Indeed, the belief in astrology, as well as the belief in daemons and magic, was practically universal for many centuries. The symbol for Taurus, the sign of Venus, whom Julius Caesar claimed as his divine ancestress, was spread by his legions through many countries. Augustus had his horoscope published, and the symbol of Capricorn, his native sign, was stamped on the coins he issued.

Astrological Handbooks

Because astrology was a highly technical subject in antiquity, it was taught from handbooks, some of which have survived. Unfortunately, none of them covers every aspect thoroughly enough for one to learn to become a practitioner from it. The authors of these handbooks were probably reluctant to divulge their craft as a whole and thus held back certain information for their more advanced students.

Here it is possible to give only a brief survey of the more important texts. Many more are extant in the great libraries of Europe, but only a fraction have been published, even though their contents are roughly known.[8]

One of the earliest texts that is still extant was written under Augustus and Tiberius at the beginning of the first century A.D. It is not a handbook at all, but a didactic poem written in hexameters. About its author, Manilius, nothing is known. Since didactic poems are not meant to be exhaustive technical treatises, it is not surprising that no one could learn from this work how to cast a nativity. It offers a good deal of technical information, but for the most part it deals with the philosophical basis of astrology and the beauty of astrological concepts. It might be called an invitation to study the subject more thoroughly from other sources, but it does not take the place of such a work.[9]

Ptolemy, whose *Tetrabiblos* was written in the first half of the second century A.D., was one of the greatest scientists of his age as well as a fine mathematician and an able astronomical observer. In this work he attempts to prove "scientifically" the influence of the stars on human life and on life on earth in general. At the beginning he deals with critics and skeptics (anticipating some of the arguments of Sextus Empiricus *Against the Astrologers*, which was written c. A.D. 200). Then he states some of the basic doctrines of astrology. The planets have their properties through sharing one or more of the four elemental qualities: hot, cold, dry and moist. Elsewhere he deals with more technical questions, such as the determination of the exact time of birth by means of an astrolabe—no other devices are fully reliable.

Vettius Valens, the author of *Anthologiae* (*Excerpts*), lived at about the same time as Ptolemy. His voluminous work comes closer to a systematic textbook than those just mentioned, even though the title suggests that it is not complete. It seems to have been written for a fairly advanced practicing astrologer who wanted to add to his experience.

Firmicus Maternus (c. A.D. 335) wrote an introduction to astrolo-

gy entitled *Libri Matheseos*.[10] Like Ptolemy, he deals with such philosophical questions as destiny versus free will and finds a compromise along
Neoplatonist lines: the soul, being divine, is not wholly dependent on the
powers represented or indicated by the stars. In a slightly different form,
this argument would also appeal to a Christian, and it seems that Firmicus did convert to Christianity at one point in his life.[11] He quotes
many older authorities—Nechepso, Petosiris, and others—but tries to
give the elementary information that they omitted, especially as far as the
technique of casting a horoscope is concerned.

From the time of Augustus we have a strange piece of classroom
eloquence composed by Arellius Fuscus [*no. 97*], a celebrated professor of
rhetoric, for the benefit of his students.[12] It is based on a story about
Alexander the Great, who was warned by the Chaldeans (i.e., astrologers) against entering the city of Babylon (Plut., *Alex.* 73, etc.). The story
gains its point from the fact that Alexander died in Babylon in 323 B.C.
Arellius, however, pretends to be one of Alexander's advisers, urging
him to disregard the warnings, and he does it in such a way as to discredit
astrology and the techniques of so-called divination altogether.

Pliny the Elder, who preserves so much magical lore, attacks
astrology (*Nat. Hist.* 2.6 [= p. 189 of the Loeb Library ed.]). He denies any
close alliance or "sympathy" between the stars and mankind; he ridicules
the traditional symbolism that connects bright stars with riches, and to
him the "celestial mechanism" is just that. At the same time he seems to
believe in an influence of the stars that has not yet been discovered (least
of all by astrologers): "their nature is eternal; they weave into the fabric of
the world and mingle with its weft." This beautiful image was used by a
skeptic who would have liked to believe.

Astrology was primarily an occult science or discipline based on
mathematics and very complex rules of interpretation, but it coexisted
with a more popular brand or version. Not everyone who believed in the
influence of the stars could possibly have understood the whole system
and cast horoscopes himself. We find the most amazing misunderstandings and oversimplifications of astrological doctrine in the banquet scene
(ch. 39) of Petronius' novel *Satyricon*, which was written in the time of
Nero. There the author makes fun of a half-educated *nouveau riche* called
Trimalchio, who tries to impress his guests with unusual dishes and fancy
table talk. He tells them, among other things, that people born under the
sign of Aries will own many sheep and have a lot of wool, but they might
also turn out to be quarrelsome pedants. According to the same
pseudoauthority, those born under the sign of Libra will become drug-
gists or butchers, because scales will be their indispensable tool. This kind
of primitive astrology was probably practiced widely throughout antiquity, but it seems like a parody of the "royal" tradition of the serious

astrologers. A good example of practical astrology is the horoscope of Hadrian, who was born in A.D. 76 and died as emperor of Rome in A.D. 138.[13]

The Christian Attitude toward Astrology

For a long time the attitude of the Christian Church toward astrology was ambiguous. We have seen that in the apocryphal Wisdom of Solomon, which was probably written by a Hellenized Jew in Alexandria around the time of Christ's birth, Solomon claims to have received from God all sorts of occult knowledge, including "the changes of the solstices and the vicissitudes of the seasons; the cycles of the years and the positions of the stars."[14] This, no doubt, is a paraphrase of astrology as it was understood in Alexandria at the time. Although the Wisdom of Solomon was and is not universally acknowledged as canonical, it had great influence on early Christian writers; Augustine quotes it almost eight hundred times.

There is no evidence that Jesus and his disciples believed in the power of the stars, but the story of Jesus' birth, as told in the Gospel according to Matthew (2:1–12)—not in the other Gospels—brings the *magi* from the East to Bethlehem because they had seen a star that announced to them the birth of the king of the Jews. As pointed out before, these were priest-kings, or Chaldeans, and their knowledge of occult science, including astrology, could easily be defined in terms of chapter 7 of the Wisdom of Solomon; in fact, the Solomon of Wisdom is a combination of the historical Solomon with an oriental priest-king who has occult knowledge, and the book spells out the powers that were commonly ascribed to such "divine men" at the time of the birth of Christ.

Since the *magi* recognized in the new-born child a fellow king worthy of their adoration, they must have already seen in him powers that they themselves possessed. Hence, if Jesus had grown up to become a priest-king of this particular type, he would have been the perfect *magus*, the perfect exorcist, the perfect astrologer, but also a great secular ruler. Not all of this was in the stars—or in the Star—and yet the stars did not lie. The story is so much a part of the Christian tradition that it would seem to confirm a general belief in the role of heavenly bodies as messengers of great events rather than as divine powers and agents, which is, in fact, a compromise between Judaism and the astral religion of other Near Eastern civilizations. The only power is with Yahweh, but one should not ignore the signs in the sky.

The "darkness over the whole land" which began while Christ was hanging on the cross and ended shortly before he died is reported by Matthew (27:45), Mark (15:33), and Luke (23:44–45). It may be understood as an eclipse of the sun (at least this seems to be Luke's interpretation, though the text is not certain). If viewed in this way, it would form an antithesis to the bright star that shone at the time of Christ's birth. Thus, Christ's birth and death are seen as cosmic events; the universe could not be indifferent to such happenings.

Curious passages are found in the Book of Revelation: at the beginning (2:28) Jesus promises to the faithful ones the morning star; toward the end (22:16) he himself is compared to the morning star; elsewhere (1:20) stars serve as symbols for angels.[15] This has an interesting parallel. In a magical papyrus (*PGM* 1:74–75) a star is called an angel, which could reflect the belief held by contemporary Platonists (Philo Judaeus, *Plant.* 12, among others) that the stars are living beings endowed with reason.

In his Letter to the Galatians (4:3ff.) Paul chastises the Christian congregations in Galatia for still "worshiping the elements" (*ta stoicheia*) and observing special days, months, seasons, and years. The meaning of *elements* is much disputed, but one plausible explanation is that Paul has in mind the "heavenly bodies," and the special occasions the Galatians still observe are the old pagan festivals connected with the sun, the moon, and other heavenly bodies, for the calendar is based on their motions. Paul warns the Galatians not to make a special celebration to honor the new moon, for instance, because this comes dangerously close to the old astral religion, which is incompatible with the Word of God.

In a well-known passage in his Letter to the Romans (8:38–39) Paul writes: "I am convinced that neither death nor life nor angels nor (supernatural) powers, that neither the present nor the future nor (cosmic) forces above or below, that no other creature can separate us from the love of God which is in Christ Jesus, our Lord." He uses the words *archai* and *dynameis, hypsoma* and *bathos,* which I have translated as "(supernatural) powers" and "(cosmic) forces above and below." He probably meant the angelic and daemonic powers who were thought to be organized like an army or a political hierarchy, but he may also have been thinking of the stars and their influence, because *hypsoma* and *bathos* are astrological terms. What Paul tells the Christians in Rome is not to be afraid of daemons or other supernatural powers, some of which may be embodied in stars as astral spirits and thus endowed with a semidivine status.

We have seen that the Scriptures do not offer a clear position on astrology, although Paul certainly regarded it as a threat. His concern shows how deeply rooted these ancient beliefs were.

No wonder we find conflicting views among the early Christian writers. Origen (c. A.D. 185–255), who was perhaps as much a Platonist as a Christian, believed, like Philo, that the stars are rational (or spiritual) beings that take an interest in humans and foretell many things, although they do not cause events to happen. He argued, however, that astrology as a science is beyond human powers. God taught it only to the angels;

the astrology practiced on earth is inspired by evil spirits and therefore is
not only worthless but dangerous.[16]

Similarly, Tertullian (c. A.D. 160–225) considered astrology to be
an art invented by the fallen angels; no Christian should consult one of its
practitioners. In his view the Magi had been astrologers, but that did not
make the art itself respectable. It had been allowed to exist until the birth
of Christ, but anyone who practiced it afterward exposed himself to the
wrath of God. In this case Tertullian wholeheartedly agreed with the
Roman law that made it a crime for astrologers to enter Rome.[17]

Augustine (A.D. 354–430), in his later years, attacked astrology,
although as a young man he had believed in fate as spelled out by the
movements of the sun and the moon and the other planets.

Manicheanism was a form of gnosis named after Mani, a religious
teacher who was born c. A.D. 216 in Babylonia. The religion he taught was
similar to Christianity but it contained many elements that the Church
rejected. Mani believed that there was a powerful principle of evil in the
world, as opposed to God, the principle of good. He also believed that
human lives were ruled by the stars, and since the stars themselves were
either daemons or the tools of daemons, man needed a religion that
included astrological lore to deal effectively with these powers.[18]

Mani's doctrine appealed to Augustine for a short time, but Augustine eventually turned away from it completely. Some of the most
eloquent pages he ever wrote are devoted to a refutation of astrology, as
can be seen in the first seven chapters of Book 5 of his *City of God*.

Augustine's main argument concerns babies who are born at
almost the same time—particularly twins—but whose lives turn out totally differently: one becomes a senator, the other a slave, for instance.
Such cases had been studied by Stoics who believed in astrology—by
Posidonius, for example—and they had seemed satisfied by the evidence. Their critics were not, however. To silence the critics, a Roman
Neo-Pythagorean, a contemporary of Cicero's by the name of Publius
Nigidius, devised an ingenious experiment. He assembled a group of
skeptics around a potter's wheel and, after whirling the wheel with all his
strength, tried to strike it as fast as he could at a spot he had already
marked.[19] But this proved impossible, for the wheel turned too fast, and
the old and new marks did not coincide; in fact, they were at a considerable distance from each other. According to Nigidius, this showed that
twins cannot have identical personalities and destinies, because the celestial spheres revolve with such incredible speed that even a few minutes or
seconds make all the difference in the world. The experiment must have
impressed Nigidius' friends, for they called him "Nigidius Figulus," or
"Nigidius the Potter," and that is how he is described in scholarly works
to this day.

More than three centuries after Nigidius' death, Augustine was still concerned about the possible merit of the experiment, and he proceeded to refute it, saying that it was more fragile than the pottery made by the rotation of the wheel.

The Stars and the Belief in Fate

Astrology and fatalism[20] seem to go together; many philosophers and theologians have found this combination appealing; others have objected to astrology on the grounds that it excludes free will. The poet James Kirkup has expressed the dilemma as follows: "I like to believe in astrology; at the same time I feel I shouldn't. But there is something in the fixed order of the stars and in their peculiar aspect at the moment of our birth which is inevitable and fated. I believe in the stars as some rationalists believe in God."[21]

The ancient concept of fate or destiny (*heimarmene*) had its roots in religion,[22] but it was developed by the Stoics, who defined it as the law according to which all things that have happened have happened, all that are happening are happening, and all that will happen will happen. To the Stoics, at least to most of them, the stars were an expression of this concept because they moved according to eternal laws. Hence, almost all Stoics believed in astrology.

Stoic fate is not blind, however. It is rational, and in itself it is a manifestation of the cosmic *logos*, which is divine. This doctrine of fate and necessity was one of the main points of controversy between the Stoa and other philosophical schools, especially the Platonists and the followers of Aristotle, who wished to maintain the autonomy of the human soul and the transcendence and providence of God.[23]

Strangely enough, the astrologer who claimed that he was able to predict someone's fate accurately also believed that he could help that person accept what was foreordained. This acceptance of the inevitable was an important tenet of Stoic ethics. It is reflected in Vettius Valens in a passage which shows that an astrologer could play a role analogous to a modern psychiatrist [*no. 115*]. While announcing a disaster, he might actually soften the blow.

Astrologers who were also practitioners of magic could break or counteract the influence of the stars and offer a way out by recruiting the help of supernatural powers.[24] Christianity and the Mystery Religions also provided a release from the shackles of determinism through salvation. But the belief that magic "can upset right and wrong, but not human destiny" (Hor., *Epod.* 5 [no. 6]) is documented as well.

Notes on Astrological Technique

The principles and the technique of astrological prediction have not changed a great deal since the late Hellenistic period. We no longer believe in a geocentric universe; three new planets (Uranus, Neptune, and Pluto) have been discovered; and because of the "precession of the equinoxes" the sun is no longer in Aries during the time that it is supposed to be there, from March 21 to April 20; and yet a horoscope today is still, as it was then, "a geocentric map of the solar system at a given moment of time,"[25] and its interpretation follows pretty much the same lines that the ancient astrologers followed.

One of the most important elements of the horoscope is the "ascendant," the degree of the ecliptic that is rising at the moment of birth. Today this is considered to be one of thirty degrees of one of twelve constellations. Originally it may have been a particular star within the constellation, for it was called *horoskopos* 'watcher of the hour'. The ascendant determines the so-called First house, and this brings us to a curious construction. While the "planets" (which included the sun and the moon) and the twelve signs of the zodiac correspond to heavenly bodies (though the sum of our planets is no longer that of the ancients, and the signs of the zodiac are no longer where they are supposed to be), the division of a chart into twelve houses has no basis in the universe as we know it. This division is based on spherical trigonometry, which in itself must be a mystery to many astrologers. Several systems of establishing the houses are used today, but none of them, it appears, predates the Renaissance. The ancient systems were much simpler.

What is remarkable about the principle of the zodiac is the fact that it catches in a net, as it were, the main areas or aspects of a person's character and life. The first house, determined by the ascendant, tells the astrologer what he wants to know about the personality, the self, its potential and its realizations. Any planets that happen to be in that section of space at the time of birth will have a special influence on the person's character and destiny.

The second and third houses are easily found after the ascendant has been determined. If Taurus is the ascendant, the second house is in Gemini, the third in Cancer, and so on. The twelfth house will take us back to the sign just preceding the ascendant, in this case Aries.

The second house gives information about the person's property and possessions, his or her financial success. The third house concerns brothers and sisters, but also one's peer group and education. The fourth house has to do with parents, the home, one's roots. The fifth house tells about one's loves, one's children, one's hobbies (a curious but not totally illogical correlation). The sixth house indicates one's health, but also the hard work one has to do. The seventh house is the house of marriage, partnerships, and (ironically) enemies. One is almost tempted to say that in such traditional lore the wisdom of long experience is evident; one has only to think of family relationships in Greek tragedy! The eighth house is the house of death, the subject's, but also that of the people from whom he may inherit. The ninth house was thought to relate to a person's intellectual and spiritual life, his philosophy and religion, but also his travels; there is some logic in this, too, for at least since Herodotus, the chief way to extend one's horizon intellectually was to travel to countries with ancient traditions; there were very few public libraries where one could consult the latest reference works. The tenth house offered clues to one's domicile, profession, social life, status, and conduct of life in general. The eleventh house revealed the nature of one's friendships (as distinguished from the loves revealed by the fifth house), but also, it seems, one's political associations and hence one's political ambitions, for the ancient system of patronage was nominally a "friendship," but it could also be a kind of "mafia." Finally, the twelfth house, graphically close to the first, was the house of troubles and tribulations, illness and betrayal, enemies and disgrace.

Even from this brief survey it becomes clear that the ancient system of twelve houses preserves a great deal of human experience. At one time there were only eight houses, but as life became more complex, the number apparently had to be increased. Life today is even more complex, and still the ancient system has something to say. It certainly has the capacity to receive many thousands of interpretations. At the very least, it would serve the astrologer as a kind of reminder as he considers the answers to possible questions asked of him. At the same time, it is a great psychological tool, one that was designed long before modern psychology and psychiatry evolved.

The other elements to be considered in interpreting the chart of the Zodiac are, as mentioned above, the planets located or placed in the signs. Each of the planets has its "house" or "houses," which in this case means the sign or signs of the zodiac in which it feels at home: for the sun this is Leo; for the moon it is Cancer; for the others there are two favorite domiciles, one diurnal, one nocturnal. The planets have their greatest and most beneficial influence if they are in the appropriate house at the time of birth—for instance, if Venus is in Libra and the birth takes place during the day, or if Jupiter is in Pisces and the birth takes place at night.

The locations of the planets in the signs of the zodiac and in the twelve trigonometric houses are important, but so, too, are the "aspects": the number of degrees between one planet and another, one planet and the "cusps" (the dividing lines between one house and another). Opposition (180° or thereabouts) and tetragon (ideally 90°) are considered unfavorable, whereas trigon (c. 120°) and sextile (ideally 60°) are considered favorable.

Since it takes the sun about thirty days to pass through one sign of the zodiac, and an enormous number of people with different characters and destinies are born during that time, each sign is subdivided into three decans, or 10° segments roughly corresponding to the ten days the sun seemed to spend there. These decans modify the general character of the sign. One particular planet is in charge of it, but there is also great variety as to the names and functions of the planets.

Notes

1. Neugebauer, *The Exact Sciences in Antiquity*, p. 164.
2. Bidez and Cumont, *Les Mages hellénisés*.
3. Saggs, *The Greatness That Was Babylon*, p. 459.
4. Ibid., p. 455.
5. A. Sachs, in *Journal of Cuneiform Studies* 6 (1953): 57.
6. Neugebauer, *The Exact Sciences in Antiquity*, pp. 178ff.; Nilsson, *Geschichte der griechischen Religion*, 1:268.
7. Nock, *Essays on Religion in the Ancient World*, 1:497.
8. The *Catalogus Codicum Astrologicorum Graecorum* surveys the mass of material in astrological handbooks that is preserved in many libraries. The first volumes of the catalog were compiled under the direction of F. Cumont (Brussels); 12 vols. have been published since 1898.
9. G. P. Goold has produced a fine text and an excellent translation of Manilius (Cambridge: Loeb Classical Library, Harvard University Press, 1977).
10. Firmicus' handbook has been translated by J. R. Bram under the title *Ancient Astrology* (Park Ridge, N.J.: Noyes, 1975).
11. The treatise *Why Paganism is Wrong* (*De Errore Profanarum Religionum*), also ascribed to Firmicus, seems to indicate that at one time he was a Christian. It was not impossible to be a Christian and a believer in astrology, though the Church officially condemned astrological doctrine.
12. On Seneca's *Suasoriae* 3.7 [*no. 97*] see Cumont, *Astrology and Religion*, pp. 148–49; and L. Bieler, in *Wiener Studien* 52 (1935): 84ff.
13. Neugebauer and Van Hoesen, *Greek Horoscopes*, pp. 90ff.
14. D. Winston, trans., *The Wisdom of Solomon*, Anchor Bible Series, vol. 43 (Garden City, N.Y.: Doubleday, 1979), 7:18–19.
15. See F. Boll, *Aus der Offenbarung Johannis* (Leipzig: Teubner, 1914), pp. 47ff.
16. Thorndike, *A History of Magic and Experimental Science*, 1:436ff.
17. Ibid., pp. 462ff.
18. J. J. O'Meara, *An Augustine Reader* (Garden City, N.Y.: Image Books, 1973), pp. 13ff., 128–29, 319ff.
19. This experiment, briefly reported by Augustine in *City of God* 5.3, has not been properly interpreted, I believe. Nigidius must have smeared some ink on his finger, set the wheel in motion, and touched it. He then tried to touch that same spot again as the wheel was still spinning.
20. See M. David, *Les Dieux et le destin en Babylonie* (Paris: Presses Universitaires, 1949); Onians, *Origins of European Thought*, pp. 303ff.
21. J. Kirkup, *Sorrows, Passions, and Alarms* (London: Collins, 1959), p. 93.
22. Fatalism is the only philosophical principle underlying fairy tales, according to Krappe, *The Science of Folklore*, p. 28. Sometimes the fairies are only agents of fate; certainly there is a linguistic link between the words *fairy* and *fate*.

23. J. Dillon, *The Middle Platonists* (Ithaca, N.Y.: Cornell University Press, 1977),
     p. 208; G. Luck, in *American Journal of Philology* 101 (1980): 373ff.
24. Arn., *Adv. Gent.* 2.13.62.
25. See MacNeice, *Astrology,* p. 244. This excellent work has not received the
     attention it deserves. The chapter on ancient astrology is especially valuable.

Texts

97

This is an extract from a *suasoria*, a type of rhetorical exercise that formed an important part of higher education in the Early Roman Empire. Students had to pretend that they were persuading a mythical or historical character to take, or not to take, a certain course of action, after which the teacher would give his own version. Such exercises were considered a good preparation for a career in politics. This piece is taken from a collection of excerpts from model speeches made by famous professors of rhetoric in the Augustan Age. In this instance the professor is Arellius Fuscus, one of the teachers who had a certain amount of influence on the poet Ovid, who is said to have excelled in this genre.

What we have is a brief outline of the original speech, some parts of which were more developed than others. It was written down many years later by Seneca the Elder, father of the famous philosopher. It states very clearly the case against astrology—in fact, against all forms of prophecy and prediction. In some parts the Latin text is corrupt, and even where it seems reasonably certain, one cannot always be sure of the meaning.

Arellius first builds up the typical diviner as a kind of superhuman being who surely descends from the gods or the stars (or at least pretends that he does). It is the same kind of irony that we find in Propertius' *Elegies* 4.7, where a Persian or Egyptian astrologer boasts about his divine ancestors. The Latin words *agnoscat suum uates deum* must therefore mean "let the god [i.e., Apollo] acknowledge the prophet as his own [i.e., his descendant]," not "the god must acknowledge him as a prophet," for the latter could be taken for granted.

The second paragraph begins with the words "If all this were [really] true, why do not men in every generation pursue these studies?" By "these studies" Arellius Fuscus means "all the known techniques of predicting the future" or "all the fraudulent claims that seers make." If astrology were an exact science in which all forecasts came true, everyone would want to be an astrologer. In fact, most people at that time knew a little about astrology—perhaps interpreting it in a garbled, nonsensical way, like the uneducated *nouveau riche*, Trimalchio, in Petronius' *Satyricon* (ch. 35), but usually understanding enough to follow the technical explanations of a professional astrologer.

In the same context Arellius calls the astrologers "those who throw themselves into the battle of the Fates" (reading *proelia* rather than *pignora*, the mechanical repetition of a word that made sense a few lines before but none whatsoever here). This, too, is ironic: the astrologers see themselves as the heroes or protagonists in a sort of cosmic battle, fighting to save their clients from the impact of fate.

Astrologers also like to advertise themselves as psychotherapists, because they can prepare their clients for the blows that fate has in store for them. But their false predictions, Arellius argues, make nervous wrecks of many who are told that they will die soon, but who live on and on in fear and anxiety. Others are given the hope of a long life, but instead meet an early death without being prepared for it; they, too, are fooled by the practitioners of a pseudoscience.

Seneca the Elder, *Suasoriae* 3.7.4 (from a speech by Arellius Fuscus)

What kind of a man is this who pretends to know the future? Surely the lot of a person who chants prophecies at the order of a god must be very unusual. He cannot be content with the womb from which the rest of us—those who know nothing of the future—are born. No doubt the person who reveals the commands of a god is marked with some divine symbol. Yes, of course: a seer stirs up fear in a king, in the ruler of the universe! That man whose privilege it is to frighten Alexander must be great himself, must stand high above the common lot of mankind. Let him name the stars among his ancestors! Let the god acknowledge the prophet as his own [son or progeny]! He who reveals the future to the nations cannot live his life within the same boundaries [as ordinary men]; his personality must be outside all the necessities of fate.

If all this were true, why do not men in every generation pursue these studies? Why do we not from childhood approach nature and the gods as far as that is possible? After all, the stars are accessible, and we can mix with gods! Why do we sweat away at eloquence? It is useless. Why do we get calloused hands from handling weapons? It is dangerous. Can there be a better investment of talent than knowledge of the future? But those who "throw themselves into the battle of the Fates," as they say, want to know about your birthday, and consider the first hour of your life the indicator of all the years to follow. They observe the motions of the stars, the directions in which they move: whether the Sun stood in threatening opposition or shone kindly on the nativity; whether the child received the full light [of the Moon], the beginning of her waxing, or whether the Moon was obscured [at the time] and hid her head in darkness; whether Saturn invited the newborn child to become a farmer, Mars a soldier to go to war, Mercury a successful businessman, or Venus graciously promised her favors, or Jupiter would carry the child from humble origins to tremendous heights. So many gods swarming about one head!

So they predict the future? To many they have promised a long life, and yet the day [of death] was suddenly upon them without any warning; to others they have predicted an early death, and yet they lived on, plagued by pointless fears [text uncertain]. To some they have promised a happy life, but Fortune quickly sent them all kinds of harm.

You see, we share an uncertain fate, and these are all fictions concocted by clever astrologers, without any truth in them. Will there be a place on earth, Alexander, that has not witnessed a victory of yours? The Ocean stood open to you, and Babylon should be closed?

98

Manilius, a Stoic, is the author of a didactic poem on astrology. We know very little about him, except that he must have lived under Augustus and Tiberius. His poem, in five books, is by no means a complete introduction to astrology. It deals with certain aspects, leaving others out, and it offers digressions that are often of great interest to us but not strictly necessary from a technical point of view. Manilius may never have intended to cover the whole subject, or he may not have had a chance to finish his work. He, like Lucretius, the Epicurean, offered more than technical or philosophical instruction: he wanted to convert his readers to his own world view. While Lucretius preached Epicureanism as a kind of religion, Manilius preached an astral religion based on Stoic ideas, a religion that promised insight into the nature of the universe.

In the present text Manilius describes astrology as a gift of the god Hermes. If this is not the Greek Hermes but the Egyptian Hermes Trismegistus, it means that Manilius considered astrology to be an Egyptian science, revealed to the priests long ago and kept secret. By studying the divinely revealed principles and applying them to practical matters, these priests established, over the centuries, the science of astrology as Manilius knew it. At the beginning of the long process there was revelation, but afterward a good deal of empirical research was done by men.

According to Manilius, the progress of astrology is just one chapter in the general progress of human civilization. He takes it for granted that magic and the other occult sciences produce concrete results, because they proceed from scientific facts and apply well-tested techniques.

Manilius 1.25–112

It was by a gift of the gods that the earth was permitted a more intimate knowledge of the universe. For if they had wanted to keep it a secret, who would have been clever enough to steal the cosmic mystery that controls everything? Having but a human mind, who could have attempted such a gigantic task, wishing to appear to be a god against the will of the gods and reveal the movements of the heavenly bodies in the zenith and the nadir, underneath the earth, and describe how the stars obey their orbits as they travel through space? You, god of Cyllene [Hermes], are the author and the origin of this great sacred tradition. Thanks to you, we know the farther reaches of the sky, the constellations, the names and movements of the stars, their importance and their influence. You wanted to enlarge the face of the universe; you wanted the power of nature, not only its appearance, to be revered; you wanted mankind to find out in what way god was supreme.

Nature, too, offered her powers and revealed herself. She did not find it beneath her dignity to inspire the minds of kings; she made them touch the summits that are close to heaven. They brought civilization to the savage peoples in the East whose lands are divided by the Euphrates and flooded by the Nile, where the universe returns and soars away, high above the cities of dark nations.

Then the priests who offered worship in temples all their lives and who were chosen to express the prayers of the people obtained by their service the favor of the gods. The very presence of the divine power kindled their pure minds, and god himself brought god into their hearts and revealed himself to his servants.

These were the men who established our noble science. They were the first to see, through their art, how fate depends on the wandering stars. Over the course of many centuries they assigned with persistent care to each period of time the events connected with it: the day on which someone is born, the kind of life he shall lead, the influence of every hour on the laws of destiny, and the enormous differences made by small motions. They explored every aspect of the sky as the stars returned to their original positions. They assigned to the unchangeable sequences of the fates the specific influence of certain configurations. As a result, experience, applied in different ways, produced an art; examples pointed the way; from long observation it was discovered that the stars control the whole world by mysterious laws, that the world itself moves by an eternal principle, and that we can, by reliable signs, recognize the ups and downs of fate.

Before this, life had been primitive and ignorant. People had looked at the outward appearance of the creation without any understanding; with amazement they had stared at the strange new light of the universe. Sometimes they mourned as though they had lost it; then again they were glad because the stars seemed to be born again [text uncertain]. They could not understand the reasons why the days varied in length and why the nights did not always fill a standard measure of time; why the length of shadows was unequal, depending on whether the sun was withdrawing or returning. Ingenuity had not yet taught mankind crafts and arts. The earth lay wasted and fallow under ignorant farmers. There was gold in the hills, but no one went there. The ocean, undisturbed, hid unknown worlds: men did not dare entrust their lives to the sea and their prayers to the winds; they thought what little knowledge they had [was] sufficient.

As time went by, the human mind grew sharper. Hard work made the poor creatures more ingenious. The heavy lot that each man had to carry forced him to look out for himself. They began to specialize and competed intellectually, and whatever [through] intelligence and experience they discovered by trial, they happily communicated and contributed to the common good. Their speech—barbarous before—now conformed to rules of its own. The soil—uncultivated before—was now worked over for all kinds of crops. The roving sailor traveled across the sea, uncharted before, and connected by trade routes countries that had not known of each other before. Gradual progress led to the development of the arts of war and peace, for experience always generates one skill from the other. Not to mention the commonplace: men learned to understand the language of birds, to predict the future from entrails, to break snakes by incantations, to conjure up ghosts and stir the depths of Acheron, to transform day into night, night into day. Human intelligence, always eager to learn, overcame everything by trying hard, and human reason did not set an end or a limit to its efforts until it had climbed up to the sky and grasped the mysteries of nature by its principles and saw everything there is to see.

Men understood why clouds are shaken by the impact of tremendous thunderclaps, why snowflakes in winter are softer than hail in summer, why flames come out of the ground and why the solid earth quakes, why rain pours down, what cause produces winds. Reason delivered us from the awesome feeling that nature inspires: it took Jupiter's lightning and thundering power away and assigned the noise to the winds, the flame to the clouds. After human reason had connected every phenomenon with its true cause, it set out to explore the structure of the universe, starting at the bottom, and attempted to grasp the whole sky; it identified the shapes, gave the stars their names, observed the cycles in which they traveled according to eternal laws. It realized that everything moves according to the divine power and the aspects of heaven and that the stars by their manifold configurations influence our destinies.

99

Near the beginning of his poem Manilius places a Stoic cosmogony. It is a dramatic account of the creation of the world, comparable to certain passages in Lucretius and to the beginning of Ovid's *Metamorphoses*. These poets clearly influenced Manilius, but his account is of the elements in rapid motion for a time, until they find their place in the universe: fire soars up to the etherial zones, earth leaps through water, and so on. The drama of creation is presented in a truly spectacular manner. One idea that emerges is typically Stoic: Nature knows her business quite well and is no "blundering novice"; all the philosopher has to do is study her ways.

The suspension of the earth in space seems to have been a scientific problem much discussed in Manilius' day. He offers a simple explanation. The earth is round, and so is the universe that rotates around it. The sun, the moon, all the planets, are round, and so are the gods. As the universe travels through space (an amazingly modern concept), its rotation produces a kind of centrifugal action. Manilius or the author he is following may have seen a simple physical experiment demonstrating such an action, but one should keep in mind that Manilius' views were not shared by most of his contemporaries.

At the end of the passage, Manilius affirms his belief in a cosmic god whose spirit (*pneuma*) is the breath of the universe. This divine element is immanent in the world and keeps it alive, as it were. The whole cosmos is one huge living and breathing organism, according to this concept, and just as in the human body the condition of one part may affect another part, what happens in one region of the universe may affect what happens in another region. This is a clear statement of the principle of "cosmic sympathy," which is so important in astrology and in the occult sciences in general. Since this principle is often attributed to Posidonius, who firmly believed in all kinds of divination, it is possible that Manilius used him as a source.

Manilius 1.149–254 (154 placed before 159, and 167 placed after 214)

Flying fire soared upward to the etherial zones, spread along the very top of the starry sky, and made from panels of flames the walls of the world. Next, spirit sank down and became light breezes and spread out air through the middle of the empty space of the world. The third element expanded [in the form of] water and floating waves and poured out the ocean born from the whole sea. This happened so that water might breathe out and exhale the light breezes and feed the air, which draws its seeds from it [the water]; also, that the wind might nourish the fire, which is placed directly under the stars. Finally, earth drifted to the bottom, ball-shaped because of its weight: slime, mixed with drifting sand, took shape as the light liquid gradually evaporated. More moisture withdrew and became pure water, and so the oceans were filtered, and land built up, and flat expanses of water came to lie next to hollow valleys. Mountains emerged from the seas. The earth, though still locked on all sides by the ocean, leapt through the waves, and it remained stable because the firmament kept at every point the same distance from it, and by falling from all sides preserved the middle and lowest part from falling. (For bodies hit by blows coming from inside remain as they are, and because of the centripetal force, they cannot move very far.)

If the earth did not hang in balance, the sun would not, as the stars appear in the sky, drive its chariot from the point of its setting and would not return to its rising; nor would the moon, below the horizon, pursue a course through space; nor would the morning star shine during the early hours of a day after having given its light as evening star at the end of a day. Actually, the earth has not been thrown down to the lowest point. It remains suspended in the center. This is why the whole space [around it] allows passage, so that the firmament may set underneath the earth and rise again. For I cannot believe that the stars that appear at the horizon rise by coincidence, nor that the firmament is created anew again and again, nor that the sun dies every day and is reborn. Over the centuries the shape of the constellations has remained the same. The same sun has risen from the same quarter of the sky. The moon has gone through its phases over the same number of days. Nature keeps to the ways that she herself has made. She is no blundering novice. The days travel around the earth with the light that never fails and show the same hours now to these, and now to other, regions of the earth. If you travel eastward, the East moves constantly farther away, as does the West if you travel westward. What is true for the sun is true for the sky.

Why should one be surprised that the earth is suspended? The firmament itself is suspended, too, and not supported by any base. This is clear from its very movement and from the fact that it travels fast through space. The sun moves without support, as it skillfully directs its chariot now this way and now that, keeping within its turning points in the sky. The moon and the stars travel through cosmic space. Similarly, in accordance with celestial laws, the earth is suspended. Therefore, the earth has been allotted a hollow space in the center of the atmosphere, equidistant at every point from the nadir. It is not flattened out in a plain, but has the shape of a sphere, which rises and falls at the same time at every point. This is its natural shape. Thus, the universe itself, because it turns round and round, gives a spherical shape to the stars. We see that the sun and the moon are round, spherical: the moon is looking for light for its extended body, but its globe as a whole does not receive the sun's rays, which hit it at an oblique angle. This is the lasting, abiding form, very much like that of the gods. It has no beginning, no end, in itself, but is like itself on its whole surface, identical with itself throughout. Similarly, the earth stays round, imitating the shape of the universe, and being the lowest of all heavenly bodies, remains in the very center.

For this reason we cannot see all the constellations from every point of the earth. You will never spot the shining light of Canopus until you have crossed the sea and reached the banks of the Nile. Those who live directly under the Bear look for it in vain: they inhabit the slopes of our globe, and the curves of the terrain in between deprive them of the sky and limit their view. The moon proves that the earth is round. When, at night, it is plunged into dark shadows, undergoing an eclipse, it does not frighten all the nations at the same time. First the countries in the East go without your light; then those that are directly under the center of the sky . . . ; finally the brass is struck among the nations of the West. If the earth were flat, the moon would rise only once over the whole world, and its eclipse would be bewailed everywhere at the same time. But since the outline of the earth follows a gentle curve, the moon appears now to these lands, now to others, rising and setting at the same time. It moves along a belly-shaped orbit, and it combines an upward with a downward motion. It comes up over some horizons and leaves others behind. Hence we conclude that the earth is round.

On its surface live many different tribes of men and wild beasts and birds of the air. One inhabitable zone stretches toward the North, another is situated in the Southern regions: it actually lies beneath our feet, but it imagines itself above us because the terrain hides the gradual slope, and the path ascends and descends at the same time. When the sun has reached the Western horizon and looks down on our part of the world, a new day wakes up sleeping cities in that other part and brings back to them with the light of day their round of daily duties. By now, there is night for us, and we invite slumber into our bodies. The ocean divides and at the same time connects the two regions.

This organic structure of the huge universe, its individual parts composed of different elements—air, fire, earth, and the flat sea—is ruled by the divine power of spirit. God breathes through the whole in a mystic way and governs it by mysterious means. He controls the mutual relationships between all parts through which one [part] transmits its strength to another and [in turn] receives another's strength. As a result, cosmic sympathy reigns forever among a variety of phenomena.

100

In his defense of astrology as a part of Stoic doctrine, Manilius naturally has to attack Epicurus. The Epicureans did not deny that gods existed, but they rejected any involvement of the gods in human affairs. The Stoics, on the other hand, believed that there was a permanent force in the history of the world, and that it excluded the element of chance. The constellations that Manilius saw in the sky at the beginning of our era were the same constellations that the Greeks had seen during the Trojan War. To Manilius, this permanence was definitely the expression of a divine will.

But in the course of history the world had seen striking changes. The descendants of the vanquished Trojans had conquered the descendants of the victorious Greeks. This, too, had happened in accordance with the divine will. Thus, for Manilius, nothing is left to chance; everything happens according to a cosmic scheme, and astrology is the science that explores this scheme.

Manilius 1.474–531

It is easy to recognize the bright constellations, for they do not show any deviation in their settings and risings. They all come up at regular times to display their own stars, and appearances and disappearances follow a certain order. Nothing in this immense structure is more marvelous than this principle and the fact that everything obeys certain laws. Nowhere does confusion interfere. Nothing deviates in any direction or moves in a larger or smaller orb or changes its course. Is there anything else so overwhelming in appearance, yet so sure in its rhythm?

To me no argument seems as forceful as this, for it shows that the world moves in accordance with a divine power and is, in itself, god, and has not been put together at the whim of chance. But this is what Epicurus wants us to believe: he first built up the walls of the universe from tiny seeds and dissolved them into these seeds again. He also thought that the seas and the land and the stars in the sky, as well as the ether, consisted of atoms, and that in the vast space whole worlds were formed and dissolved again and new worlds created. He also said that everything would return to the state of atoms and change its appearance. But who could believe that such huge conglomerations of matter could be created from tiny particles without a divine will, and that the world is the result of casual combination? If chance gave us this universe, let chance govern it! But then why do we see the stars rise in a regular rhythm and accomplish their course as if it had been ordered by a command, never hurrying ahead, never lagging behind? Why do the same stars always grace the summer nights, the same stars always the winter nights? Why does every day impose a certain configuration upon the sky as it comes and a certain configuration as it goes? When the Greeks sacked Troy, the Bear and Orion already moved frontally toward each other; the Bear was content to move in a circle at the top, Orion to ascend toward her from the opposite direction as she turned away, always running over the whole firmament to meet her. Even then men were able to tell the time of dark night by the constellations, and the sky had established a clock of its own. How many realms have tumbled since the sack of Troy? How many nations have been led into captivity? How many times has Fortuna distributed slavery and supremacy throughout the world and reappeared in a different shape? Did it not rekindle the ashes of Troy and give [the Trojans] supreme power without a thought of what had happened? And now it is the turn of Greece to be weighed down by the fate of Asia Minor! Why bother to enumerate the centuries and tell how many times the fiery sun has come back to illuminate the world on its varying course? Everything born under the law of mortality must change. The earth does not realize that it is ravaged by the passage of time and that it changes its face over the centuries. But the firmament remains intact: it conserves all its elements; long periods of time do not increase it nor old age diminish it; nor does it swerve from its movement the least bit or lag in its course. It will always be the same because it always was the same. Our forefathers did not see it changed; our descendants will not see it changed. It is god: he will never change. The sun never takes a detour toward the Bears that lie across the sky. It does not change its direction, going from West to East, bringing the dawn to lands that have never seen it. The moon does not grow beyond its normal sphere of light but keeps the rhythm of its waxing and waning. The stars that are attached to the sky do not fall down on the earth but accomplish their orbits in measured periods of time. All this is not the work of chance but the planning of a supreme god.

101

The Milky Way did not play an important role in ancient astrological theory, but as a striking celestial phenomenon it had to be discussed. After reviewing some older theories, Manilius revives one that Cicero's Greek source in the *Republic* 6.16 had proposed: the Milky Way is the place in heaven where the souls of heroes go when they die. These souls are of the same substance as the stars themselves, and so, through their affinity, will be drawn to them. The catalog of great Roman statesmen and soldiers, following Greek heroes, statesmen, and philosophers, ends with Augustus, who is still alive at the time Manilius' text is written, but who is promised by the poet a preeminent place in heaven after his death. Manilius must have read Cicero's "Dream of Scipio" (*De Republ.*, bk. 6) as well as the passage in Virgil's *Aeneid* (6.756ff.) in which Anchises points out to his son in the underworld the series of heroes who will shape Roman history for centuries to come.

From the following text it would seem that theories of life after death were also a part of astrological doctrine. If one believed in the survival of the individual soul (not all Stoics did), the souls had to be ranked in some way. Thus the Milky Way offered itself as a convenient dwelling place for superior souls. It was prominent and visible—the very opposite of Hades, the great "Invisible One."

Manilius 1.758–804

[*The author first presents five theories about the origin of the Milky Way, some physical, some mythical; he then gives a different kind of explanation.*]

Or could it be that the souls of heroes, of great men who are worthy of heaven, once they are freed from their bodies and released from the earthly sphere, come here to inhabit a heaven of their own, living "ether years" and enjoying the firmament . . . ?

[*The poet then lists heroes of Greek myth, including Peleus, Achilles, Agamemnon, and adds one historical figure, Alexander the Great. Then Greek statesmen and philosophers are mentioned. A catalog of great Roman soldiers and statesmen follows. Manilius notes that Augustus is still among the living, but that one day*] Augustus will rule heaven, with Jupiter Tonans as his companion, through the signs of the Zodiac. In the assembly of the gods he will see great Quirinus . . . on an even higher level than the Milky Way. Up there is the seat of the gods; here is the seat of those who, almost divine and close to the gods, follow their example through their outstanding achievements.

102

Manilius speaks once more of the "mutual sympathy" that reigns in the universe and of the "sum total of things," which always remains the same, thus anticipating a law of modern physics, it seems. Manilius believes in a supreme god who has created the universe and keeps it moving, but as he puts it, "movement feeds the creation: it does not change it"—a remarkable observation.

Manilius 2.60–79

I shall sing of the god who rules mysteriously over nature, the god who permeates the sky, the land, and the sea and who governs the whole immense structure with a unifying bond. I shall sing how the life of the whole universe is based on mutual sympathy and how it moves by the force of reason because a single spirit inhabits all its parts and radiates through the whole world, spreading itself through everything and giving it the shape of a living creature. If the whole mechanism were not built firmly out of sympathetic elements and did not obey a supreme master, and if providence did not rule the tremendous potential of the universe, the earth would not be stable nor would the stars observe their orbits (in fact, the universe would go astray and move aimlessly or else stand still and motionless); nor would the constellations keep their set courses, nor would the night flee the day and then, in turn, chase the day. The rains would not nourish the earth, nor the winds the upper air, nor the sea the clouds, the rivers the sea, the ocean the springs. Nor would the sum total of things remain the same forever through all its parts, having been arranged in a fair manner by the creator to make sure that the waves would not dry up nor the land sink nor the heaven in its motion shrink or extend beyond its normal dimensions. Movement feeds the creation: it does not change it. . . .

103

Manilius now develops the concept of "cosmic sympathy" in an attempt to prove the validity of astrology as a science. Part of his proof is empirical: thus he speaks of sea creatures that change their shapes according to the movement of the moon. Such data had been compiled by Posidonius.

Some of the thoughts expressed in this passage are beautiful and profound and seem to belong to an ancient philosophical tradition that emerges and reemerges throughout antiquity and cannot be traced to a specific school. The rhetorical question "Who could know heaven except by the grace of heaven?" is very similar to Plotinus' axiom that the human eye must have an element of the sun in it in order to see the light of the sun.

But Manilius also operates with a concept dear to the Stoics, the *consensus gentium,* the "agreement of all nations." His argument becomes rather emotional and rhetorical, although in the end he professes not to care whether the majority of mankind listens to him. He must have encountered more than a few skeptics in his lifetime, but he is content to "sing" (i.e., write his verse) for the chosen few.

Manilius 2.80–149

Thus everything is organized throughout the whole world and follows a master. This god, and the reason that controls everything, brings down from the heavenly stars the creatures of the earth. Though the stars are very distant and remote, he makes us feel their influence, as they give to the peoples their ways of life and destinies and to every person a character of his own. We do not have to look far for proof: this is why the sky affects the farmland, why it gives and takes away various crops, why it moves the sea by ebb and tide. This constant motion of the sea is sometimes caused by the moon, sometimes provoked by her withdrawal to another part, and sometimes depends on the yearly course of the sun through the year. This is why certain creatures at the bottom of the sea, imprisoned in a shell, change their shape according to the movement of the moon, imitating your waxing, Delia, and your waning. This is why you, too, turn your face back to your brother's chariot and then turn it away again, reflecting the amount of light he left you or gave you: you are a star at the expense of a star. Finally, take the cattle and the dumb animals on earth: they will never know anything about themselves and the laws of nature, but when nature reminds them, they lift up their souls to the heaven, which is their father; they watch the stars and cleanse their bodies when they see the horns of the waxing moon. They foresee the coming of storms, the return of fair weather. Who can doubt after this that man is connected with heaven . . . [something appears to be missing from the text] . . . man to whom nature gave wonderful gifts: the power of speech, a superior intelligence, and a quick mind? Does not god descend into man alone and dwell in him and seek himself? Not to mention other arts to which is given such an enviable power, a gift beyond our estate . . . (not to mention the fact that nothing is given by a law of equal distribution which shows that the universe is the work of one creator, not of matter; not to mention the fact that fate is predetermined and inescapable, and that it is the characteristic of matter to suffer, of heaven to exert pressure) . . . who could know heaven except by the grace of heaven? Who could find god unless he were part of god himself? Who could actually see and grasp in his limited mind the enormous structure of this vault that stretches into infinity, the dances of the stars, the never-ending wars of planets and signs . . . (and land and sea under the sky and what is under them), . . . if nature had not blessed our minds with a special vision and had turned a mind related to her toward herself and taught us this marvelous science? How, if not by something that comes from heaven and invites us to heaven and to the sacred fellowship of nature? Who could deny that it would be sacrilege to grasp heaven against its will, to capture it, so to speak, and drag it down into one's soul? But there is no need for long digressions to prove something which is manifest: people do believe in our science, and that must give it authority and weight. Our science never deceives itself nor does it deceive anyone. The method must be followed according to rule, and it is trusted for the right reasons. Things happen as they were foretold. Who would dare to denounce as false what Fortuna confirms? Whose vote would win against such an overwhelming majority?

All this I would like to carry with inspired breath in my song as high as the stars. I do not compose poems in the crowd and for the crowd. Alone, free, I shall drive my chariot, as if racing on an empty course, and no one will come from the opposite direction or drive along with me on the same track. I shall sing a theme for heaven to hear, and the stars will marvel and the world rejoice at the song of its poet. I shall also sing for those to whom the stars generously granted knowledge of their ways and their meaning: a very small group in the whole world. But large is the crowd that loves wealth and gold, power and the insignia of power, a life of leisure full of soft luxury, sweet and entertaining music and pleasant sounds that touch the ears. These things are understood with much less effort than the doctrine of fate. But to learn thoroughly the law of fate is also part of fate.

104

Ancient astrology was a science, but it was, at the same time, more and less than its practitioners claimed. Much of it was based on mathematical calculations, but the result of these, the chart, had to be interpreted according to a complex system of rules, and that part was more an art than a science; it could not be learned entirely from textbooks but required a certain amount of experience, and a dose of intuition certainly helped. The astrologer often had a chance to talk to the client and assess him, just as the dream interpreter did. It was different, of course, when a baby was born and the nativity had to be cast then and there.

By Manilius' time the astrologer had become a sort of personal adviser, a psychotherapist. His contact with many different types of clients over the years must have given him an excellent opportunity to study human nature. Manilius may have lived through the last years of the Civil War, and this experience may have convinced him that the world is ruled by conflict, by strife. At the same time, friendship and love—the highest values in life, though difficult to attain—are guaranteed by the stars.

We seem to hear the voice of a disillusioned practitioner of the ancient art of astrology who has lived through difficult times and has shared the secrets of many clients. His experience confirms what his astrological studies tell him: to hate may often seem easier than to love, but it is love that we must recognize as the great cosmic force.

Manilius 2.567–607

The many different relationships between the signs cause enmities and produce hostility in so many ways and in corresponding numbers. For this reason nature has never created out of herself anything that could be more important, more precious than the bonds of friendship. Throughout so many generations of men, so many ages and periods, among so many wars and afflictions, even in times of peace, whenever the situation calls for a friend, it is almost impossible to find one. There was only one Pylades, only one Orestes who offered to die for the friend; in centuries theirs was the only competition for death; it was unique in that one wanted to die and the other refused to yield. [And yet two men were able to follow their example: punishment could barely find guilt to punish; the bondsman wished that the accused would not return, and the accused feared that the bondsman would gain him his freedom?] But how large is the sum of crimes throughout the centuries! How utterly impossible to absolve earth from its burden of hate! Sons had their fathers murdered for money, and the tombs of mothers . . . [something is missing from the text] Phoebus brought darkness and deserted the earth. Why mention the sack of cities, the betrayal of temples, disasters of all kinds in the midst of peace, poisonous mixtures, ambushes in the marketplace, slaughter inside the city walls and a conspiracy that lurks beneath the cloak of friendship? Evil is everywhere among the people, and the whole world is full of insanity. Right and wrong are confused, and injustice makes brutal use of the law itself; crime is more powerful than punishment. No wonder: under many signs men are born for discord; hence peace has disappeared from the world; the bond of trust is rarely found and is given to few; the earth is caught in a conflict with itself, just as heaven is; the human race is ruled by the law of strife.

105

Though Manilius believes in gods, he also operates with the concept of Nature, *physis*. It is difficult to say whether Nature is a separate entity or just a convenient term to designate all that is divine and creative and permanent in the universe. Perhaps it is a compromise between traditional polytheism, a more advanced form of Stoicism, and the specific world view of the astrologers, who might be bound by Stoic doctrine, but who, in Manilius' time, were more likely to be eclectics. That the universe controls itself is a fundamental idea in this context, and "Nature" seems to be just a convenient term for an autonomous, all-embracing organism in which every thought, every dream, every experience, and every action is somehow located and accounted for. Astrology, therefore, can be considered a symbolic language that expresses this truth.

For many ancient philosophers, the nature of the universe was not a scientific fact to be explored by scientific means; it was a mystery, and once fully experienced and understood, it would furnish them with a set of rules to deal with practical problems such as assessing someone's personality and predicting someone's future.

Manilius 3.47–66

Nature, the origin of everything and the guardian of mysteries, built up the enormous structures that form the walls of the world and encircled our globe, which hangs exactly in the center, with a widespread flock of stars. By certain laws she organized heterogeneous parts—air, earth, fire, floating water—into a unity and ordered them to feed one another so that harmony would rule all these discordant principles and the world might endure, held together by the bonds of a reciprocal covenant. To make sure that nothing was missing from the overall scheme and that everything belonging to the universe was controlled by the universe itself, Nature also made the lives and the destinies of mortals dependent upon the stars. In their never-tiring motion Nature wanted them to be responsible for all decisive events: the glory of light, fame. . . . Every possible situation, every activity, every achievement, every skill, every circumstance that might possibly happen in a human life was embraced in her lot by Nature and arranged in as many portions as there are stars placed by her. She established special relations for everyone, assigned special gifts. She led in a firm order through the stars the whole estate of a person. . . .

106

Manilius here discusses the twelve "houses" into which the astrologers divided the space around the earth. These regions are represented by twelve radii in the standard astrological charts today, with the earth at the center. Unlike the signs of the zodiac, however, they do not correspond to anything in nature: they are a construction. Each house represents an aspect of a person's character and life.

Different methods of predicting someone's life span were used by the astrologers. This one is based on two rules. First, the astrologer considers the ascendant, that is, the first house. If the first house coincides with Aries (i.e., if the sign of Aries is rising at the moment of birth), this adds 10 2/3 years to the life of the individual. This is not the whole life span, for the position of the moon also must be considered. If the moon is in the first house in a favorable position (i.e., in a sign that agrees with her), this grants a life span of 78 years. It is not clear from the context whether these two figures have to be added: 78 + 10 2/3 = 88 2/3. This seems a rather high figure, considering the average life expectancy at that time. If one adds the life spans granted by all twelve houses and divides by 12, one arrives at an average of just under 55 years. The highest figure is 78, and this would have been considered a ripe old age in Manilius' time. In Cicero's "Dream of Scipio" (*De Republ.* 6.12), which Manilius probably had read, Scipio Africanus the Elder predicts to Scipio Africanus the Younger his death at the age of 56; he gives special significance to this product of 7 × 8, numbers that he calls "perfect." Thus, ancient numerology confirms astrology.

Manilius 3.560–617

I have shown what kind of life, throughout distinct periods of time, comes our way at any given moment. I have also shown to what star each year, each month, each day, each hour, belongs. Now I must explain another principle that applies to the span of a person's life: it tells how many years each sign is supposed to grant. You must consider this theory carefully and keep in mind the figures if you wish to predict the length of a life by the stars. Aries gives 10 2/3 years, Taurus 12 2/3, Gemini 14 2/3, Cancer 16 2/3, Leo 18 2/3, Virgo 20 2/3, and Libra the same number. Scorpio equals the number of years that Leo gives, and those of Sagittarius correspond to those of Cancer. Capricorn gives 14 2/3, Aquarius 12 2/3. Aries and Pisces not only share their borderline but also their power: they both give 10 2/3 years.

In order to understand the calculation in determining the length of life, it is not enough to learn the fixed number of years given by each sign. The "temples" [houses] and "parts" of the sky also have their own gifts to grant, and they add their specific amounts in a well-defined sequence when the whole configuration of stars is right. Now I shall discuss only the decrees of the "temples"; later, when the whole structure of the universe has been clearly understood and the different sections are not scattered here and there in a confusing fashion, the whole combination with its distinct powers will be approached. [Something seems to be missing from the text here.]

If the Moon is in a favorable position in the "temple" of the first cardinal point, where the sky returns to the earth, and if it is rising and holds the ascendant, the course of life will be increased to 80 years minus 2. When it is placed in the zenith, it will be the same number (i.e., 80) minus 3. In the region of its setting it is less generous than 80 by 5 (i.e., 75 years). At its very lowest point it is considered to give 60 years plus 12. The trigon of the horoscope [i.e., of the ascendant], which rose first and is on the right side, grants 60 plus 8. The trigon on the left, the one that follows the preceding signs, gives 60 plus 3. The third "temple" from the horoscope, which is also the one next to the zenith, gives 60 years minus 3. The "temple" that appears below, separated by an equal distance, grants as its gift a life of 50 years. The place directly under the rising horoscope allows 40 years to come and go, adds 2 more and leaves you still young. The one that precedes the zone of the rising quarter gives 23 years to those who are born under it and snatches them away when they have just tasted the bloom of youth. The "temple" just above the setting allows 30 years and increases them by 3. The "temple" at the very bottom brings death in childhood: those born at such a time will die at the age of 12, their bodies still undeveloped.

107

Manilius is an astrologer but he is also a philosopher. In the manner of the philosophers of his age, he offers help and advice to those who are confused, distressed, or worried about the future. Lucretius, over a half-century before, had offered the same kind of service, from the Epicurean point of view, in his poem *On Nature*, which Manilius clearly knew. But Manilius is a Stoic; he believes in fate and in divine Providence. Since there is nothing we can do to change the realities of life, and since everything is for the best, even if we do not see it right away, we ought to accept everything that happens to us. This, in fact, is the secret of happiness. Stop worrying about the future, Manilius says: what must be, will be, and there is no way you can influence fate.

Although Lucretius and Manilius belong to different schools of thought, they tell us indirectly how unhappy, how neurotic, the Romans of the Late Republic and the Early Empire were. We may assume that most of the mental and emotional disorders known to modern psychiatry existed in one form or another in antiquity, even if they were not recognized or described in scientific terms. Most physicians probably did not know how to treat them. In extreme cases exorcists were called in, and for the milder forms of depression or neurosis philosophers were available, but some philosophers, like Apollonius of Tyana, were also exorcists and had the reputation of being sorcerers. Philosophers in general not only lectured; they also listened to their students when they talked about their problems, and offered them advice.

Life had its complexities then as now, and when Manilius says "We always act as if we are about to live, but we never live," we feel the truth of this today as his contemporaries must have felt it.

Manilius deals particularly with the *paradoxa* of fate. History as he knows it, from the heroic age to Augustan Rome, is full of *paradoxa*. The unexpected, the unpredictable, always happens, yet astrologers claim to be able to predict even unforeseen events. Fate decreed that the ancient power of Troy would survive in one man, Aeneas, and because he landed in Italy, Rome, once a small village, became the center of an empire.

The poet sounds rather smug as he looks down the flight of the centuries and concludes that all this had to happen as it did for the greater glory of Rome. But the lesson he states applies to any person who may feel that some failure or defeat is final and that the future has nothing in store. "Don't despair," the Stoic philosopher says, "and don't try to change what cannot be changed. Put your trust in divine Providence; it will work for you as it did for Rome."

A certain amount of historical lore and personal experience has gone into this diatribe, which is meant to comfort ordinary people in the daily disappointments and frustrations of their lives. After stating his case as forcefully as possible, Manilius adds a caveat: fate cannot be used as an excuse for crime, nor should the good and virtuous lose their rewards, for it could be said that fate acts through them. This is clearly an attempt to reconcile Stoicism with the legal and moral conventions of the time.

Manilius 4.1–118

Why do we waste the years of our lives worrying? Why do we torture ourselves with fears and vain desires? We grow old before our time with constant anxieties, and we lose the life that we want to prolong. Since there is no limit to our wishes, we can never be happy. We always act as if we are about to live, but we never live. The more someone owns, the poorer he is, because he wants even more: he does not count what he already has but only wishes for what he does not have. Nature needs and demands but little for itself, but we in our prayers build up a high structure from which to fall. With our profits we buy luxuries, and with a life of luxury, extortion. It is the ultimate price of wealth to squander wealth.

Set your minds free, mortal men, let your cares go and deliver your lives from all this pointless fuss. Fate rules the world; everything is bound by certain laws; eternities are sealed by predetermined events. We die the moment we are born, and on the beginning depends the end. Fate is the source of wealth and power and, more often than not, poverty: it gives us at our birth abilities and character, vices and virtues, losses and gains. No one can renounce what is given nor claim what is denied to him. No one can catch Fortune by praying against her will or escape her if she comes close to him. Everyone must bear his appointed lot.

Would the flames have given way before Aeneas? Would Troy, triumphant on the very day of its destruction, have survived in one man if Fate did not make the laws of life and death? Would the she-wolf of Mars have nursed the twins exposed to die? Would Rome have grown out of shacks? Would shepherds have brought the thunder to the Capitoline hill? Would Jupiter have agreed to being locked up in his citadel? Would the world have been conquered by a conquered people? Would Mucius have extinguished the fire with blood from his wounds and returned victorious to Rome? Would Horatius single-handedly have barred the bridge and the city to the attacking enemy? Would a young woman have canceled a treaty? Would three brothers have been killed by the heroism of one? No army won such a victory: Rome relied on a single hero, and it was brought down, even though fate decreed that it should rule the world.

Why mention Cannae and the enemy army close to the walls of Rome? Why mention Varro, who was great because he fled, and Fabius, who was great because he delayed? Did not the fortress of Carthage after the battle of Lake Trasimene admit defeat, although it could have won the war? Did not Hannibal, imagining that he had been caught in our net, pay for the downfall of his race with an inglorious death? Think of the battles in Latium and think of Rome fighting against herself. Think of the civil wars and of the Cimbrian helpless in the presence of Marius, who was helpless in prison himself. This was the man who became an exile after having been consul many times, and he was consul again after having been an exile. His downfall was like that of Libya, where he went into hiding, but then he came out of the ruins of Carthage and conquered Rome. Never would Fortuna have allowed this, had it not been decreed by Fate.

Pompey, you had overthrown Mithridates' empire. You had cleared the sea of pirates. You had been awarded triumphs after wars that had ranged over the whole world. You could now claim the title "the Great." Who would have believed that you were murdered on the shores of Egypt, with only a little wood from a shipwreck to burn your corpse, the remnants of a shattered boat serving as a pyre? Can there be such a complete reversal without the decree of Fate? Julius Caesar was born of heaven and returned to heaven, but after his victory, when he had successfully ended the civil war and held high office in times of peace, he could not escape the violence predicted so many times: holding in his hand information about the conspiracy and a list of names, he obliterated with his own blood, before the eyes of the whole Senate, the evidence. Why? Because Fate must prevail.

Should I list cities destroyed, kings overthrown? Need I mention Croesus on the pyre, or Priam's headless corpse on the shore, with not even Troy as his pyre? And Xerxes, whose shipwreck was more terrible than any sea could inflict? Should I bring up the king of Rome whose mother was a slave girl? Fire that was rescued from fire and flames that destroyed a temple but gave way to a man?

How often does sudden death come to the bodies of the strong! How often does death run from itself and roam through the flames! Some have been carried out for burial but return from the grave: they were given two lives, others barely one. You see, a trivial ailment can kill and a more serious one will get better. Medical science is helpless, logic and experience baffled, therapy harmful, neglect beneficial, and procrastination often stops the disease. Food can be dangerous, poison harmless.

Sons turn out worse than their fathers or rise above their parents: they keep a nature of their own. Success [of a royal house?] comes with one man and goes with another. One who is madly in love can either swim across the sea or ruin Troy. Another's serious manner is well suited to the framing of laws. See, sons kill their fathers, parents their children, and brothers meet armed in bloody combat. All this violence is not the work of men: they are forced to commit these atrocities; they are driven to their own punishment and the mutilation of their limbs.

Not every age has brought forth a Decius or a Camillus or a Cato, whose spirits remained unconquered in defeat. The raw material is there in abundance, but it will do nothing against the will of fate. The poor may not necessarily expect to live fewer years, nor can immense wealth buy a long life. Fortuna carries a dead body from a stately home; she commands a pyre and orders a tomb for exalted persons. How great is the power that orders the powerful around.

Is it not true that virtue can be unhappy and vice successful, that rashly conceived actions are rewarded and careful planning fails? Fortuna does not judge the merits of a case and support the deserving; she moves casually and indiscriminately among the crowd.

So there is something else, something greater that forces and controls us and subjects all that is mortal to laws of its own. To the men that are born from it, it assigns the years they will live and the ups and downs of their fortunes. Often it joins the bodies of animals and men, and such a birth will not grow from the seed; for what do we have in common with beasts? When was an adulterer ever punished for his sin by a monstrous birth? It is the stars that introduce new shapes; it is heaven that crossbreeds features. After all, if there were no chain of Fate, why would it be handed down to us? Why, at certain times, are all things that will come to pass prophesied?

And yet this theory does not go so far as to defend a crime or to cheat virtue of the rewards that it deserves. No one will hate poisonous plants the less because they do not grow of their own free will but from a particular seed; nor will tasty food be less popular because Nature, not a deliberate choice, gave us these crops. In the same way, men's merits deserve greater glory because they owe their achievements to heaven. On the other hand, we must hate the wicked even more because they are destined for crime and punishment. It does not matter where crime originates; it is still crime. The very fact that I interpret Fate in this way is ordained by Fate.

108

At the beginning of his astrological handbook, Ptolemy attempts to explain in scientific terms why astrology works. To us, this kind of explanation may not seem scientific. After all, scientists have recognized that the sun is not a planet, and new planets have been identified in the solar system, planets whose specific influences remain to be determined. Nevertheless, in Ptolemy's day, this explanation was the best he could come up with, and his authority was such that his theories were widely accepted. Astrology, Ptolemy argued, was partly empirical, partly intuitive, partly theoretical. From experience, its practitioners seem to have been convinced that, generally speaking, it produced results. Perhaps they forgot their failures and remembered only their successes. But skeptical outsiders demanded some sort of proof, and since statistics of failure and success were hard to evaluate, if they were kept at all, theories like Ptolemy's had to be devised in order to impress the skeptics.

Ptolemy operates with two concepts—that of the "etherial substance," borrowed from Aristotle, and that of "cosmic sympathy," borrowed from Posidonius—but he also offers some empirical evidence. The influence of the sun and the moon on all sorts of natural processes on earth was recognized and could be substantiated by many observations. Since in astrological terms the sun and the moon were "planets," all planets were thought to influence organic and inorganic conditions on earth.

This particular section of Ptolemy's work is more of a diatribe than a manual. It is aimed at skeptics and critics, and while it uses traditional material (e.g., it points to the farmer's almanac), it also introduces a scientific hypothesis.

Ptolemy, *Tetrabiblus* 1.2.1–3

It is quite clear to everyone and can be explained briefly that a specific force emanates and spreads from the everlasting etherial substance and that it moves toward the whole region about the earth. This region is constantly subject to change because the main elements of the sublunar [lower] sphere, fire and air, are surrounded and controlled by motions in the [upper] etherial region. But they themselves surround and control everything else, earth and water and the plants and the creatures that live on earth and in water. Somehow the sun, together with the atmosphere, always influences everything on earth, not only by the changes that take place during the seasons each year—creatures being born, plants bearing fruit, waters flowing, bodies changing—but also by its daily course around the earth when it gives out heat, moisture, dryness, and fresh air in a logical order and in accordance with its configurations in relation to the zenith. The moon, being closest to the earth, releases a tremendous discharge on the earth. Most inanimate things and animate creatures live in sympathy with the moon and change along with it: rivers increase and diminish their flow according to the light of the moon; oceans turn their tides in accordance with the rising and setting of the moon; plants and living beings as a whole or in part grow and shrink in rhythm with the moon. The transitions of fixed stars and planets also produce important conditions in the atmosphere—heat, wind, snow—which in turn influence accordingly what happens on earth. Furthermore, their aspects in relation to each other, as they meet and mix their influences, create many different developments. The power of the sun prevails if one looks at the overall structure of quality [text uncertain], but the other heavenly bodies, to a certain degree, either contribute to this or oppose it. The moon does this more obviously and more continually—for instance, when it is new, at quarter, or full. The other stars do this at greater intervals and less obviously—for example, in their risings and settings and their mutual approaches. If you look at it this way, it must seem logical to you not only that things already fully formed are by necessity affected by the motions of these heavenly bodies but that the germination of the seed and its maturity are shaped and formed according to the condition of the atmosphere at the time. The more observant farmers and shepherds make guesses about the winds that blow at the time of fertilization and the sowing of the seeds, and they can tell about the quality of the outcome. The more important events predicted by the more obvious aspects of the sun and the moon are registered not by trained scientists but by careful observers in general. For instance, we look at future events, and some of them are caused by a major force and a simpler order, and this is obvious even to untrained minds, well, even to some animals. I am talking of the seasons and the winds as they happen year after year. The sun is generally held responsible for these things. Things that are less generally known are seen necessarily by trained observers. Sailors, for instance, know the peculiar signs of winds and storms as they come up in certain intervals, caused by the aspects of the moon and the fixed stars with the sun. . . .

109

Like Manilius [no. 98], Ptolemy believes that astrology is a divine art, and that it is revealed to mankind as a special favor of the gods. How, then, can it go wrong, as it admittedly sometimes does? The art itself is not to blame, Ptolemy argues; rather, the fault lies with the imperfect human beings who practice it. To illustrate the problem, he compares astrology with the art of navigation and with medical science. We do not discredit navigation as an art because navigators sometimes make mistakes. What Ptolemy says here about the "beauty" of astrology, he also says in a short poem [no. 113].

We see from this excerpt (as from no. 97) that the art which Ptolemy, Manilius, and others thought divine had its critics in antiquity. Among other things, these critics objected to the habit astrologers had of finding out as much as possible about the native, his family, his background, and so on, instead of limiting themselves to the information they found in the stars. In reply to this, Ptolemy remarks that physicians, too, interest themselves in certain aspects of an illness which are, strictly speaking, outside the realm of medical science. The whole person must be considered, he says. Artemidorus gives the same advice to the interpreter of dreams.

Ptolemy, *Tetrabiblus* 1.2.5

. . . It would be wrong to dismiss this type of [astrological] prediction completely only because it sometimes can be wrong. After all, we do not discredit the art of navigation as such simply because it is often imperfect.

When we deal with any art, but especially when we deal with a divine art, we must accept what is possible and be happy with it. It would be wrong to demand—in a typically human, haphazard manner—everything from it and to expect final answers, which it cannot give, instead of quietly appreciating its beauty. We do not blame physicians who talk about the disease in general and about the patient's "idiosyncrasy" when they examine him. Why should we object to astrologers when they include in their diagnosis the native's nationality, country of origin, manner of upbringing, and other given circumstances?

110

According to Ptolemy, medical astrology was first developed in Egypt, and it seems to have been a fairly sophisticated discipline. The physician-astrologer would examine the patient and also cast his nativity, which would give him additional information about the patient's state of health. The stars might tell him about the weak points in the patient's organism, or they might warm him of an impending crisis. If, after having made a prognosis, the physician-astrologer hesitated to choose between two types of treatment, the stars might indicate which one was preferable. Again we see the doctrine of sympathy and antipathy at work.

Ancient medicine obviously was not the science it is today, and so the combination of medicine and astrology should not surprise us. If, in a given society, most people believed that the stars either cause or indicate human illness, along with everything else that happens to human beings, this society would also expect the stars to reveal the cures for the illness, and a physician who ignored astrology altogether might have fewer patients than one who weighed the influences of the stars in his diagnosis.

Ptolemy, *Tetrabiblus* 1.3

As far as [astrological] predictions are concerned, it seems that even if they are not infallible, their potential at least is most impressive. Similarly, prevention works in some cases, even if it does not take care of everything; and even if these cases are few and insignificant, they should be welcomed and appreciated and considered an unusual benefit.

The Egyptians were aware of this. They developed this technique further than anyone else by thoroughly combining medicine with astrological prognosis. They would never have established certain means of prevention or protection or preservation against conditions that exist or are about to exist in the atmosphere, in general or specifically, if they had not been convinced that the future could not be changed or influenced. In fact, they placed the possibility of reacting by a series of natural abilities right after the theory of fate. They combined with the possibility of prediction the useful and beneficial part of the method they called "medical astrology" because they wanted to find out, thanks to astrology, the specific nature of the mixtures in matter and the things that are bound to happen because of the atmosphere and their individual causes. They felt that without this knowledge any remedies must fail, since the same remedies would not be appropriate for all bodies and all affections. On the other hand, their medical knowledge of sympathetic or antipathetic forces in each case and their knowledge of a preventive therapy for an impending illness as well as the cure for an existing disease enabled them almost always to prescribe the correct treatment.

111

The ancient astrologers made an effort to determine the moment of their clients' birth as closely as possible because they knew that the nature of the universe was changing from second to second. The conventional time-measuring devices used in everyday life were not accurate enough; only an astrolabe would do. The term *astrolabe* originally meant "star-taking," and the instrument used by Ptolemy himself may have been a very simple affair. In the Middle Ages three distinct types of astrolabe emerged: (1) a portable armil, that is, an instrument consisting of a metal ring fixed in the plane of the equator, sometimes crossed by another ring in the plane of the meridian; (2) a planisphere, that is, a polar projection of part of the celestial sphere; (3) a graduated brass ring with a movable index turning upon the center.

The ancients probably knew at least one of these types, but Ptolemy is not very explicit about how to use them. In his time the astrologers still observed the sky, but they also had charts and ephemerids, and they kept records of striking celestial phenomena. They noted the exact time when the moon was full, and so on. Thus the "astral time" of a person's birth could be defined in terms of the lapse in time since the most recent phenomenon was recorded.

Ptolemy, *Tetrabiblus* 3.2

Often there is a problem about the foremost and principal fact, the fraction of the hour of birth. In general, only observation by a "horoscopic" [i.e., hour-watching] astrolabe at the very moment of birth can, for a trained observer, give the exact time. Almost all other "horoscopic" instruments that most serious astrologers use are in many ways capable of errors: sundials, because of their incorrect position or the incorrect angle of the "gnomon" [i.e., a pin or triangular plate that casts a shadow]; water clocks, because of the stoppage and irregular flow of the water for various reasons, or just by accident. Thus it seems necessary to explain first how to find by a natural, logical method the degree of the zodiac which would be rising, using as a premise the . . . , given the degree of the hour known nearest to [the time of] birth, which is determined by the method of "ascensions." We must take the syzygy [i.e., conjunction or opposition] of two heavenly bodies immediately preceding the birth—it may be a new moon or a full moon—and when we have determined the exact degree of both luminaries [i.e., sun and moon] if it is a new moon, or, if it is a full moon, the exact degree of the one that is above the earth, we must see what stars control it at the time of birth.

112

Mars and Saturn are generally considered "bad" planets, but their harmful influence can be weakened if they are in "honorable" positions at the time of birth, that is, in a sign where they feel at home—for example, Mars in Aries, Saturn in Aquarius. If both are in hostile signs, they produce the types of people that Ptolemy lists, or perhaps one should say that they create the disposition toward a criminal career.

Ptolemy, *Tetrabiblus* 3.13

Saturn associated with Mars in honorable positions produces people who are neither good nor bad: they are hard-working, outspoken busybodies, boastful cowards, austere in their conduct, pitiless, contemptuous, rough, quarrelsome, foolhardy troublemakers, schemers, hijackers, stubborn in their anger, inexorable demagogues, tyrants, greedy, and they hate their fellow citizens. . . .

In the opposite positions [Mars and Saturn make]: robbers, pirates, counterfeiters, wretches, profiteers, atheists . . . thieves, perjurers, murderers, eaters of unlawful food, criminals, killers, poisoners, robbers of temples and graves, and, in general, men who are totally evil. . . .

113

This short poem by Ptolemy sums up what might be called the religious feeling that here and there shines through in Ptolemy's technical handbook [see *no. 109*]. It is not so much an awareness of the power that his craft gives him. It is not a feeling of humility in the face of the universe. It is a religious experience: by interpreting the will of the gods from the movements of the stars, Ptolemy feels that he is directly in touch with the gods.

It has been said that Kepler, the greatest astronomer and astrologer of the seventeenth century, died of malnutrition because he charged such modest fees that he could not pay the grocer's bills. But in his work, too, one encounters a spirit of exaltation which transcends the worries of everyday life.

Ptolemy, *Anthologia Palatina* 9.577

I know that I am mortal, the creature of one day. But when I explore the winding courses of the stars I no longer touch with my feet the earth: I am standing near Zeus himself, drinking my fill of Ambrosia, the food of the gods.

114

This text from the second or third century A.D. was once part of an astrological handbook. It deals with the various constellations of the planets: conjunction (0° distant), opposition (180° distant), and trine (120° distant). The significance of each constellation depends on its own nature (trines are usually favorable), the nature of the planets involved, and the positions of the planets in the signs of the zodiac. The astrologer's art consists in weighing all these factors and in determining their overall meaning.

The symbolism behind this particular reading is fairly obvious: Mercury indicates good opportunities, especially in business deals; Jupiter stands for power, prestige, and authority; Mars suggests aggressiveness. Such symbolism works in different ways on different levels, however, and much depends on the native's position in life.

Tebtunis Papyri, nr. 276

. . . If, moreover, Mercury is in conjunction, and Saturn is in an irregular situation, . . . from an unfavorable circumstance. If Mars, at the same time, is in opposition to Saturn, while the constellation [?] mentioned before continues to exist, [this will wipe out?] the profits of transactions. Saturn in trine with Mars signifies [bad] fortune. Jupiter in trine or in conjunction with Mars makes great kingdoms and empires. Venus in conjunction with Mars brings about fornication and adultery; if, moreover, Mercury is in conjunction with them, they produce scandalous lusts. If Mercury is in conjunction with them, this causes successful business transactions, or [it means that] a man will earn a living by . . . or by his wits [text uncertain]. . . . If Mars appears in trine with Jupiter or Saturn, this produces great happiness, and he [the native] will acquire great wealth and . . . . If Jupiter and Saturn form this aspect, and Mars comes in conjunction with either . . . he will obtain [wealth] and collect a fortune but spend it and lose everything. If Jupiter, Mercury, and Venus are in conjunction, they bring about glory and empires and great prosperity; if the conjunction takes place at the morning rising [of Venus], that person will have prosperity from youth onward.

115

Vettius Valens, an astrologer of the second century A.D., considers his function to be to tell his client the truth about his future and to help him face that truth. Most people are unable or unwilling to accept their fate; in fact, they like to trick themselves by believing in Chance and cherishing Hope and letting these pseudodivinities control their lives. We are always ready to hope that Fate will not be as harsh as the serious astrologer predicts, and we are more than willing to anticipate a sudden change in Fate due to Chance. Our prayers may foster new hopes, but these hopes are in vain. We must try to be good soldiers of Fate and obey orders as best we can. Or, using another image, we must be like the professional actors, who play their roles and leave the stage when the plot demands their exit. During the performance we must play the role assigned to us by Fate and make the best of it, even if we do not like it.

The self-discipline that Vettius Valens demands here is the self-discipline of Stoic ethics, and his message is essentially the same as Manilius' [*no. 107*].

Vettius Valens, *Anthologiae* 5.9 (= p. 219 Kroll)

Fate has decreed for every human being the unalterable realization of his horoscope, fortifying it with many causes of good and bad things to come. Because of them, two self-begotten goddesses, Hope and Chance, act as the servants of Destiny. They rule our lives. By compulsion and deception they make us accept what has been decreed. One of them [Chance] manifests herself to all through the outcome of the horoscope, showing herself sometimes as good and kind, sometimes as dark and cruel. Some she raises up in order to throw them down; others she flings into obscurity to lift them up in greater splendor. The other [Hope] is neither dark nor serene; she hides herself and goes around in disguise and smiles at everyone like a flatterer and points out to them many attractive prospects that are impossible to attain. By such deceit she rules most people, and they, though tricked by her and dependent on pleasure, let themselves be pulled back to her, and full of hope they believe that their wishes will be fulfilled; and then they experience what they do not expect. Sometimes Hope offers firm expectations, but actually she has abandoned you already and is gone to others. She seems to be close to everyone, and yet she stays with no one.

Those who are not familiar with astrological forecasts and have no wish to study them are driven away and enslaved by the goddesses mentioned above; they undergo every kind of punishment and suffer gladly. Some find part of their expectations fulfilled, so they put up higher stakes and wait for a permanently favorable outcome, without realizing how unstable things are and how easily accidents can happen. Some who have been disappointed in their expectations, not just occasionally but again and again, surrender body and soul to passion and live dishonored and disgraced, or else they exist as the slaves of fickle Chance and treacherous Hope and never are able to achieve anything in life. But those who make truth and the forecasting of the future their profession acquire a soul that is free and not subject to slavery. They despise Chance, do not persist in hoping, are not afraid of death, and live unperturbed. They have trained their souls to be brave and are not puffed up by prosperity nor depressed by adversity but accept contentedly what comes their way. Since they have renounced all kinds of pleasure and flattery, they have become good soldiers of Fate.

For it is impossible by prayers or sacrifice to overcome the foundation that was laid in the beginning and substitute another more to one's liking. Whatever is in store for us will happen even if we do not pray for it; what is not fated will not happen, despite our prayers. Like actors on the stage who change their masks according to the poet's text and calmly play kings or robbers or farmers or common folk or gods, so, too, we must act the characters that Fate has assigned to us and adapt ourselves to what happens in any given situation, even if we do not agree. For if one refuses, "he will suffer anyway and get no credit" [Cleanth., frag. 527 Arnim].

116

In his textbook Vettius Valens tells us about the joys of astrological research. The following passage reads almost like a prose paraphrase of Ptolemy's short poem [*no. 113*]. To these men, astrology was clearly more than a profession, more than a science: it was a vocation, and it left them no time, nor any desire, for the popular pastimes and amusements of the day, such as horse races, concerts, plays, the ballet. Vettius Valens seems to believe that all so-called pleasant experiences contain in themselves, or are inevitably followed by, an element of pain. This is not true in the case of the investigation of the sky: it conveys an experience of pure joy. This might be said of any kind of research that demands hard work and long hours, progresses slowly, but brings, as a reward, great insights and discoveries. Some alchemists speak of their craft in equally enthusiastic terms.

Vettius Valens, *Anthologiae* 6.1 (= p. 242 Kroll)

I never got carried away by the various kinds of horse races or by the sharp crack of the whip, or by the rhythmic movements of dancers, nor did I enjoy the superficial charm of flutes and poetry and melodious songs or anything else that attracts an audience by a certain art or by jokes. I never took part in any harmful or useful occupations that were divided between pleasure and pain. I had nothing to do with disgraceful and troublesome . . . [at least one word seems to be missing in the Greek text]. But once I had experienced the divine and reverent contemplation of celestial phenomena, I wished to cleanse my character of every kind of vice and pollution and leave my soul immortal. I felt that I was communicating with divine beings, and I acquired a sober mind for research.

117

In his lectures Plotinus, the most eminent Neoplatonist, dealt with magic and occult science in general. He himself appears to have had "psychic" gifts, and he was once told that he had a guardian spirit of a higher order than most mortals, and he was also able to protect himself against powerful black magic (Porph., *Plot.*, chs. 53–55, 56–60).

Among the lectures of the master which Porphyry—himself a serious student of occult practices—published in six groups of nine books called the *Enneads*, there is one dealing with astrology (3.1.5). In this context Plotinus does not reject the possibility that the stars may guide our lives; in fact, he accepts the Stoic doctrine of "cosmic sympathy" which underlies much of astrological thought. But for him the stars do not act as causes by themselves; they are only indicators of things to come. They cannot direct our mind, our will, nor can they shape our character. Since the stars are divine beings, they certainly cannot be held responsible for the evil in this world.

If this is the case, Plotinus must assume the existence of a power higher than the stars, a power that rules or influences both the stars and our destinies, and the stars must merely function as a set of cosmic instruments giving important information to those who are able to read them correctly.

For Plotinus all modes of being are determined by a kind of expansion or "overflow" of a single impersonal and immaterial force that he calls "The One" or "The Good." The problem of evil would require a special discussion: Plotinus considers it essentially a form of nonbeing represented by the world of the senses insofar as it has a material base; thus he eliminates the concept of an evil cosmic soul as an antagonist of "The Good."

In this particular lecture Plotinus wishes to restrict and reduce the exaggerated claims of the astrologers without actually denouncing their craft. As he sees it, there is such a thing as heredity, and beyond heredity and the powers above there is something that we may call "our own," that is, our own individuality. Thus, one's life, one's personality, may be the product of all three influences.

It would follow from this statement that not everything in a person's character and life can be seen in the stars, and that the astrologer who relies only on the stars is bound to give us false or incomplete information about ourselves.

Plotinus seems familiar with the principles and techniques of contemporary astrology. He must have read at least one of the current manuals and noted a number of fallacies in order to discuss them in his lecture. He probably also had contacts with some practitioners through his students. Hence, in spite of his criticism, he may be considered a reliable source, and his treatment of the subject fills a few gaps in our knowledge of ancient astrology.

Plotinus, *Enneads* 3.1.5

But perhaps . . . the motion, the course, of the stars controls and guides every single thing, depending on the relative position of the planets, their aspects, their risings, settings, and conjunctions. On this basis people predict everything that will happen in the universe concerning every single person, and especially his destiny and his personality. They say that one can see the other living beings and the plants grow and diminish because of their sympathy with the planets, and that they are affected by the planets in other ways as well. Moreover, they claim that the regions of the earth are different from one another in regard to their relationship to the universe, especially to the sun. Living creatures in general, as well as plants, conform to their regions, as do human shapes, sizes, colors, tempers, desires, ways of life, and characters. Hence the motion of the universe controls everything.

In answer to this one must say that . . . [the partisans of astrology] ascribe to . . . [other] principles what is ours—acts of will, passions, weaknesses, impulses—but give us nothing and leave us like rolling stones, not like human beings who have work of their own to do in accordance with their own nature. Surely one must give to us our due; at the same time, some influences from the universe obviously join what is our own and belong to us. One ought also to distinguish between the things we do ourselves and the things we experience out of necessity, and not attribute everything to these [cosmic forces]. No doubt something reaches us from those regions and from the differences in the atmosphere—for instance, heat and cold in our individual temperature—but something also comes from our parents. We are certainly like our parents in our appearance and also in the irrational impulses of our soul. On the other hand, even if people are similar to their parents in appearance, you may see a great deal of difference in their character, their way of thinking—not corresponding to the regions—so that phenomena of this kind probably come from another principle. Our resistances to our physical temperaments and to our desires might also be mentioned at this point. But the astrologers look at the constellations of the stars and tell us what is happening to every individual, using this as evidence that the events were caused by them, as if the birds, for instance, were the cause of what they [merely] indicate, as would everything the diviners look at when they predict the future. . . .

Whatever an astrologer predicts, looking at the positions occupied by the stars at the moment of someone's birth, is supposed to happen, not only because the stars suggest it but also because they bring it about. And when they talk about a person's noble birth—meaning that he comes from a distinguished line of fathers and mothers—how is it possible to say this if the parents already had what the astrologers predict from a particular constellation? They also tell the fate of the parents from the nativity of the children and the character and fate of the children from the nativity of the parents—children that are not yet born!—and they predict the death of a brother from the horoscope of his brother, what will happen to the husband from the horoscope of his wife, and vice versa. Well, how could the position of the stars in relation to an individual cause what has been predicted from the horoscope of the parents? Either the situation as it existed earlier will have to be the cause, or if it is not, the later one cannot be the cause either. Moreover, the likeness between parents and children shows that good looks and bad looks are inherited and are not caused by the movement of the stars. It is only reasonable to assume that all kinds of living creatures are born at the same time as men, and that all of them ought to have the same fate, since they share the same position of the stars. How are men and other living creatures produced at the same time by certain constellations?

But in truth all individual things come into being in accordance with their own nature: a horse because it comes from a horse; a human being because he or she comes from a human being, and any particular human being because he or she comes from the same type of human being. Admitting that the movement of the universe contributes something—though it must leave the main contribution to the parents—admitting also that the stars act on the physical parts of us in many physical ways, giving us heat and coolness and the physical mixtures resulting from those: how can they influence our character, our way of life, and that which is least dependent on physical mixtures, such as becoming a teacher or a geometrician or a gambler or an inventor? And how could a bad character be sent by the stars? They are divine, after all. . . .

No, we must say that the stars move for the preservation of the universe. But they also offer another service: Those who look at their constellations, as if they were a kind of writing, those who can read this kind of writing, read the future from their patterns, interpreting their meaning by the systematic use of the principle of analogy, just as if someone said: "When the bird flies high, it means outstanding deeds."

118

In this lecture Plotinus continues his discussion of astrological doctrines. During the years of his teaching he often returned to the same themes, approaching them from different angles. Like Socrates, he seems to have formed his thoughts as he moved along, but he preferred the monologue to the dialogue form. Again we see that he was familiar with his subject.

It seems absurd to him to say that the stars are angry at men and punish them by making them unattractive or poor or sickly or wicked. (We should remember that the planets were named after the Greco-Roman gods, who had divine power but not divine love and compassion, and who were, in fact, ruled by every human passion and emotion.) Many people in Plotinus' age probably had no difficulty believing that astral gods actually caused all the evils in the world—sickness, crime, war—because they were angry. But this, Plotinus says, is unthinkable.

There is another possibility: The stars are not favorable or unfavorable per se, but they emit a positive or a negative radiation, depending on their position in the universe. Or else some are favorable, others unfavorable, all the time, but their positions modify the intensity of their (positive or negative) radiation.

Plotinus sums up the various doctrines of the astrologers before he delivers his attack on them. First, he considers whether or not the planets have souls. Obviously, if they have souls they also have a will of their own, and they can intentionally hurt us. But they are divine beings and therefore they do not want to hurt us. They certainly cannot be bribed. If the planets have no will of their own, they might conceivably be forced by their positions and constellations to affect us adversely. Plotinus here seems to refer to that part of astrological doctrine which establishes some kind of pecking order in heaven. A planet may be basically benign but may also be temporarily demoted within the celestial hierarchy and may even be forced to do something bad.

This whole concept of a celestial empire in which everyone has a certain position but can move up or down, having greater authorities above and lesser authorities below, reflects somehow the hierarchical structure of the great powers of the ancient world: Babylonia, Egypt, Persia, Rome. In such a hierarchy it was possible for a good and enlightened official or commander to hurt the people under him because an order had come from above. It was also possible for a wicked and corrupt governor to do something good, against his will, because he was bound by his instructions. The way huge political and administrative structures had functioned over many centuries must have influenced people's thinking about the greatest structure of all—the universe. They could probably best conceive of it in terms of their own day-to-day experiences in their small world.

In his lecture, Plotinus attacks this kind of model of the universe. He refuses to see the planets as exalted heavenly bureaucrats who are unfair to ordinary people because of pressure from above or because they happen to be in a bad mood at a particular time.

In the first printed edition of the *Enneads*, as well as in an early Latin translation, a curious passage (par. 12) appears following paragraph 5. It seems to defend astrology against the kind of criticism that Plotinus levels at it, although it never attacks his main doctrine. Scholars have suggested that this is a short paper delivered by one of Plotinus' students. Ancient philosophers sometimes encouraged their students to contradict them and to try to build a strong case against them, for the sake of argument, as an exercise in dialectics. The teacher was thus forced to find new arguments for his own position or to refute the objections that seemed to weaken it. Paragraph 12 could well be the summary of such a critique, found among the papers of the master and edited along with them. It could also be an excerpt that he himself composed as he read an astrological treatise, planning to use it in class as an *aide-mémoire*. At any rate, it seems to belong here, not after paragraph 11, where most editors place it. The paragraph traditionally numbered 6 does not continue the argument of paragraph 5, but appears to be a rebuttal to paragraph 12.

Plotinus, *Enneads* 2.3.1–5, 12, 6

1. I have said elsewhere [*Enn.* 3.1.5] that the course of the stars indicates what is going to happen in individual cases, but does not itself, as most people think, cause everything to happen. My argument offered some proofs, but now I must discuss it more accurately and in more detail, for to think of it this way or that makes quite a bit of difference.

People say that the planets in their courses not only cause things in general, such as poverty, wealth, health, and sickness, but also ugliness and beauty, and, what is most important, vices and virtues and also the actions that result from them in every given case, on every given occasion, just as if they were angry at men over matters in which men do not wrong them, since men are the way they are because the planets made them that way.

It is also said that the planets give benefits to people not because they love them but because they [the planets] are either unpleasantly or pleasantly affected according to the place they have reached in their course. It is also said that they are in a different mood when they are in their zenith and when they are descending.

But what is most important: People say that some of the planets are good and others bad and that those which are supposed to be good give bad gifts and the good ones become evil. People also think that the planets, when they look at each other, cause one thing, but when they do not look at each other, something else, as if they were not independent but produced one result [?] looking at each other, another one [?] not looking at each other.

They also think that a planet is good when he looks at such and such another planet, but if he looks at a different one, he deteriorates, and that it makes a difference whether he looks at him in such and such an aspect or in another one. They also believe that the mixture of all planets is different again, just as a blend of various liquids is different from any of the ingredients. These and others of this kind are the general opinions. We now ought to examine and discuss each point individually; this might be a good starting point.

2. Should we assume that these bodies that go around in their courses have souls or not? For if they have no souls, they offer nothing but heat or cold. Now, if we assume that some stars are cold, they will influence our destiny only as far as our bodies are concerned, since there is a bodily motion in our direction, one which would not produce a significant change in our bodies, since the effluence from every single star is the same and since they are mixed together into a unity on earth, so that there are only local differences, depending on our distance from the stars. The cold star will have the same kind of influence, but according to its different nature. How, then, can they make some people wise, some foolish, some school teachers, others professors of rhetoric, others kithara-players and professionals in other arts, and also some rich, some poor? How can the stars be responsible for the other things which do not have their cause and origin in a blend of bodies? How, for example, can they give a person such and such a brother, a father, a son, a wife, make a person prosper for the time being, or become a general, a king? But if the stars have souls and do all this on purpose, what have we done to them that they would hurt us, especially since they are established in a divine region and are divine themselves? That which makes men evil does not belong to them, nor does anything good or bad happen to them either because of our happiness or our misery.

3. "The planets do not do these things of their own free will but because they are forced by their positions and aspects." But if they are forced, all of them surely ought to do the same things in the same positions and under the same aspects. What difference can it actually make to a planet if it passes now through this portion of the zodiac, now through that? It does not even move along the zodiac itself, but far below it, and wherever it may be, it is in the region of heaven. It would be ridiculous for a planet to become different according to each sign through which it passes and to hand out different gifts and to be different when it is rising, when it is at the center, and when it is declining. For it certainly does not enjoy being at the center, nor is it distressed or inactive when it declines. Another planet does not grow angry when it is rising, nor is it in a good

mood when it is declining. One of them is even better when it is declining. For each individual planet is, at any given time, at the center as far as some are concerned, but declining as far as others are concerned, and when it is declining for some, it is at the center for others. Surely it cannot be, at the same time, cheerful and depressed, angry and benevolent. And, of course, it is absurd to say that some of them are cheerful when setting, others when rising. For this would mean, again, that they can be cheerful and depressed at the same time. And then: why would their grief hurt us? But it is totally inadmissible that they should be cheerful at one time and depressed at another. They are always in a serene state and enjoy the good they have and the good they see. Each has its own life all by itself, and each has its own good in its action. This has nothing to do with us. Generally speaking, living creatures that have no relationship to us can affect us only incidentally, not through their main activity. Their activity is not aimed at us at all, except that they, like birds, may incidentally act as signs.

4. It is also absurd to say that a planet is happy when it looks at [forms an aspect with] another planet, and that another planet feels differently looking at another one. What enmity could there be between them? About what? Why should it make a difference whether two planets form an aspect of 120° or 180° or 90°? And why should one form an aspect of this sort with another and then, when it is in another sign of the zodiac, nearer to it, not form any aspect at all? Generally speaking, how can they ever do what they are supposed to do? How can each one act by itself? How can all of them together produce an effect that is different from their individual effects? They certainly do not form an agreement between themselves and then act against us, executing their decision and reaching some sort of compromise. None of them forcefully prevents the influence of another, and none of them concedes to another under pressure a field of action. And to say that one planet is glad when he is in the region of another, while the other is affected quite differently when he is in the region of the former—is it not like saying that two people like each other, adding that A likes B while B hates A?

5. Astrologers also claim that one of the planets is cold, stating in addition that the farther away from us it is, the better for us, as if its evil influence on us were in its being cold; and yet it ought to be good for us when it is in the opposite sign of the zodiac. They also teach that the hot and the cold planet in opposition are both dangerous for us; actually there ought to be a mixture [of temperatures]. They say that one planet enjoys the day and becomes good as it warms up whereas another one being fiery enjoys the night, as if it were not always day for them, I mean light, and as if the other planet, being high above the earth's shadow, could ever be overtaken by darkness. Their theory that the full moon in conjunction with such and such a planet is favorable, but unfavorable when she is

waning—this theory could be turned upside down, if this sort of thing is admissible at all. For when she is full as far as we are concerned, she would be dark to that planet which moves above her in the other hemisphere, and when she is waning, as far as we are concerned, she would be full from the point of view of that planet; so she ought to do the opposite when she is waning [as far as we are concerned], since she looks at that other planet with her full light. To the moon herself it would make absolutely no difference what phase she is in, since one half of her is always illuminated. It might make a difference if she were getting warm, according to their theory. But the moon could get warm even if she were dark from our point of view. . . .

12. The side of the moon which looks toward us is dark in relation to the regions of the earth. It does not hurt the regions above. But since that [which is above] does not help, being far away, this [i.e., the conjunction] is supposed to be less favorable. When the moon is full it is sufficient for what is below, even if that planet is far away. When the moon shows her unlighted side to the fiery planet she is considered good for us. . . . The bodies of living creatures that come from there [the higher regions] vary according to their temperature, but none of them is cold. Their position indicates this. The planet called Jupiter has a well-balanced blend of fire, and so does Venus. For this reason, because of their similarity, they are supposed to be harmonious. They are alien in nature to the planet called Mars because of its mixture and to Saturn because of its distance. Mercury, being indifferent, assimilates himself to all, it seems. All of them contribute their share to the whole, and their relationship with one another is such that it benefits the whole, as does each individual part in one single living creature. They are there for its sake, as, for instance, the gallbladder serves the whole body, but also the organ next to it, for it is its duty to arouse an impulse and also to keep the whole body and the organ next to it from dangerous excess. Similarly, there must be, in the universe, some such organ whose function it is to produce sweetness. There also are eyes. Everything shares a common experience through its irrational part: thus it is one and there is one single harmony.

6. But it is surely total nonsense when astrologers call this planet Mars and this one [reading *Aphroditēn tēnde themenous*] Venus and make them responsible for adultery when they form a certain aspect, as if they satisfied their mutual desire from the wantonness of human beings. Assuming that they look at each other, how could anyone accept that they enjoy the sight but nothing else beyond that? What kind of life is this for the planets, anyway? Innumerable living creatures are born and exist, and to each the planets are supposed to allot such and such a thing: to give them fame, make them wealthy or poor or frivolous, and transfer all their activities to them. How can the planets possibly be responsible for all this?

·VI·

ALCHEMY

Introduction

The word *alchemy* is derived from the Arabic *alkimya*, which consists of *al* 'the' and a pre-Arabic noun, probably Egyptian *kamt, quemt,* or *chemi,* all of which seem to mean "black" or "black stuff" and could refer to the mud of the Nile, but apparently also to a black powder produced from quicksilver in a metal-manufacturing process developed in Egypt. At one time this particular powder was thought to be the basic substance of all metals.

Alchemy, the forerunner of chemistry, was an occult philosophy or science that sought to bring the macrocosm (the universe) into a close relationship with the microcosm (the human being). It was based on the magical law of sympathy and contained elements of astrology, mysticism, religion, and theosophy. A good deal of ancient alchemy is "scientific" and highly technical in nature. Special apparatuses were constructed and applied under conditions that are reminiscent of modern research. But the ultimate goals of alchemy were not always "scientific" from the present-day point of view. Whatever important discoveries were made seem to have been more or less accidental and were not always fully recognized. Some were even kept secret, then forgotten, and had to be discovered again centuries later.

What were the main purposes of alchemy? The transmutation of baser metals into silver and gold; the creation of an elixir of life to prolong it; the creation of a human being (*homunculus*). All these were useful, negotiable achievements that could give enormous power and wealth to the alchemist or to the king who employed him. At the same time, the alchemist seems to have worked on the discovery of his own soul—its purification and perfection.

Let us look at the practical aims in more detail. That precious metals such as gold and silver could be produced from baser ones like copper, iron, lead, and tin was, of course, an illusion, but even fake silver and gold were of great commercial value, as is costume jewelry today. Royalty, nobility, and the rich wore the real thing, but the rest of the people for the most part were quite happy with an imitation. A superficial coloring of the baser metals—perhaps by adding small quantities of real gold or silver—already enabled alchemists to coat objects and thereby approximate the shining quality of silver or gold. The alchemists also came up with alloys that looked enough like precious metals to deceive anyone except a real expert.

In Egypt goldsmiths and metallurgists had worked with various metals for centuries. When Hellenistic Egypt attracted Greek scientists, no doubt new progress was made. It has been suggested that magic in general, as well as astrology and other occult sciences and techniques, developed in Hellenistic Egypt as a result of an exchange of ideas between Egyptian practitioners and Greek scientists. The same might be said about alchemy. Presumably, as in the case of astrology, many ideas and traditions had been generated in Mesopotamia but later drifted toward Egypt, and by that time Greek scientists had arrived in Egypt. This reconstruction is largely speculative. It would seem, however, that any ancient knowledge available at the time of Alexander's conquest could have been developed by disciples of Alexander's own teacher, Aristotle, who had been invited by the Ptolemies to come to Egypt and work there.

All ancient civilizations were fascinated by gold—how to find it in the crust of the earth; how to wash it, fuse it, refine it; and if it did not occur naturally, how to find ways of producing it artificially. Alchemy was no doubt encouraged by the kings of Egypt because it helped create new industries, especially the production of jewelry and cosmetics.

The oldest extant tract on alchemy, the *Papyrus Ebers*, a 68-foot roll discovered in the necropolis of Thebes, sometimes called the oldest book in the world, is an important document for *iatrochemistry*, that is, the medical use of chemistry or alchemy. It contains more than 800 prescriptions and recipes. One is entitled "a delightful remedy against death" and recommends half an onion mixed with the froth of beer. There is nothing magical about this, for both onions and beer were popular among the Egyptians. Other recipes are clearly based on the laws of sympathy, antipathy, or analogy. To protect one's clothes against mice, one had to rub cat's fat into them; just as living cats kept the mice away, the fat of a dead one worked as a protection. Some of the potions were given symbolic names—for instance, "dragon's blood"—to indicate their power.

Such recipes were kept in the royal archives and in temple libraries for centuries. They were jealously guarded, in the same way that industrial secrets are guarded today, to keep ahead of the competition, but also because they were thought to be based on divine revelation. In later antiquity, Hermes Trismegistus, a combination of the Egyptian god Thoth and the Greek god Hermes, emerged as the god who had dis-

covered alchemy and the other occult sciences and taught them to mankind. By this time alchemy had undergone the influence of Neo-
Pythagoreanism, and the belief in numbers as symbols of cosmic forces
had begun to play a role.

The Two Aspects of Alchemy

It is important to distinguish between the two aspects of ancient alchemy.
On the one hand, it was an applied science, and its aims were practical
and commercial. On the other hand, it was almost a religion, a mystic way
of life. For us, it may be difficult to reconcile these two aspects, for at any
given time or in any given practitioner one of the two aspects may have
eclipsed the other. Perhaps we should use the term *alchemy* only when
referring to the combination of the two aspects and speak of *ancient chemistry* when the religious element is absent.

The Practical Side

Let us look first at the practical aspect. The alchemists were working on
drugs that could restore health and prolong life. They also developed
dyes and colors. We know that Tyrian purple, for instance, was much in
demand in the days of the Roman Empire because of its richness and
resistance to the wear of washing. The manufacturing process, which is
roughly understood today, was a secret of the Tyrians, and as long as they
maintained their monopoly, their profits must have been enormous. To
compete, alchemists in other countries tried to develop dyes that were as
attractive as Tyrian purple but easier to make and therefore cheaper, and
to a certain extent they succeeded, for the indigo-dyed wrappings of
some mummies are still amazingly fresh today.

In Hellenistic times Egypt also had an important cosmetics indus-
try. Perfumes, lotions, and different kings of makeup (rouge for the
cheeks, black powder to darken the eyebrows) were exported to other
countries.

The ultimate aim of the alchemists seems to have been to imitate
and accelerate the processes that occur more slowly and less perfectly in
nature, to achieve the same results faster and thus less expensively. One
could say that they were trying to improve upon nature, to use natural
resources in the most rational way.

Chemical processes such as oxidation, reduction, solution,
smelting, and alloying were known to the ancient alchemists. Sulfur and
mercury showed the most spectacular effects as far as changes in color
and substance were concerned; hence, they were among the most popular. The fermentation of barley into beer had been known for thousands
of years in the Middle East; the fermentation of grape juice into wine was
known to the Greeks of the heroic age; and the distillation of spirits may
have been discovered by an Egyptian alchemist toward the end of antiq-

uity, though the technique was apparently forgotten soon afterward and had to be rediscovered in the Middle Ages. The word *alcohol* is Arabic, but it originally designated the fine metallic powder (usually powdered antimony) that Near Eastern women put on their eyelids.

Some of the apparatuses used are known. The *alembic* is a simple distilling apparatus invented by Cleopatra (probably not the queen). Its name is derived from an Arabic word that preserves the Greek *ambix* 'cup' or 'beaker', and it consisted of the *cucurbit* 'gourd-shaped vessel', and the *ambix* 'cap', which fed the distilled product into a receiver. According to tradition, the first double boiler also was invented by a woman, Mary the Jewess (it is still called *bain-marie* in French), and consisted of a flat vessel full of hot water in or over which other vessels could be placed so that their contents might be warmed, evaporated, or dried. The *kerotakis* was a closed vessel in which thin leaves of copper and other metals were exposed to the action of various vapors, for instance, the vapor of mercury. This device appears to have been a kind of *alembic*, or *circulatory*, that is, a still or retort that had its neck or necks bent back so as to enter its lower part. The *athanor* ('furnace' in Arabic) was a small domed tower that contained an egg-shaped glass vessel lying in a sandbath over a fire; a constant heat could be maintained using this apparatus.

Many other simple devices continued in use throughout the Middle Ages. The earliest alchemistic tracts were written in Egyptian, but in the Hellenistic period the most important textbooks seem to have been in Greek. From Greek they were translated into Arabic, and from Arabic into Latin. Thus, an enormous body of information—or misinformation—has reached the West, some of it in Greek, some only in translation.

The Spiritual or Mystical Side

The mystical side of alchemy is about as well documented as its practical side. It is marked by a quest for spiritual perfection, just as the search for precious metals involved the perfecting and refinement of raw materials. The process is best illustrated by the aphorism, "Out of other things you will never make the One, until you have first become the One yourself."

Many alchemic operations can be understood as sacrificial offerings, as ceremonies to be accomplished after the alchemist himself has been initiated into some higher mysteries. A long period of spiritual preparation is indispensable. The ultimate goal of this process, as in the mystery religions, is salvation. Thus alchemy appears to be a Hellenistic form of mysticism. Since the soul is divine in origin but tied to matter in this world and isolated from its spiritual home, it must, as far as possible, purify the divine spirit inherent in it from the contamination by matter.[1]

In his search for the *materia prima*, the alchemist discovers hidden powers within his own soul. The symbols he draws and studies help him explore his collective unconscious; the reading and rereading of books derived from divine revelation may create a certain drowsiness of intox-ication; watching the chemical processes in his laboratory for hours on end may produce a kind of trance or an exhaustion that leads to trance.[2]

Thus alchemy can be more than a science; it can be a way of life, like religion or magic. Even when there are no tangible results, the al-chemist goes on reading, praying, meditating, and distilling. Perhaps he will make an important discovery, but it will come more or less by acci-dent, as a by-product. Lead never turns into gold, and the philosopher's stone never materializes, but the search for perfection continues.

The alchemist's quest to improve matter, or to ennoble baser substances, appealed to those who had been trained in the great philo-sophical schools of Greece—to the Platonists, who believed that the cre-ation was basically good, and to the Aristotelians, who believed that nature, though not perfect, strives toward perfections. Indeed, some of the basic philosophical principles of alchemy were no doubt derived from earlier thought. The unity of all things, or rather their unity within diver-sity, had been postulated by the Eleatic School in the sixth century B.C. For the alchemists this principle was symbolized by the *Ouroboros*, the ser-pent that "eats its tail" and that carries the legend *hen to pan* 'all is one'. The legend has been explained or paraphrased: "One is all, and by it all, and for it all, and if one does not contain all, all is nothing." This rendering reflects the position of Plotinus, who said: "Everything is everywhere and everything is everything and every single thing is everything" (*Enn.* 5.8.4).

Unifying Concepts

Within the unity of all things there are opposites, such as the four ele-ments—fire and water, air and earth—a doctrine that was known in India and Egypt long before the time of Aristotle. But these opposites are not absolute; one can be transformed into another, and the principle of change, transformation or transmutation, plays an important role in al-chemy. Solid water (ice) resembles earth, whereas vaporized water (steam) resembles air, yet water and steam are the same substance. Fire can be thought of as the energy that brings about changes by the heat it produces: fuel is consumed, and the substance that boils in the apparatus changes in character. To the four material elements Aristotle added a fifth, the *quinta essentia,* or ether, a purer form of fire or air, the substance of which the heavenly bodies were thought to be composed, but which is also found in different degrees of admixture in the animal, vegetable, and mineral worlds.

The principle of transformation was clearly all-important to the alchemists. According to Ovid, it was one of the great cosmic laws, and in his *Metamorphoses* he traces the theme from the creation of the world—the transformation of chaos into cosmos—to the transfiguration of Julius Caesar into a star: *In nova fert animus mutatas dicere formas.* There are also hundreds of stories in Greek mythology telling of people being transformed into animals, trees, or stars.

Seeds become flowers and trees, caterpillars become butterflies, and human life from birth to death is a series of transformations or transitions. There is some wonderful magic at work in the universe, some real, some fantastic, like Ovid's fairy tales. If the unity of matter is accepted and the possibility of a powerful transforming agent is admitted, anything can become anything else. In a sense the gods of antiquity were the greatest alchemists; if nothing else worked, a prayer might produce results, and when there were results, the alchemist—like the astrologer or the magician—felt that he himself was a god: this was his reward.

In truth, we have come full circle. Alchemy and magic are closely related; in fact, it is probably impossible to separate them. Many magical texts could be classified as alchemistic recipes. Alchemy and astrology also are related. During alchemistic operations the stars had to be watched, the names of the "planets" were transferred to certain metals, and the astrological symbols of these metals served to designate them: the Sun was gold, the Moon silver; Mars was iron, Mercury quicksilver; Saturn was lead, Jupiter tin.[3]

Notes

1. Festugière, *La Révélation d'Hermès Trismégiste* (Paris: Lecoffre, 1949), 1:260ff.
2. "Pray, read, read, read, reread, work, and you will find" (*ora, lege, lege, lege, relege, labora, et invenies*) is another aphorism. The mystic aspect of alchemy was described by the American scholar E. A. Hitchcock in *Remarks on Alchemy and the Alchemists* (Boston, 1857). See also T. Burckhardt, *Alchemy: Science of the Cosmos, Science of the Soul,* trans. W. Stoddart (Baltimore: Penguin Books, 1967); and Biedermann, *Handlexikon der magischen Künste,* 2nd ed.
3. Les Belles Lettres (Paris) is planning a new edition of Greek alchemistic texts (the Budé series) in twelve volumes, with introductions, French translations, and notes. The first volume, edited by R. Halleux, with an introduction by H.-D. Saffrey, was published in 1981 under the title *Les Alchimistes grecs.*

Texts

119

The *Ouroboros,* the snake that bites its own tail, is a symbol often used by alchemists. It represents the unity of all forces and processes in the cosmos. To know one thing by studying it carefully is to know everything. The macrocosm is reflected in the microcosm. The formula that supposedly explains the symbol seems to express the doctrine that the individual reality exists for the sake of universal reality, but also vice versa: the universe is there for the one thing. If the universe were not present, in a mystic sense, in the one thing, there would be no universe. The mystic language of alchemic texts presents many problems. The written texts are not enough. No doubt the ancient study of alchemy needed a teacher to interpret them and fill in the gaps.

The *Ouroboros*

One is all, and by it all, and for it all, and if one does not contain all, all is nothing.

120

The Precepts of Hermes Trismegistus were probably engraved on an emerald tablet at one point to emphasize their value. "Thrice-Greatest Hermes" is a Greek adaptation of the Egyptian god Thoth, and he was thought to have revealed to mankind all the arts and sciences, especially the occult sciences. The text of the *Precepts* is known from two versions: one in Arabic, attributed to Geber (or Jabir) Ibn Hayyan; the other in Latin. The Arabic version may reflect a lost Greek original; the Latin version is believed to depend on the Arabic.

There are thirteen precepts altogether and they are intended as a summary of the science of alchemy. The number *thirteen* may be significant as a "magic" number; but discounting (I) (a brief preface designed to impress the reader) and (XIII) (a brief summary), there are only eleven precepts.

II.   This is an affirmation that the microcosm reflects the macrocosm, and vice versa. The "wonders of the one Thing" expresses in language what the *Ouroboros* symbolizes visually: If you understand one substance perfectly, or if you can actually produce it, you understand the universe. This is a miracle, but then the world is full of miracles.

III.   The "One Being" is the supreme god at whose command (the "One Word") the world was created. This god—like the Old Testament Yahweh—can reveal his secrets to mankind, either directly or through an intermediary such as Hermes. Thanks to divine revelation, creating the tiniest substance is, in principle, equivalent to creating the universe. The alchemist is on the same level as his god. But creating one substance is only the beginning of a process that continues ad infinitum. By transformation or adaptation of the "One Thing," other substances are created.

IV.   Sun, Moon, Wind, and Earth are essential cosmic forces in any creative process. The Sun and Moon may represent gold and silver in the present context, but they could also be astrological influences that had to be considered in an alchemic operation. The Earth not only brings forth the food that we need but it also contains precious metals. The Wind spreads seeds, but it is also the Spirit, because *pneuma* in Greek covers both meanings.

V.   The "One Thing" is *the* most perfect thing in the world ("father of perfection" seems to be a Semitism, like "sons of the kingdom"). If the "One Thing" is done well, the whole world will be in fine condition.

VI.   The "power" is the divine power operating through the alchemist. "Earth" represents any solid substance that can be used for any practical purpose. In order to be completely useful to mankind, the spiritual power should be transformed into material things. This utilitarian process is not a modern concept, and alchemy is not an entirely spiritual science. Alchemy is a domain where spiritual and material forces come into contact with each other and produce something of value.

VII.   Earth is the coarse element, Fire the subtle one, but it is possible that the precepts were aimed at processes of refinement or distillation in general. To extract "Fire" from a coarser substance was one of the goals of alchemy.

VIII.   The right substance, the right apparatus, the right procedure, was not enough. The alchemist had to acquire and cultivate a certain mental attitude. Nothing could be gained without mystic experience. The ascent and descent of the soul proceed through the planetary spheres (which represent material substances as well as qualities of human character and intellect).

IX.   "Virtue" is the conventional translation of the Greek term *aretē*, which really means "effectiveness" or "power." To achieve real power the alchemist must be a visionary. The creative process in the mind is more important than the creative process in the test tube. The progress of alchemy as a science depended on new discoveries, new insights, new inventions, and these were thought to be divinely inspired.

X.   Here the act of creating a substance in the alchemist's laboratory is compared to the greatest creative act, the creation of the world by the demiurge. The alchemists liked to think of themselves as divine figures.

XI.   The "wonders that are here established" (or, "performed"?) must refer to the actual alchemistic operations described in a standard textbook or transmitted orally by a master.

XII.   Hermes Trismegistus reminds the reader that his precepts are based on divine revelation. The "three parts of cosmic philosophy" are no doubt magic, astrology, and alchemy, for these were the three domains over which the "Great Thoth" of the Egyptians presided. The statement indicates how strongly the author believed that these three occult sciences formed a unity.

The traditional Latin text of the Emerald Tablet is given by H. Kopp, *Beiträge zur Geschichte der Chemie* (Brunswick: Vieweg, 1869), pp. 376–77. The Latin and the Arabic versions are compared by J. Ruska, *Tabula Smaragdina* (Heidelberg: Winter, 1926). Among the many attempts to make sense of the text, I mention the following: F. Barrett, *Lives of the Alchymistic Philosophers* (London, 1814), pp. 383–84; E. J. Holmyard, in *Nature* 112 (1923): 525–26; T. L. Davis, in *Journal of Chemical Education* 3 (1926): 863–75; R. Steele and D. W. Singer, in *Proceedings of the Royal Society of Medicine* 21 (1928): 41–57; M. Gaster, in *The Quest* 21 (1930): 165–69; L. Thorndike, in *Isis* 27 (1937): 53–62.

The Precepts of Hermes Trismegistus

I.   What I say is not fictitious but reliable and true.

II.   What is below is like that which is above, and what is above is like that which is below. They work to accomplish the wonders of the One Thing.

III.   As all things were created by the One Word of the One Being, so all things were created by the One Thing by adaptation.

IV.   Its father is the Sun and its mother the Moon. The Wind carries it in its belly. Its nurse is the Earth.

V.   It is the father of Perfection in the whole world.

VI.   The power is strong if it is changed into Earth.

VII.   Separate Earth from Fire, the subtle from the coarse, but be prudent and circumspect as you do it.

VIII.   Use your mind to its full extent and rise from Earth to Heaven, and then again descend to Earth and combine the powers of what is above and what is below. Thus you will win glory in the whole world, and obscurity will leave you at once.

IX.   This has more virtue than Virtue itself, because it controls every subtle thing and penetrates every solid thing.

X.   This is the way the world was created.

XI.   This is the origin of the wonders that are here established [or, performed?].

XII.   This is why I am called "Thrice-Greatest Hermes," for I possess the three parts of cosmic philosophy.

XIII.   What I had to say about the operation of the Sun is completed.

121

Zosimus of Panopolis (today Akhmim, on the east bank of the Nile in Egypt) is considered one of the great alchemists of the early Christian era. Scholars believe that he lived in Alexandria at some time during the fourth century A.D. and used its prestigious library. We know that he traveled to Rome at least once, for his own account of the trip survives in a manuscript in Cambridge, England.

The present text is part of his work *On Completion*. It is corrupt in several places, even where the context is clear, and therefore the translation remains tentative.

The work is dedicated to Theosebeia, presumably a wealthy lady who was interested in Zosimus' alchemic researches. He makes it clear to her that the kings of Egypt had traditionally sponsored this kind of research, but under the strictest conditions of secrecy. He obviously has in mind the Ptolemies, who ruled Egypt from 323 B.C. until 30 B.C. We do not know whether these Macedonian kings continued an older tradition, but they clearly recognized the value of the natural resources of the country, and they encouraged scientific and technological research. Hellenistic Egypt manufactured metals, jewelry, textiles, perfumes, papyrus, and other goods on a large scale, and its economy depended on the export of these goods throughout the Mediterranean region. Some of these industries were royal monopolies, and the manufacturing processes were carefully guarded secrets. The research chemists who worked for the crown were not allowed to publish the results of their work. Any important discoveries were exploited by the government. In modern terms, the kings owned the patents. Similarly, all mining rights were owned by the government.

All this we learn from Zosimus a few centuries later. He defends the early alchemists who wrote about their work but were prohibited from publishing their most important discoveries. Only the Jews, he says, were the exception to this rule—they did not respect the prohibition. There was a large Jewish community in Alexandria. We know of the Jewish philosopher Philo. And a Jewish alchemist, Mary, is credited with the invention of the water bath, which is still called *bain-marie* in French cookbooks. Thus some Jewish scientists of the Ptolemaic period were not loyal subjects of the crown, according to Zosimus. At the same time, he credits them with preserving in clandestine fashion valuable knowledge that would otherwise have been lost completely when Cleopatra's empire collapsed. No doubt a good deal of Hellenistic technology was lost at that time because it had been kept secret. The enforced secrecy may explain why the fairly sophisticated chemistry of the period was classified as magic tinged with mysticism.

Zosimus, *On Completion*, excerpts (= 2:231–37 and 3:239–46 Berthelot)

Here is confirmed the Book of Truth.
Zosimus to Theosebeia greetings!
Madam, the whole kingdom of Egypt depends on these two arts: that of the appropriate things and that of the minerals. For the so-called "Divine Art," whether in its dogmatic, philosophical part, or in that part which is mostly guesswork [reading *hypopteuousa* for *hypopiptousa*], has been given to its guardians for [their] support, and not only itself, but also those four arts which are called "Liberal Arts" and the "Arts and Crafts." Their creative application belongs [?] to the kings. Thus, if the king agrees [?], he who has a share of this knowledge from his ancestors, either by oral tradition [?] or having deciphered it from the slabs . . . but even he who had a full knowledge of these things did not practice them, for he would have been punished. In the same way, the workmen who knew how to strike the coins of the kingdom were not allowed to do this for

themselves; they would have been punished. Similarly, under the kings of Egypt those who knew the technique of "cooking" and the secret of the "procedure" did not practice this for themselves but served the Egyptian kings, working to fill their treasuries. They had their own inspectors and supervisors, and there was strict control as far as "cooking" was concerned, not only in itself, but also in respect to the gold mines. For if anything was found by digging, the law in Egypt demanded that it be officially registered.

Some blame Democritus and the ancient authors [in general] that they did not mention those arts but only the "Liberal Arts." But why blame them? They could not do otherwise, since they depended [?] on the kings of Egypt and boasted to be among the "Prophets" of the first order. How could they have revealed, and have made public, knowledge that was reserved for the kings [?], thus giving to others the power that controls wealth? And even if they could have done it [?], they were jealous of their knowledge. Only to the Jews did they secretly explain these techniques and write and hand them down [for them]. This is why we find that Theophilus, son of Theogenes, has recorded the locations of gold mines, and Mary [the Jewess] has described [alchemic] ovens, and other Jews similarly.

122

The Greek text of the *Book of Comarius* reads like a translation from another language, or perhaps it was written by someone whose Greek was inadequate. It is certainly far removed from classical Greek. There are, in addition, textual corruptions introduced by the scribes. Texts that were put to practical use were often tampered with. The successive owners of such handbooks were no doubt practicing alchemists themselves, and they probably annotated their copies. Or if they copied a text, they were likely to leave out material that was of little interest to them. Hence, these treatises have survived in different versions or "recensions," and it is therefore impossible to reconstruct an archetype.

An additional problem is created by the apparently deliberate gaps left in such texts by authors who were unwilling to reveal all the secrets of their art and who therefore forced their readers to study with a teacher. Certain things are to be explained later, but the explanations never come, either because the text is incomplete or because the author forgets his promise. (We encounter the same difficulty in astrological literature: none of the treatises we have is a complete textbook enabling the beginner to become a master in a series of steps, following practical examples. This was apparently not the way these subjects were taught.)

The *Book of Comarius* is dedicated to "Cleopatra the Divine," also called "the wise woman," but not necessarily the famous queen. The prayer at the beginning, with its unmistakably Christian character, must be considered a later addition, perhaps by a Byzantine monk who copied (or edited) a pagan treatise. For a long time alchemy was not banned by the Church as a form of magic: on the contrary, as centers of learning, the monasteries were probably among the few places where alchemy could be studied and where texts were available. The prayer at the beginning of this text was perhaps designed to give an edifying character to the work and to place it above suspicion.

Comarius begins with a brief cosmogony and then turns to practical matters such as metals, colors, and apparatuses. A group of philosophers (i.e., scientists) is then introduced, and Cleopatra delivers to them the knowledge she has received from Comarius.

From the more practical precepts, the reader is led to general discourses on the wonders of nature. The symbolism is rich, the language mystic, and the frequent exhortations to the reader to listen to what clearly cannot really be understood increase one's frustration. In the concluding section, alchemy is described as providing a key to the mystery of resurrection, another reason for a Christian to study the subject, though the concept of resurrection is older than the Gospels.

Book of Comarius, Philosopher and High Priest Who Was Teaching Cleopatra the Divine the Sacred Art of the Philosopher's Stone, excerpts (= 2:278–87 and 3:289–99 Berthelot)

Lord, God of all powers, Creator of all of nature, creator and maker of all the celestial and supercelestial beings, blessed and eternal ruler! We celebrate you, we bless you, we praise you, we worship the sublimity of your kingdom. For you are the beginning and the end, and every creature visible and invisible obeys you, because you have created them. Since your eternal kingdom has been created as something which is subject to you [?], we implore you, most merciful ruler, in the name of your unspeakable love for mankind, to illuminate our minds and our hearts so that we, too, may glorify you as our only true God and the Father of our Lord Jesus Christ, with your all-holy, good, and life-giving Spirit, now and forever and ever. Amen.

I shall begin this book with the account concerning silver and gold which was given by Comarius, the philosopher, and Cleopatra, the wise woman. The book at hand does not include the demonstrations concerning lights and substances. In this book we have the teaching of Comarius, the philosopher, addressed to Cleopatra, the wise woman.

Comarius, the philosopher, teaches the mystical philosophy to Cleopatra. He is sitting on a throne. He has devoted himself to the mystical philosophy [?]. Even now [?] he has spoken to those who understand mystical insight, and with his hand he has shown that everything is One and consists of four elements.

As an [intellectual] exercise he said: "The earth has been established above the waters, the waters on the tops of mountains. Now, take the earth that is above the waters, Cleopatra, and make a spiritual body from it, the spirit of alum. These things are like the earth and the fire, in respect of their warmth to the fire, in respect of their dryness to the earth. The waters that are on the mountain tops are like the air in respect of their coldness, like the water in respect of their wetness. . . . Look, from one pearl, Cleopatra, and from another one you have the whole [technique of] dyeing."

Cleopatra took what Comarius had written and began to put into practice the applications of other philosophers, to divide into four parts the beautiful philosophy [?], the one [that teaches that] the matter derived from the natures, as it has been taught and discovered, and an idea of the operations of its difference [?]. Thus [they say?], searching for the beautiful philosophy we have found that it is divided into four parts, and thus we have discovered [?] the general idea of the nature of each of them, the first having blackness, the second whiteness, the third yellowness, the fourth [?] purpleness or refinement. On the other hand, each of these things does not exist from its own general nature [?], but they depend [?] generally on the elements, [and so?] we have a center from which we can proceed systematically. Thus, in between the blackness and the whiteness, the yellowness and the purpleness [?] or refinement, there is the maceration and the washing [out?] of the species. Between the whiteness and the yellowness there is the technique of casting gold, and between the yellowness and the whiteness there is the duality of the composition.

The work is accomplished by the application of the breast-shaped apparatus, the first experiment consisting in separating the liquids from the oxides [?], and this takes a long time.

Next comes the maceration, which consists [?] of the mixture of water and wet oxide [?].

Third, the dissolution of the species, which are burned seven times in an "Askelon vessel." This is how one operates the whitening process and the blackening process of the species by the action of the fire.

Number four is the yellowing process by which one mixes [the substance?] with other yellow liquids and produces wax [?] for the yellowing, in order to achieve the desired goal.

Number five is the fusion, which leads from the yellowing to the gilding.

For the yellowing one must, as mentioned above, divide the composition into two halves. Once it has been halved, one of the parts is mixed with yellow and white liquids, and then you can blend it for any purpose you have in mind.

Again, if the fermentation is a refinement [of the species?], that is to say that refinement and fermentation [constitute the?] perfect transmutation of the composition of the gilding.

This is the way that you, too, must proceed, my friends, when you want to approach this beautiful technique. Look at the nature of plants and their origin. Some descend from the mountains and grow from the earth; some ascend from the valleys; others come from the plains. Look how they develop, for you will [must?] harvest them at special times, on special days; you will pick them from the islands of the sea and from the highest place. Look at the air that is at their service and the nourishment that surrounds them, to make sure that they are not harmed and do not die. Look at the divine water that moistens them and the air that governs them, once they have been incorporated into one essence.

Ostanes and his followers answered Cleopatra: "In you is hidden the whole terrible and strange mystery. Enlighten us in general, but especially about the elements. Tell us how the highest descends toward the lowest, and how the lowest ascends toward the highest and how the one in the middle approaches the highest to unite itself with it and what is the element (that acts) on them. And (tell us) how the blessed waters descend from above in order to see the dead that are lying around, in chains, oppressed in darkness and obscurity inside Hades, and how the remedy of life reaches them and wakes them up from sleep and awakens them to an awakening [reading *eis gregorsin* for *tois ktetorsin* vel sim.], and how the new waters flow toward them, at the beginning of the couch [or, descent?] and born on the couch [or, descent?] and approaching with the fire, and a cloud carries them, and out of the sea ascends the cloud that carries the waters."

Considering what had been revealed to them, the philosophers rejoiced.

Cleopatra said to them: "When the waters come they awaken the bodies and the spirits that are enclosed in them and are weak. For again they suffer oppression, and again they will be shut up in Hades, and in a short while they grow and ascend and put on different glorious colors like flowers in spring, and spring itself rejoices and is glad at the beauty they wear.

"For to you who are wise I say this: When you take plants and elements and stones from their places they appear to be mature and [yet they are] not mature; for the fire tests everything. When they are clothed in glory and in shining colors from the fire, then you will see them as greater ones through their hidden glory, and [you will see] their exquisite beauty, and fusion [will be] transformed into divinity, for they get nourished in the fire, just as an embryo, nourished in its mother's womb, grows slowly. When the appointed month is near, it is not prevented from coming out. Such also is the power of this admirable art. They are hurt in

Hades and in the tomb in which they lie by waves and ripples that follow each other, but when the tomb is opened, they will ascend from Hades like the babe from the womb. When the philosophers have contemplated the beauty [of this], just like a loving mother [contemplates] the baby to which she has given birth, they seek to nourish, like a baby, this art, [but] with water instead of milk. For the art imitates [or, is like] the baby and, like the baby, it takes shape, and (there comes a time) when it is perfect in every respect. Here you have the sealed mystery.

"From now on I shall tell you clearly where the elements and plants lie. But first I shall speak in riddles: Climb to the top of the ladder, up the mountain covered with trees, and see: there is a stone on top. Take the arsenic from the stone and use it for whitening divinely. And see: in the middle of the mountain, underneath the arsenic, there is its bride [mercury?, or yellow arsenic, as opposed to the white one?], with whom it unites itself and in whom it finds its pleasure. Nature rejoices in nature, and outside of it there is no union. Descend to the Egyptian Sea and bring back from the sand, from the source, the so-called natron. Unite it with these substances, and they bring out the all-coloring beauty; outside of it there is no union, for the bride is its measure. See, nature corresponds to nature, and when you have assembled everything in an equal proportion, then natures conquer natures and rejoice in one another.

"Look, scientists, and understand. Here you have the fulfillment of the technique of bridegroom and bride having been joined and becoming one. Here you have the plants and their varieties. Look, I have told you the whole truth, and I shall tell it to you again. You must look and understand that from the sea ascend the clouds carrying the blessed waters, and they refresh the earth and make the seeds and the flowers grow. Similarly, our cloud, coming out of our element and carrying the divine waters, refreshes the plants and the elements and does not need anything that is produced by any other soil.

"Here you have the strange mystery, brothers, the completely unknown [mystery]; here you have the truth that has been revealed to you. Look how you sprinkle your soil, how you sprinkle your soil and make your seeds grow in order to harvest the harvest when it is ripe.

"Now listen and understand and judge correctly what I say: Take from the four elements the highest arsenic and the lowest arsenic and the highest, the white and the red, equal in weight, male and female, so that they are joined to each other. Just as the bird hatches and brings to perfection its eggs in warmth, so you, too, must hatch and polish [or, bring to perfection?] your work by taking it out and watering it in the divine waters and [warming it] in the sun and in burned places, and you must roast it in a gentle flame with the virgin milk and hold it [away] from the smoke. . . . And enclose it in Hades and move it in safety until its structure becomes more solid and does not run away from the fire. Then you take it out of it, and when the soul and the spirit have joined each other and become one, then you must throw it on solid silver, and you will have gold [of a quality] that the storehouses of the kings do not have.

"Here you have the mystery of the philosophers. Our fathers made us swear never to reveal it and never to divulge it, since it has divine shape and divine power. For divine is that which is united with the Godhead and accomplishes divine substances, in which the spirit is embodied and the mortal elements are animated; receiving the spirit that comes out of them, they dominate each other and in turn are dominated by each other. Just like the dark spirit, which is full of vanity and despondency, the one which has power over the bodies and prevents them from growing white and receiving the beauty and the color in which they were clothed by the Creator . . . (for body, spirit, and soul are weak because of the darkness that stretches over them).

"But once the dark, evil-smelling spirit itself has been disposed of, so that neither the smell nor the color of the darkness appears [any more], then the body is illuminated, and the soul and the spirit rejoice, because [reading *hoti* for *hote*] the darkness has gone away from the body. The soul calls out to the illuminated body: Wake up from Hades! Resurrect from the tomb! Come out alive from the darkness! Enter the process of becoming spiritual, of becoming divine, for the voice of resurrection has sounded, and the remedy of life has come to you. For the spirit rejoices again in the body in which he is, and so does the soul, and it runs fast and full of joy to embrace it, and it does embrace it, and the darkness does not gain power over it because it depends on light, and it cannot be separated from it forever, and it enjoys being in her house, because, hiding it in darkness, she found it filled with light. It was joined with it, since it had become divine according to her [?], and it lives in her. For it put on the light of godliness, and the darkness ran away from them, and all joined in love—the body, the soul, and the spirit—and they have become one in the one that hides the mystery. In the act of their coming together, the mystery was accomplished, the house was sealed, and a statue full of light and godliness was placed there, for the fire brought them together and transformed them, and from the lap of its womb it came forth.

"Similarly, from the womb of the waters and from the air, which ministers to them. . . . and it brought them out from the darkness into light, from grief to joy, from sickness to health, from death to life. And it clad them in divine spiritual glory, which they had never worn before, because in them the whole mystery is hidden, and the divine is there unchanged. For it is because of their courage that the bodies enter along with each other and, coming out of the earth, put on light and divine glory, because they grew according to their nature and were changed in their appearance and arose from sleep and came out of Hades. For the womb of the fire gave birth to them, and from it [the womb] they put on the glory. And it brought them to a single unity, and the image was perfected in body and soul and spirit, and they became one. For the fire was subordinated to water, [as was] the earth to the air. Similarly, the air is with the fire, and the earth is with the water, and the fire and the water are with the earth, and the water is with the air, and they are one. For from plants and sublimed vapors the One came into being, and it was created divine from nature and from the divine, capturing and controlling all of nature. Look, the natures controlled the natures, and through this they changed the natures and the bodies and everything from their nature, for he who fled entered into the one who did not flee, and he who controlled entered into the one who did not control, and they were united with each other.

"This mystery that we have learned, brothers, comes from God and from our father, Comarius, the Ancient. Look, I have told you, brothers, the whole hidden truth [handed down] from many wise men and prophets."

The philosophers said to her: "Cleopatra, you have given us ecstasies by telling us what you have. Blessed is the womb that bore you!"

Again, Cleopatra spoke to them: "What I have told you concerns heavenly bodies and divine mysteries. For through their changes and transformations they change the natures and clothe them [?] in an unknown glory, a supreme glory that they did not have before."

The sage said: "Tell us this, too, Cleopatra: Why is it written: 'The mystery of the hurricane. . . . the art is a body, and like a wheel above it; just like the mystery, and the course, and the pole above, and houses and the towers and the most glorious encampments?' "

Cleopatra said: "The philosophers were right to put it [the art] there, where it had been put by the Demiurge and the Lord of all things. And, look, I tell you that the pole will run as a result of the four elements, and that it will never stop. These things have been arranged in our own country, in Ethiopia, and from here the plants, the stones, and the sacred bodies are taken; the one that put them there was a god, not a man. Into everyone the Demiurge placed the seed of power. One greens, the other does not green; one is dry, the other wet; one tends to combine, the other to separate; one dominates, the other is subordinate; and as they meet, some dominate the others, and one rejoices in another body, and one imparts splendor to another. One single nature results which pursues and dominates all natures, and the One itself conquers the nature of fire and earth and transforms its whole nature. And look, I tell you what is beyond it: when it is perfected, it becomes a deadly drug that runs through the body. For just as it enters its own body, it circulates in the [other] bodies. For by decomposition and warmth a drug is obtained that runs unhindered through every kind of body. At this point has the art of philosophy been accomplished."

Select Bibliography

Ancient sources are mentioned in the various chapters, in the notes, and in the headnote for each translated text.

Abt, A. *Die Apologie des Apuleius von Madaura und die antike Zauberei.* Giessen: Töpelmann, 1908.

Allier, R. S. P. *Magie et religion.* Paris: Berger-Levrault, 1935.

Angus, S. *The Mystery Religions and Christianity: A Study in the Background of Early Christianity.* New York: Scribner, 1925.

———. *The Spiritual Quest of the Graeco-Roman World.* London: Murray, 1929.

Armstrong, A. H. "Was Plotinus a Magician?" *Phronesis* 1 (1955): 73ff.

Audollent, A. M. H., ed. *Defixionum Tabellae* . . . Paris: Fontemoing, 1904.

Baroja, J. Caro. *The World of the Witches.* Translated by N. Glendinning. London: Weidenfeld and Nicolson, 1964. Cf. G. Luck, *Latomus* 27 (1968): 737.

Barrett, C. K. *The New Testament Background: Selected Documents.* London: SPCK, 1958.

Bell, H. I. *Cults and Creeds in Graeco-Roman Egypt.* Liverpool: Liverpool University Press, 1952.

Bell, H. I.; Nock, A. D.; and Thompson, H. "Magical Texts from a Bilingual Papyrus in the British Museum." *Proceedings of the British Academy* 17 (1931): 235ff.

Berthelot, M. P. E. *Collection des anciens alchimistes grecs.* 3 vols. Paris: Steinheil, 1887–88.

Bertholet, A. "Das Wesen der Magie." *Nachrichten der Götting. Gesellsch. der Wissenschaften, Philos.-Histor. Klasse,* 1926–27.

Beth, K. *Religion und Magie: Ein religionsgeschichtlicher Beitrag.* 2nd ed. Leipzig: Teubner, 1927.

Bidez, J. *Vie de Porphyre.* Paris: Les Belles Lettres, 1913.

Bidez, J., and Cumont, F. *Les Mages hellénisés.* 2 vols. Paris: Les Belles Lettres, 1938.

Biedermann, H. *Handlexikon der magischen Künste.* 2nd ed. Graz: Akadem. Verlagsanstalt, 1973.

Bieler, L. *Theios Anēr: Das Bild des göttlichen Menschen in Antike und Frühchristentum.* 2 vols. Vienna: Höfels, 1935–39.

Boll, F., and Bezold, C. *Sternglaube und Sterndeutung: Die Geschichte und das Wesen der Astrologie*. Edited and revised by W. Gundel. Leipzig: Teubner, 1931.

Bonner, C. "Witchcraft in the Lecture Room of Libanius." *Transactions and Proceedings of the American Philological Association* 63 (1932): 34ff.

Bouché-Leclercq, A. *Histoire de la divination dans l'Antiquité*. 4 vols. Paris: Leroux, 1879–82.

———. *L 'Astrologie grecque*. Paris: Leroux, 1899.

Brown, P. "The Rise and Function of the Holy Man." *Journal of Roman Studies* 61 (1971): 80ff.

Bruns, I. "Der Liebeszauber bei den augusteischen Dichtern." In *Vorträge und Aufsätze*, pp. 321ff. Munich: Beck, 1905.

Burkert, W. *Lore and Science in Ancient Pythagoreanism*. Translated by E. L. Minar, Jr. Cambridge: Harvard University Press, 1972.

Butler, E. M. *Ritual Magic*. Cambridge: Cambridge University Press, 1949.

Butterfield, H. *The Origins of Modern Science*. London: Bell, 1970.

Comparetti, D. *Virgilio nel medio evo*. Florence: Seeber, 1872.

Contenau, G. *La Magie chez les Assyriens et les Babyloniens*. Paris: Payot, 1947.

Cramer, F. H. *Astrology and Politics*. Philadelphia: American Philosophical Society, 1954.

Cumont, F. *Astrology and Religion among the Greeks and Romans*. New York: Putnam, 1912.

———. "Les Anges du paganisme." *Revue de l'histoire des religions* 72 (1915): 159ff.

———. *Les Religions orientales dans le paganisme romain*. 4th ed. Paris: Leroux, 1929.

Davies, T. W. *Magic, Divination, and Demonology among the Hebrews and Their Neighbours*. London: Clarke, 1898.

Deissmann, A. *Light from the Ancient East*. Translated by R. M. Strachan. New York: Doran, 1927.

Deubner, L. "Charms and Amulets." *Encyclopaedia of Religion and Ethics* (1970 ed.), 3:433ff.

Dieterich, A. *Abraxas: Studien zur Religionsgeschichte des späteren Altertums*. Leipzig: Teubner, 1891.

Dodds, E. R. *The Greeks and the Irrational*. Berkeley and Los Angeles: University of California Press, 1951. Cf. G. Luck, *Gnomon* 24 (1953): 361ff.

———. *Pagan and Christian in an Age of Anxiety*. Cambridge: Cambridge University Press, 1965.

———. *The Ancient Concept of Progress and Other Essays on Greek Literature and Belief*. Oxford: Clarendon Press, 1973.

Doresse, J. *The Secret Books of the Egyptian Gnostics*. New York: Viking Press, 1960.

Douglas, M., ed. *Witchcraft: Confessions and Accusations*. New York: Tavistock Publications, 1970.

Edelstein, E. J., and Edelstein, L. *Asclepius: A Collection and Interpretations of the Testimonies*. 2 vols. Baltimore: Johns Hopkins Press, 1965.

Eitrem, S. "The Necromancy in the Persai of Aischylos." *Symbolae Osloenses* 6 (1928): 1ff.

———. "La Magie comme motif littéraire chez les Grecs et les Romains." *Symbolae Osloenses* 21 (1941): 39ff.

————. "La Théurgie chez les Néoplatoniciens et dans les papyrus magiques." *Symbolae Osloenses* 22 (1942): 49ff.

Ernout, A. "La Magie chez Pline l'Ancien." In *Hommage à J. Bayet*, pp. 190ff. Paris: Les Belles Lettres, 1964.

Fagan, C. *Astrological Origins*. St. Paul, Minn.: Llewellyn, 1971.

Festugière, A.-J. *L'Idéal religieux des Grecs et l'Evangile*. 2nd ed. Paris: Gabalda, 1981.

————. *La Révélation d'Hermès Trismégiste*. 4 vols. Paris: Vrin, 1944–54.

————. *Hermétisme et mystique païenne*. Paris: Aubier-Montaigne, 1967.

Festugière A.-J., and Nock, A. D., eds. and trans. *Corpus Hermeticum*. 4 vols. Paris: Les Belles Lettres, 1946–54.

Fiebig, P. W. J. *Antike Wundergeschichten*. Bonn: Marcus und Weber, 1911.

Foerster, W. *Gnosis: A Selection of Texts*. Translated by R. M. Wilson. 2 vols. Oxford: Clarendon Press, 1972.

Fowler, W. W. *The Religious Experience of the Roman People*. London: Macmillan and Co., 1922.

Frankfort, H. *Kingship and the Gods*. Chicago: University of Chicago Press, 1948.

Frazer, J. G. *The Golden Bough: A Study in Magic and Religion*. 12 vols. New York: Macmillan, 1911–15.

Frick, K. "Einführung in die alchemiegeschichtliche Literatur." *Sudhoffs Archiv* 45 (1961): 147ff.

Gadd, C. J. *Ideas of Divine Rule in the Ancient Near East*. Munich: Knaur Reprints, 1980.

Gleadow, R. *The Origin of the Zodiac*. New York: Athenaeum, 1965.

Grant, F. C. *Hellenistic Religions: The Age of Syncretism*. New York: Liberal Arts Press, 1953.

Grant, R. M. *Miracle and Natural Law in Graeco-Roman and Early Christian Thought*. Amsterdam: North Holland, 1952.

Griffith, F. L., and Thompson, H. *The Demotical Magical Papyrus of Leiden and London*. 3 vols. London: Grevel, 1904–9.

Gundel, H.-G. *Weltbild und Astrologie in den griechischen Zauberpapyri*. Munich: Beiträge zur Papyrusforschung, 1968. Cf. J. G. Griffiths, *Classical Review* 19 (1969): 358ff.

Gundel, W., and Gundel, H.-G. *Astrologumena: Die astrologische Literatur in der Antike und ihre Geschichte*. Wiesbaden: Steiner, 1966.

Hastings, J., ed. *Encyclopaedia of Religion and Ethics*. 12 vols. New York: Scribner, 1908–21.

Hatch, E. *The Influence of Greek Ideas and Usages upon the Christian Church*. Edited and revised by F. C. Grant. New York: Harper, 1957.

Holmyard, E. J. *Alchemy*. Harmondsworth: Penguin, 1957.

Hubert, H., and Mauss, M. "Esquisse d'une théorie générale de la magie." *Année sociologique* 7 (1902–3): 1ff.

Hull, J. M. *Hellenistic Magic and the Synoptic Tradition*. Studies in Biblical Theology, 2nd ser., no. 28. Naperville, Ill.: Allenson, 1974.

Jean, C.-F. *La Religion Sumérienne*. Paris: Geuthner, 1931.

Kessels, H. H. M. "Ancient Systems of Dream Identification." *Mnemosyne*, 4th ser., 22 (1969): 389ff.

Krappe, A. H. *The Science of Folklore*. 1930. Reprint. London: Methuen, 1974.

Lain Entralgo, P. *The Therapy of the Word in Classical Antiquity.* Translated by L. J.
    Rather and J. M. Sharp. New Haven, Conn.: Yale University Press, 1970.
Lawson, J. C. *Modern Greek Folklore and Ancient Greek Religion.* 1910. Reprint.
    Cambridge: Cambridge University Press, 1964.
Lexa, F. *La Magie dans l'Egypte antique.* 3 vols. Paris: Geuthner, 1923–25.
Lindsay, J. *The Origins of Alchemy in Graeco-Roman Egypt.* London: Muller, 1970.
———. *The Origins of Astrology.* London: Muller, 1971.
Luck, G. *Hexen und Zauberei in der römischen Dichtung.* Zurich: Artemis, 1962.
McCasland, S. V. *By the Finger of God.* New York: Macmillan, 1951.
MacNeice, L. *Astrology.* Garden City, N.Y.: Doubleday, 1964.
Marrett, R. R. *The Threshold of Religion.* 2nd ed. London: Methuen, 1914.
Mead, G. R. S. "Occultism." *Encyclopaedia of Religion and Ethics* (1970 ed.), 9:444ff.
Merlan, P. "Plotinus and Magic." *Isis* 44 (1953): 341ff.
Michelet, J. *La Sorcière.* 2nd ed. Brussels, 1862.
Momigliano, A., ed. *The Conflict between Paganism and Christianity in the Fourth
    Century.* Oxford: Clarendon Press, 1963.
Moule, C. F. D., ed. *Miracles: Cambridge Studies in Their Philosophy and History.*
    Cambridge: Cambridge University Press, 1965.
Neugebauer, O. E. *The Exact Sciences in Antiquity.* Princeton: Princeton University
    Press, 1951.
Neugebauer, O. E., and Van Hoesen, H. B. *Greek Horoscopes.* Philadelphia: Ameri-
    can Philosophical Society, 1959.
Nilsson, M. P. *Die Religion in den griechischen Zauberpapyri.* Lund: Gleerup, 1949.
———. *Geschichte der griechischen Religion.* 2 vols. 2nd ed. Munich: Beck, 1955.
Nock, A. D. *Essays on Religion in the Ancient World.* Edited by Z. Steward. 2 vols.
    Cambridge: Harvard University Press, 1972.
Oesterley, W. O. E. *Immortality and the Unseen World.* London: SPCK, 1921.
Onians, R. B. *The Origins of European Thought.* Cambridge: Cambridge Universtiy
    Press, 1951. Cf. H. J. Rose, *Journal of Hellenic Studies* 73/74 (1955/56): 175ff.
Petzoldt, L., ed. *Magie und Religion.* Darmstadt: Wissenschaftliche Buchge-
    sellschaft, 1978.
Préaux, J. "Virgile et le Rameau d'Or." In *Hommage à G. Dumézil* (= *Coll. Latomus* 45
    [1960]: 151ff.).
Preisendanz, K., et al., eds. *Papyri Graecae Magicae.* 3 vols. Leipzig: Teubner, 1928–
    41.
Read, J. *Prelude to Chemistry.* London: Bell, 1936.
———. *Through Alchemy to Chemistry.* London: Bell, 1957.
Reitzenstein, R. *Poimandres.* 2nd ed. Leipzig: Teubner, 1922.
Rutten, M. M. *La Science des Chaldéens.* Paris: Presses Universitaires de France,
    1960.
Saggs, H. W. F. *The Greatness That Was Babylon.* London: Sidgwick and Jackson,
    1962.
Sarton, G. *A History of Science: Hellenistic Science and Culture in the Last Three Cen-
    turies* B.C. Cambridge: Harvard University Press, 1959.
Scott-Moncrieff, P. D. *Paganism and Christianity in Egypt.* Cambridge: Cambridge
    University Press, 1913.
Smith, K. F. "Magic (Greek and Roman)." *Encyclopaedia of Religion and Ethics* (1970
    ed.), 1:265ff.

Tambornino, J. *De Antiquorum Daemonismo.* Giessen: Töpelmann, 1909.

Taylor, F. Sherwood. *The Alchemists: Founders of Modern Science.* New York: Schuman, 1949.

Thompson, R. C. *The Reports of the Magicians and Astrologers of Nineveh in the British Museum.* 2 vols. London: Luzac, 1900.

Thorndike, L. *A History of Magic and Experimental Science.* 8 vols. New York: Macmillan, 1923–58.

Thorwald, J. *Science and Secrets of Early Medicine.* Translated by R. and C. Winston. New York: Harcourt, Brace, 1963.

Tupet, A. M. *La Magie dans la poésie Latine des origines jusqu'a la fin du règne d'Auguste.* Paris: Les Belles Lettres, 1976.

Weinreich, O. *Antike Heilungswunder.* Giessen: Töpelmann, 1908.

Wiedemann, A. *Magie und Zauberei im alten Aegypten.* Berlin: Weidmann, 1905.

Witt, R. E. *Isis in the Graeco-Roman World.* Ithaca, N.Y.: Cornell University Press, 1971.

Wünsch, R. *Antike Fluchtafeln.* 2nd ed. Bonn, 1912.

Xella, R., ed. *Magia: Studi di storia delle religioni in memoria di Raffaela Garosi.* Rome: Bulzoni, 1976.

Index of Ancient Sources

*Numbers indicating sections of sources are printed in
roman type, general references to pages of this volume are
given in italics, and references to translations
are printed boldface*

AUTHORS

PAPYRI

GREEK INSCRIPTIONS

LATIN INSCRIPTIONS

General Index

Georg Luck is professor of classics at the Johns Hopkins University. He has served as editor of the *American Journal of Philology* and is the author of *The Latin Love Elegy* and a number of other books and articles dealing with ancient poets and philosophers.

THE JOHNS HOPKINS UNIVERSITY PRESS

Arcana Mundi

This book was set in Palatino text and Triset display type
by The Composing Room of Michigan, Inc.,
from a design by Cynthia W. Hotvedt.

It was printed on 50-lb. MV Eggshell Cream paper
and bound by The Maple Press Company,
York, Pennsylvania.